PMI-ACP Exam Prep
PLUS Desk Reference

John G. Stenbeck, PMP®, CSM, CSP, PMI-ACP℠
Joseph T. Drammissi, PMP®, CSM, PMI-ACP℠
Bryan Berthot, MBA, PMP®, CSPO, PMI-ACP℠

First Edition

GR8 PM

Traditional. Agile. Hybrid.

PMI-ACP Exam Prep
PLUS Desk Reference

John G. Stenbeck, PMP®, CSM, CSP, PMI-ACP^{SM}
Joseph T. Drammissi, PMP®, CSM, PMI-ACP^{SM}
Bryan Berthot, MBA, PMP®, CSPO, PMI-ACP^{SM}

Published by:
GR8PM, Inc.
7918 El Cajon Blvd. #N-326
La Mesa, CA 91942 USA
(619) 890-5807
custserv@gr8pm.com; http://www.gr8pm.com

All rights reserved. No part of this book may be reproduced or transmitted in any form or by any means, electronic or mechanical, including photocopying, recording or by any information storage and retrieval system without written permission by the author, except for the inclusion of brief quotations in a review.

Copyright© 2011-2012 by GR8PM, Inc.
1st edition.
Printed in the United States of America.

ISBN Edition: 978-0-9846693-0-1

Project Management Agile Body of Knowledge, PMABOK, Agile Process Map, and Agile PM Processes Grid are either registered trademarks or trademarks of GR8PM, Inc.

Project Management Institute, PMI, PMP, PMI-ACP, and ACP are either registered trademarks or trademarks of the Project Management Institute. Other product and company names mentioned herein may be the trademarks of their respective owners.

This book expresses the views and opinions of its authors. The information contained in this book is provided without any express, statutory, or implied warranties. Neither the authors, GR8PM, Inc., nor its resellers, or distributors will be held liable for any damages caused or alleged to be caused either directly or indirectly by this book.

Cover Art: Kim Sharp, Sharp Creative Studio, http://www.sharpcreativestudio.com/

About the Cover Photo:

We chose the photo because our company's mission is to build bridges of understanding in the project world – between traditionalists and agilists – and because we believe that project management in all its forms – traditional, agile, and hybrid – is about building bridges to the future.

The Mike O'Callaghan – Pat Tillman Memorial Bridge (Colorado River Bridge) is the central portion of the Hoover Dam Bypass Project. Construction on the nearly 2,000 foot long bridge (with a 1,060 foot twin-rib concrete arch) began in late January 2005 and traffic began using the Hoover Dam Bypass on October 19, 2010. This signature bridge spans the Black Canyon (about 1,500 feet south of the Hoover Dam), connecting the Arizona and Nevada Approach highways nearly 900 feet above the Colorado River.

Some interesting facts provided by the project manager, our colleague and friend, F. Dave Zanetell, PMP, include:

- Total Cost for the Hoover Bypass was $240 million (includes all engineering, construction and management)
- The Hoover Bypass includes 8 bridges and 5 miles of four lane approach roadway
- The Bypass approach roadways required over 3.6 million yards of rock excavation and embankment
- Bypass includes the centerpiece Mike O'Callaghan-Pat Tillman Memorial Bridge
    - Longest concrete arch in the western hemisphere
    - Fourth longest concrete arch in the world
    - Bridge length is 1,960 feet
    - Arch length is 1,060 feet
- Second tallest bridge in United States at 890 feet above the Colorado River
- Includes 290 feet of the world's tallest precast segmental columns
- Multiple Federal and State agency stakeholder team managed by the Central Federal Lands Division of FHWA.
- Project completed under the original $240 million budget without dispute or claim

We thank Dave for the information, photo, and inspiration of a remarkable project that we can all marvel over!

Acknowledgements

JOE: To my wife Nina, the source of inspiration and dreams in my life, for her unwavering faith and support in my pursuit of this goal.

BRYAN: To my wife Susan, who graciously supported and put up with me while we worked on this intense project.

JOHN: To my sons, JT and Michael, who inspire me, and my Cursillo brothers who have cheered me on, please keep praying for me.

GR8PM: As a whole we would like to thank: Kim Sharp for her creative genius and Lauren Seybert for her tireless editing, Daniel Skarda for his great illustrations and Tamara Parsons of KenType for taking our book to the next level. Peggy Couvrette for her endless support in keeping things running around us! Your contributions were invaluable in making this project a reality.

Contents at a Glance

CHAPTER 1	Agile Project Management Value Proposition	3
CHAPTER 2	Introducing Agile Project Management	15
CHAPTER 3	Initiating Projects	61
CHAPTER 4	Planning Projects – Part 1	95
CHAPTER 5	Agile Estimating	125
CHAPTER 6	Planning Projects – Part 2	145
CHAPTER 7	Iterating Projects	175
CHAPTER 8	Controlling Projects	215
CHAPTER 9	Contracting and Accounting Control	235
CHAPTER 10	Closing Projects	257
CHAPTER 11	How to Pass the Exam...*The First Try!*	279
CHAPTER 12	Comprehensive Exams	305
GLOSSARY		365
INDEX		385

Table of Contents

CHAPTER 1
Agile Project Management Value Proposition 3
Agile Value Proposition... in a Nutshell 3
Ethos of Agile Project Management 4
Agile Manifesto and the 12 Principles 6
What's In It For You? 7
Pursuing the PMI-ACP℠ 8
Why THIS Book? 9
What the Exams Test 9
About the Authors 10
Conventions & Standards Used in this Book 11

CHAPTER 2
Introducing Agile Project Management 15
Chapter Highlights 15
Overview of the Agile Project Management 16
Is Agile Really Needed? 18
Mapping Agile to the PMBOK® 19
Agile Planning and Estimating 20
Agile Execution and Control 21
The Origins of Agile Project Management 22
Application of Lean thinking to Project Management 24
Summary of Agile Frameworks & Tools 31
    1. Scrum 32
    2. Extreme Programming (XP) 33
    3. Lean Software Development 36
    4. Other Frameworks 37
    5. Test Driven Development (TDD) 43
    6. Agile Modeling (AM) 44
The Agile Process Map™ & Agile PM Processes Grid™ 45
Chapter Close-Out and Exercises 47

CHAPTER 3
Initiating Projects 61
Chapter Highlights 61
Overview of Agile Project Initiation 62
    Identify Stakeholders and Build Engagement 63
    Identify Stakeholders 64
Build Stakeholder Engagement 65
Value-Driven Delivery 68
    Document the Business Case 68
    Write Contracts 69

  Adaptive Planning 71
    Acquire the Right Team. 71
    Project Kickoff Meeting 72
    Apply Incremental Delivery Cycles. 73
  Create Team Performance Environment 74
    Recruit Coaches 74
    Understanding Agile Leadership 75
  Clarify Risk Considerations 77
    Organizational Practices 77
    Regulatory Discovery 78
    Defining Quality Standards 78
  Provide Communication Support 79
    Colocated and Distributed Teams 79
    Participatory Decision Models 79
  Invest in Continuous Improvement 82
    Define Required Ceremonies 82
  Chapter Close-Out and Exercises 83

CHAPTER 4

Planning Projects – Part 1 . . . . **95**
Chapter Highlights 95
Understanding Agile Planning 95
External Stakeholders Engagement 96
  Designing the Product Roadmap 97
  Identifying Minimal Marketable Features (MMF). 98
  Prioritizing Stories for the Project Team 98
Value-Driven Delivery 99
  Release/Iteration Plans 100
  Planning Activities. 104
  Decomposition and Progressive Elaboration 107
  Story Maps 107
Adaptive Planning 108
  User Stories 108
  Iteration Backlog 110
  Definition of Done 110
Chapter Close-Out and Exercises 112

CHAPTER 5

Agile Estimating **125**
Chapter Highlights 125
Estimation and Sizing 126
Estimation and Sizing Risks 129
Wideband Delphi 129
Planning Poker 131
Affinity Estimates 131
Chapter Close-Out and Exercises 133

CHAPTER 6

Planning Projects – Part 2 145
Chapter Highlights 145
Team Performance 146
Coaching/Facilitation 146
Collaboration/Negotiation 147
Motivation/Empowerment 148
Risk Management 148
Risk-Adjusted Backlog and Regulatory Compliance 148
Communication 149
Communication Protocols 149
Information Radiators 149
Team Space 151
Agile Tooling 152
Continuous Improvement 155
Value Stream Mapping 156
Cross-Functional Team Formation 157
Metrics Identification 158
Chapter Close-Out and Exercises 162

CHAPTER 7

Iterating Projects 175
Chapter Highlights 175
Overview of Execution 175
Product Backlog Grooming 177
Improve Value-Driven Deliverables 179
    Measuring and Using Cycle Time 179
    Measuring and Using Work-in-Process (WIP) 181
    Using Cumulative Flow Diagrams (CFDs) 183
Facilitate Adaptive Planning 185
    Create Visual Controls 185
    Apply Test-driven Practices 190
    Agile Modeling 192
    Wireframes 192
Nurture Team Performance 193
Enhance Risk Management 194
    Simplify Problem Solving 195
    Incorporate Continuous Integration 195
    Risk-based Spike 196
    Risk Burn-down Charts 198
    Verification and Validation 198
Adapt Communications 199
    Daily Stand-up, IterationReview, & Team Retrospective Meetings 199
    Osmotic Communication 201
Implement Continuous Improvement 202

    Track Metrics. 202
    Chapter Close-Out and Exercises 202

CHAPTER 8

Controlling Projects 215
Chapter Highlights. 215
External Stakeholders Engagement 216
Value-Driven Delivery. 216
Adaptive Planning 217
Team Performance 217
Risk Management. 218
Communication 221
Continuous Improvement. 222
Chapter Close-Out and Exercises 224

CHAPTER 9

Contracting and Accounting Control 235
Chapter Highlights. 235
Contracting Control 235
Accounting Control 237
Earned Value Management (EVM) 238
    EVM Basics. 239
    Agile Earned Value Management (A-EVM). 239
Chapter Close-Out and Exercises 245

CHAPTER 10

Closing Projects 257
Chapter Highlights. 257
External Stakeholders Engagement 258
Value-Driven Delivery. 258
Team Performance 258
Communication 259
Keys to Facilitating a Retrospective 263
Release and Project Retrospectives 264
Continuous Improvement. 264
Chapter Close-Out and Exercises 268

CHAPTER 11

How to Pass the Exam...the First Time! **279**
Chapter Highlights. 279
Integrate Professional and Social Responsibilities. 280
    Recognize Professional and Social Responsibilities 280
    The PMI Code of Ethics and Professional Conduct. 280
    The Four Values – Responsibility, Respect, Fairness, and Honesty . . 281
    Endorsing Responsibilities to the Profession 282
    Safeguarding Responsibilities to Customers and the Public 282
    Observing Other Responsibilities. 283
How to Pass the Exam...the First Time 283
The Key is the 5 Ps 284
What The Exam Tests 285
  A Passing Grade. 285
  Using a Testing Strategy 286
Getting to the Test 288
  Fill Out the Application 288
  Application Requirements 288
  The Testing Environment. 289
After Taking the Exam 290

CHAPTER 12

Comprehensive Exams **305**
Exam 1 306
Exam 2 327
Answers Exam 1. 348
Answers Exam 2. 356
Glossary **365**
Index **381**

CHAPTER 1

Agile Project Management Value Proposition

Agile Value Proposition ... in a Nutshell!

The playing field where human communities compete, from companies to nations, requires innovation and agility to create or maintain any competitive economic advantage. That sustainable advantage comes from systematic innovation. A strong correlation of that fact can be seen for industries from consumer electronics and pharmaceuticals to telecommunications. A mild correlation can also be seen for industries from healthcare and insurance to retail/wholesale.

So whether communities thrive, survive, or fail is directly correlated to their ability to be agile and innovative. That core driver is behind the ever increasing demand for Agile Project Managers. *That is also the agile value proposition... in a nutshell!*

Stated another way, projects allow organizations to operationalize their innovative strategic vision. Executing those projects using the ***correct*** project management framework insures those projects maximize the positive impact of the assets and people deployed to deliver them. To accomplish this, professional project managers are increasingly being tasked by their organizations to synthesize the best practices of traditional and agile frameworks into an approach that is tailored to the environmental demands facing them.

Without a solid base of Agile Project Management knowledge it is impossible for a project manager to fulfill that responsibility effectively.

Evidence strongly suggests that the future of project management is running *hybrid projects.* Tomorrow's professional project manager cannot be effective without the ability to run hybrid projects. So, in a nutshell, the Agile Project Management value proposition is the ability to manage hybrid projects because you have an understanding of both traditional and agile frameworks!

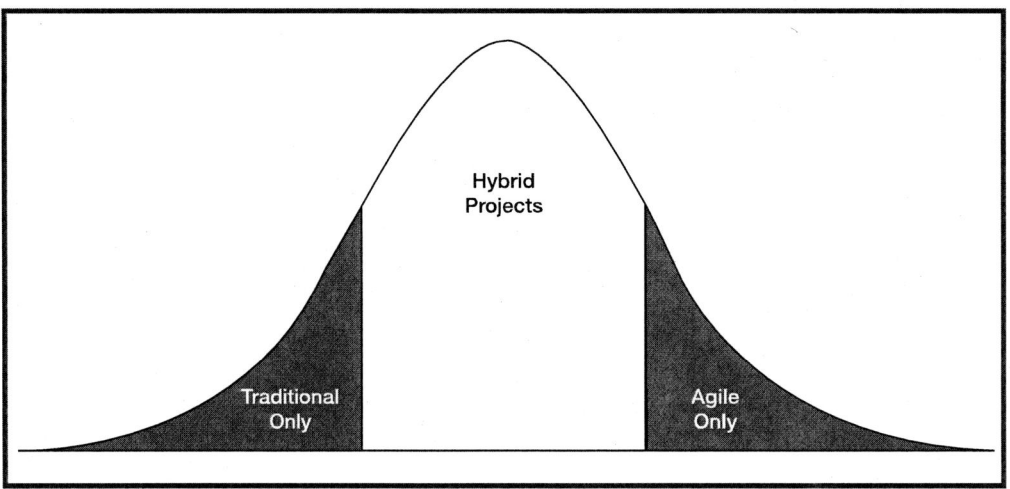

Figure 1.1 Distribution of Projects being Managed using Various Frameworks.

Ethos of Agile Project Management

When we consider the quantitative, engineering environment where most project management takes place, it might seem odd to use a word like ethos. Ethos conjures up other words like philosophy, culture, and attitude, but there is a good, solid quantitative reason for understanding, accepting, and applying the ethos of Agile Project Management.

That reason is **risk management.** A project cannot survive, much less thrive, without effective risk management, which for any project, hinges on cross-functional teams communicating effectively, a critical variable.

The agile ethos recognizes this fact as being equivalent to gravity. You can't escape it so why deny it. Instead, leverage it to create potential advantage. **The agile ethos is founded on the principle that teams must be cross-functional, can be trusted, and should be colocated, in order to optimize the chance to identify risks and reduce errors.** Such a team will experience osmotic communication about risks that are obvious to one team member, but perhaps not to other team members – often the ones that most dramatically affect the success of the project.

Unfortunately, good communication does not automatically occur in any environment and must, instead, be cultivated as part of the ethos and framework of Agile Project Management.

This basic fact has been observed hundreds of times during a simple exercise, called the "Stare and Share," conducted at numerous training seminars. The exercise has three steps. In step 1, all participants are asked to stand, choose a partner, and face the partner. They are then given 20 seconds (which always seems like a lifetime to the participants) to "visually study their partner." In step 2, they are instructed to stand back-to-back (so they cannot see each other) and to change three things about their appearance. In step 3, they are asked to turn so they can each see their partner once again, and then identify the three changes their partner made. At no time are the participants told not to collaborate, and they are even referred to as "partners" repeatedly throughout the instructions. Nevertheless, there are normally less than one-third of the participants who identify all three changes, and less than five percent who ask for, or reveal, the changes to one another.

This human trait impacts many project teams. Critical information – information vital to success – will not be shared automatically, unless the people assigned to the project unite as a team. Commitment to one another's success does not begin until a team is born! Catalyzing as a team, therefore, is critical to success and only happens when communication is properly facilitated.

So the *quantitative* goal of having colocated, a cross-functional, trusted team is to reduce project risk by reducing the unknown about the project. The situation before a team catalyzes can be seen in Figure 1.2. The illustration shows that as long as the project is worked on by a group of people who have not become a "team," the relationship between what is known and unknown remains static. That produces a significant "blind spot," where things that are not known by the PM overlap with things that are not known by the team (i.e., the bottom right quadrant).

The situation after a team catalyzes can be seen in the next illustration, Figure 1.3. When a team environment exists, everyone is committed to being responsible for the project's success or failure. That is because relationships formed when the team made the **hard commitment** to the **iteration goal** (a process that will be explained in Chapter 4). Those relationships engage everyone to remain vigilant, watching for areas of risk "owned" by other team members – as naturally as soldiers covering each other's back in combat. Most importantly, the automatic disclosure of observations, insights, and information occurs.

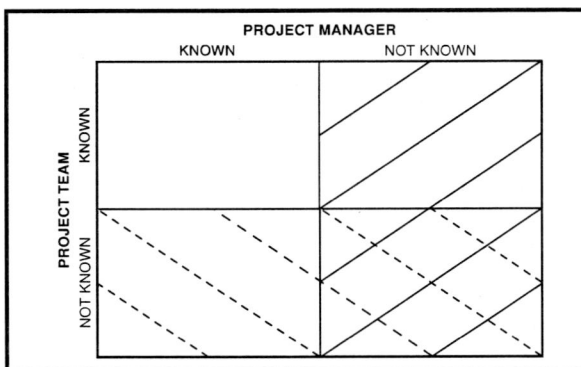

Figure 1.2 Risk Before Team Formation.

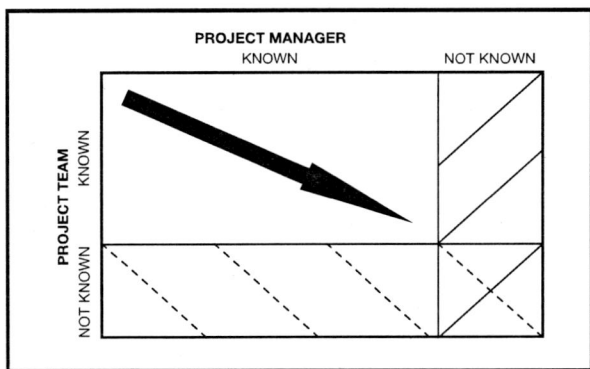

Figure 1.3 Risk After Team Formation.

This reduces the resulting blind spot, increasing the general level of knowledge about the project. The way this happens can almost be described as triangulation. As members of the team share their knowledge, other members can integrate that with their knowledge base and then share their own observations and insights. In the process, risks that had been unrecognized, and therefore unknown, are identified by triangulating their position. This occurs much like the navigation of early mariners using a sextant and the stars. Two data points are used to help identify a third. Precisely because trusted, cross-functional teams supply a mix of skills, risk and errors are reduced. So risk is diminished and the opportunity for success is enhanced. **In the agile ethos, empowering teams is central to realizing the goal of a successful project.**

Another facet of the agile ethos is commitment to a culture of **continuous improvement.** The commitment to continuous improvement shows up in many of the practices, ceremonies, and tools used in Agile Project Management in order to ensure long-term sustainable benefits which translate into competitive advantage for the customer, not just quicker project deliverables in the short term.

The agile ethos was expressed originally in the Agile Manifesto and then expanded in the Principles behind the Agile Manifesto (i.e., "The 12 Principles").

Agile Manifesto and the 12 Principles

One of the seminal events in the rise of Agile Project Management occurred in February 2001, at the Snowbird resort in Utah. Seventeen luminaries in the field of software development met to discuss the need for alternatives to the failure-prone project management processes then being used. Perhaps no one was more surprised than the participants when they achieved a meeting of the minds and all agreed to sign the Manifesto for Agile Software Development, now commonly referred to as the Agile Manifesto.

The group named itself *The Agile Alliance* and published the Manifesto for Agile Software Development *(See below)*. It outlines the fundamental beliefs that reinforce agile software development, a precursor to Agile Project Management.

Manifesto for Agile Software Development[1]

We are uncovering better ways of developing software by doing it and helping others do it. Through this work we have come to value:

> Individuals and interactions over processes and tools
> Working software over comprehensive documentation
> Customer collaboration over contract negotiation
> Responding to change over following a plan

That is, while there is value in the items on the right, we value the items on the left more.

 Notice that the central word in the Agile Manifesto is "over." The manifesto does not support the common, erroneous interpretations that it supports individuals and interactions "instead of" or "rejecting" processes and tools. Great damage has been done to the value of Agile Project Management by imposters claiming their focus is working software "not" comprehensive documentation, or customer collaboration "without needing" contract negotiation, or responding to change "without" following a plan. Proponents of such approaches are simply not agile, in spirit or in fact!

The Agile Alliance also published the ***Principles behind the Agile Manifesto***, which stated the following.

We follow these principles:

- Our highest priority is to satisfy the customer through early and continuous delivery of valuable software.
- Welcome changing requirements, even late in development. Agile processes harness change for the customer's competitive advantage.
- Deliver working software frequently, from a couple of weeks to a couple of months, with a preference to the shorter timescale.

- Business people and developers must work together daily throughout the project.
- Build projects around motivated individuals. Give them the environment and support they need, and trust them to get the job done.
- The most efficient and effective method of conveying information to and within a development team is face-to-face conversation.
- Working software is the primary measure of progress.
- Agile processes promote sustainable development. The sponsors, developers, and users should be able to maintain a constant pace indefinitely.
- Continuous attention to technical excellence and good design enhances Agility.
- Simplicity – the art of maximizing the amount of work not done – is essential.
- The best architectures, requirements, and designs emerge from self-organizing teams.
- At regular intervals, the team reflects on how to become more effective, then tunes and adjusts its behavior accordingly.

While the ethos of agile, as imbued in the promise of the Manifesto, is laudable and includes some serious wisdom, the Manifesto, the Agile Alliance, and the many organizations it spawned have not fulfilled the potential of agile. In a certain sense they became a victim of their own success.

Basically, the insights that human beings are far more than biological machines and that the solution to our complex problems won't be found in the level of thinking that got us here (to paraphrase a famous quote attributed to Einstein), are absolutely valid and form the core of the agile ethos.

The resulting problem becomes that agile has been misinterpreted and misused to justify all kinds of bad thinking and bad behavior under the banner of letting teams "be productive." Some agile evangelists have suffered from a myopic viewpoint that lost sight of the need to be able to do things at the enterprise, portfolio, and program levels. It seems that their fear of slipping back down the path of the old command-and-control approaches has led them to believe it is a dichotomous choice. If the choice were between using agile teams or submitting to command-and-control processes their position might be reasonable. However, the best solution to the situation is not "either/or," the best solution is "both/and."

Holding onto the ethos of agile and using the insight that Lean provides, allows for a framework and processes that are an intelligent balance for flexible, effective teams and long term organizational stability. This understanding comes into focus when the beliefs, principles, and paradigms on which a framework is built, are carefully examined and appropriately applied.

As you study for the ACP exam, we hope your goal will be to embrace the ethos of agile and to employ it with the maturity that your studies should stimulate.

What's In It for You?

Congratulations! You are taking an exciting first step toward becoming an Agile Certified Practitioner (PMI-ACP[SM]). As you are probably already aware, getting that next promotion and raise, or that next job, often hinges on demonstrating command of the most desirable skills in today's hyper-competitive workplace. According to the 2010 Role Delineation Study (RDS) completed by the Project Management Institute (PMI), the knowledge, skills, tools, and techniques used in agile are an important part of being a professional project manager (PM)[2]. Also, a quick look at postings for PM jobs on major employment websites like Monster or CareerBuilder confirms that Agile Project Management is a skill set that is in high demand among employers today. This book helps you become a subject matter expert (SME) in Agile Project Management opening doors to career opportunity!

Using this book helps you unlock the potential of the ACP because it is more than just an exam preparation book. It is a ***Desk Reference*** for the ***Project Management Agile Body of Knowledge***™ (PMABOK™). It serves as a handy source of "how to" knowledge and best practices as you lead your teams and organization to the next level of agility and competitive advantage!

The best way to demonstrate your expertise is to acquire the ACP certification from PMI, and this book gives you a ***100% Money-back, 1st Time Pass, Guarantee!*** We know this book contains everything you need to pass. We believe you will use it to adequately prepare ***and we trust you!*** So if you don't pass the exam the first time – for any reason – just send us the original notice from Prometric showing you did not pass, your book and the purchase receipt, and we will send you a refund…***no questions asked!***

Again, congratulations on taking that important first step!

Pursuing the PMI-ACP^{SM}

This book will help you acquire the benefits available to anyone using or wanting to use Agile Project Management methods. It is good for people who are familiar with basic agile concepts as well as those who are not. Many Scrum Masters will discover "how to" information that applies the "Shu Ha Ri" theory they learned in their certification class to the real world challenges they are facing.

This book is for:

- Program Managers and Project Managers
- Scrum Masters and Product Owners
- Project Team Members – Engineers, Analysts, Developers, and Testers
- Customers, General and Senior Management
- Partners, Vendors, and Contractors
- College and University Instructors

In today's competitive job market, the ACP certification provides career-enhancing advantages beyond those offered by Scrum which is the dominant agile framework being practiced. Since all three authors of this book hold Scrum Alliance certifications, we obviously recognize Scrum's value.

Figure 1.4 compares the PMI-ACP^{SM} certification to the two best-known Scrum Alliance certifications (the Certified Scrum Professional and Certified Scrum Master). It is apparent from the comparison that the ACP goes beyond Scrum. Obtaining the ACP certification demonstrates to employers that one is a professional project manager who is familiar with Scrum, Extreme Programming (XP) and Lean Software Development frameworks. It also signifies the competency to work in environments where the versatility to tailor hybrid solutions beyond any single agile framework is important. Passing the ACP exam provides credible validation of expertise which spans a wide breadth of agile frameworks, tools, and techniques.

Frameworks Covered:	Agile Certified Professional (PMI-ACP^{SM})	Certified Scrum Professional (CSP)	Certified Scrum Master (CSM)
• Scrum	✓	✓	✓
• XP	✓		
• Lean	✓		
• Other Frameworks	✓		
Agile PM Education	21 hours; Taught by any PM education provider	Be current holder of CSM, CSPO, or CSD certification	16 hours; Must be taught by Certified Scrum Trainers
Work Experience	2,000 PM hours; 1,500 agile hours (Non-overlapping)	2,000 hours of Scrum-related work in the past two years	No requirement; 2 day class
Industry Orientation	Industry neutral	Software development	Software development
Exam Details	120 questions 3 hours Pass/Fail	150 questions 3 hours Pass/Fail	35 question evaluation 1 hour No Fail
Exam Administration	Proctored by a PMI contractor	Proctored by a Scrum Alliance contractor	Class instructor
Credential Expiration	3 year cycle; Must earn 30 PDUs in agile PM per cycle	2 year cycle; Continuing education required to retain certification	2 year cycle; Must retake evaluation to retain certification

Figure 1.4 Comparison of the PMI-ACPSM and Scrum Certifications.

Why THIS Book?

At GR8PM (pronounced "Great PM") we view Traditional, Agile, and Hybrid project management frameworks as complementary tools that every professional project manager needs to know. Selecting and using the right framework is a significant first step to delivering a successful project. We also know all successful PMs are pragmatists and once they have good command of the framework and its tools, they will make the right choice in applying the best approach to leading their project to success!

GR8PM also knows that employers and client organizations want the assurance of well trained professionals in their organizations. Therefore, we created this world-class exam preparation book for the new Agile Certified Practitioner (PMI-ACP^{SM}) and went a step beyond. In addition to doing an in-depth analysis of all 11 books listed by PMI as the basis of the test, we used our own expertise to create a useful, accessible digest of the Project Management Agile Body of Knowledge™ (PMABOK™). **That means this book will help you pass the exam and even more importantly, succeed in using agile methods as a professional project manager!**

With our experience and analysis reduced to writing, we applied the concepts of Accelerated Adult Learning Theory to the instructional design of this book to ensure it would give students the most help possible.

In a nutshell, Accelerated Adult Learning Theory, which was pioneered around 1980, confirmed what most people would see as common sense.[3] Specifically that **people learn in three different ways – visual, auditory, and tactile.** That research also confirmed that engaging all three ways creates the greatest learning and long-term memory retention. Each way of learning, or learning modality, is like a different type of radio broadcast – AM, FM, or Satellite. You find different music and different programs in each type of broadcast and tune to those stations for different reasons. Similarly, people use different ways of learning in different situations. Sometimes, visual learning works best. Other times, auditory learning is the best approach. And in some situations, tactile learning is needed. Often, how energetic or how tired an individual feels will impact which type of learning works best. Without a doubt, the absolutely best and longest-lasting type of learning takes place when all three ways are stimulated.

This book is designed to capitalize on the findings of Accelerated Adult Learning Theory and engage you in visual, auditory, and tactile ways of learning. Specifically, you will find explanations, illustrations, suggestions for writing notes and flashcards, and test questions throughout this manual. The explanations and activities provided will stimulate each type of learning modality and result in a thorough, long-lasting understanding of the material and concepts of Agile Project Management.

What the Exam Tests

First of all, please be very clear about one thing: *exactly what the ACP exam will test is not disclosed by PMI* and will continue to be "under development" for the foreseeable future time. PMI's initial pilot is over and the test is now administered and scored using industry-standard methods as with the PMP exam.

The ACP is different from PMI's other exams, like those for the PMP, CAPM, PgMP, and other certifications, because those can be traced back to *A Guide to the Project Management Body of Knowledge (PMBOK®) Fourth Edition*[4]. Unfortunately, there was no similar, authoritative guide for the Project Management Agile Body of Knowledge until this book was written.

This book provides a comprehensive explanation of everything that can reasonably be expected to appear on the exam. And in Chapter 11 we present a detailed discussion of what to expect.

About the Authors

This manual was created through the combined efforts of:

- John Stenbeck, PMP, CSM, CSP, PMI-ACP
- Joseph T. Drammissi, MSPM, PMP, CSM, PMI-ACP
- Bryan Berthot, MBA, PMP, CSM, CSPO, CPHIMS, PMI-ACP

We studied and analyzed all 11 books (3,888 pages) specified by PMI and then condensed that material into a usable format for both exam preparation and a daily Desk Reference.

John G. Stenbeck, PMP, CSM, CSP, PMI-ACP, is a Principal at GR8PM, Inc., with a combined background in information technology (IT), accounting, and operations. He has the ability to manage large, complex projects to success where others have failed. John has extensive experience implementing enterprise resource planning (ERP) systems at firms in the aerospace, shipbuilding, and construction industries.

John is an Adjunct Instructor for the University of California San Diego's School of Extended Studies, where he teaches project management in the Systems Engineering Certificate program. As a trainer, he has taught numerous public and corporate on-site programs to over 6,500 students. John helps technical professionals in the high technology, aerospace, defense, financial services, and bio-pharmaceutical industries master project management and executive leadership skills.

Over the past fifteen years, he has managed projects for a host of companies including Booz Allen Hamilton, Inc., Guinness Bass Import Company, Hewlett-Packard Company, Oracle Corp., Qualcomm, Inc., and Visa – Smart Cards.

John is certified by the Project Management Institute (PMI) as a Project Management Professional (PMP) and an Agile Certified Practitioner (PMI-ACP), and by the Scrum Alliance as a Certified Scrum Master (CSM) and a Certified Scrum Professional (CSP). Moreover, he has an ITIL v.3 Foundations certification. John graduated from San Diego State University with a BS in Business Administration, with an emphasis in Accounting. John has also authored seven nationally delivered training programs.

John is the immediate Past President for the PMI-San Diego Chapter and has been a very popular, highly-rated, frequent speaker at PMI Leadership Institute Meetings and Global Congresses for more than five years.

Joseph T. Drammissi, PMP, CSM, PMI-ACP, is a Principal at GR8PM, Inc., with expertise from a wide range of experience in both defense and commercial organizations, as well as in environments ranging from research and development to manufacturing.

Joe has worked as a design engineer, systems engineer, project manager, and program manager and is familiar with all aspects of the process from start to finish. He has designed products and systems ranging from oceanographic winches and underwater fiber optic cable deployment systems to solid state commercial lasers, gamma ray scanners, and bomb detection systems. Additionally, Joe has managed projects and programs producing complex RF subsystems, video exploitation systems, mail scanning systems, programmable power supplies, and synthetic aperture radar (SAR) systems for use on unmanned aeronautical vehicles (UAVs). He has the ability to manage large, complex projects as well as small, high-intensity turnaround projects.

The companies Joe has served share a business process environment that can be characterized as engineer-to-order (ETO) or configure-to-order (CTO). He also has expertise using Earned Value Management (EVM) in an environment governed by the Defense Federal Acquisition Regulations (DFARs).

As an Adjunct Instructor for University of California – San Diego's School of Extended Studies, Joe teaches in the Project Management Professional Certificate Program. He has also delivered corporate on-site training and is a sought after speaker on project management. Joe gives back to PMI as the Vice President of Professional Development for the San Diego Chapter where he is actively building vibrant, high value-added programs for its members.

Joe is certified by the Project Management Institute (PMI) as a Project Management Professional (PMP) and by the Scrum Alliance as a Certified Scrum Master (CSM). He holds professional certificates in Project Management and Systems Engineering from University of California – San Diego. He graduated from San Diego State University with a BS in Mechanical Engineering and will graduate from the University of Wisconsin with an MS in Project Management in 2012.

**Bryan Berthot, MBA, PMP, CSPO, CPHIMS, PMI-ACP,** is the President of Berthot Consulting LLC, a firm specializing in corporate training, organizational assessments of project management best practices, and Agile and Scrum coaching. He has over twenty years of experience in healthcare and information technology. Bryan has worked as a systems analyst, Extreme Programmer, database administrator, and project manager. An accomplished project management practitioner, he has led software development and business process improvement projects in both the corporate world and in the public sector. While at the National Institute of Mental Health (NIMH), Bryan co-authored a widely cited validation study of the Psychiatric Symptom Assessment Scale (PSAS), a clinical instrument used to evaluate psychiatric inpatients.

Over the past fifteen years, he has managed projects for several healthcare companies, including Ligand Pharmaceuticals, UnitedHealth Group, and Primary Provider Management Company.

As a project management educator, Bryan has trained thousands of project managers at the undergraduate and graduate levels, as well as middle and senior corporate levels. He has taught at the University of Maryland University College Graduate School of Business and Technology, at UC-San Diego Extension, at San Diego State University, and at many PMI chapters.

Bryan received his MBA from the University of Maryland University College. He is both a Project Management Professional (PMP) and an Agile Certified Practitioner (PMI-ACP). Bryan is also a Certified Scrum Master (CSM), a Certified Scrum Product Owner (CSPO), and a Certified Professional in Healthcare Information and Management Systems (CPHIMS).

Bryan currently serves as VP of Finance for the PMI-San Diego Chapter and is a frequent speaker at project management events.

Conventions & Standards Used in this Book

Chapter Highlights
At the beginning of each chapter, you will find an overview of the significant information introduced and covered within. You can use the summary to identify the critical content you need to know before you proceed or as a quick reference guide in the future.

Chapter Endnotes
The extensive endnotes included in this ACP Exam Prep book allow it to also be used as a Desk Reference for the Project Management Agile Body of Knowledge™, helping you locate useful source information. Although the endnotes may only be marginally helpful for exam preparation, they will be invaluable long after the pain of the exam has faded! That is when your boss and coworkers will expect you to be an expert in all things agile, and you will refer to the source material contained in the endnotes time and time again.

Key Notes
Throughout the book, the Key Note icon (shown on the left) is used to call your attention to important facts to master for the exam, as well as for daily practical reasons.

Flashcard Moments

Also throughout the book, we will use the Flashcard icon (shown on the left) to call your attention to important facts that are a good choice for creating flashcards. As we mentioned before, Adult Learning Theory has shown that learning through various channels increases retention and mastery. The act of writing a flashcard impacts learning on two channels – writing and then subsequent review. You can also buy pre-printed flashcards on-line at our website.

Agile PM Processes Grid™ Exercise

One of the best test preparation exercises a student can do is the Agile Project Management Processes Grid™ exercise. It gives students a chance to see how much content they have retained and can process from memory onto a blank sheet of paper, which will be provided by the proctor at the testing site. At the end of each chapter, you should take a blank sheet of paper and spend no more than 3 minutes seeing how much of the grid you can reproduce from memory.

It is an excellent self-assessment of what you have retained to that point from studying.

Terminology Matching Exercise

Every chapter has a terminology matching exercise to help reinforce your mastery of the agile lexicon that you will see on the ACP exam. It is also important because mastery of the "common language" enables successful interaction with other professionals in the field. The sooner you learn it, the sooner you will be on the road to success!

Crossword Puzzles & Word Searches

Also, you will find Crossword Puzzles and Word Searches at the end of each chapter. These exercises are designed to help reinforce key concepts and terminology in a fun and challenging manner.

Chapter Practice Test & Answers

At the end of every chapter, 20 questions were designed to test your command of that chapter's specific material. These questions come from our database of over 1,000 questions and are based on chapter terms, formulas, calculations, and concepts. They will test both your knowledge and ability to handle various question formats, such as multiple-choice, fill in the blank, and application to scenarios – all of which you can expect to find on the actual certification exam.

The answers to the test questions are included for your review and edification. In the answer key, you will find explanations of both the right and the wrong answers. You can then use these answers to assess your understanding or interpretation of the subject that the question covers.

Chapter End Notes

[1] Copyright © 2001 Kent Beck, Mike Beedle, Arie van Bennekum, Alistair Cockburn, Ward Cunningham, Martin Fowler, James Grenning, Jim Highsmith, Andrew Hunt, Ron Jeffries, Jon Kern, Brian Marick, Robert C. Martin, Steve Mellor, Ken Schwaber, Jeff Sutherland, and Dave Thomas; this declaration may be freely copied in any form, but only in its entirety through this notice.

[2] PMI conducts a role delineation study (RDS) every five to seven years to ensure their credentials reflect contemporary practice and evolve to meet the current needs of the profession and practitioner. PMI also does it to comply with the PMP credential's accreditation against the ISO 17024 standard. The RDS was completed in 2010.

[3] See, for example, the work of Dr. Georgi Lozanov, and the research published by Dewey, Glasser, Hunter, Bloom, Goodlad, Gardner, Stallings, and others.

[4] Project Management Institute. (2008). A guide to the project management body of knowledge (PMBOK® guide), Fourth edition. Newtown Square, PA: Author.

Introducing Agile Project Management

Chapter Highlights

In this Chapter we will begin with an overview of Agile Project Management and provide a quick, familiar example to help you create a high-level mental map of the subject. Then we will explore the idea of mapping Agile to the PMBOK® and review both agile planning and estimating as well as agile execution and control practices. With that mental map in place, we will cover the origins of Agile Project Management, the history of Lean systems thinking, and the application of Lean thinking to project management.

We will conclude by summarizing the agile frameworks and tools on PMI's ACP Examination Content Outline, plus a few other frameworks, including:

- Scrum
- Extreme Programming (XP)
- Lean Software Development (LSD)
- Other Agile Frameworks
- Test Driven Development (TDD)
- Agile Modeling (AM)

Lastly, we will introduce the ***Agile Project Management Processes Grid***™, a tool for ACP Exam preparation.

Overview of Agile Project Management

A Quick Familiar Example

Years of teaching experience have shown that sharing a quick, familiar example at the 50,000 foot level helps students create a mental map as they study Agile Project Management in greater depth. Below is an example of agile processes being applied in a situation that will be familiar to you.

You and three of your friends are hosting a dinner party together. Your project objective is to put on a successful party and remain friends afterwards! You are a cross-functional team because each of you has a different skill set. One is good at making cocktails, another is good at hors d'oeuvres, the third is good at entrees, and the fourth is good at desserts. Your team is not independently wealthy so it cannot simply outsource all of the work to a catering company. Consequently, you will be doing the work yourselves. To be successful, you want to establish mutual accountability as well as task integration so that there is support for each of you when it is time for the next deliverable.

The first agile principle in this example is that the team must have the necessary skills to complete the project. Agile is not a silver bullet! If a team does not have the required skills, even agile cannot help it successfully complete projects. **The second agile principle here is that the team must be self-organized, highly-trusted, and accountable.**

Because your team is also required on other projects (such as going to work) the team has agreed to use 4 iterations (in the evening) to complete the project. They are:

- Wednesday – Plan and acquire resources
- Thursday – Produce sub-components
- Friday – Complete and deliver the party
- Saturday – Clean up and do a retrospective before the next party

An *iteration* is simply a *timebox* within which work will be completed. In the agile world, work is done in iterations and a release can be the output of a single iteration or the output of several iterations that are inter-related by design choices.

> **Iteration #1** for your party is planning. Your team sits down and talks about what kinds of cocktails, hors d'oeuvres, entrées, and desserts you will serve. Based on the outcome of that discussion, the team prepares a shopping list of ingredients needing to be purchased in order to put on a successful dinner party. Each store where the team will shop is put on a separate piece of paper and assigned to a team member to purchase those items.
>
> At the conclusion of iteration #1, the theme of the party, shopping lists, and a plan for its delivery have been established. These deliverables are referred to as a *potentially shippable product increment.* If a blizzard should blow into town on Thursday and prevent the party on Friday, the team has still produced a result, or output, which is useful when the project is resumed.
>
> This agile principle is incremental building and frequent delivery of *potentially shippable product increments.* A potentially shippable product increment is anything that has value because the customer can see or use it to understand project progress. It may also have reference value for the team after an unexpected delay in order to restart the project. Also, a foreshadowing of the practice of *user stories* can be seen in the shopping lists. User stories are written documents that help the team understand what work needs to be done.

Iteration #2 is preparation and logistics, specifically food preparation and set-up. Because you are working as a cross-functional team, you gather in the kitchen and help each other with washing, peeling, chopping, and storing the food ingredients you will use the following night.

At the end of iteration #2, you, once again, have an increment of value in a deliverable. All of the sub-components have been prepared or created and stored in the refrigerator.

If you should get an unexpected call that three of your guests missed their plane, forcing the party to be postponed until Saturday night, the iteration was still successful. The team produced a result, or output, which demonstrates project progress and is useful when the project is resumed. Furthermore, if the party was postponed for a week and some of the prep had to be redone due to spoilage, it would be similar to the work required to ramp a project back up after it has been stopped.

The agile principles seen here are colocated work space (the kitchen) and also interrelated yet independent deliverables that demonstrate project progress.

Iteration #3 is execution; welcoming your guests and enjoying dinner with them. Everything goes as planned, good conversation occurs, and you enjoy your guests and the time around the table together. You have delivered (or consumed) another potentially shippable product increment.

In the **agile vocabulary,** we would refer to **Friday's output** as both a **potentially shippable product increment** and as a **release.** It's considered a release because it was the cumulative effort of the first 3 iterations and it was delivered to the customer – your friends. A key idea in Agile Project Management is that a release can be planned one of two ways. This example demonstrated one approach, where the release deadline was known and fixed and therefore the exact feature set was subject to some adjustment if needed. The focus was to deliver something the customer valued when it was promised. For our example, the release was set for Friday and the customer (your friends) expected a deliverable of food and festivities, which they received.

The second approach to release planning is to define specifically what will be delivered and then analyze when it can be completed. After all, at a high level, the only way to fix both the scope and the date is to vary quality, and in **agile, quality is never varied** – it must be a working piece of functionality.

Iteration #4 is cleaning up with a retrospective meeting immediately afterwards. With agile in a normal environment – not the daily iterations we described here – **the team holds two meetings at the end of each iteration.** The first meeting is the **review meeting** where the potentially shippable product increment is presented to all interested stakeholders for their review and feedback. The review meeting is **product focused.** In our example, the customers ate the meal and were satisfied with the product, which was, in effect, a review meeting. The second meeting, which only the team attends, is the **retrospective meeting.** The retrospective meeting is **process focused.** The team uses that time to identify ways to improve how they create deliverables.

Because the project was completed by a cross-functional team, they also managed to remain friends, fulfilling a key objective. The project is complete, everyone is happy, and the experience with Agile Project Management has been both educational and successful.

This simplified example illustrates some of the key concepts and challenges of Agile Project Management. One of those key concepts is the idea of breaking up larger projects into interrelated, incremental deliverables. Those deliverables must be related and integrated in a fashion that continuously delivers value by building units of the solution. Each unit must be independent and build on prior work to move towards the final comprehensive solution. Finding the people in any organization who have the level of expertise needed to plan those types of increments is a very real challenge.

Is Agile Really Needed?

Even though there is an early precursor of agile in the concept of rolling wave planning, the last major tool recognized in the Project Management Institute's ***"A Guide to the Project Management Body of Knowledge (PMBOK® Guide Second Edition)*** was the Critical Chain in 1997[1]. That fact raises the first question we should ask, "What has changed since then?" Consider the following:

- Google launched in September, 1998
- The iPod was unveiled in October, 2001
- The BlackBerry "smartphone" was released in January, 2002
- NASA's Phoenix lander extracted Martian ice in June, 2007
- The iPad was introduced in April, 2010

Interestingly, the Apple iPad provides a "classic case study" in Agile Project Management. In Lean and agile terminology, it was a full function device that included the **minimum marketable feature** set, yet it was not a full feature tablet PC. Because it was focused on what the customer wanted, it sold 3 million devices in 80 days and almost 15 million devices in the 8 months of 2010, taking 75 percent market share of tablet PCs by the end of the year. That meant that it sold more units than all other tablet PCs combined.

The success of the iPad speaks eloquently to the success that agile enables. It also challenges organizational leaders who may feel an expectation for them to produce achievements like Steve Jobs.[2]

Even PMI acknowledged the increased demands and complexity of the project management universe when they moved beyond the long-cherished Iron Triangle – time, cost, scope – that was a part of every edition of the PMBOK through the Third Edition. With the release of the PMBOK, Fourth Edition, PMI took the traditional view of time, cost, scope, and added quality, risk, and customer satisfaction. The triangle became a hexagon in order to express the increased complexity that project managers now face in the everyday world. Soon project managers around the world will be speaking about the *"Hell-of-a-Hexagon"* that replaced the *"Iron Triangle."* (See Figure 2.1.)

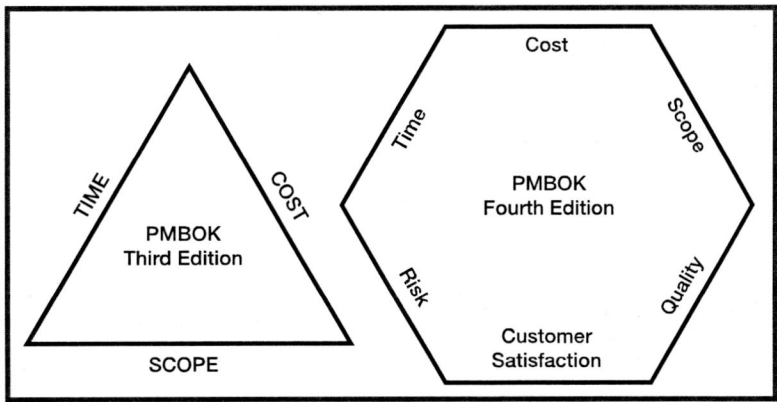

Figure 2.1 Comparing the "Iron Triangle" to the New "Hell of a Hexagon."

There is an abundance of additional evidence that points to the added complexity faced by project managers. Consider the high project failure rates documented over the last couple of decades by the Standish Group in the aptly named CHAOS Reports.[3] Or consider the report from Standish that proved only 20% of the features being delivered to users are in the "Always" or "Often Used" categories, while only 16% are "Sometimes Used," and a full 64% fall into the "Rarely" and "Never Used" categories.

Mapping Agile to the PMBOK®

Under the "Traditional" project management umbrella, PMI is the industry leader. PMI has the largest membership base, by far, of any professional user group for project managers and has developed the most recognized and best-respected credentials and certifications for practitioners in the project management field. There are, however, a host of smaller regional and local players that offer competing membership and certification choices. Regardless, PMI remains the leader and dominates the trends in identifying best practices because of its extensive research grants and educational scholarships.

Under the "Agile" project management umbrella, the Scrum Alliance (SA) is the biggest player because it has the largest membership base specifically in the agile sphere. It developed and controls the most recognized certification – the Certified Scrum Master (CSM) – for practitioners in the agile PM discipline. However, a host of smaller regional and local players offer competing memberships and certifications as well. (See Figure 2.2)

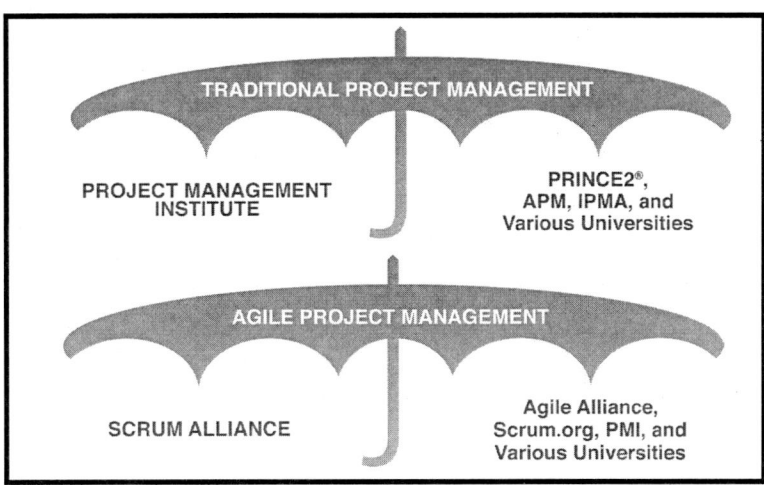

Figure 2.2 A Comparison of Traditional and Agile PM Industry Participants.

Because of the high profile that the SA has in the agile sphere, it is common to refer to Scrum and agile interchangeably – much like Kleenex® and facial tissue – but it is not always accurate to do so. ***Scrum*** is a variant, flavor, or approach within agile, however agile preceded Scrum and is broader than Scrum. Agile also includes several other notable frameworks, such as ***Extreme Programming*** (XP), ***Lean Software Development*** (LSD), and ***Feature Driven Development*** (FDD). Agile also has a group of others that make up a minute part of the market, including ***Crystal, Dynamic Systems Development Method*** (DSDM), ***Agile Unified Process*** (AUP), and ***Spiral.*** Finally, although the SA is the current leader in the agile space, PMI's new ACP certification can be expected to challenge their position and eventually dominate the landscape over the next few years.

Agile Planning and Estimating

In order to compare traditional planning and estimating to agile, we have to first understand the assumptions that underpin each method.

In the traditional world of project management represented by the PMBOK®, the first assumption is that scope can and should be defined at the very beginning of the project (Figure 2.3). Although some evidence challenges the validity of assuming that scope can be accurately defined at the beginning of a project, it continues to be the starting assumption for traditional project management. PMs who have worked on large, complex projects have experienced change order process controls, change management boards, and any number of other tactics deployed to manage and control changes in scope. Despite all the effort to manage scope changes, it often proves futile. Nonetheless, **traditional project management starts with an assumption that well-defined scope is possible.**

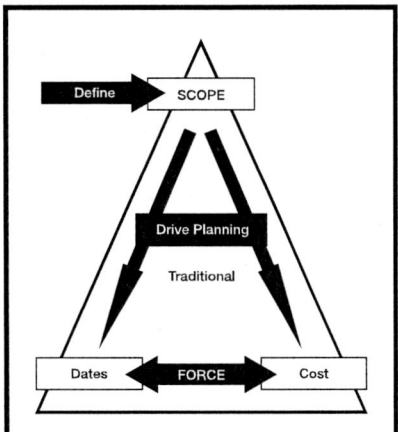

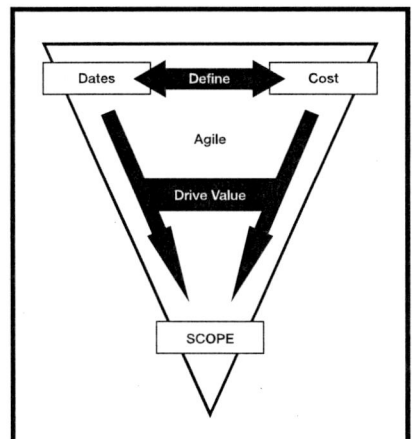

Figure 2.3 Traditional PM Assumptions. Figure 2.4 Agile PM Assumptions.

This first assumption of well-defined scope drives the next assumption that desired dates and cost constraints can be honored. Once again, PMs who have worked on large complex projects often report the futility experienced when trying to get dates and costs to conform to a plan.

By comparison, the **first assumption for agile** methodologies is that the **customer clearly knows the date they wish to receive the solution and also the cost constraints that must be observed** (Figure 2.4). Because the customer knows these two pieces of data *firmly*, agile methodologies use dates and costs as the starting point for planning and estimating. Agile then proceeds based on the assumption that rigorous communication with the customer will drive value by refining project scope as development makes the options, and their costs, clearer.

Working with the customer, the **agile team strives to drive value by prioritizing the most important aspects of the project scope and developing them first.** In agile, planning and estimating is focused on creating accurate estimates that are reliable because they are within an appropriate, manageable, near-term time horizon. Beyond the near term horizon, agile estimating and planning focuses on avoiding the expensive illusion of false precision. Instead it uses tools, techniques, and tactics that provide robust, reliable planning at an intelligent, appropriate cost. The agile tools, techniques, and tactics used to do so will be covered in greater detail in subsequent chapters.

Before we move on, it is worthwhile to point out, as many traditional project manager's would, that anyone who has worked on large complex projects knows that having an available, involved, and rational customer may be more elusive than trying to get dates and costs to conform to a plan that reflects changing external realities.

Agile Execution and Control

Execution and control in Agile Project Management relies on the use of **timeboxes** and **feedback cycles.** There are several types of timeboxes employed in Agile Project Management.

The highest level timebox is referred to as a *roadmap.* An agile roadmap is most equivalent to a program plan in the traditional project management world. Roadmaps are composed of release plans, the next lower level timebox in Agile Project Management. The size of the timebox represented by a roadmap is the sum of the release plans within the roadmap (See Figure 2.5).

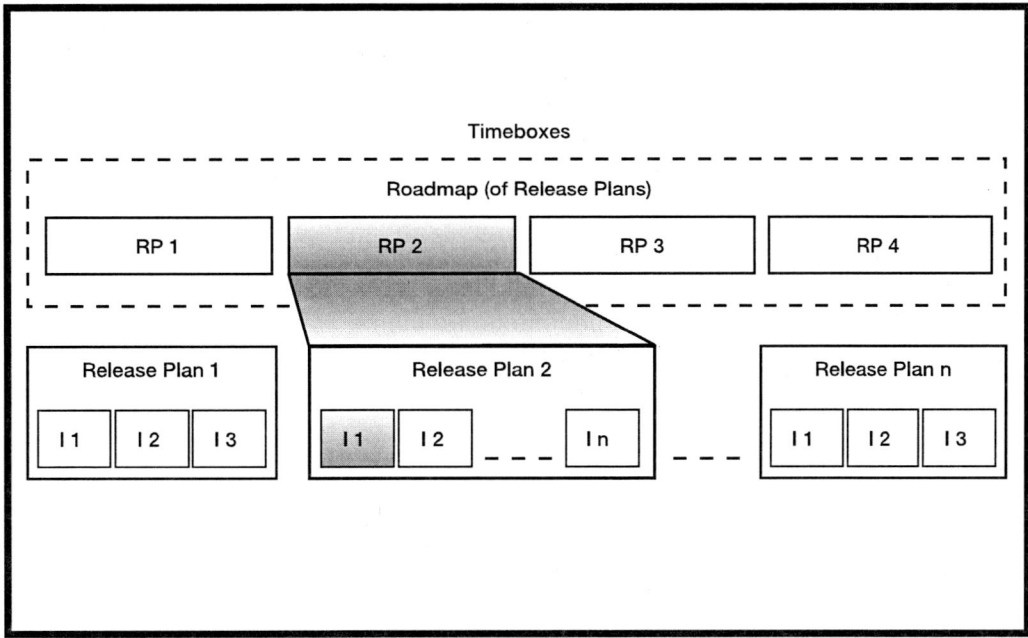

Figure 2.5 Agile Roadmap of Release Plans.

A *release plan* is a timebox equivalent to a project schedule in the traditional project management world. Release plans identify specific feature sets that represent a recognizable, logical component of the overall solution. Quite often, release plans represent the point at which deliverables can be used or implemented by customers. Release plans are composed of iteration plans. The size of the timebox represented by a release plan is the sum of the iterations within that release.

An *iteration plan* is the third timebox. Iteration plans are unique because they are a combination of a timebox and detailed work effort descriptions (See Figure 2.6). Each iteration contains the **user stories,** which describe the work effort for specific features or components that will be created by the agile team. Within iteration plans, user stories are decomposed into tasks, which can be estimated for the amount of work required to complete them. Iteration plans define the work that will be done in that specific timebox. Iteration plans are rolled up into release plans.

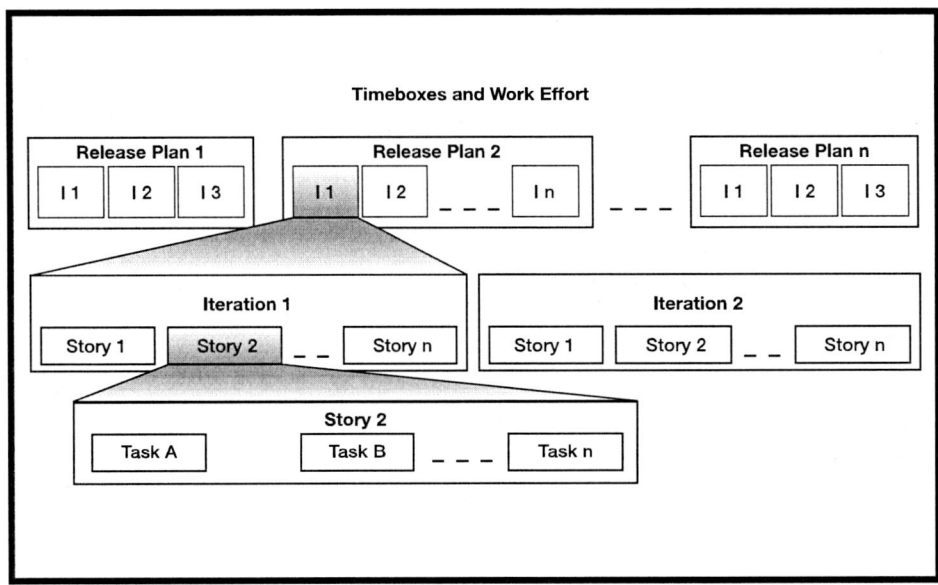

Figure 2.6 The Iteration (or Sprint) Plan.

By definition, the size of the timebox for an iteration is stable. Based on organizational norms or rules, an iteration timebox will typically be defined as either two, three, or four weeks. Once the timebox for iterations has been defined, it remains fixed because rhythm helps the team increase speed, while stability helps the team improve quality over time.

Feedback cycles occur at several distinct points in the process.

 One of those points is the *daily meeting* for the agile team. The daily meeting is sometimes referred to as a stand-up meeting or a Scrum meeting and is held to synchronize the activities of all of the team members. It also allows measurement of work progress against the iteration plan.

 Another of those feedback points is the iteration *review meeting,* which occurs at the end of each iteration timebox and is **product** centric. At the end of each iteration, the agile team presents the completed deliverables to all interested stakeholders. This allows the stakeholders to see the most recent work product of the team and give feedback on how well it meets their needs and expectations. It provides transparency between the stakeholders' needs and the agile team's work, allowing adaptation to occur while it is easier and less expensive to make changes.

 The third feedback point is the iteration retrospective meeting. The retrospective also occurs at the end of each iteration and is process centric. During the retrospective meeting, the agile team, Scrum Master, and Product Owner discuss process improvement ideas. It provides an opportunity for all members of the team to identify what changes would produce better work products, reduce errors, or improve communications.

The Origins of Agile Project Management

History of Lean Systems Thinking

Although arguments can be made that rigorous process thinking went into building the pyramids and many other significant accomplishments of antiquity, Henry Ford and his team of engineers – in particular Henry Gantt – are considered the first to truly integrate an entire production process. Around 1913 they integrated the ideas of interchangeable parts, standardized work units, and automated conveyors in order to produce what they described as production flow. The dramatic productivity gains made with a moving assembly line were revolutionary.

The revolution went beyond mere productivity gains and created insight into the theoretical foundations of mass-production manufacturing. Ford used process sequencing, single-purpose machines, and control-gate decision points to deliver required parts and sub-assemblies directly to the assembly line. Each of these ideas was a revolutionary break from prior standard practices of process grouping, general purpose machines, and batch-production decision points, which delivered parts still needing subassembly to the assembly line.

However, there were two significant problems with Ford's approach. First, the production system could not accommodate variability and second, the manufacturing machines could not handle complexity. This was epitomized in Henry Ford's, now infamous, statement that customers could have a Model T in any color they wanted...as long as they wanted black! But color wasn't the only limitation. All Model T chassis had to be essentially identical even though customers could choose one of four body styles. Because the single purpose machines only worked on a single part, changes were not possible and the model cycle for the Model T ended up being longer than 15 years. In the end Ford's system, while much more efficient than his competitors, lost out to other automakers who responded with many models and many options for each model.

The production systems of Ford's competitors handled variability and complexity, but at the cost of much longer throughput times. Their larger, faster machines lowered costs per unit but continually increased throughput times and inventories. Compounding the problem, the lag time between process steps, because of the complex routing of parts, required immense management effort that eventually spawned the computerized Materials Requirements Planning (MRP) systems that have become common.

In the midst of this manufacturing milieu, Sakichi Toyoda, founder of Toyota, and his son Kiichiro Toyoda, worked to build upon what the Ford had done using ideas from W. Edwards Deming.[4] Although they were unimpressed when they observed an American mass production assembly line, they were struck by an idea while shopping in a supermarket. They observed the simple idea where a customer took whatever soda they wanted and it was automatically replenished to await the next time a customer decided to take one.

As the Toyodas and Taiichi Ohno studied this situation, it occurred to them that a series of simple innovations might make it possible to provide both continuity in process flow and a wide variety in product offerings.[5] The result was the Toyota Production System (TPS).

The revolutionary idea within the Toyota Production System was that the focus should be shifted from individual machines and their utilization, to optimizing the product flow through the whole manufacturing process. Using concepts that aligned parts and sub-assembly production to the actual volume needed, applied self-monitored quality, and integrated process sequencing with quick changeovers, TPS created a system where each step "requested" materials from the previous upstream step to meet current needs. The outcome was low cost, high variety, high quality, and very short throughput times, which allowed them to respond to changing customer desires. As an added benefit, managing the immense MRP systems became much simpler and more accurate.

Today the ideas developed by W. Edwards Deming and the Toyota Production System are generally referred to as *"Lean."* The concepts of Lean were first described by James Womack in the book *The Machine That Changed the World*.[6] A few years later, Womack and Daniel T. Jones defined the five core Lean principles in their classic Lean Thinking.[7]

The Five Core Lean Principles are:
1. Define the value the customer desires.
2. For each product, identify the value stream that provides customer value and challenge all of the wasted steps not directly providing it.
3. After removing the wasted steps, make the remaining value-added steps flow continuously through to the product.
4. Wherever possible, use "pulling" between steps to create continuous flow.
5. Continuously move toward perfection by reducing the number of steps, and the amount of time and information needed, to provide the customer value.

Because these five principles provide the theoretical foundation that influenced Agile Project Management, they are important to know and remember.

The terms pushing and pulling are Lean manufacturing concepts. ***Pushing*** signifies a "make to stock" (MTS) supply chain philosophy where production is not based on actual demand. Pulling is a "make to order" (MTO) approach where production is based on actual demand.

Lean thinking has spread through every industry, and nearly every country, causing leaders to adapt the tools and principles from manufacturing into services, healthcare, construction, and even charitable, institutional, and government settings. But Lean has only begun to influence senior managers and leaders compared to what the future will likely hold as time-to-market becomes a critical competitive differentiator.

The Lean principles summarized above have evolved into a set of core beliefs that should also be well understood in preparation for the ACP exam. Those core beliefs can be articulated as:

- The measure of success for any system or process is the amount of time between when ideas come in and when value is received by the customer.
- Any ad hoc system or process will produce unacceptable delay in customer value because it cannot be studied or improved upon. Therefore, processes must be defined in order to improve customer value.

- Most process errors are caused by the system, not the people who work in the system. Therefore, the people doing the work are the best qualified to define how to improve the system.
- The goal is to optimize the whole system, not merely improve individual steps. Therefore, optimizing the whole system or process by looking at when steps occur is a better path to improvement than trying to optimize the efficiency of each step.
- Because the goal is to optimize the whole system and because the people doing the work are the best qualified to improve the system, management must work with the team in order for the system to improve.
- Teams, as well as systems, have inherent capacity limits that cannot be violated without subverting quality and sustainability. Therefore, teams are most efficient when the amount of work expected is within their capacity and efficiency is best improved by minimizing the amount of non-value or low-value work in process at any time.

These core beliefs create an agile paradigm where managers and teams work together toward the goal of maximum customer value. That fact is true whether the Lean principles are applied to software development, healthcare delivery, professional service delivery or any other field.

Application of Lean Thinking to Project Management

Proponents of traditional project management cite its success in the fields of engineering and construction as an indicator of its applicability to fields like software development. Since teams take requirements and build products that customers can use (not unlike engineering, construction, or other fields of product/service development and delivery), the theory implies traditional project management should work well. There are a number of problems with this thought process.

First, unlike construction where detailed blueprints are available before construction begins, or engineering where models or algorithms are available to specify specific processes before manufacturing begins, software development usually starts without clearly defined requirements or models that hold the rules for the complex variables that are involved.

Second, the immense variability and complexity of developing software makes the challenges faced by Ford pale in comparison. The variability is driven by the constraint of being human, which is to say we cannot perfectly perceive the best solution to a complex problem without going through incremental stages of development. The complexity is fueled by the wide range of variables, such as situational context and multiple platforms (i.e., PC, web, and mobile), which the solution must handle.

However, success in the software world – with all of its immense variability and complexity – has proven that Lean systems thinking, as embodied in Agile Project Management, can clarify what solution is needed and the process of discovery that can produce it. **Because the end goal is delivering value to a customer, Lean and agile processes are applicable to a great many fields outside software development.**

Applying the basic principles from Lean Manufacturing to project management requires the practitioner to **accept the idea that fast, flexible flow in the development process** – sometimes called the **development pipeline** – is possible. Many new practitioners have great skepticism about the whole idea that their specific industry could be modeled or managed as a fast, flexible pipeline. They discount that a value stream could be mapped or that mapping and refining it using Lean concepts as a guide would bear any useful benefits.

In order to help you prepare for the ACP exam, as well as prepare to apply Lean concepts in the workplace, we will now describe the Agile Project Management practices that are implied in Lean thinking. As we do this, you will see how agile practices have grown out of Lean principles. The reason for developing this understanding is twofold; first, when a question on the ACP exam describes a situation where an agile practitioner has found himself in a situation where standard agile practices won't work, you can use the Lean principles to guide you to the right answer and second, the development of this understanding will lead to better responses to workplace challenges.

Agile Project Management begins with the Lean concept that creating a sustainable stream of products requires directing business resources and focusing development teams so that results are based on **prioritized business needs which are defined to create customer value.** That, in turn, requires focusing on speeding up time-to-market by removing delays in the development process.

Another important concept implied by Lean, but made an explicit goal in Agile Project Management, is to **improve communication.** Quantitatively, improved communication reduces risk while also improving quality and dramatically increasing the likelihood of achieving real customer value.

Unfortunately, Agile Project Management practices tend to focus on communication at the local level – within the team, with the customer, and to a lesser degree, between multiple teams. Current Agile Project Management practices offer only limited support for improving communication across the enterprise or across the entire value stream. This weakness is being addressed by new practices in agile program and portfolio management.

Agile Project Management also embraces the Lean concepts of **deferring commitment** and **eliminating waste** as good ideas. Many practitioners are distracted by those word choices and fail to consider the evidence before making a judgment. But, as we mentioned earlier, when one considers the high project failure rates documented by the Standish Group in the CHAOS Reports and their research that showed 64 percent of the features being delivered to users fall into the "Rarely" or "Never Used" categories, the only viable conclusion is that when the Lean concepts of eliminating waste and deferring commitment are properly understood, they create value.

 In Lean, and therefore also in Agile Project Management, ***deferring commitment*** means that decisions are made at the **right time,** sometimes referred to as the "last responsible moment." Although this idea is counter-intuitive to many project managers because traditional project management has spent decades developing massive specifications at the beginning of a project, it is entirely sensible. Ask any experienced project manager whether it is better to (a) plan and estimate a project when very little is known about the problem or solution, or (b) plan and estimate a project when good information is known, and they will laugh at you because the answer is so obvious! Millions of change orders – change orders that could have been avoided – also validate the sensibility of this concept.

The concept is to **resist making decisions too early,** when needed information is not available, simply to create a sense of security or precision that will often turn out to be false. Conversely, the concept also warns against making decisions too late and incurring avoidable, higher costs, which usually occurs because the decision maker was too risk averse and wanted more accurate information used in the estimate.

The financial rationale for deferring commitments is quite straightforward. It is well known that with the application of additional effort – that is, time spent by resources that are usually expensive and in short supply – the accuracy of any estimate can be increased. As shown in Figure 2.7, 10 hours spent on an estimate might create 80% accuracy, while spending 20 hours might improve the accuracy to 90%. The problem is that a 12% improvement in accuracy (i.e. (90% - 80%)/80%), has required a 100% increase in cost, from 10 to 20 hours.

If that wasn't onerous enough, consider the fact that the **value of any estimate decreases with the passage of time.** Estimates are most valuable early in the project when little is known, and least valuable late in the project when much is known. So the focus in **Agile Project Management is to produce detailed estimates only when enough is known to get useful accuracy at a reasonable cost.** In Agile Project Management deferring commitment can be readily applied in defining requirements and doing analysis and estimating.

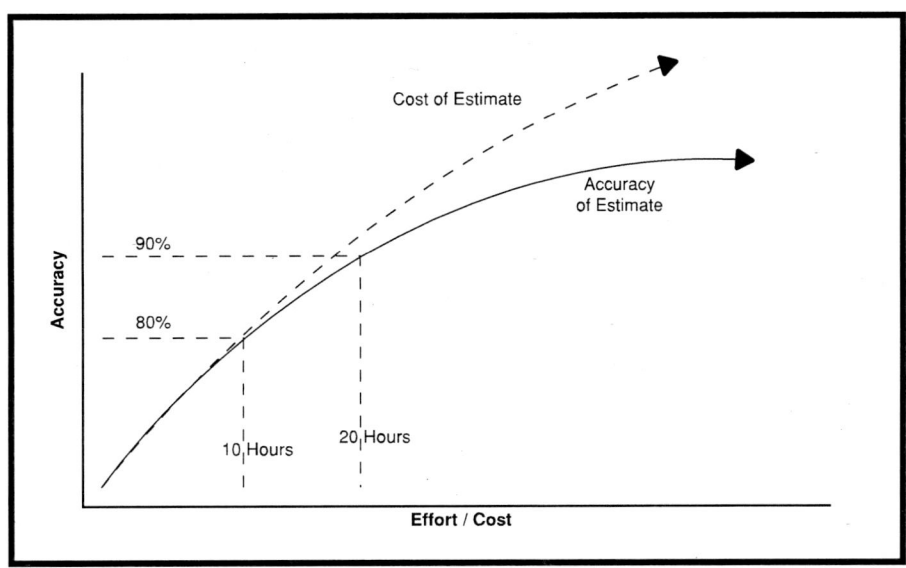

Figure 2.7 Accuracy Versus Cost of Estimate.

The goal of defining requirements and creating estimates should be to prioritize where resources are invested. If we simply stop to consider whether it is really necessary to define every single customer requirement, the answer should be a clear, "No." What we need is great clarity about the requirements that will impact development resources on a reasonable time horizon – 60, 90, or 120 days.

Some requirements are more important, more urgent, or more technically complex than others. As a guide, **Agile Project Management should start with those requirements that are the most important to the customer, involve safety, and create technical risk for things like scalability.** Then, once those priorities are defined, move to requirements that improve marketability, performance, and flexibility. Finally, focus should shift to requirements that leverage opportunity or create comfort and luxury.

Recognize that commitments cost money because they spend time doing some kind of work, which can never be restored or the cost undone. Therefore, commitments should be spent doing work on the requirements that will bring the greatest value to the customer. Agile Project Management directs resources to the requirements that customers define as most important.

As we have shown, **Agile Project Management embraces deferring commitment.** Now, let's see why the concept of eliminating waste is a good idea.

Most of the projects being managed today involve a considerable degree of architectural or technical risk, with risk being a good indicator of potential waste. After all, few things are as wasteful as building the wrong thing or building something no one will ever use. Therefore, **eliminating waste has primary importance** as a guideline for the Agile Project Management practitioner.

Waste comes in many forms. In software, it is code that is more complex than needed, causing undue defects and creating extra quality control work. In manufacturing, it is non-value-added work spent to create a product. In other contexts, waste is unneeded paperwork or documentation, or missing paperwork or documentation that creates errors or rework, or a failure to create clarity that would have increased the speed at which the deliverable could have been created. Wherever waste is, Agile Project Management seeks ways to improve the system and eliminate it, because it is likely that errors will be repeated until the system that caused it is fixed.

Lean asserts that the most common and perhaps largest waste in traditional project management is the effort spent on detailed planning done too early in the project. To consider this idea from a Lean point of view, ask yourself, "When is it best to estimate, when little is known about the problem and solution domains or when much is known?" The answer is so obvious that when we ask that question in class, many students are hesitant to answer because they suspect it is a trick question.

Most project managers would acknowledge, especially on large, long projects, that accurate information is the least available during the early stages. Customers often have only a vague notion of how to describe the best solution. They often use the phrase, "I'll know it when I see it," which is referred to as the "IKIWISI syndrome" (pronounced icky-whizzy) to express their lack of clarity. Yet, this is when traditional project management often produces detailed requirements documents, very specific contract language, and detailed project plans.

Agile Project Management avoids this type of waste using a technique called emergent design. **Emergent design limits resource commitments and costs to those features that are currently necessary.** A comparison of the two concepts is shown in Figure 2.8, where a traditional waterfall approach that begins with a large effort to define everything and ever smaller efforts spent on elaboration over time, is contrasted with an agile approach, which only elaborates those things that are needed for reasonable clarity on a practical time horizon, such as 60, 90, or 120 days.

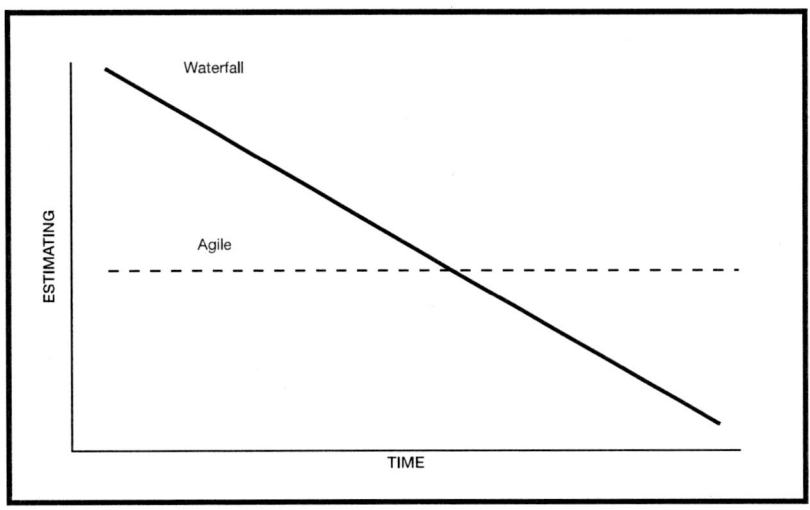

Figure 2.8 Estimating Effort/Resources over Time.

Emergent design has a dual meaning. It means that results emerge from an internal creative work process rather than being the result of an external blueprint. It also means that the design artifactsare more than the sum of the parts or a permutation of existing factors cobbled together by a team. It implies that the design process is creative and cannot be done by rote or by accident so it must be intentional.

 When emergent design is applied in software development, it also integrates the discipline of *design patterns* to create application architecture that is durable and flexible, as well as automated acceptance and unit testing, to improve code clarity and reduce defects. **The use of design patterns enables code to more easily adapt to change by reducing complexity.** Reduced complexity is achieved by limiting coding to defined, current needs. Automated testing validates the design pattern, making the code safer to change should the need arise. Therefore, emergent design and automated testing combine to enable the deferral of commitments until implementation variables are reasonably understood.

 A central tenet of Agile Project Management is that knowledge about the context of the problem and the variables of its solution are discovered and created as an integral part of the development process. **Agile Project Management solutions are created, built, or developed in stages so that as the customer uncovers specific real needs (remember IKIWISI?) the team can design and write code accordingly.** The analogy below may help clarify your understanding.

According to a recent article, at any given moment there are 500,000 passengers riding in airplanes over the United States. Due to factors like headwinds and crosswinds and collision avoidance routing, each of those flights is off course more than 90% of the time. The reason the vast number of those flights – or projects – are completed as intended is because the pilot uses accurate, transparent, real-time data to make minor course corrections as needed.

 In Agile Project Management, the person who is the *voice of the customer,* called the *Product Owner* in the Scrum lexicon and *customer/proxy* in this book, is continuously taking in stakeholder feedback data and using it to provide the team with minor course corrections.

By doing Agile Project Management this way, the team delivers value quickly and avoids building things of little (or no) value. Remember that creating customer value is more of a discovery process than a building process. Software, buildings or medical devices have little inherent value. Value occurs when any of these enable the delivery of a product or service that solves a customer problem. Therefore, it may be more useful to think of product or service development – whether the deliverables are tangible or intangible – as a set of activities used to uncover the real needs, and the real problems, of customers and furthering the strategic goals of the organization by addressing them.

Applying Lean to Agile Project Management implies accepting the mindset that it is necessary to deliver increments of the solution, early and often, so that the customer can experience specific aspects of the solution and reduce IKIWISI at each stage.

 Delivering increments early and often requires development to be done in iterations, which is referred to as *iterative development.*

The financial reason for doing iterative development is that customer value can be realized more quickly. Doing so improves market penetration, generates greater credibility for the business, creates strong customer loyalty, and increases profit margins. It also typically allows revenue streams to begin sooner, which, in turn, offsets the cost of subsequent development and reduces the total capital commitment required, directly increasing return on investment (ROI).

The financial benefits of Agile Project Management demonstrate the value of Lean's focus on time and timing. Time is one of the core focuses in a Lean approach. Instead of the traditional project management focus on resource utilization – which has driven matrix-type organizational structures and multitasking of workers – **Lean zeroes in on reducing the elapsed time from idea generation to delivery of value to the customer.** Of course, since time is money, when the team goes faster by using an improved system or process, costs go down.

Agile Project Management also uses the Lean focus on time and timing to reduce risk, in part, by eliminating delays that create waste. For example, some common delays that create waste in software are: requirements waiting to be verified as correct, work stoppages because a clarification is needed from a customer or analyst, and waiting for code that has been written, but needs to be tested. In healthcare, some common examples of waste are: delays experienced when a patient is waiting for insurance coverage to be verified as correct, when a pharmacy can't dispense a prescription because a clarification is needed from the doctor, and when a pharmaceutical has passed testing, but is waiting to be approved by a regulator. These delays represent both risk and waste because delays increase the likelihood that something will be misunderstood and, in turn, multiply the potential of something going wrong.

By using iterative development steps, Agile Project Management creates the ability to make minor changes that move in the direction of the real solution without wasting effort. Borrowing from the Lean Manufacturing vocabulary, agile seeks to **minimize work-in-process (WIP).**

For Agile Project Management, WIP means those things that are described as 60% done or 80% done, or some other percent done in a traditional project status meeting. Because the customer cannot reduce IKIWISI and progress toward the real solution cannot be accurately measured, WIP has no value even though it has cost.

Whereas a traditional project may spends months or years going from 20% done to 30% done to 90% done, it isn't until it is 100% done that the customer can truly ascertain if real value has been created. There are myriad examples of projects that accumulated astronomical costs while in a state of WIP only to be judged by the customer as having no value when the deliverables were finished. In those cases, the work done by the team has gone directly from WIP to waste, and despite elaborate risk management protocols, potential risk germinated into very real problems.

One well known example of this was Motorola's multibillion-dollar venture into satellite-based phones – the Iridium project. While some might argue that Iridium was a success from a technical perspective, despite remarkable financial forecasts and intense project management, the entire venture turned out to be a financial debacle because it failed to deliver customer value.

This could have been avoided by using Agile Project Management's iterative development process, where the customer is given something at the end of each iteration that can be used, seen, applied or sampled, in order to produce clarity about needed course adjustments. The impact is organic risk mitigation and systematic value generation.

Summary of Agile Frameworks & Tools

As was previously stated, Lean provided a foundation upon which agile methodologies have developed. Likewise, agile provided a foundation, which is broader than Scrum, upon which the Scrum framework has developed into the most used framework with the largest association of practitioners.

 A key point to note is that the lexicon used in this book is the most common taxonomy of *methodologies, frameworks, and processes.* (see figure 2.9) Methodologies provide the philosophical foundation for organizing frameworks, and in project management the two dominant choices are traditional, as embodied in the PMBOK®, and Agile. *Methods* are used to create and define *frameworks* as logical foundations. Frameworks are used to develop *processes,* which are the practical "how to" protocols used to guide things like sponsoring, organizing, funding, and controlling projects.

Methodology	Traditional		Agile			
Framework	PMBOK®	PRINCE2	SCRUM	XP	LEAN	CRYSTAL
Process	Proprietary		Framework Specific			

Table 2.9 A Taxonomy of Project Management Methodologies, Frameworks, and Processes.

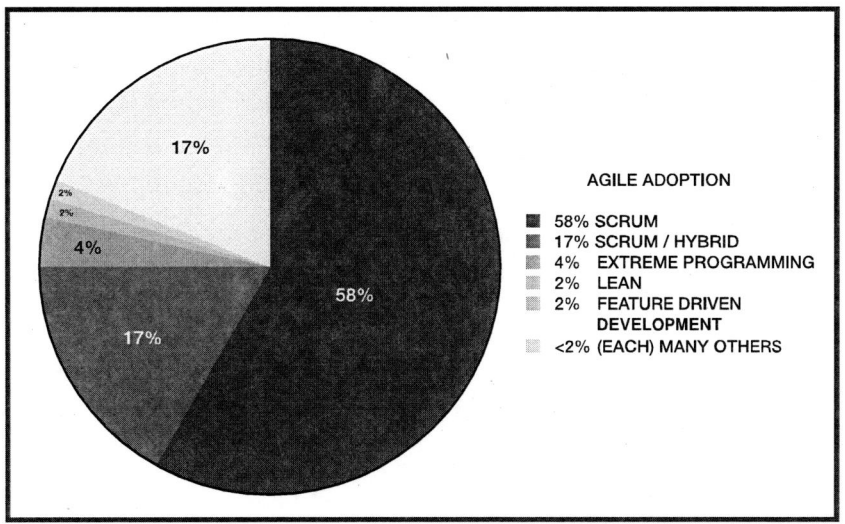

Figure 2.10 Agile Adoption by Framework.

Research indicates that the most common frameworks are Scrum, Scrum Hybrids, Extreme Programming (XP), Lean Software Development, and Feature Driven Development (FDD)[8]. These data are presented in Figure 2.10. There are also a host of other frameworks that each hold a very small market share, including Agile Unified Process (AUP), Crystal, Dynamic Systems Development Method (DSDM), and Spiral.

Each of the agile frameworks started in a specific context, which influenced how they applied Lean principles. In order to properly prepare for the ACP exam, and also to clarify which framework to start with when an organization first adopts Agile Project Management, we will briefly describe the various agile frameworks here.

Here, we summarize:
1. **Scrum,**
2. **Extreme Programming**
3. **Lean Software Development**
4. **Other Frameworks**
5. **Test Driven Development**
6. **Agile Modeling (AM)**

because PMI has specifically named them in its announcements for the ACP exam.

1. Scrum

(NOTE: As mentioned above, because Scrum is the dominant approach in Agile Project Management, we will develop an in-depth explanation of it in later chapters, but we will introduce and summarize it here.)

Scrum is a project management framework that uses iterative cycles and incremental deliverables to develop solutions. Scrum has been used extensively for agile software development, and more recently has begun to move into engineering, construction, and medical/pharmaceutical organizations.

The seeds of Scrum were planted in 1986 when Hirotaka Takeuchi and Ikujiro Nonaka wrote about a new approach to product development that increased speed and flexibility.[9] They described a holistic or "rugby" approach of one cross-functional team moving through multiple overlapping phases, "passing the ball back and forth," similar to what happens in a rugby Scrum.

However, the Scrum name first appeared in 1991 when Peter DeGrace and Leslie Stahl first referred to this as the "Scrum approach" in their book ***Wicked Problems, Righteous Solutions.***[10] But Jeff Sutherland, John Scumniotales and Jeff McKenna were the first to refer to it using the single word "Scrum" as the name of the approach they developed at the Easel Corporation.

In 1995, Jeff Sutherland and Ken Schwaber, another early luminary, collaborated in writing, sharing experiences and suggesting industry best practices. Their work became the first public presentation of what is now known as Scrum.

The Scrum framework is intended to be lightweight and contain a minimal set of practices and roles that can be customized after it has been learned and implemented.

In the Scrum framework, work is done during specified timeboxes, referred to as "sprints" (a synonym for iterations), which are typically between two and four weeks in length. Deliverables, referred to as "potentially shippable product" increments, are expected at the end of each sprint.

The ethos or heart of Scrum lies in the mutual commitments exchanged between the organization and the team. The organization agrees that the size of the timebox for all sprints, and the specific deliverables for each sprint, will be stable or frozen. In exchange for the organization's promise to allow the team to focus and work uninterrupted, the team commits to delivering the specific deliverables at the end of the sprint regardless of unknown challenges that may surface while they are in the process of creating the deliverables. In essence, the organization promises to be reliable, giving the team a stable work environment for the period of the sprint, and the team promises to be as creative as necessary to solve the problem and conquer the unknown.

The main roles in Scrum are:
Scrum Master (SM) – The SM ensures the process is understood and followed, shielding the team from outside interference and removing impediments for the team.
- **Product Owner (PO)** – The PO is the "voice of the customer" representing the stakeholders and the business, and setting the priorities for deliverables.
- **Team** – The Team is a cross-functional group, which creates solutions by analyzing, designing, developing, testing, and implementing deliverables. It is assumed that the team has all the needed skills, is highly trusted, and self-managing.

Scrum supports self-organizing teams by preferring colocation of all team members so that immediate verbal communication is possible between all the subject matter experts on the team.

One **key principle in Scrum,** which is shared by the other frameworks, is that during a project, **customers need to be able to change their minds about requirements,** and the best way to meet those emerging needs is a combination of short term stability (during the sprint) and long term flexibility (outside the sprint). Scrum and other agile frameworks accept that complex problems cannot be fully defined in advance; they use the scientifically validated empirical process control approach – transparency, inspection, and adaptation – to focus the team on quickly delivering results that move through the cone of uncertainty towards a solution in the midst of emerging requirements.

Again, because Scrum and Scrum Hybrids are the framework being used by 75% of organizations implementing agile, it will be highlighted throughout this book. At this point, however, we will move on to summarizing the other frameworks.

2. Extreme Programming (XP)

Second to Scrum, in adoption rate and marketplace usage, is Extreme Programming (XP).

XP began as a response to two major changes in software development. First, new object-oriented programming methods began to replace procedural programming as the approach favored by businesses. Second, speed-to-market became a strategic growth issue as the Internet and the dot-com boom realigned the competitive business landscape. Shorter product life-cycles demanded agility to handle rapidly changing customer requirements, creating an environment that was incompatible with traditional software development.

XP was intended to respond to these pressures and optimize business value. Because full implementation of XP requires a very mature operating environment and also very high levels of discipline, it is only well-suited to a limited number of organizations.

The ideas for Extreme Programming were formalized by Kent Beck in his book on the method, *Extreme Programming Explained.*[11] As its name implies, the context in which XP started was software, so it is a programmer-centric framework focused on technical practices that promote skillful software development. Also as its name implies, XP applies techniques and practices with extreme rigor as long as doing so improves results.

Beginning in 1999, a very elementary "XP System Map," as shown in Figure 2.11, has been used to illustrate the core XP concepts.[12]

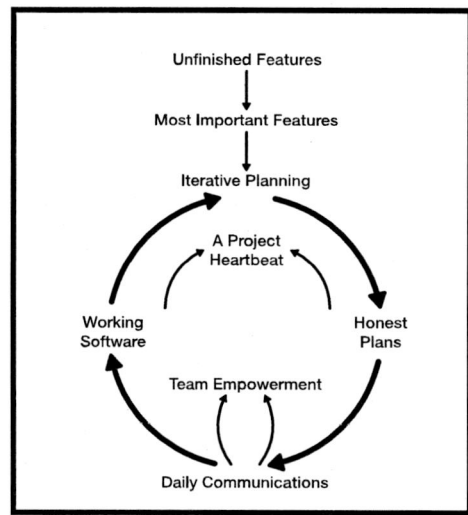

Figure 2.11. The XP System Map.

Over the course of time, this has expanded with best practices emerging, such as continuous code reviews, pair programming, unit testing, modularity, bottom-up design, incremental design patterns and refactoring of all code.

XP currently defines five basic activities within the software development process:

- *Coding* - As one might expect given the context of its start, XP states that the most important product of the development process is software code because without code, there is no working product.
- *Testing* - Testing, and predictably lots of it. Since the most valuable product is code, testing has extreme value because the more flaws it can eliminate, the more working code (and therefore value) can be delivered.
- *Listening* - Listening, although common sense, is a departure from the expected "short list" for the stereotype of "propeller heads." In XP, programmers listen to what "business logic" the customer needs so they can understand those needs well enough to discern the technical aspects of a viable solution, unless it is discovered that the problem cannot be solved.
- *Designing* - Designing, specifically for simplicity. The goal is to limit system complexity at the threshold where it is mandatory, and no more than that, and prevent dependencies becoming unclear. XP seeks to avoid that trap by creating modular designs that organize the system logic with the minimum amount of dependencies.
- *Communicating* - Communication is, again, unexpected for the stereotype. Whereas listening defined programmer behavior towards customers, communicating to the customer expresses the need to have system requirements from the customer for the developers.

The XP goal is to rapidly create and distribute organizational knowledge to the development team, creating a unified view with the customers and users of the system.

 For the ACP exam, students should note that the roles on an XP project include:

- *Customer:* The customer creates and prioritizes the stories to be developed. Unlike other agile frameworks, the customer can vary the release date by adding or removing stories from the backlog to be delivered in any given release. Similar to other frameworks, the customer sets the development priorities.

- *Programmer:* The programmers estimate stories, accept responsibility for tasks, write tests, and write code, usually working in pairs.
- *Coach:* The coach, while preferred, is optional and monitors the process, mentors the team on XP processes and techniques, and helps the team identify and focus on risks and optimization opportunities.
- *Tracker:* The tracker, another preferred, but optional position, monitors team progress and warns when redistributing tasks might be required to adjust the schedule. Sometimes a programmer "doubles" as tracker for the same pair, and sometimes a programmer serves as tracker for a different pair.

The following are considered the *12 Core Practices of XP:*

- Planning Game: The **Planning Game** is a technique used to elicit new requirements from the customer, with the team then giving an estimate of the effort required to develop and implement it.
- *Small releases:* Begin with the smallest useful feature set. Release early and often, adding a few features each time.
- *Product theme:* Each project has an underlying theme or metaphor, which provides an easily remembered naming convention.
- *Simple design:* Employ the simplest possible design to get the job done.
- *Test-driven development (TDD):* Write a test before adding a feature. When the suite runs, the job is done. We will discuss TDD in more detail later.
- *Refactoring:* **Refactoring** refers to constantly improving a product's internal design (e.g., rewriting code) without changing its behavior to make the product more reliable and adaptable.
- *Pair programming:* **Pair programming** is a technique where two programmers work together on one computer. The first programmer types in code while the second programmer reviews each line of code as it is written. The first programmer is called the driver. The second programmer is called the observer or navigator. They switch roles frequently. The observer considers things like potential problems with strategic choices, as well as ideas for improvements. The driver focuses all of his or her attention on tactical choices and completing the current programming task.
- *Collective code ownership:* This is a practice where everyone shares responsibility for the quality of the code, allowing anyone to make necessary changes anywhere.
- *Continuous integration:* With **continuous integration,** all product changes (i.e., to the code base) are integrated at least daily. Unit tests have to run at 100% both pre and post-integration.
- *Forty hour work week:* The development team works a standard 40 hour week. A maximum of one week of overtime is allowed. If additional overtime is needed, this is considered a serious failure of the agile process and must be evaluated.
- *On site customer:* The development team has continuous access to an on site customer. For commercial software with many stakeholders, a proxy may be used.
- *Coding standards:* Everyone codes to the same standards and conventions.

Agile, in general, has a goal of using *face-to-face* (F2F) and **osmotic communication.** This is typically achieved through colocation arrangements described as a "caves and commons" area.

The team is located together where they have a "commons" area everyone shares to facilitate instant or immediate communication. The co-locate area also has "caves," which provide private space for when team members need to retreat and focus in order to solve a challenging issue. This type of arrangement fosters osmotic communication; team members regularly pick up important data "by osmosis" – data which they otherwise might not get.

 Osmotic communication can be described as a team member picking up pieces of a conversation in a common area and then being able to make a meaningful contribution even though he or she was not fully engaged in the discussion.

Another view on the term osmotic communication draws on science where an element moves through a semi-permeable membrane into another organism. In agile, the experience of team learning has been described as an almost effortless or unconscious assimilation or diffusion of knowledge that seemed "osmotic." The explanation seems to be that the mind becomes semi-permeable when it is engaged in solving a problem. So simply being immersed in an environment where team discussions are happening around the person whose mind is so engaged, causes information to flow in or act upon the mind.

Among the common criticisms of XP are problems with requirements stability, lack of documented design specifications at the architectural or systems level, and lack of a document trail defining compromises made to solve user conflicts. There is also controversy about the "reality" of XP practices such as the demand to have the customer/proxy on-site, or the requirement to have a unified customer viewpoint versus a single programming organization. Because scalability is often required in today's globally distributed world, XP has been perceived as having limited value by many organizations.

3. Lean Software Development

As with XP, the name of the Lean Software Development (LSD) framework gives away the context of its start up. **The goal of the LSD framework is to eliminate any unnecessary burden or overhead from the software development process.** Unlike other agile development frameworks, LSD is concerned with how the organization perceives and articulates the systems they want, and that concern shows up during requirements gathering and documentation efforts.

The original LSD framework descends from the work of W. Edward Deming, with more recent improvements being drawn from the Theory of Constraints. Lean manufacturing – and hence the name, Lean Software Development – grew out of Deming's work on Total Quality Management (TQM). TQM emphasized the importance of process and the absolute truth that the people using the process are the ones who must build and improve it. TQM is very quantitative and metric centric, so it is no surprise that metrics play a significant role in LSD as well.

The newer additions to LSD come from the work of Dr. Eliyahu M. Goldratt on the Theory of Constraints (TOC).[13] The TOC stressed the need to first identify constraints and then remove, or at least improve the constraints, in order to improve the business organization, which is a self-contained system.

Therefore LSD processes pursue the goal of defining, developing, and delivering complex software systems that exactly meet the competitive business challenge. The emphasis on the project management aspects of software development, rather than the technical ones, means LSD shares thinking with Scrum. Both frameworks seek to manage costs and improve the project's ROI.

Because of LSD's focus on gathering the correct requirements (those with the biggest impact to the business) and defining them with great clarity and completeness so they can be verified, the customer plays a central, critical role. Continuous customer feedback regarding the functional requirements needed to create business value, also helps identify missing, conflicting, and incomplete requirements.

More so than many other agile frameworks, LSD uses the focus on requirements to create an abundance of quantitative metrics to guide configuration and management decisions so that project failure can be avoided. Because LSD focuses on the "root cause" of issues such as resource constraints, teams lacking the correct skills, and excessive team membership churn, it often creates political discomfort. That discomfort will be most pronounced in organizations where projects are executed within departmental silos, or other insulated settings.

Unlike other frameworks that have semi-strict role definitions, LSD uses a more cross-functional approach. Team members are cross-trained on functional and technical facets of the system, as well as on the business problems to be solved or business value the system features are expected to provide to the customer.

Because **LSD focuses** more on the project management side and requires few specific technical practices, it can be integrated rather easily with other agile frameworks such as XP, which focuses on the technical facets of software development.

The **LSD framework** upholds seven principles, which began in Lean manufacturing and have been extended in its approach to project management. The principles are:

1. **Eliminate Waste** – It does not add customer value so eliminate it!
2. **Build Quality In** – Validate all assumptions and use metrics throughout the process to ensure practices create value, otherwise discard them.
3. **Create Knowledge** – Use short iterative cycles to get continuous feedback and ensure focus is on the right things.
4. **Defer Commitment** – Don't make decisions until a clear understanding of the problem, the solution choices, and the tradeoffs of each are available.
5. **Deliver Fast** – Identify business issues as quickly as possible and then deliver a system or feature that solves them.
6. **Respect People** – Only the employees using the system can improve it, so empower the team to succeed by enabling them to improve it.
7. **Optimize the Whole** – Always use cross-functional teams so important or critical facets of the problem aren't overlooked and the solution design will solve it.

4. Other Frameworks

While these frameworks are not specifically mentioned by PMI as part of the knowledge base required for the ACP exam, probably because they hold such a small market share, it is nonetheless worthwhile to have a cursory understanding of Feature Driven Development (FDD), Agile Unified Process (AUP), and Crystal.

The other frameworks – Dynamic Systems Development Method (DSDM), Essential Unified Process (EssUP), Open Unified Process (OpenUP), and Spiral – make up such a minute part of the market that we will not cover them.

Feature Driven Development (FDD)

Among the various agile frameworks, Feature Driven Development (FDD) may be the most "tightly wrapped." Whereas other frameworks begin with a set of principles or processes, the FDD core is the domain model.

Defining the domain model is a mandatory first step for FDD. Creating it requires that domain knowledge be collected from subject matter experts (SMEs), referred to as Domain Experts, and then integrated into a cohesive model that accurately represents the problem domain. Using the Domain Model, validated requirements are analyzed and a plan is drawn up to create the solution and determine the resources needed to build it.

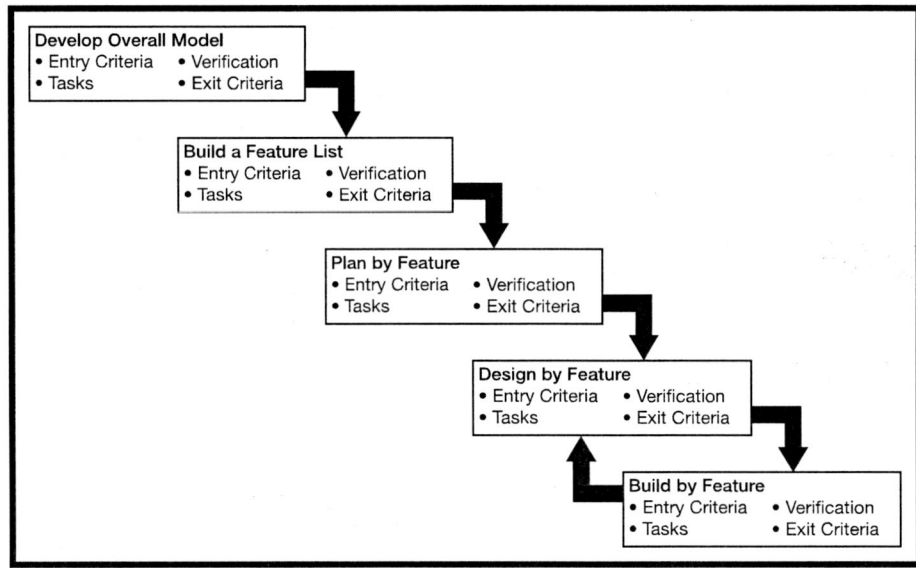

Figure 2.12 Feature Driven Development Process Map.

Typically requirements are gathered using a top-down approach where general business practices are defined as Subject Areas. Subject Areas are decomposed into business activities that are defined as Feature Sets. Feature Sets are decomposed into tasks, defined as Features, that can be clearly specified and accurately estimated.

The development activities of building the features drive the team's work (hence the name, Feature Driven Development) through iterations that are typically no more than two weeks long. Sets of features are developed, one after the other in successive iterations. For reporting purposes, data is collected at the feature level and rolled up into Feature Sets, and Feature Sets can then be rolled up into Subject Areas.

As shown in Figure 2.12, the **FDD framework requires five steps** that must be followed in order to create a very specific process. The steps are:

1. Develop Overall (Domain) Model
2. Build a Feature List
3. Plan by *Feature*
4. Design by *Feature*
5. Build by *Feature*

In the FDD framework everything is planned, designed, built, and managed at the feature level. Other levels like feature sets, domain areas, and requirements lists are available for higher-level planning and reporting, but the "master key" is the feature.

In FDD a feature is defined as a small, client-valued function. It is expressed as an *action* that causes a *result* to an object. The formula for defining features is written in the form:<action><result> [of|to|for|from] <object>, where the information in the square brackets is optional and used to make the feature statement easier to read. For example, a feature statement might read, "Calculate monthly payment for car loan." The verb "calculate" is the <action>, the noun "monthly payment" is the <result>, and the noun "car loan" is the <object>.

FDD also defines more specific roles and responsibilities than most other agile frameworks. The **nine roles are:**

1. **Project Manager** – The PM is responsible for all administrative, financial, and reporting facets of the project
2. **Chief Architect** – The CA controls the design of the Domain Model and solution (system or process) and manages the technical architecture, design sessions, and code reviews.
3. **Development Manager** – The DM manages daily development activities, coordinates the development team, and resolves resource issues.
4. **Chief Programmer** – The CP is a senior developer who is responsible for a specific Feature Set and manages their design and development activities.
5. **Class Owner** – The CO is a developer who reports to the CP and designs, codes, tests, and documents features as they are implemented.
6. **Domain Expert** – The DE is a business SME and stakeholder who defines requirements as features that the solution must provide. Business analysts are the most common DEs, but anyone with knowledge of how the system will impact the business can be a DE.
7. **Tester** – The Tester is responsible for validating that features perform as defined.
8. **Deployer** – The Deployer manages the data definitions and conversions and supports the deployment of code to the various platforms.
9. **Technical Writer** – The TW creates and maintains the documentation that users will need to operate the system.

Because of the number and specificity of the roles in FDD, it does not use the principle of ***shared ownership of code*** and ***artifacts*** the way other agile frameworks do.

For the ACP exam, students want to know the definitions of shared ownership of code and artifacts:

Shared ownership of code, also known as collective code ownership, means every programmer is allowed to change any part of the code. Therefore, every programmer is responsible for all the code. Pair programming supports this idea because as programmers work in various pairs, they get exposed to all the code in the system. Advocates say this is a major advantage because it speeds up development and any errors in the code are fixed by programmers when they encounter them. The obvious risk comes from programmers who do not see subtle dependencies. Well-defined unit tests are used to address this issue.

Artifacts are the data records that document a record of the projects inputs, outputs, and progress points. In Scrum, the four principal artifacts are the Product Backlog, Release Burn-down, Iteration Backlog, and Iteration Burn-down. Artifacts may be kept electronically, but are intended to be used as visible information displays.

Another unique aspect of FDD is the very specific report style used to report project progress. Most agile frameworks use lists to track requirements and work done. In FDD, all lists correlate to specific features while also using a Feature Set Progress Report. The Feature Set Progress Report tracks feature development progress by subject area using specific color codes and percentage complete. Light green means the Feature Set is on schedule, dark green means the Feature Set has been completed, and grey means the Feature Set is behind schedule. Feature progress is rolled up into a table showing progress against Feature Set milestones in the Feature Set Progress Report.

Features are completed a line graph showing the project's total progress by day or week. The exact state of each feature is documented in a table with **six specific milestones.** They are:

1. Domain Walkthrough
2. Design
3. Design Inspection
4. Code
5. Code Inspection
6. Promote to Build

From these steps, stakeholders can see how the project is progressing.

Agile Unified Process (AUP)

The Agile Unified Process (AUP) framework is a simplified version of the Rational Unified Process (RUP). The RUP is an iterative software development framework created by the Rational Software Corporation, a division of IBM, and developed by Scott Ambler and Larry Constantine.[14] It is generally considered a "high ceremony" framework because it specifies many activities and artifacts for each project. The AUP defined an easier-to-use approach for developing software based on integration of agile techniques and concepts. The AUP includes test driven development (TDD), agile modeling, agile change management, and code refactoring techniques to improve productivity.

The AUP is based on six philosophies, which are:

1. **Competence** – The team knows what it's doing. They won't read detailed process documentation, instead will apply high-level guidance and standards.
2. **Simplicity** – Describe things concisely on a few pages, not reams of pages.
3. **Agility** – The AUP conforms to the values and principles of the Agile Alliance.
4. **Activity** – Focus on only the high-value activities that count. Ignore the noise.
5. **Tools** – Simple tools are often the best, so AUP is independent of any toolset. AUP recommends using the tools best suited for the job.
6. **Tailor** – AUP works best when tailored to the needs defined by the context.

The AUP kept the four major phases of the UP, which are:

1. **Inception** – Inception cultivates a shared understanding of the project scope and defines architectural choices.
2. **Elaboration** – Elaboration develops the understanding of the system into requirements and validates architectural choices.
3. **Construction** – Construction occurs until system development is completed.
4. **Transition** – Transition all testing and system deployment to production.

These phases occur serially and conclude after a specified milestone is accomplished. The AUP made a significant change to the UP when it defined two types of iterations. The first is a development release iteration that reaches the Transition milestone when it is deployed to a non-production environment, such as a quality-assurance and testing environment. The second is a production release iteration that reaches the Transition milestone when it is deployed to the production environment.

The AUP simplified the RUP by focusing on seven disciplines, which are:

1. **Model** – Use a model to represent the organization's business approach, the problem domain, and any viable solution to solve the problem.
2. **Implement** – Code the model(s) into executable code and perform unit testing.
3. **Test** – Apply additional tests to find defects, validate the system design works, verify the requirements are satisfied, and ensure code quality.
4. **Deploy** – Plan and deliver the system for end users.
5. **Configuration Management** – Control all project artifacts, including version tracking and change management.
6. **Project Management** – Provide project management, including scope, resource, risk and progress management, and coordination of external interfaces, to achieve an on time, on budget completion.
7. **Environment** – Provide process guidance standards and ensure needed tools are available for the team.

Risk management in **AUP prefers that high-risk elements be prioritized early in development.** For example, the core architecture is developed during the Elaboration phase to validate requirements, assumptions, and address technical risks. AUP also uses a risk list to document and manage risks throughout the development process.

Crystal

Among the agile frameworks, Crystal is the only one that is actually a family of frameworks that vary based on project size and criticality. Crystal was named by the author, Alistair Cockburn, in his book *Crystal Clear: A Human-Powered Methodology for Small Teams.*[15] Each specific framework within the family is designated by a color that correlates to the hardness of a geological crystal, thereby implying the project's size and criticality.

In **Crystal, size is defined by the number of people involved in a project.** As team size grows, more formality or ceremony is added to the structure, artifacts, and management. In Crystal, criticality is defined as the potential damage the system can cause. For example, an operating room system malfunction can cause far more damage than a video game controller that misfires. As project criticality increases, the formality of control needs to increase to guarantee that requirements are fulfilled.

Cockburn once stated that even though the Crystal frameworks share elements, they are not expected to be upward or downward compatible. For example, a Crystal Clear project does not transition to a Crystal Maroon project because of an increase in size and criticality. Instead should the project become Maroon, the project should adopt the Maroon framework, not expand the prior Crystal Clear practices.

This approach offsets a significant weakness in Crystal. The only authoritatively published specific information for applying Crystal is for the Clear and Orange levels, with some discussion of a variant called Crystal Orange Web, surfacing recently. Cockburn has dismissed this criticism saying, in effect, if you feel you need details you don't have adequate background to use Crystal. We find that response less than satisfying. Nonetheless, Crystal does encapsulate some insightful thinking.

Regardless of which Crystal version is chosen, they all share seven key principles. The seven key principles are:

1. **Frequent Delivery** – FD means stakeholders and customers receive deliverables every couple of months, at a minimum. Large deliverables may not go into the production

environment, but intermediate versions of them should be available in a test environment where stakeholders and customers can provide feedback.

2. **Continual Feedback** – CF means the team meets on a regular basis to discuss project activities with stakeholders and uses feedback to confirm that the project is headed in the desired direction or make adjustments as needed.
3. **Constant Communication** – CC means that on small projects the team is colocated in the same room, while larger projects are colocated in the same facility or on the same campus. CC also means that teams have frequent access to the persons defining requirements.
4. **Safety** – Safety is recognized in Crystal in two forms. The first form, which is common to most agile frameworks, recognizes the need for a "safe zone" where team members can communicate without fear of reprisal. This allows hard truths that might impact the overall process to be brought to light early, because team effectiveness suffers without access to the truth during the project. The second form, which is unique to Crystal, recognizes that some software projects affect end-user safety. For example, a weapons system is far more critical than a music organizer.
5. **Focus** – The top two or three priorities are clearly shared with the team and the team is given uninterrupted time to complete them.
6. **Access** – As with most agile frameworks, the team must have adequate access to end users of the system while it is being built.
7. **Automated Tests and Integration** – Testing and integration must be supported by automated versioning, testing, and integration of system components.

Determining the Crystal framework to use for a project is done on a grid like Figure 2.13. The horizontal, X-axis, is divided into five columns defined by colors correlated to size, ranging from Clear to Maroon. The numbers in the cells are the upper size limit of the project team. As the project team size increases the framework choice moves from left to right, from Clear to Maroon, because the project is expected to be harder.

	CLEAR L = 6	YELLOW L = 20	ORANGE L = 40	RED L = 80	MAROON L = 200
(L) Life	L6	L20	L40	L80	L200
(E) Essential Money	E6	E20	E40	E80	E200
(D) Discretionary Money	D6	D20	D40	D80	D200
(C) Comfort	C6	C20	C40	C80	C200

Figure 2.13 The Crystal Family of Frameworks.

The vertical, Y-axis, is divided into four rows, correlated to criticality, which rise from the bottom upward, and noted as "C" for Comfort issues, "D" for Discretionary Money issues, "E" for Essential Money issues, and "L" for Life impacting issues. As the criticality of a project increases the framework choice moves from the bottom to the top of the column because the framework must adapt to the additional requirements and artifacts needed.

In the Crystal Clear framework, roles are limited and all team members are expected to be colocated in the same room. The most important role is the Senior Designer who makes all the technical decisions. The team decides what artifacts will be produced and what coding standards and test practices will be followed because project milestones are actual working software, not documents. Other duties such as project management, business analysis, and testing are shared by the Sponsor and Programmer(s). Working software is expected to be released every 60 to 90 days, even if work is performed in shorter iterations.

Nothing has been published regarding the Crystal Yellow framework.

In the Crystal Orange framework the number of roles increases, and can vary between organizations and projects, but typically include the Sponsor, Project Manager, Business Analyst, Architect, Designer(s), Programmer(s), QA Engineer, and Tester(s). There is greater formality about what artifacts will be produced and what coding standards and test practices will be followed. Working software is expected to be released every 90 to 120 days, even if work is performed in shorter iterations.

Crystal Orange defines the artifacts and deliverables as:

- Requirements Document
- Release Sequence (Schedule)
- Project Schedule
- Status Reports
- User Interface Design Document (if a UI is delivered)
- Object Model(s)
- User Documentation or Manual
- Test Cases

Nothing has been published regarding the Crystal Red and Maroon frameworks.

5. Test Driven Development (TDD)

Test-driven development (TDD) is a software development process; an Agile Project Management tool, not a framework. It is used in *conjunction* with a framework.

TDD has grown out of the test-first concepts of extreme programming, and more recently has enjoyed general interest on its own. The most common usage occurs when automating an existing manual process that has a current testing process. It is also applied to improve legacy code developed with older languages.

TDD uses repetition of very short development cycles where a developer writes test preconditions, test controls, and test reporting based on predicted outcomes that define a desired improvement or new function. The developer then writes code and uses automated testing software tools to monitor the execution of the code to test the *actual* outcomes against the *predicted* outcomes. If the code fails the automated test case, the developer refines it until code is produced that passes. As a final step the code is *refactored*, processed by a tool that makes small changes in the code that do not modify its functionality, but improves attributes like readability, complexity, maintainability, and compliance with architecture or object model standards for extensibility – until the new code meets established standards.

In TDD, the programmer focuses on passing the immediate test and only then considers how to handle exceptions, errors, and rare circumstances. It is easy to jump to the conclusion that TDD only provides validation of the correctness of code, but it is useful to recognize that it can also drive program design. The discipline of understanding how customers will use specific functionality, which is needed to create the test cases, raises awareness and concern about the interface before implementation occurs and drives design in a beneficial direction.

However, TDD can be difficult to apply with programs that integrate to databases, where full functional tests are required to determine success or failure or where code is dependent on specific network configurations. It also has a possibly significant weakness because tests are created by the developer who is also solving them. Therefore tests may miss the developer's "blind spots" regarding user specifications. And, of course, management may object that the tests increase overhead and maintenance.

6. Agile Modeling (AM)

Agile Modeling (AM) is also not a framework, but a modeling *tool* for software development projects. It is used in conjunction with a framework.

 For the ACP exam, students should note that **AM is a collection of values, principles, and practices used to create models for software development projects.** It is intended to be an effective, light-weight approach that is tailored *into* a framework such as Scrum, XP, or Lean. AM creates effective models that support development of solutions using a performance-based approach.

The basic **AM principle is to create multiple models in small increments** because any given model is bound to include some inaccuracies. The practice is to create an abstract representation of the software then prove or disprove its performance with code that actually works or does not work. Using the right artifacts from each model, the team improves its understanding of the situation, and iterates to the next model and artifacts, to follow a continuous forward march to a usable solution. Active stakeholder participation in AM is critical because the project stakeholders know what the result of a successful model will be and can provide the feedback needed to improve between each one.

The principle of *applied simplicity* is used in AM to focus on the practice of only creating models for the current facet of the problem and avoiding large, detailed models. The principle of open communication is practiced in AM by displaying models on walls or Wiki's, embracing collective ownership of artifacts, following modeling standards, and using group-based model development.

AM suggests doing just enough modeling to understand the scope of the problem and the architecture of possible solutions, then using development iterations to improve those models until a solution can be created.

The Agile Process Map™ & Agile PM Processes Grid™

Agile Process Map™

Now that you have been exposed to a significant part of the agile lexicon, it is time to put those ideas together in an Agile Process Map™ that can be used to guide and integrate the detailed learning in the rest of this course.

As you may have gathered from what you have learned so far, the agile worldview centers around the team's work as the point of value creation. So from the team-centric view, the macro perspective is a process that moves from a "steady state" to a "transition state" to a "steady state."

The first steady state encompasses the activities of the customer/proxy, or in Scrum vernacular the Product Owner (PO), who is receiving, analyzing, and prioritizing the features required for a successful solution. That work is kept in an artifact referred to in Scrum as the ***product backlog.*** The Product Backlog is equivalent to the product specification or requirements list in traditional project management. It is, however, significantly different because the PO is continuously ***grooming*** it based on information being received from internal and external sources. As priorities change, system features can be promoted or demoted. As the project moves forward, features that were on the future horizon enter the current horizon and are analyzed and estimated. So the Product Backlog is in a state of flux, but from the team's perspective it is in a steady state. That is because the team interacts with the Product Backlog only at the beginning of each iteration in order to negotiate with the PO and decide which features will be included in the next iteration. Once those features are agreed upon and fully committed to, they cannot be changed. This is shown in Figure 2.14.

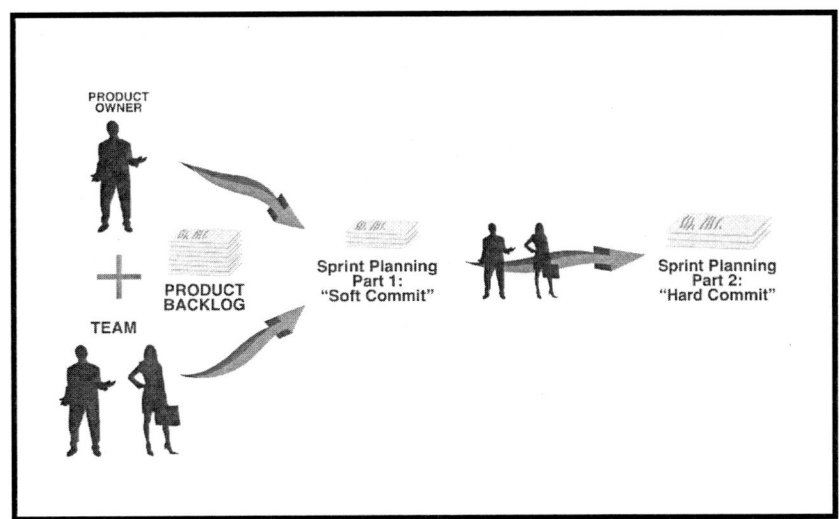

Figure 2.14 Steady State #1.

So for the PO, the backlog is in a state of transition, but for the team that flux is outside their concern. Once the team has fully committed to the ***Iteration Backlog,*** which is the portion of the Product Backlog being developed in the current iteration, enters a state of transition. The team has committed to doing whatever is necessary to change the current state of those features into the future state as the goal of that iteration. At this point, conversely, for the PO the iteration (or in Scrum vernacular sprint) backlog is in a steady state and may not be changed.

The desired future state of those features is, by definition, the potentially shippable product increment, which is the goal of that iteration. The team will focus all of its energy on building that part of the solution or system and at the end of the iteration, will demonstrate for all interested stakeholders what has been created at a review meeting. The **review meeting** is a product-centric meeting where acceptance of the deliverables and considerations for future enhancements is discussed. As far as the team is concerned, once they have demonstrated that the features work as agreed upon at the beginning of the iteration, the second steady state has been achieved. This is illustrated in Figure 2.15.

Between those two steady states is the state of transition, which is where the agile team lives its life. In the state of transition, there are only two constants – the duration and the goal of the iteration. Everything else is in a constant state of change, **driving the need for the team's daily meeting to synchronize and plan.** Each day when the team meets, each member briefly explains what they have done since the last meeting, what they will do before the next meeting, and any impediments interfering with their ability to be effective and productive. The team will use that information to self-manage. They will re-plan as needed, synchronize hand-offs, rally to support one another, and also hold one another accountable. Each day, each member is expected to make reasonable progress towards the fully committed, agreed-upon iteration goal. As needed, the team will also meet with the PO to clarify questions or concerns about elements, components or behaviors of the system in order to make sure it will meet the ***definition of done*** that the PO supplied at the beginning. Sometimes discoveries or insights will come out of the daily meeting. Those discoveries and insights are forwarded to the PO for use in grooming the Product Backlog.

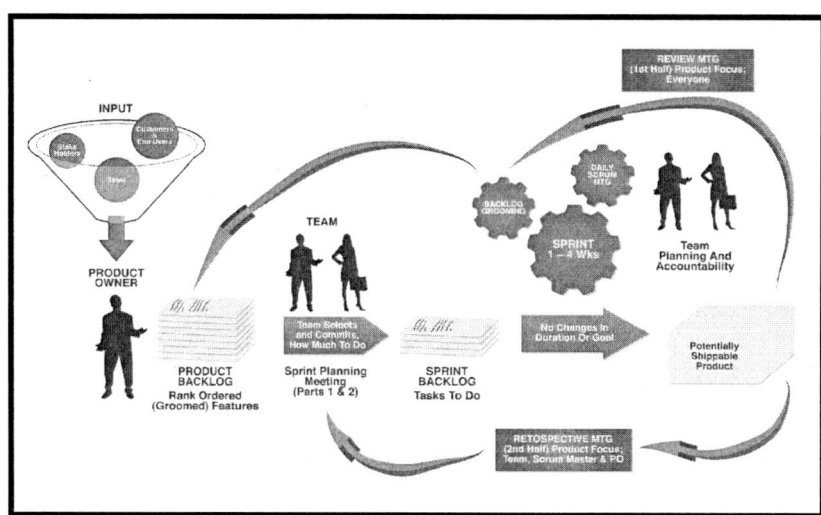

Figure 2.15 The Agile Process Map™ Shows the Second Steady State.

By having daily results that are measurable, external control is unnecessary because internal self-discipline has been created.

The final part of the process is the **retrospective meeting.** The retrospective meeting is attended by the team – and sometimes the PO – only. It is a process-centric meeting where the team identifies how it can improve its process of creating potentially shippable product increments. Typically, the review meeting and the retrospective meeting are the first and second halves of a single meeting for the team.

Agile Project Management Processes Grid™ for the ACP Exam

In 1986 PMI produced the first draft of the world changing *A Guide to the Project Management Body of Knowledge.* Throughout the ensuing 25 years, project management professionals have had to master the dreaded PMBOK® Framework grid in order to survive the rite of passage called the PMP Exam. Project management may not be rocket science, but that's not because the PMP exam is easier!

In 2010, PMI took another historic step by announcing that it would embrace the agile methodology as a source of credible, valuable, and necessary frameworks and tools for project management professionals to have in their repertoire of skills. In 2011, PMI announced a formidable process for demonstrating the acquisition of those skills with a new path to certification that includes the (some would say, soon to be dreaded) ACP Exam.

As mentioned earlier, our purpose in writing this book was twofold. Our first focus was to help students adequately and efficiently prepare for the ACP exam. Secondly, we knew students would benefit from having a Desk Reference to support their work handling daily challenges of being an agile PM. In order to fulfill the first requirement of passing the exam, we created the Agile Project Management Processes Grid™, which is also a useful reference tool while you are working.

It is with great pride that we introduce the ***Agile Project Management Processes Grid***™*!*

Using the Agile Project Management Processes Grid™

As we mentioned earlier, one of the best test preparation exercises a student can do is to practice reproducing the Agile PM Processes Grid™ from memory. It gives students a chance to see how much content they have retained, and most importantly can process from memory onto a blank sheet of paper. It is an excellent self-assessment of what you have retained to that point from studying.

Because the testing center will provide several blank sheets of paper or a small whiteboard with dry marker and eraser, anything the student can quickly reproduce or brain dump is an aid in passing the test as stress builds up. At the end of each chapter, the student will be challenged to take 3 minutes and see how much of the grid they can reproduce from memory. When the 3 minute time limit expires, use the grid above to correct what you did and study specific additional cells to add to it the next time.

It is an exercise well suited to repeating and practicing over lunch, during breaks, and periodically throughout the day. Doing so extends your study time and reinforces your learning.

 Memorizing the Agile PM Processes Grid™ can be immensely simplified by using an age old practice called mnemonics. **Mnemonics** are a technique for assisting human recall by using or similar device. The grid has processes and areas of knowledge and skill that identify the columns and rows. To apply a mnemonic device a student takes the first letter of each process name and creates a sentence where each word starts with the same letter. The trick is to make it as visual and memorable as possible so weird and wild is helpful.

Knowledge & Skills Areas	Agile Project Management Processes Grid™				
	Initiate	**Plan**	**Iterate**	**Control**	**Close**
External Stakeholders Engagement	• Stakeholders Identification • Vision Statement • Project Data Sheet • Active Listening	• Product Roadmap • Minimally Marketable Feature (MMF) • Prioritization	• Product Backlog Grooming	• Product Demonstrations	• Deliverables Acceptance
Value-Driven Delivery	• Value Analysis • Business Case • Contracts	• Release / Iteration Plans • Planning Activities • Decomposition • Progressive Elaboration	• Cycle Time Measurement • Work-in-Process (WIP) Limits • Cumulative Flow Diagrams	• Product Feedback • Accounting and Contracting Control • Earned Value Mgt. (EVM)	• Product Release
Adaptive Planning	• Team Acquisition • Project Kick-off Meeting • Incremental Delivery • Time Boxing	• User Stories • Iteration Backlog • Definition of Done • Estimation • Sizing • Wideband Delphi • Planning Poker • Story Points • Ideal Days • Affinity Estimates	• Burn Down Charts • Task / Kanban Boards • Test-driven Practices • Agile Modeling • Wireframes	• Information Radiators Monitoring	
Team Performance	• Coach Recruiting • Servant / Adaptive Leadership • Emotional Intelligence	• Coaching / Facilitation • Collaboration / Negotiation • Motivation / Empowerment	• Coaching / Mentoring • Conflict Resolution	• Task Board / Burn Down Charts Updates • Velocity	• Team Evaluations • Performance Incentives • Self assessment
Risk Management	• Organizational Practices • Regulatory Discovery • Quality Standards	• Risk-adjusted Backlog • Regulatory Compliance	• Problem Solving • Continuous Integration • Risk-based Spike • Risk Burn Down Charts • Verification and Validation	• Obstacle Removal • Variance and Trend Analysis • Escaped Defects	
Communication	• Colocated / Distributed • Participatory Decision Making	• Communication Protocols • Information Radiator • Team Space • Agile Tooling	• Daily Stand-up, Iteration Review, and Team Retrospectives • Osmotic Communication	• Knowledge Sharing	• Retrospectives (Project, Release, and Iteration Levels)
Continuous Improvement	• Identify Agile Ceremonies	• Value Stream Mapping • Cross-functional Team Formation • Metric Definition	• Metric Tracking	• Process Analysis	• Process Tailoring

Figure 2.16 Agile Project Management Processes Grid™

For example, the processes start with the letters I, P, I, C, and C so five possible mnemonics are:

- **I Prefer Ice Cold Cheese!**
- **I Plan Intently to Control Costs**
- **I Pondered Inscrutable Clairvoyant Clues**
- **I Prefer Ingesting Cold Chivas!**
- **Intoxicated Pink Iguanas Came Calling**

The knowledge areas can be represented with the letters S (for stakeholders), V, A, T, R, C, and I (for improvement) so five possible mnemonics are:

- Students Variously Attempted To Recall Critical Information
- Stately Venetian Attorneys Tried Recalling Circus Invocations
- Super Venomous Angels Tortured Recalcitrant Crowned Idiots
- Saturated Vermin Attempted To Reverse Course Instinctively
- Simply Venturing Abroad Teaches Reasonable Civilians Insight

Two common mistakes need to be pointed out. First is not choosing a single, specific mnemonic and committing it to memory. It is counterproductive to try to use multiple mnemonics because it creates mental clutter and confusion. Make a decision, pick one, and then keep playing with it in your mind until it sticks like the Disney song "It's a Small World After All." Second is making it mundane. The mnemonic needs to be visually wild or better yet a crazy mental cartoon with motion and sound.

With your mnemonic ready, you draw 5 vertical lines, and 7 horizontal lines to divide up the paper, then write the first letter at the top of each column and the beginning of each row, and begin filling in everything you can remember. With each cycle your recollection will grow stronger!

Chapter Close-Out

Agile PM Processes Grid™ Exercise

Please take out a blank piece of paper, set a timer for no more than 3 minutes, and see how much of the grid you can reproduce from memory. To make the most of this Agile PM Processes Grid™ exercise, please simulate being in the testing environment. Close your book and all your notes. Visualize the Proctor handing you the blank sheets of paper and taking your seat in the testing site. Begin by drawing the grid, 6 columns and 8 rows, and then fill in everything you can. After the 3 minutes ends, use your book and notes to complete the grid. Study it as you do so.

Terminology Matching Exercise

In the blank column to the left of the Term, fill in the letter that identifies the correct definition or description.

	Term		Definition / Description
	1. Retrospective	A	An artifact similar to the product specification or requirements list in traditional project management.
	2. WIP	B	A family of agile frameworks that vary based on project size and criticality.
	3. Planning Game	C	Possibly the most "tightly wrapped" agile framework.
	4. FDD	D	Work-In-Process
	5. Crystal	E	An XP method for eliciting customer requirements.
	6. TDD	F	A process-focused meeting the team uses to identify ways to improve how they create deliverables.
	7. Product Backlog	G	A software development process that is an Agile Project Management tool, not a framework.
	8. Timebox	H	A project management framework that uses iterative cycles and incremental deliverables to develop solutions.
	9. Iteration	I	The customer/proxy that represents the stakeholders and the business and sets the priorities.
	10. Scrum	J	There are several types used in Agile Project Management; the highest level one is a roadmap.
	11. User Stories	K	A list of features to be developed in the current iteration
	12. Product Owner	L	Records of project inputs, outputs, and progress points
	13. Scrum Master	M	Written documentation that helps the team understand what work needs to be done.
	14. Artifacts	N	Ensures the process is understood and followed, shields the team from interference, and removes impediments.
	15. Iteration Backlog	O	A time-box within which work is completed.

Crossword Puzzle

Hints:

ACROSS
- 3 A list of features to be developed in the current iteration.
- 6 Possibly the most "tightly wrapped" agile framework.
- 7 Documentation that helps the team understand what work needs to be done.
- 11 A process-focused meeting used to improve the team creates deliverables.
- 12 A framework that uses iterative cycles and incremental delivery of solutions.
- 13 Records of project inputs, outputs, and progress points.
- 14 A family of agile frameworks that vary based on project size and criticality
- 15 An XP method for eliciting customer requirements.

DOWN
- 1 Several types are used in Agile Project Management; the highest level one is a roadmap.
- 2 Work-In-Process
- 4 An artifact similar to the product specification list in traditional project management.
- 5 A software development process that is an Agile Project Management tool.
- 8 Ensures the process is followed and shields the team from interference.
- 9 A time-box within which work is completed.
- 10 The "voice of the customer" that represents the stakeholders and the **business.**

Word Search

Word Search - 15 Words to find:
- ARTIFACTS
- ITERATION
- PRODUCT OWNER
- SCRUM MASTER
- TIMEBOX
- CRYSTAL
- PLANNINGGAME
- RETROSPECTIVE
- PRINTBACKLOG
- USERSTORIES
- FDD
- PRODUCTBACKLOG
- SCRUM
- TDD
- WIP

```
R N G L T M T I P S P R I N T _ B A C K L O G
U E R A E D N C A K T S G R E O G U K L N O R
A R T I F A C T S C N A A R R O M C I O P U F
E C W R D R _ M D T A R C T L P A M I G E T A
T R D T O O T S S U A G M K U B E T L R A M P
D Y S S O S T V D P C S C P _ A A R E L R E N
S S T O T _ P K N A _ A C T A R N I U O T F E
I T C X R T T E N R B W C R E S R T Y P I _ S
T E G R C G U R C _ A U P T U O R N G _ F B O
E R D A U T W S T T D S I L G T D R F D A A _
R S R E L M A C E O P U L E T I X _ A A U P I
A C R Y S _ U P R R M S C R U M _ M A S T E R
T P A _ V D O P R C _ D C A R E T _ O U R T C
P L W I O P T A A O E S T D D _ E F N S E F B
L A I R R B D T _ T D E T L M B _ C W E T D M
P N P R T I M E _ W T U T O O O U D K R R U N
C N R C R Y S T A L G C C A R X O S R _ O O B
R I C N T G R L G S M U S T T I T R G S S C A
_ N I R S B I R U E G U P C _ U E L A T P E U
N G P O P L A N N I N G _ G _ O W S S O E C T
M _ S P R I N T _ B A C K L O _ W L P R C E O
I G S S C R U M _ M A S _ I S U I N N A T M A
P A C E T F D D D N I D P _ R N O S E D I O _
D M A _ G P T I M E _ E W I P C N T C R V T R
A E W _ R _ N R K A S F C G L D _ N T E E A L
```

Chapter Practice Test

1. When applying Extreme Programming (XP) methods, the phrase "last possible moment" refers to _____.

    A. The moment at which failing to make a decision eliminates an important alternative
    B. The moment at which time the project is officially late
    C. The end of an iteration
    D. The latest possible release date

2. A period, usually 2 to 4 weeks, in which the project team codes and tests one or more small features resulting in potentially releasable software is referred to as _____.

    A. An iteration
    B. A timebox
    C. A story
    D. A theme

3. Anything that has value because the customer can see it or use it to understand project progress could be referred to as a _____.

    A. User story
    B. Potentially shippable product increment
    C. Release
    D. Timebox

4. A meeting where the potentially shippable product increment is presented to all interested stakeholders for their review and feedback is best described as a(n) _____.

    A. Retrospective meeting
    B. Planning meeting
    C. Review meeting
    D. Acceptance meeting

5. A meeting that is process-focused and used by the team to identify ways to improve how they create deliverables is best described as a(n) _____.

    A. Acceptance meeting
    B. Planning meeting
    C. Review meeting
    D. Retrospective meeting

6. One of the most widely recognized agile certifications is the Certified Scrum Master (CSM) certification. This certification is issued by the _____.

    A. Agile Alliance
    B. Scrum Alliance
    C. Project Management Institute (PMI)
    D. Master Certification Alliance (MCA)

7. Which of the following is not considered one of the various agile frameworks?

    A. Extreme Programming (XP)
    B. Lean Software development (LSD)
    C. Test Driven Development (TDD)
    D. Feature Driven Development (FDD)

8. _____ is the highest level timebox and is composed of release plans.

    A. An iteration
    B. A sprint
    C. A roadmap
    D. A story

9. A lower level timebox that identifies specific feature sets representing a recognizable, logical component of the overall solution and often the point at which deliverables can be used or implemented by the customer is referred to as _____.

    A. An iteration
    B. A release plan
    C. A roadmap
    D. A story

10. Release plans are composed of _____.

    A. Iteration plans
    B. Story points
    C. Roadmaps
    D. Customer requirements

11. In the Scrum world, _____ is a term often used in place of iteration.

    A. Release
    B. Story
    C. Roadmap
    D. Sprint

12. Of the following terms, which is not considered part of the feedback cycle?

    A. Monthly project review
    B. Daily stand up meeting
    C. Review meeting
    D. Retrospective meeting

13. The phrase _____ means that decisions are made at the right time and is sometimes referred to as the "last responsible moment."

    A. Progressive elaboration
    B. Deferring commitment
    C. Rolling wave planning
    D. Last minute sprint (LMS)

14. The phrase describing the agile practice of delivering increments of the solution early and often is referred to as _____.

    A. Progressive elaboration
    B. Deferring commitment
    C. Rolling wave planning
    D. Iterative development

15. Agile project methodologies seek to reduce work-in-process (WIP) because _____.

    A. WIP is disruptive to iteration planning
    B. WIP has cost, but no value
    C. WIP helps learning and is actually encouraged
    D. Deferring commitment requires that WIP be minimized

16. In the Scrum framework of Agile Project Management, the _____ ensures the process is understood and followed, shields the team from outside interference, and removes impediments for the team.

    A. Product Owner
    B. Scrum Master
    C. Project Manager
    D. On-site customer/proxy

17. In the Scrum framework of Agile Project Management, the _____ is the "voice of the customer" representing the stakeholders and the business, and setting the priorities for deliverables.

    A. Product Owner
    B. Scrum Master
    C. Project Manager
    D. Lead Programmer

18. Osmotic communication is something that agile and XP encourage and leverage to their advantage. Which of the following is necessary in order for osmotic communication to occur?

    A. All team members must be trained in osmotic communication
    B. At least one team member must be remotely located
    C. All team members must be colocated
    D. There must be an on-site customer/proxy on the team

19. An Extreme Programming (XP) technique in which two programmers work together on a single computer is referred to as _____.

    A. Tandem programming
    B. Pair programming
    C. Extreme programming
    D. Feature driven programming

20. A tool that is a collection of values, principles, and practices used to create models for software development projects is referred to as _____.

    A. Agile modeling
    B. Pair programming
    C. Extreme programming
    D. Test driven development

Answers – Terminology Matching

1:F, 2:D, 3:E, 4:C, 5:B, 6:G, 7:A, 8:J, 9:O , 10:H , 11:M , 12:I , 13:N ,14:L , 15:K

Answers – Crossword Puzzle

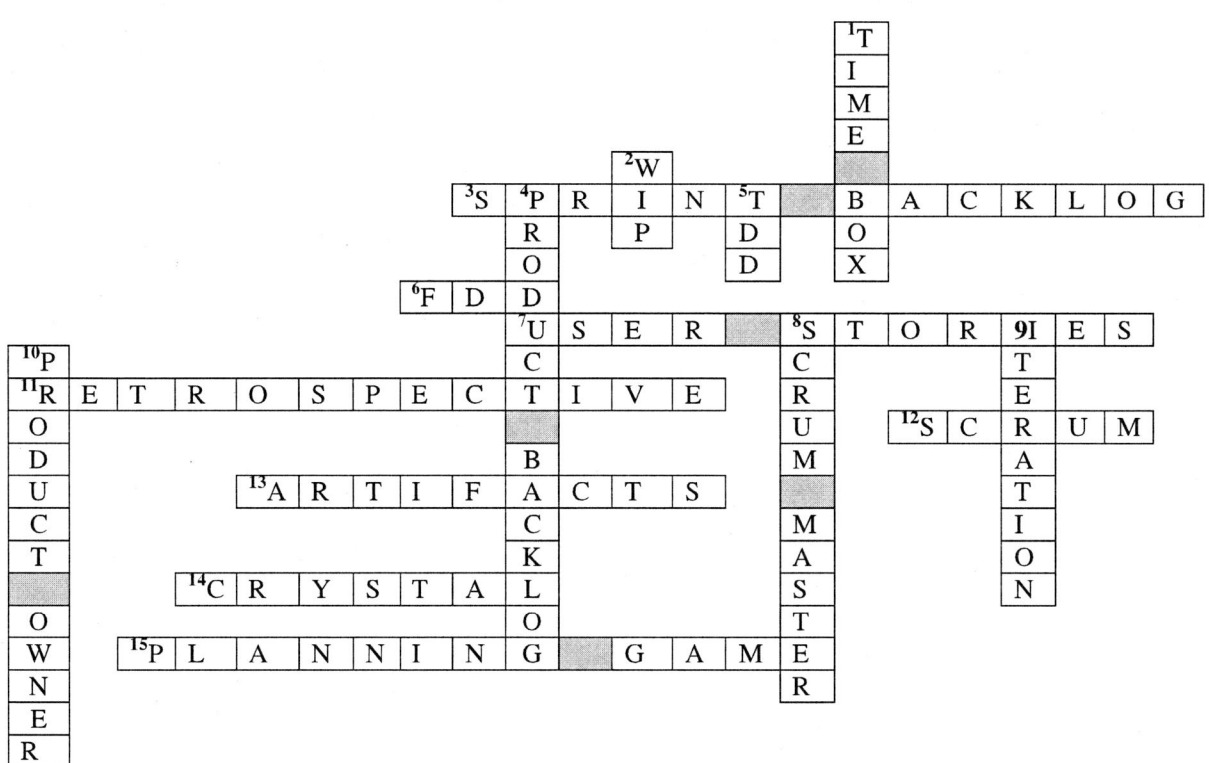

Answers – Word Search

Word Search - 15 Words to find:

- ARTIFACTS
- ITERATION
- PRODUCT OWNER
- SCRUM MASTER
- TIMEBOX
- CRYSTAL
- PLANNINGGAME
- RETROSPECTIVE
- PRINTBACKLOG
- USERSTORIES
- FDD
- PRODUCTBACKLOG
- SCRUM
- TDD
- WIP

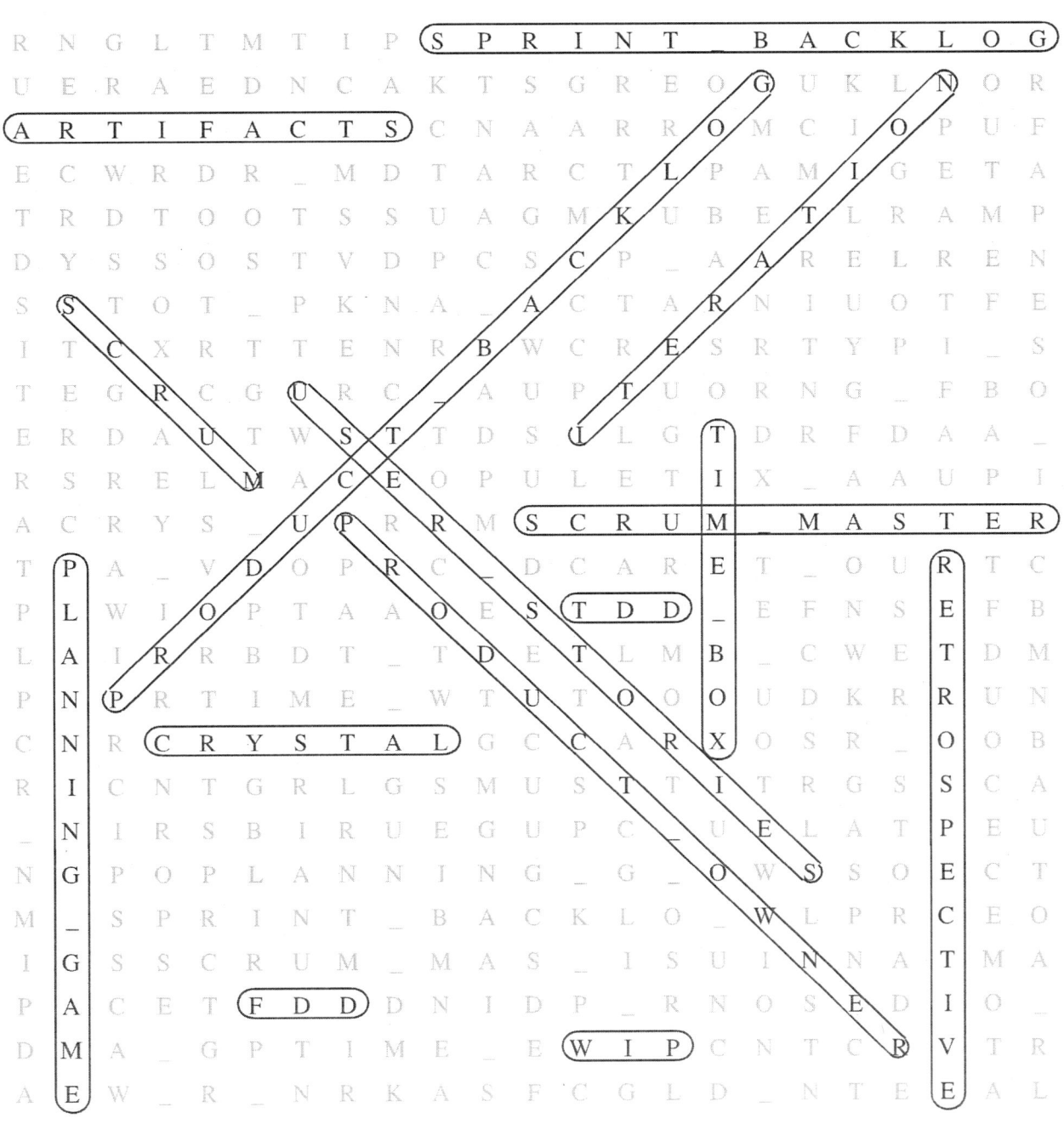

CHAPTER 2: Introducing Agile Project Management   57

Answers – Practice Test

1. **A.** In their book *Software Development: An Agile Toolkit for Software Development Managers,* authors Mary and Tom Poppendieck note that the last *responsible* moment, is not the last *possible* moment. The difference hinges on when not making a decision will eliminate an important alternative. **B, C,** and **D** may all be beyond the last responsible moment.

2. **A.** Iterations, or sprints, are timeboxes used to deliver working products. **B** is incorrect because it is too generic. **C** and **D** are incorrect because they are not timeboxes.

3. **B.** A potentially shippable product increment is anything that has value because the customer can be shown it or use it to understand project progress. **A** is incorrect because it does not show project progress. **C** and **D** are completely irrelevant terms.

4. **C.** The first meeting is the Review meeting where the potentially shippable product increment is presented to all interested stakeholders for their review and feedback. **A, B** and **D** are other types of meetings.

5. **D.** The second meeting, which only the team attends, is the Retrospective meeting. The Retrospective meeting is process-focused and used to identify ways to improve how they create deliverables. **A, B** and **C** are other types of meetings.

6. **B.** Under the "Agile" project management umbrella, the Scrum Alliance (SA) is the biggest player. SA has the largest membership base, specifically in the agile sphere. It has developed and controls the most recognized certification – the Certified Scrum Master (CSM) – for practitioners in the agile PM discipline. **A** and **C** offer other certifications, and **D** is completely fictitious.

7. **C.** Test-driven development (TDD) is a software development process, an Agile Project Management *tool*, not a framework. **A, B** and **D** are agile frameworks, known as Extreme Programming (XP), Lean Software Development (LSD), and Feature Driven Development (FDD).

8. **C.** The highest level timebox is referred to as a roadmap. **A** and **B** offer lower level timeboxes. **D** is not a timebox.

9. **B.** Release plans identify specific feature sets that represent a recognizable, logical component of the overall solution. Quite often release plans represent the point at which deliverables can be used or implemented by customers. **A** and **C** offer other timeboxes. **D** is not a timebox.

10. **A.** Release plans are composed of iteration (or sprint) plans. The size of the timebox represented by a Release Plan is the sum of the iterations within that release. **B** and **D** are content in the Release, but are less correct. **C** is not part of a Release Plan.

11. **D.** The term Sprint is used in place of the word iteration and is more common in the Scrum environment. **A, B** and **C** are terms for other things.

12. **A.** Monthly project reviews are part of traditional project management, not agile. **B, C** and **D** – daily stand up, review and retrospective meetings – are all part of the frequent agile feedback cycles.

13. **B.** In Lean, and therefore also in Agile Project Management, deferring commitment means that decisions are made at the right time, sometimes referred to as the "last responsible moment." **A, C** and **D** are simply incorrect.

14. **D.** Delivering increments early and often requires development to be done in iterations, which is referred to as iterative development. **A, B** and **C** are simply incorrect.

15. **B.** For Agile Project Management, WIP means those things that are described as 60% done or 80% done, or some other percent done in a traditional project status meeting. Since WIP cannot be shown as a completed incremental solution, WIP has no value even though it has cost. **A** and **C** are incorrect because WIP is neither disruptive nor an aid to learning. **D** is incorrect as deferring commitment sometimes creates reduced WIP.

16. **B.** The Scrum Master ensures the process is understood and followed, shields the team from outside interference, and removes impediments for the team. **A, C** and **D** are incorrect because they are other roles with other duties.

17. **A.** The Product Owner is the "voice of the customer" representing the stakeholders and the business by setting the priorities for deliverables. **B, C** and **D** are incorrect because they are other roles with other duties.

18. **C.** Osmotic communication requires that the team members be colocated. **A** and **B** are incorrect because they are untrue. **D** is incorrect because an on-site customer/proxy is not required, although desirable, for osmotic communication.

19. **B.** Pair programming is a technique where two programmers work together on one computer. **A, C** and **D** are incorrect because they are fictitious or untrue.

20. **A.** Agile Modeling (AM) is also not a framework, but a modeling tool for software development projects. It is used in conjunction with a framework and is a collection of values, principles, and practices used to create models for software development projects. **B, C** and **D** are incorrect because they are fictitious or untrue.

Chapter End Notes

[1] Goldratt, E. M. (1997). *Critical chain*. Great Barrington, MA: The North River Press.

[2] Steven Paul "Steve" Jobs (February 24, 1955 – October 5, 2011) was a visionary widely recognized as a charismatic pioneer of the personal computer revolution. He was co-founder, chairman, and chief executive officer of Apple Inc.

[3] See for example *CHAOS 2009 Report Summary*, Boston, MA, April 23, 2009, The Standish Group International, Inc. (www.standishgroup.com)

[4] William Edwards Deming (October 14, 1900 – December 20, 1993) is perhaps best known for his work in Japan. He taught how to improve product quality through the application of statistical methods. Deming made a significant contribution to Japan's later reputation for innovative high-quality products. Despite being a hero in Japan, he was only beginning to br recognized in the U.S. at the time of his death

[5] Taiichi Ohno (February 29, 1912 – May 28, 1990) is considered to be the father of the Toyota Production System, which became Lean Manufacturing in the U.S.

[6] Womack, J. P., Jones, D. T., & Roos, D. (1990). *The machine that changed the world: Based on the Massachusetts Institute of Technology 5-million-dollar 5-year study on the future of the automobile*. New York: Rawson Associates.

[7] Womack, J. P., & Jones, D. T. (1996). *Lean thinking: Banish waste and create wealth in your corporation*. New York: Simon & Schuster.

[8] *5th Annual State of Agile Development Survey Results* (©qaSignature, Inc. 2011): This fifth annual survey was conducted between August 11 and October 31, 2010. It includes information from 4,770 participants from 91 countries. Data was analyzed and prepared into a summary report by Analysis.Net Research, an independent survey consultancy.

[9] Takeuchi, H., & Nonaka, I. (1986, January-February). *The new new product development game*. Harvard Business Review, 64(1), 137-146.

[10] DeGrace, P., & Stahl, L. H. (1990). *Wicked problems, righteous solutions: A catalogue of modern software engineering paradigms*. New York: Prentice Hall.

[11] Beck, K., & Andres, C. (2004). *Extreme programming explained: Embrace change, Second edition*. Boston: Addison-Wesley Professional.

[12] http://www.extremeprogramming.org

[13] Goldratt, E. M. (1999). *Theory of constraints*. Great Barrington, MA: The North River Press.

[14] Scott W. Ambler and Larry Constantine wrote a collection of books in 2000 that became the foundation of Unified Process (UP) theory and practices. Those books included *The Unified Process Elaboration Phase: Best Practices in Implementing the UP*, *The Unified Process Construction Phase: Best Practices in Implementing the UP*, *The Unified Process Inception Phase: Best Practices for Implementing the UP*, and *The Unified Process Transition and Production Phases: Best Practices in Implementing the UP*.

[15] Cockburn, A. (2004). *Crystal clear: A human-powered methodology for small teams*. Boston: Addison-Wesley Professional.

CHAPTER 3

Initiating Projects

Chapter Highlights

In this chapter, we will build on the overview from the prior chapter. We will have an in-depth discussion of **Initiate, the first process in the Agile Project Management Processes Grid™**. We will describe how to identify stakeholders and build their engagement, how to create value-driven deliveries using adaptive planning, how to enable team performance and clarify risk, and how to support effective communication and continuous improvement.

Overview of Agile Project Initiation

The process of initiating projects in an agile framework is just as important as it is in a traditional framework, if not more so. It is, however, quite different because of its focus on prioritized, cyclical, iterative development. As you will recall from Chapter 2, when we compared the traditional and agile approaches to estimating, as shown in Figure 2.8, the traditional approach started with a large effort to elaborate everything in detail. The agile approach meanwhile, elaborated in detail only those things that had been prioritized and were on a practical time horizon, such as 60, 90, or 120 days, noting everything beyond that point on the time horizon with appropriate placeholder user stories for future elaboration.

Philosophically, the big difference lies with a traditional focus on **what** will be done versus an agile focus on what to do **when**. The **traditional** planning framework is **task-centric** and the **agile** framework is **value-centric**. Having the Product Owner prioritize the user stories is central to the process. Doing so creates stakeholder engagement and enables value-driven delivery cycles.

Process Overview

The Agile Process Map™ introduced in Chapter 2 (Figure 2.16) illustrated the overall process flow of Agile Project Management. That flow diagram helped you create a mental map of the entire process of managing projects in an agile way. In this chapter, we will expand upon that flow diagram and drill down into the process of initiating a single, distinct project.

Initiating single, discrete projects in an agile fashion is a micro version of the macro view that you learned in Chapter 2. The process requires taking input from stakeholders and setting priorities according to their values. In order to do that successfully, the agile framework recognizes and responds to the demand to engage stakeholders in structured, meaningful discussions helping them clarify and articulate their values and priorities. The output of collecting, refining, and prioritizing input from stakeholders, customers, end users, and the team is a product backlog, as you can see in Figure 3.1.

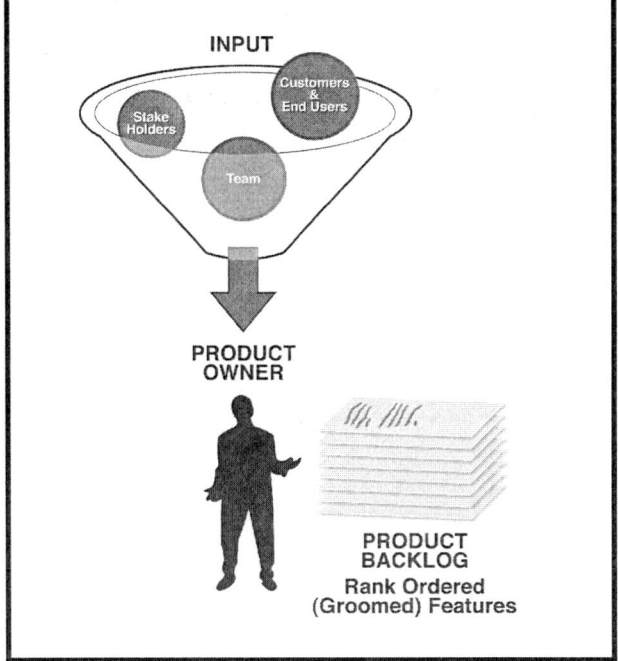

Figure 3.1 The Product Backlog Consists of the Features that are Prioritized and Groomed by the Product Owner.

Although primary responsibility for creating the product backlog belongs to the Product Owner, it is done in collaboration with the agile team. **The product backlog represents the vision for the entire product as decided by the customer/proxy.** It is continually being improved as new insights are gained and documented, typically in the form of user stories. The agile values of transparency and adaptability underpin this approach.

In Scrum, as well as most other agile frameworks, the process of negotiating the iteration backlog is done in an iteration planning meeting. A portion of the product backlog is selected for the iteration backlog through a negotiated process where the agile team and the Product Owner discuss and refine their mutual understanding of exactly what will be delivered at the end of the iteration. The negotiating process during the iteration planning meeting usually has two steps.

In Step 1, the Product Owner describes what she/he feels can and should be included in the iteration. It is helpful to note that prior to Step 1, as part of the Agile Project Management process that occurs parallel to, but outside of, the iteration specific practices, the Product Owner spends time with the team to **size** user stories that are high on the prioritized product backlog and on the near-term time horizon. Using that preliminary information regarding size, the Product Owner presents what they believe can and should be included in the iteration. During Step 1, after the Product Owner describes what should be included in the iteration, the team clarifies the exact meaning of each user story. In particular, they want a ***definition of done*** for each story that includes specific metrics or acceptance criteria. Based on the mutual understanding that has been established, the team makes a ***soft commitment*** to a specific set of features for the iteration backlog.

Step 2 follows directly after the soft commitment while the Product Owner is still immediately available to clarify any unexpected, additional questions. The team discusses the approach they will use to create the deliverables, decomposes the user stories into tasks, and performs detailed estimating of each task. In mature agile environments, the team also performs a capacity analysis to confirm that enough hours are available from each of the required resources to be able to successfully achieve the iteration goal. Once the team has finalized their analysis and agreed they can succeed, they make a ***hard commitment*** to the specific set of features that will be delivered to the Product Owner at the end of the iteration. The hard commitment signals that the iteration has been initiated.

The process of collecting and refining user requirements into the product backlog then negotiating an agreement about which requirements are the highest priority and will be delivered at the end of the iteration, is the process that creates an environment where stakeholder engagement is possible.

Identify Stakeholders and Build Engagement

Every project comes into existence because of the action of one or more key stakeholders. Many project managers get into trouble because they assume those initiators are the only stakeholders with which they need to be concerned and they couldn't be more wrong.

It is important to identify all of the stakeholders because they hold the power to provide or deny access to the resources needed by the agile team to fulfill the vision of the project. Many times key indirect stakeholders are overlooked. In doing so, many projects have run into major, potentially fatal, obstacles or even sabotage from stakeholders whose participation was required, but missed because it was not recognized.

In order to accurately identify all of the stakeholders for a project, a clear vision of the product, regardless of whether it is tangible or intangible, must be defined. Three of the tools commonly used in the process of defining and clarifying the vision for a releasable product are the ***product vision box***, the ***project data sheet***, and the ***flexibility matrix***[1]. The product vision box and the project data sheet will be explained in depth in Chapter 7, Iterating projects – Part 2, but we will define them briefly here.

A **product vision box** can be thought of as the product box on a store shelf. It has whatever graphic images and narrative content is necessary to convey to the customer what they can expect from the product. Significantly, it is in end user language and not techno-jargon.

A **project data sheet (PDS)**, by comparison, captures a project's objectives in a minimalist document.[2] Typically it is a one-page summary of the key objectives, capabilities, and information needed to understand the purpose and progress of the project.

A **flexibility matrix** is a simple tool that helps the customer/proxy clarify how to handle the unavoidable tradeoffs that may arise in the future and communicate that perspective to the team. The matrix clarifies which constraints are flexible and which are not, hence the name. It allows the customer/proxy to establish a top-level decision tool for making tradeoff decisions when the typical resource, time, or cost conflicts arise during execution.

As the customer gathers information about the project vision, she solicits customer views on tradeoffs and documents the results in the matrix. Because the matrix will be used throughout the project to decide tradeoffs, getting it settled early in the project is key to avoiding difficult or impossible negotiations later. Once people decide their position on a specific tradeoff, the effort to get cooperation becomes much more difficult without a flexibility matrix.

As stated earlier, philosophically the agile framework is process-centric. **The process goal is to create stakeholder engagement and value-driven delivery cycles.** If we want to build agile products, we need adaptive teams that include all stakeholders. Stakeholders are referred to as the customer and represented by the customer/proxy.

Identify Stakeholders

Many consultants describe listing stakeholders and their interests in a project as the "most obvious secret to success" that is commonly overlooked. They know a great many budget-busting, project-imperiling change requests occur simply because the team lacked a written list of stakeholders and their interests. In fact, whole categories of mistakes can be avoided if this simple, yet profound, step is taken during development and before system delivery.

The stakeholder list includes those directly involved, like the client, the end users, management, channel partners, and supply-chain vendors. But it also includes those indirectly impacted, like technical or logistical support and interest groups.

The identification process can be rather informal, but it must be serious and reasonably thorough. It must include the favorable stakeholders, like project champions, the opposing stakeholders, sometimes called parasitic participants, and the independent stakeholders who can be influenced to support the project by the actions of the team.

In order to be valuable, the identification process needs to answer questions that will spur the team to think broadly about all of the stakeholders. Questions like:

- Who will the solution benefit?
- Who may be burdened by the solution?
- What groups or organization will use the system?
- How will the solution, and future improvements, be delivered?

Once the stakeholders have been properly identified, the process of engaging them can begin.

Build Stakeholder Engagement

The process of building stakeholder engagement in an agile framework is based on assumptions that differ rather starkly with the assumptions in the traditional framework. The traditional approach, as illustrated in Figure 3.2, assumes that the path from the problem to the solution is a direct, almost stair-step, process. The evidence of many projects, however, suggests that most customers need an opportunity to interact with the solution in the early stages in order to clarify their own understanding of the problem and accurately define the best solution. Agile frameworks, by comparison, assume that customers must traverse through an ambiguous process where they move between experiences that sub-optimally solve their problem in order to find the experiences that optimally solve it.

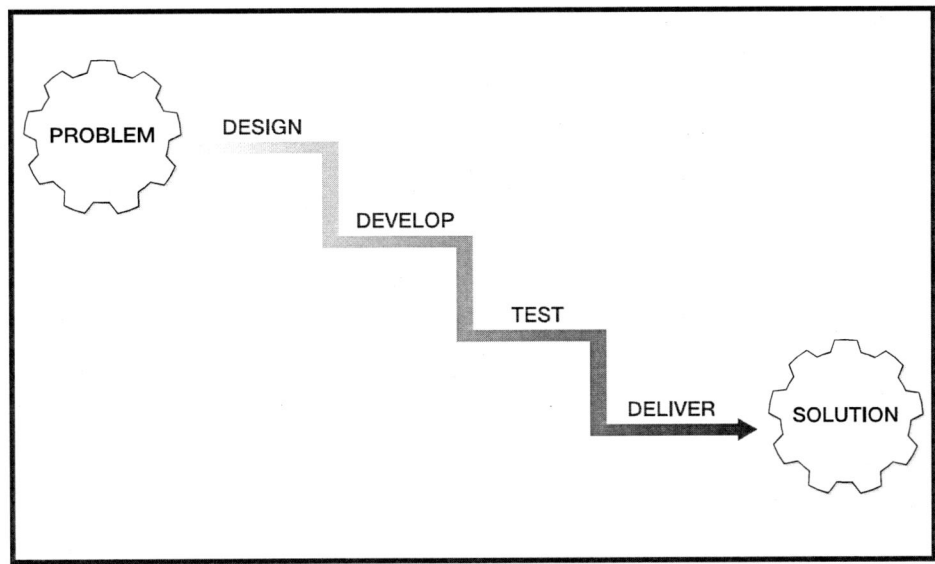

Figure 3.2 The Traditional Development Approach.

While customers interact with the team, their focus oscillates back and forth as they find the real boundaries of their problem and clarify the solution to it. Along the way, the solution moves from what they thought at the beginning to what they really need. Stakeholders, because of the limits of their humanity, need to be meaningfully engaged with the deliverables in order to move through this *cone of uncertainty* and find the optimal solution. (See Figure 3.3.)

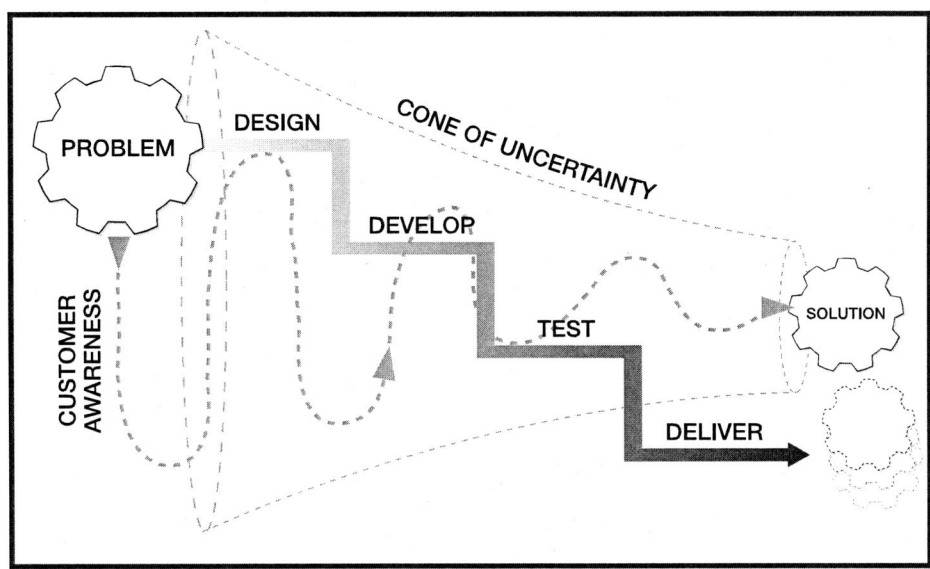

Figure 3.3 The Agile Development Approach.

It is no wonder that many traditional projects have had the sad experience of delivering precisely what was specified only to have the customer say it is not what they wanted. Sometimes it is the IKIWISI syndrome, sometimes it is the changing competitive landscape, sometimes it is the changing internal political landscape, but most often it is a combination of all three factors, causing the best solution to be imperceptible at the beginning of the project.

Two corollaries of the agile approach to finding solutions are point-based engineering (PBE) and Toyota's set-based concurrent engineering (SBCE). PBE is used to encourage experimentation in product development and approaches product design as a sequence of decisions, narrowing and focusing prior decisions for subsequent ones, thus refining a broad marketing vision into a releasable product. SBCE maintains groups, sets or collections of design options throughout the design process and defers design decisions to the latest, responsible moment along the way to a releasable product.

All three approaches – agile, PBE, and SBCE – recognize that customers and product development must both work through a cone of uncertainty in order to identify the best possible solution.

 It is impossible to be an Agile Project Manager without acquiring and maintaining a clear perspective of the key stakeholder values. Interestingly, the idea of key stakeholder values includes both the values of key stakeholders and the key values of all stakeholders. It is important to solicit, remember, and understand both and it is impossible to do so without a framework that engages stakeholders in participatory decision making.

Two keys to stakeholder engagement are successful information transfer and building trust. The Communications Effectiveness Pyramid, illustrated in Figure 3.4, shows that face-to-face (F2F) communication is more effective and thus preferable to other modes of communication.[3] This preference must be balanced using the ***barely sufficient*** philosophy suggested by Cockburn, which advocates doing only what is necessary to achieve success.[4] For example, if a stakeholder cannot be physically present at a retrospective meeting for face-to-face communication, then the next best mode of communication (i.e., a teleconference) must be accepted as sufficient.

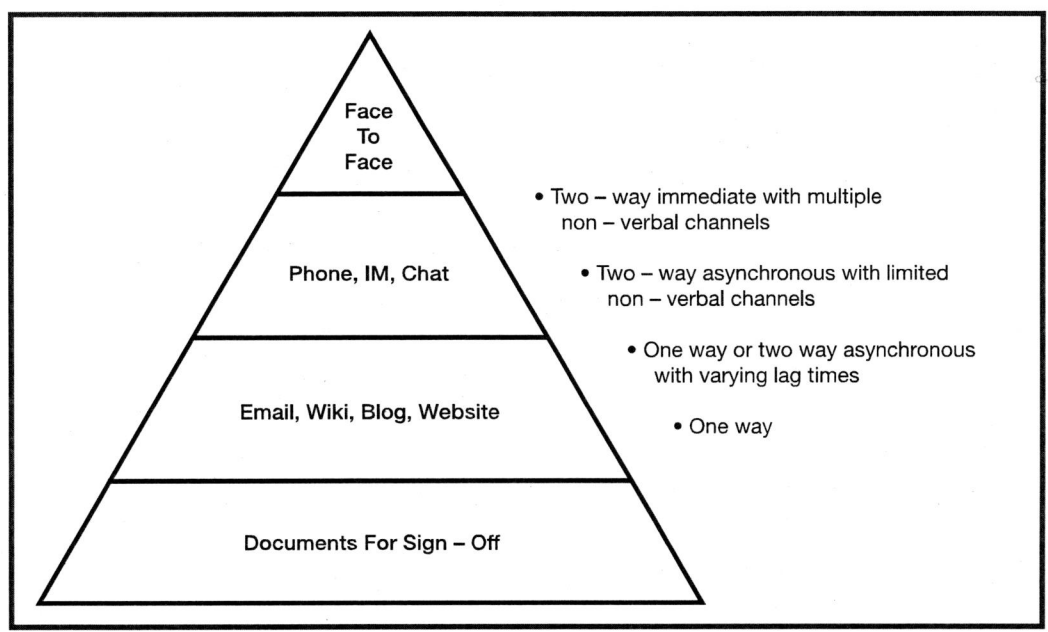

Figure 3.4 The Communications Effectiveness Pyramid.

Another example of a barely sufficient choice for agile teams is the preference for colocation. In all cases, colocation is preferable to a geographically distributed team. But when colocation is not possible, using teleconferences and instant messaging to be successful must be accepted as sufficient. Is it preferable to co-locate team members? Yes. Is it mandatory? No! Unless, of course, if the team is unsuccessful due to a breakdown in information transfer. Then the minimum threshold of barely sufficient has not been met and the lack of communication effectiveness must be addressed and resolved.

Building trust occurs when an agile team delivers a quality product according to schedule. Weick's principle of ***small wins*** tells us that delivering a quality product at regular intervals - even if the project scope is small - is a motivating reward for the project team.[5] Just as importantly, it inspires confidence in stakeholders. For the stakeholders, seeing a demonstration where their product vision is being realized, motivates them to increase their participation in the project. Stakeholders thus become more engaged once they see the commitment of the project team being manifested in "potentially shippable increments" of progress!

Acquiring and maintaining a clear perspective of stakeholder values requires an Agile Project Manager to develop active listening skills and apply them professionally.

We have all heard that a good listener strives to completely understand what another is saying. In fact, an Agile Project Manager must not only understand what is being said, but more importantly, what is meant by what is being said. In the end, an Agile Project Manager may disagree with whether the stakeholder's need is real, but before they act to manage the situation, they must know exactly what is requested. Therefore, listening is one of the most useful skills agile PMs can have. How well they listen has a major impact on the quality of stakeholder engagement.

 Active listening intentionally focuses on who is speaking in order to understand what is said and what is meant. As the listener, the Agile Project Manager is then able to document a user story to the stakeholder's satisfaction. Doing so improves mutual understanding and leads to the transparency and adaptability required in Agile Project Management.

In order to improve your active listening skills apply the following model:

STEP 1 – *Receive*. Remove any barriers – physical or mental – that may limit the attention you give to hearing the message. This may mean asking the stakeholder to wait a moment while you complete a task so you can give them your undivided attention. It may mean moving into a quieter or more private location so important or confidential information can be shared.

STEP 2 – *Analyze*. Deciphering, sometimes called unpacking, the stakeholder's words involves analyzing the speaker's vocabulary and word usage to correctly interpret them while decoding their non-verbal signals. It also means taking care to confirm context variables – like cultural norms, technical baselines, and legal requirements – in order to prevent any misunderstanding.

STEP 3 – *Evaluate*. Only after being certain to receive and analyze the stakeholder's message, should it be evaluated for missing information, which is needed in order to have a clear and complete picture. It is also at this step that the Agile Project Manager decides what options exist to appropriately handle the information received.

STEP 4 – *Handle*. Only after ascertaining that the message was accurately received and appropriate options were analyzed, is the final step taken – handling the request. Handling may be a verbal response to a stakeholder's concern about an issue or a physical response, such as documenting a story card for a future more in-depth discussion. Both let the speaker know you have gotten their message and how it will be addressed.

Note that the first letter of each step – R, A, E, H – spells "Hear" in reverse.

Value-Driven Delivery

Document the Business Case

A ***business case*** is a written document that explains how the use of resources is aligned with the accomplishment of a goal or the implementation of a needed change. A compelling business case leaves no doubt that benefits far outweigh the costs and risks. (Teaching exactly how to create one is outside of the scope of this book, but a summary explanation is appropriate and included here.)

The acceptance criteria for a business case include:

1. Providing the context and background of the business environment and need
2. Outlining the options for meeting those needs, and recommending a solution
3. Defining success metrics for the proposed solution and an analysis of the related cost\benefit and financial ratios
4. Presenting a compelling case for change that secures executive support
5. Securing executive approval prior to moving forward

The business case should include a business model snapshot showing:

1. Critical success factors and goals
2. Process maps of the current and future processes, including:
   - Roles and responsibilities

- Business rules
- Workflows and/or Swim-lane diagrams
3. Opportunities for process improvement

The process map is a high-level visual picture of the major process steps down to the individual sub-processes. However, individual sub-process steps are detailed within a procedures document. It is used to improve understanding of business processes by breaking them down into simple visual steps in order to better identify potential problem areas, gaps and opportunities for improvement. An effective process map is not only accurate; it must also be easy to read and understand.

 The goal is to define the problem the project seeks to address and identify impacted stakeholders, systems and business processes. In so doing, the scope of the project is clarified and indirect stakeholders are often identified.

Write Contracts

As a solution provider or customer or supplier, at the beginning of a project there is too much at stake to work without a contract. No matter how much the Agile Manifesto values customer collaboration above contracts, legal departments the world over are going to insist contracts are necessary. In fact a contract is just a way to define the rules for working together and communicating. Good rules increase the probability of success for both parties, while bad rules inhibit successful progress. So the question is not, "Contract or no contract?" The question is, "Which contract best conforms to the needs of an agile project?"

To answer that question, we must consider both the purpose of the project and the context of its delivery in order to define the contents – the rules – that need to be in the contract. Because one size does not fit all, the best approach is to understand various criteria for evaluating agile contracts.

One basic agile principle to keep in mind is that contracts produce no added value for the customer. They are simply a necessary formality which can be used to create a win-win relationship with customers through good communication. But, by definition, contracts are a waste product, so any time spent negotiating and writing them should be optimized to improve communication and reduce cost.

Also keep in mind that a contract divides shared risk and defines trust points between the parties. Who pays how much if things are more difficult than expected and who benefits how much if the project goes well both hinge on those trust points and must be articulated well. Unrealistic promises or demands, poorly defined time frames or functional expectations, and win-lose tactics all undermine the probability of project success. The most common result of an inequitable contract is compromised quality, which leads to suffering for both parties.

Criteria for evaluating contract suitability include:

1. Does the contract include defined project objectives?
   - Is the elevator statement and product vision included (or promised as an addendum with a time constraint)?
   - Is the project data sheet format included (and promised when complete as an addendum with a time constraint)?
2. Are key roles and responsibilities defined to foster cooperation?
   - Is the agile framework and/or process defined?
   - Is the Product Owner designated, with a clear statement of responsibilities?

- Are the key team roles – and any specific personnel – defined, with a clear statement of responsibilities?
3. How is scope delivery defined, and how is it linked to invoicing and payment?
   - How will scope be managed? (i.e., Backlog grooming and by whom; Iteration-level addendums)
   - Is the contract "staged" with checkpoints for visibility and customer go/no-go decisions?
   - Does the contract include an "end of iteration, cancel-for-convenience" clause for both parties?
4. How are risks and rewards divided between customer and provider?
   - Is cost responsibility shared using a target cost principle (like at Toyota) so that when the target cost has been met, both parties bear the excess cost of changes?
   - Are bonus, penalty, early termination and late delivery clauses documented?

Examples of possible contracts include:

- Agile Iteration Contract
- Time and Materials Contract
- Phased Development

Agile Iteration Contract

Scope Management: Mutual, based on the team delivering agreed upon features to defined quality standards by iteration end, and the Product Owner not changing the iteration backlog before iteration end.

Risk Management: Mutual, using product backlog grooming and iteration backlog commitment negotiations. Scope can only be varied between iterations and within the boundaries of the overall project scope.

Communication Management: Project scope is confirmed at the start of each iteration in order to build trust. The iteration scope is documented as an addendum to the contract also.

Invoicing & Payment Management: Either based on a time and materials agreement or an earned value agreement, usually with a not-to-exceed cost ceiling for the iteration or release.

Time and Materials

Scope Management: Not defined; dependent. When the customer doesn't see value they can decide to stop paying so the project comes to an end. A cooperative effort, driven by the customer's limited budget and the provider's desire for more business, focuses both parties on creating value.

Risk Management: Customer carries all change management risk. The budget may be used up without achieving expected business value and the customer may not get everything that was sought. Insuring that only valid effort and expenses are invoiced and paid is important.

Communication Management: Interdependent need to actively prevent dissatisfaction.

Invoicing & Payment Management: Work for an agreed upon time period then invoice the customer. Variations may include a cost ceiling to limit the customer's financial risk.

Phased Development

Scope Management: Scope is typically funded on a quarterly basis and additional funding is approved following each successful release. Knowing another release will occur, next quarter, or not, guides feature selection for the timebox.

Risk Management: Mutual, but limited to one quarter's development costs and a second quarter's budget (contingent funding).

Communication Management: Interdependent need to secure additional funding approval drives both customer and provider to insure each release is successful.

Invoicing & Payment Management: Invoicing for agreed upon work is paid within funding limit using iteration contract addendums.

The contract is a very important foundation for a successful project. The Agile Manifesto was spot on when it stated, "Customer collaboration over contract negotiation." Contract negotiation is fundamentally important and must be done. But it should be done with the perspective that a vibrant working relationship between the parties must be a result that is more important than the contract document.

Adaptive Planning

Acquire the Right Team

Earlier we said that Agile Project Management is not a silver bullet because without the right skills on the team, nothing can help. Later we noted that effective risk management hinges the actions of cross-functional teams and that the agile ethos recognizes teams must be trusted in order to optimize the chance to identify risks and reduce errors. We also pointed out that the seventh principle in the LSD framework is "Optimize the Whole" by always using cross-functional teams so important or critical facets of the problem aren't overlooked. So the question is not, "Can we have a cross-functional team with the right skills?" We know the answer is that we must have a cross-functional team with the right skills. The question is, "How do we go about getting that particular team?"

The first part of the answer to that question is actually a reality check. If the project is number 103 on the company's priority list then the Agile Project Manager must frame the team requirements within that reality. The crucial key is to use the business case and flexibility matrix, described above, to solicit the executive sponsorship needed to clarify the tactical reality with the Product Owner.

The second part of getting the particular team the project needs requires evaluating potential (or assigned) team members according to key factors such as:

- **Ability** – What specific competencies do they provide?
- **Availability** – What is their availability and what are their competing commitments? Are they local or remote?
- **Cost** – How appropriate is their cost given the budget constraint?
- **Chemistry** – How well do their work style preferences align with the team culture and environment?
- **Experience** – What similar or related work have they done? What time and quality constraints were the prior project under?

In many, if not most organizations, whether they use a traditional or agile framework, one of the biggest challenges to getting the proper team is pre-assignment. **Pre-assignment** of team members is necessary when the project is dependent on specific expertise and that expertise is in short supply. Sometimes pre-assignment is defined as a part of the contract and must be honored. But it happens many other times when there is limited rationale for accepting it. In those circumstances – and maybe in the situations just described – the project manager must evaluate carefully whether critical skills are missing from the team and take steps to correct the problem.

It may also be necessary for the project manager to act in order to insure the project receives competent staff on a timely basis, and team members don't have their bandwidth constricted due to new work assignments. A professional Agile Project Manager must be willing and able to negotiate as toughly as required to provide for project success.

The desired result is the right person in the right role at the right time. Until the team has that result, the Agile Project Manager must continue to negotiate and secure those people for the project team.

Project Kickoff Meeting

In traditional project management, most projects start with a kickoff meeting. In an agile framework it is necessary to do likewise, however, the way the meeting is conducted and its goal are dissimilar from the traditional approach. An agile project kick-off meeting has several key objectives that provide the framework for an agenda, including:

- Establish ground rules
- Have the project vision presented by the customer/proxy
- Review the high-level business case
- Document the one or two dozen key features
- Project setup and release and iteration planning

An agile project kickoff meeting begins with identifying the agile framework that will be used and agreeing upon behavioral-collaboration rules the team expects of one another. Because each team and the context of each project is different, this step articulates what all team members can expect while working together on the project. Discussion of development standards and team member roles are included. Experience has shown that skipping this step will cause issues throughout the project, starting with the next parts of the kick-off meeting.

 One rather interesting difference between an agile kick-off and a more typical traditional one is that the team helps the customer/proxy clarify their vision through discussions and important group exercises. The exercises include developing the product vision box and writing the **elevator statement** (which is covered in Chapter 7) and the project data sheet.[6] The goal of the meeting goes beyond presenting the "big picture" and drives to getting every team member aligned with a clear understanding of what is being developed. The desired outcome is a clearly defined scope that is documented at a very high level in one or two dozen key features. Those are all very large pieces of information with minimal detail, but clear connections to one another and to the strategic objective embodied in the business case. The farther out on the time horizon the feature is, the broader the feature definition. The purpose is to orient the new project team to the business reasons driving the project.

Typically the kick-off meeting, to this point, has run about two hours and senior stakeholders start to get anxious for it to end. However, the team needs more time, up to a full day depending on the size of the project, to effectively finish the process. Therefore, a common practice is to publish an understanding that when this point is reached in the agenda, there will be a short refreshment break and senior managers may leave. Project set-up and release and iteration planning begins after the break and may take the rest of the day.

Planning project set-up involves defining environmental needs for getting the project off to a good start. Whereas release and iteration planning involves identifying any required proof-of-concept work as well as laying out subsequent iterations. Defining the probable total iterations allows the customer/proxy to make needed future planning decisions regarding feature priority.

When teams are not colocated, every effort should be made to bring them together for the kick-off meeting. Agile emphasizes face-to-face communication because of its many benefits. But given the reality of remote teams and budget constraints, this is the time for selective use of available resources. The kick-off meeting should receive high priority because the shared decisions will guide and focus the team throughout the rest of the project.

Apply Incremental Delivery Cycles

The "early and often" principle of iterative development has often been called "deliver fast," but we feel it is better to think of it as "remove delays." The focus is on adding value to the customer without delay and since delays represent waste, removing them will result in faster delivery. While the benefits of delivering fast are clear, it is essential that this is done in a sustainable manner.

Using Adaptive Planning Norms

Adaptive planning, as commonly practiced, entails incremental delivery cycles or iterations. Each iteration is a single timebox during which specific, agreed upon deliverables will be constructed and demonstrated to the stakeholders.

In order for this approach to work effectively and efficiently, it is imperative that norms and expectations be defined, communicated, and understood. Then they must be rationally and consistently applied. That means key variables must be consciously chosen and clearly articulated.

The first of those key variables is the length of time for each timebox. The balance point for choosing each length is providing desired flexibility while avoiding unneeded cost. Because each iteration begins and ends with specific planning and review activities, there is a type of "overhead" that is fixed and must be carried by the work delivered during the iteration. This means that if the work accomplished per team member, per day is essentially the same for both a two-week and a four-week iteration, then the planning and review costs – which will occur twice as often for the two-week iteration – will in fact be twice as high.

This does not mean that longer iterations are automatically more desirable. **Iteration length should be chosen to optimize the amount, frequency, and timeliness of feedback shared by the agile team and the customer/proxy.**[7] Since the feedback loop is a key control, limiting the risk of the team spending time and effort incorrectly developing a product or service due to a misunderstanding of the customer/proxy vision, shorter iterations may save a significant amount of rework.

An additional aspect to consider when choosing the iteration length is how it may, or may not, facilitate customer engagement. Customer and key stakeholder engagement is critical to successful Agile Project Management and customer engagement entails a certain amount of needs gratification. So, depending on the organizational audience, shorter iterations may be advisable if that keeps them excited about and engaged in the progress being made to fulfill their vision. Remember, the value of that engagement and feedback must be weighed against whether it is less than or more than the "cost" associated with shorter iterations though.

Ultimately there are trade-offs in every situation, but a norm must be established because having consistent timeboxes enables the team to develop a rhythm that increases both speed and quality.

Defining Timeboxes

As we said earlier, there are several types of timeboxes employed in Agile Project Management. The roadmap is most equivalent to program level planning and is decomposed into release plans, which are most equivalent to project schedules in traditional project management. Release plans are composed of iteration plans. The iteration plan is a combination of a timebox and work effort *(See Figure 2.6)*. By definition, the size of the timebox for an iteration is stable and typically defined as either two, three or four weeks.

How to prepare for the first iteration since it's the first timebox is a common question. Everyone recognizes that beginning a project requires certain resources and without them we move towards project failure, not success. Prior to the first iteration, a clearly defined vision is the first thing needed to identify, at a high level, the types of work the team will be required to accomplish. The vision is simply decomposed into the categories of work, not the details, and the general degree of skill required in each category so that a proper cross-functional team can be defined.

The second thing needed is a team with the right knowledge, experience, skills, tools, and processes to effectively produce the deliverables. A colocated environment is preferred and it must have at least the minimum tools and workspace (even virtually) so the team can function.

The third requirements protocols for creating and supporting visibility amongst the team as it creates the deliverables. We will discuss communication requirements in more detail shortly.

And lastly, high-level architectural outlines are needed to facilitate planning for at least the first two iterations (aka "**Just Enough**"), handle questions when needed during those iterations (aka "**Just In Time**"), and meet any regulatory requirements (aka "**Just Because**"). The architectural outlines must be adequate to guide emergent design and incremental delivery of business value.

Create Team Performance Environment

Recruit Coaches

It might seem strange to start talking about team performance by suggesting a coach since many agile teams work without ever having a coach. However, research clearly shows un-coached teams are much less likely to achieve optimal performance. For example, it is generally expected that the average Scrum team will manage a 35% productivity improvement. Compare that with the various properly coached teams that experienced 300% to 400% improvements at Yahoo, according to Gabrielle Benefield in *Rolling Out Agile in a Large Enterprise*.[8]

An agile coach, whether they are an internal company resource or an outsourced expert, has three key roles. They act as a trainer, a consultant and an advisor who extends what was learned in classes to the specific environment the team will encounter. The coach is there to help the team apply an agile framework to the particular setting and impediments they face. Sometimes that means adapting the framework while other times that means challenging existing norms.

Top notch coaches aim for knowledge transfer to the team who is responsible for making the work happen. They focus on facilitating teams to create change and improve delivery. They understand they must help the team rethink basic assumptions and mental models about their environment and quite often focus on making individuals and teams solve their own problems using non-directive techniques.

Internal coaches have the advantage of knowing the corporate culture and history as well as the team. External coaches often bring a new perspective and broad-scope process customization expertise that enables them to challenge assumptions and suggest alternatives more comfortably. Some situations are best served by one or the other.

Understanding Agile Leadership

In the traditional environment, the project manager utilizes directive, command-and-control tactics, such as assigning tasks to team members.[9] The Agile Project Manager, however, relies on facilitation efforts and servant leadership to help the team achieve its goals. **Servant leadership** includes a number of skills and techniques, all aimed at developing and facilitating the agile project team. They include:

- Creating an environment of **personal safety** where team members may both innovate and come to friendly disagreements; one where the Agile Project Manager and the team support the individual.[10]
- Mentoring team members on the agile framework as well as on general management and technical skills, allowing the team to become cross-functional and self-organizing.
- Facilitating (and *not* controlling) team meetings, including release planning meetings, daily stand-ups, demonstrations, reflection workshops, reviews, and retrospectives.
- Guiding the team, when necessary, to foster appropriate value-based decisions.
- Removing obstacles that impede progress or facilitating the effort of team members to do so.

As the agile team matures, it moves along the continuum from the directed traditional team to the self-organizing agile team that cross-functional, and highly motivated to succeed. When the team reaches this state, the Agile Project Manager can act largely as a consultant, serving the team as a facilitator when called upon. Ideally, the Agile Project Manager will not conduct individual performance reviews as this is considered a conflict of interest, violating the servant leadership role.

The Agile Project Manager also fosters **adaptive leadership** within the organization. Such efforts include:

- Adapting to (and, in the agile spirit, embracing) change. On projects, many things are subject to change, including requirements, priorities, customers, workforce, and organizational goals. The Agile Project Manager and the team, in consultation with the customer/proxy, must decide which changes to respond to during an iteration, and which to defer until an iteration is complete. "Locking down" an iteration is an example of a decision to prevent unapproved scope changes that ultimately escalate costs.

- Adapting actions to guide agile process outcomes. A team may implement improvements based on interim reflection workshops and retrospective meetings. Such *adaptive actions* may include things like reducing features, adding an iteration, creating another agile team, or identifying a new metric.
- Adapting the agile framework to the work environment and the customer/proxy. For example, over time, an agile team may decide to customize its numbering schema for estimating story points instead of adhering strictly to the Fibonacci sequence.[11]

Part of adaptive leadership can best be described using a term that has become both a cliché and a source of contention – emotional intelligence. But it is important for an Agile Project Manager to not be distracted by that word choice because, as Jim Highsmith points out, "Management research shows that mood or "emotional intelligence" in leaders has a much larger impact on performance than we may have imagined."[12]

 Popularized by Daniel Goleman, *emotional intelligence (EI)* distinguishes an effective leader from a merely competent one and is characterized by the presence of its components – self-awareness, self-regulation, motivation, empathy, and social skills.[13]

The Agile Project Manager must recognize that their emotional intelligence is contagious and will dramatically impact the team's success. Because the team will experience both highs and lows, quite often with unexpected volatility, during the project, supporting appropriate responses and discouraging inappropriate ones is critical. Group dynamics that are conducive to creating desirable, emergent results at the edge of chaos where most teams must work are fundamental to optimal productivity.

 A best practice technique used by many professional Agile Project Managers is defining the team's *rules of engagement,* or ground rules. The rules establish norms and expectations for team member's treatment of one another. The team discusses, develops, defines, documents, and posts the rules in a prominent place. Then it enforces and adapts the rules over time. Doing so fosters an interdependent accountability based on self-discipline.

The rules do not discourage the healthy, necessary conflict and contention of emergent design, but foster and direct it in positive ways. Great teams feed on the energy of diverse ideas in contention to produce the highest quality results.

Examples of common rules of engagement include:

- Everyone participates
- Respect differences
- Attack issues, not people
- Everyone has an equal voice
- Everyone has valuable contribution to make
- Honor confidentiality and privacy within the team

Cultivating an agile team spirit enables exciting productivity. It does so in part because the healthy contention of emergent design brings important risks into focus so the team can mitigate and resolve them.

Clarify Risk Considerations

Organizational Practices

During project initiation, the focus of risk management is to enable the team to make realistic, long-term commitments. Despite the uncertainties that surround every project, customers need reliable schedule commitments so they can integrate the deliverables into their business plans.

Risk management must take into account both the generic risks that are common to all projects and the unique risks specific to the project. A best practice first step for doing so is to have the team – preferably including the customer/proxy – brainstorm a list of possible catastrophic events that could impact the project. While it is not likely that any of the catastrophes will happen, they hold the seeds or root causes that will manifest themselves in smaller risk events.

Creating the list should be an exercise that is simultaneously serious and fun. A large dose of good natured conjecture will produce a broad range of ideas, which can be sorted out afterwards. After gathering the team and passing out index cards, encourage them to use dynamic, dramatic, negative futuristic thinking to write down and call out any notion that might lead to project failure.

Writing any of the following common questions on a flipchart or whiteboard where everyone can see them will help stimulate the team's thinking.

- When you have a nightmare about the project what is happening? *(Academy Award for Best Screen Play goes to the winner.)*
- Imagine that a year after the project's disastrous demise you are on **60 Minutes** being asked what went wrong. Describe what happened? *(Pulitzer Prize in Investigative Reporting goes to the winner.)*
- Visualize the best possible outcome for the project. Can you describe the opposite? *(Screen credit as a Co-Creator of an episode of **The Simpsons** goes to the winner.)*
- Can you describe a scenario of utter project failure and avoid blaming anyone? *(Teflon Don award goes to the winner.)*

The point is to inspire serious fun while digging up possible risks by reading index cards aloud encouraging further insights and team collaboration. Reading the cards aloud can be assigned to a neutral facilitator if the team prefers anonymity.

Once the list of catastrophic scenarios has been brainstormed, the follow up is to analyze them for possible root causes either immediately after or in a subsequent meeting.

The risk analysis can typically be done by a smaller cross-section of the team, freeing up the remainder to work on other tasks.

The final step in the initiating processes to create a risk matrix that shows the probability of a risk occurring and its impact, usually at the high, medium, and low level of granularity. Some teams extend this first assessment with numerical values that are calculated by multiplying the risk probabilities by the rough order of magnitude of risk the impact. During the planning process, this basic risk profile will be expanded and detailed, so it will be covered in more depth in Chapter 4.

The focus of these organizational practices is to help teams focus on avoiding risk by identifying them early. One particular category of risk is regulatory and it needs a fuller discussion.

Regulatory Discovery

Many organizations must comply with governmental regulations. Compliance is mandatory so implementing an agile framework must include documentation that auditors judge to be at the "right" level. Mike Cohn made a good point of this when he developed the idea of a "Relative Penalty" in weighting priorities. He shared how one of his clients "joked that the only downside to not implementing the feature was that the CEO might spend some time in prison."[14] Because she wasn't the CEO, the feature had a relative benefit of 1, but a relative penalty (i.e., risk) of 9 for the CEO.

So part of understanding customer needs includes identifying all stakeholders, internal and external, like audit staff and regulators, and insuring that the team is made aware of audit needs, like documentation versions and trails.

Documenting user stories can often still be done on index or note cards provided there is a proper protocol for tracking them throughout their lifecycle for auditing purposes. In addition to tracking the stories, there may be a requirement to track testing plans, results and constraints along the continuum of rights, with a trail such as read, read/write, and read/write/change for regulators like the Food and Drug Administration (FDA).

An Agile Project Manager must guard against the common organizational drift towards compliance as an implicit, primary focus. Compliance activities mitigate risks like financial fraud, product liability, and construction defects. Compliance is legitimate work, but project managers are responsible for exercising oversight and challenging customers when they lose sight of real value driven by real need and slip into wasteful drift. The best strategy is to minimize wasteful compliance and then direct needed compliance away from the critical path, critical team members, and critical resources.

Compliance isn't a zero sum game as long as the Agile Project Manager does reasonable discovery and exercises discretion to produce only documentation that contributes to deliverables, now and in the future, and fulfills required compliance mandates.

Lynne Nix, founder and president of Knowledge Structures, has a saying summing this up perfectly. She says, "A little documentation goes a long way... if it's the right documentation."[15]

Defining Quality Standards

Quality is inherent when an agile framework is implemented correctly because only working solutions are delivered. It is also the first "shortcut" teams turn to when making progress becomes daunting. Therefore, it is crucial during project initiation to define the quality standards that must be applied. That means appropriate definitions of acceptance test requirements for each class or category of artifacts is needed so the team will know what level of validation their work will require.

A common challenge for quality professionals is adjusting work processes to fit the collaborative, iterative, incremental manner in which deliverables are created. Specifically, because agile frameworks focus on upfront quality-in design and development, the level-of-effort will be higher than customary. Balancing that early investment are the later savings when there is less need for quality assurance activities, such as reviews and inspections. Also, because deliverables emerge, quality professionals must adjust to what is sometimes perceived as "incomplete" artifacts in the early iterations and help find ways to work with in-process artifacts.

Another challenge is defining standards for the iteration review meetings. The review meeting shows the working solution at that time and demonstrates explicit progress toward key stakeholder goals, so standards are usually pretty clear. What is often less clear are expectations regarding stakeholders providing feedback the team can use. If the demo occurs in a regulated environment, a more formally defined process may be needed to satisfy quality criteria.

It is well known that the cost to fix a defect rises exponentially the later it is discovered. Following standards and guidelines is an important quality technique that leads to greater consistency and work quality while reducing cost by eliminating rework. Agile frameworks recognize this and promote doing so as a best practice. Agile teams should be following enterprise-level guidelines, which should be tailored versions of industry guidelines, in order to reduce the likelihood of poorly conceived quality standards.

Provide Communication Support

Colocated and Distributed Teams

Whether an agile team is colocated or distributed, communication support must be provided by design and not by accident. Colocated teams enjoy a host of advantages and require only normal levels of support. The real challenge is in supporting communication for distributed teams. Key factors that must be considered include:

- Synchronizing communication
- Enabling collaboration
- Providing enough communication bandwidth

Remember that the foremost purpose of the daily meeting is help the team synchronize their communication. The most common challenge for remote teams are the verbal language and accent issues due to the **lack of visual clues.** Because so much communication is non-verbal, the lack of visual clues creates a huge risk of misunderstanding. Two solutions to this challenge are, first, to invest in a good headset (and/or hearing aid!) because vocal clues are very subtle, and second, use detailed written communication preceding the call. Because English is the lingua franca of many business teams, and because not everyone has a good "ear" for hearing past the accents of those speaking English as a second language, encourage the use of detailed written communication that can be distributed before the conference call or tele-meeting. Doing so allows other teammates to use the written word to develop an "ear" for the spoken word, vastly increasing the quality of communication occurring.

Remember that we live on a round globe with an ever moving cycle of night and day that works against enabling collaboration because of time zones. There are many ways to deal with this issue including shifting core hours to find an overlap and using asynchronous communication like emails and wikis. But a proven best practice is to modularize using a development hierarchy that distributes project-level pieces first, then theme-level pieces second, team-level pieces third, followed by feature-level pieces, and lastly function-level pieces (i.e., Developers, QA, Testers, etc.).

Providing enough communication bandwidth to achieve actual knowledge sharing is also a challenge. Solutions to this challenge include rotating developers across projects, features, and modules, using groupware tools like blogs and wikis, and investing in commercial Agile Project Management tools.

Participatory Decision Models

Agile leaders seeking to optimize team performance also need to use a participatory decision-making model in order to make sure each team member's voice is heard.

Participatory decision making is a creative process where ownership of decisions belongs to the team, and where finding effective options that everyone can support is the focus.

Over the last ten years, Agile Project Management frameworks have enjoyed a meteoric rise in interest because of the way they have improved operating outcomes for so many organizations. One of the variables easily identified as a significant contributor to that success is participatory decision making. As stated previously, the agile ethos recognizes that the solutions to the significant, complex problems faced by most organizations cannot be solved by human beings acting like biological machines. Organizations need the creative, non-linear, and imaginative insights that only come from fully engaged people.

Consider the situation as a puzzle in the form of a question. Who is best qualified and most responsible for the solution that will best meet the customer's needs? Is it best to have management interpret the customer's needs as an intermediary for the team doing the work or for the team to communicate directly with the customer?

For many decades, going back to Henry Ford, the answer from business has clearly been "management." To Ford, management was much more intelligent than workers and only they could be trusted to decide how to improve the manufacture of cars. He had very little respect for workers and no concept whatsoever for the knowledge workers that currently deliver results in today's organizations.

Today's projects have a threefold difficulty with Ford's thinking model. First, while Ford's policy allowed for setting up a very good static process for building one kind of car, it offered no flexibility, an absolute requirement for achieving success on today's projects. Recall Ford's famous statement that people could have "any color they wanted as long as it was black." That simply won't do!

Second, in Ford's workplace, management may have known better what was happening on the manufacturing line, but on projects, the knowledge workers dealing with the environmental challenges always understand how to solve the problem better than management, who is usually one step removed from the actual point of production. In Agile Project Management, the process is dynamic, always changing to meet an evolving challenge, as the team moves through the cone of uncertainty.

Third, and finally, when Ford was running his plants, a job's most important value was the paycheck that provided for the worker's family. Today, research has shown that monetary compensation is not the number one factor for most knowledge workers. The question of compensation has to be made neutral, but knowledge workers are also looking for engagement, challenge, and meaning in their work. Therefore, due to the massive investment in education and training required to make knowledge workers productive, any company using Ford's approach would be plagued by difficulties trying to keep workers motivated.

So if Ford's approach is no longer viable, what is the alternative? Peter Drucker emphasized the need for organizations to empower the knowledge worker to make decisions that they – more so than management – are in the best position to make; and also to avoid having the knowledge workers leave, damaging the organization.[16] In Jim Collins's famous book, *Good to Great,* an outline of the answer is also identified.[17] The great organizations he describes engage in rigorous debate, often over extended periods of time, using dialogue, not coercion, to interrogate the truth down to the brutal facts, in a way that allows individuals to be extremely interactive, until the best solution is identified. We also see it implied in Roger Martin's article, *The Opposable Mind: How Successful*

Leaders Win Through Integrative Thinking, where he describes how real leaders, great leaders, tolerate and embrace ambiguity as long as necessary during discussion because they refuse to be limited by "either/or" choices.[18]

The agile methodology and its many frameworks have embraced participatory decision making as the alternative to Ford's thinking model.

Because the quality of the solution delivered by an agile team is based on the trust and respect needed to enable a free flow of information, a vigorous discussion and active participation by *every* member is needed for the participatory decision-making process to be engaged and fostered to maturity in the agile ethos. Experience has shown that if any of those key components is left out, ineffective, poor quality results follow. Experience has also shown that it is difficult to develop the sophisticated leadership skill needed to facilitate, influence, and coach a team into the healthy, durable relationships required for participatory decision making.

Participatory decision making either helps the team operate smoothly or mires it in a swamp of indecision, and the difference is largely dependent on who is leading. If the leader shies away from the discussion necessary to get the structural engineer to challenge the architect, then the building can't be built cost-effectively. If the construction manager has to attend too many meetings, in the name of "coordination," the project gets hopelessly behind schedule because the team doesn't have access to the customer/proxy when needed. The ends of the continuum – too little and too much – can both cripple participatory decision making.

Leadership is critical to effective decision making in an agile project environment where thousands of decisions must be made using information that is often vague. Customer desires are unclear. Technology is untried in the exact situation. Eight or nine out of ten decisions can paralyze the team because the fuzziness makes them oscillate between choices. Often times, once the required, healthy, vigorous debate has occurred and the team has reached an impasse because the ambiguity engulfs them, the leader has to step forward. An effective leader acknowledges the ambiguity, takes responsibility for the impact of the decision – whatever it may be – and enables the team to resume productive activities by making the decision.

Fortunately, as Agile Project Management has matured, it has developed a number of tools and techniques aiding the team in achieving remarkably participatory decision making.

Earlier in this chapter, we said that most agile frameworks use a negotiating process to choose the iteration backlog during a two-step iteration planning meeting where the agile team and the Product Owner discuss and refine their mutual understanding of exactly what will be delivered at the end of the iteration. That negotiating process is a participatory decision making tool where the Product Owner describes user stories that should be included in the iteration, the team asks questions to clarify the exact meaning of each user story, and specific metrics or acceptance criteria are defined. That sterile description probably does not provide an accurate portrait of the vigor with which the actual debate occurs while a mutual understanding is being elaborated. Because the team will be making *commitments* based on the iteration backlog, they have a keen, vested interested in participating in how it is defined.

Earlier we also mentioned that prior to iteration planning meetings, part of the Agile Project Management process involved the Product Owner spending time with the team to elaborate and size the user stories that are high on the prioritized product backlog. Elaborating the user stories, as well as sizing them, are both also participatory decision making tools. We will detail the exact process of writing and elaborating user stories when we cover Planning Projects. We will also detail the exact process of sizing them in the chapter on Estimating. For this chapter's purpose, we will summarize the processes here in order to clarify how they act as participatory decision making tools.

By definition, all projects begin with incomplete requirements. The goal of sizing is to give the team and the customer/proxy a quick, relative measure of the effort involved with delivering a particular user story. The process, at a high level, simply assesses how big, complex, and risky a story is compared to other stories and then assigns it a value referred to as *story points*. Sizing allows for adequate and appropriate planning, focusing the team on what is needed to accurately estimate high priority components on a time horizon that is near enough to be accurately understood and applied.

The process of sizing integrates customer and team ideas about stories, subjects them to energetic discussion, analyzes them according to the customer's vision, and begins to align them with time and other constraints. The result is decision-making that is unlocked by dedicated participation. This balances agility in decision making with ownership and accountability, a hallmark of participatory decision making.

Invest in Continuous Improvement

Define Required Ceremonies

During project initiation the seeds of continuous improvement are planted by defining required ceremonies. In Scrum there are three key ceremonies: Sprint Planning, Sprint Review/Retrospective, and the Daily Meeting. Other agile frameworks have variations that typically include these three and may add a few more. The important thing is to know which ceremonies are needed by the team and stakeholders and then articulate them during project initiation.

It's important to remember that **agile frameworks intend to deliver the right product for the current need, which may be different than the need that existed when the project began.** That means agile teams must be open to, and embrace, the changes that emerge as they move forward. Ceremonies act as the gravitational force that keeps the team working to deliver the right product for the customer/proxy who defines the solution's orbit.

The process of initiating projects in an agile framework is a prioritized, cyclical, iterative process that elaborates in detail only those things on a practical time horizon. Having the customer/proxy prioritize the user stories is central to the process and creates stakeholder engagement and value-driven delivery cycles. In order to do that successfully, the agile framework recognizes and responds to the need to engage stakeholders in structured, meaningful discussions, helping them clarify and articulate their values and priorities. The output of collecting, refining, and prioritizing input from stakeholders, customers, end users, and the team produces an actionable, high-value product backlog.

Chapter Close-Out

Agile PM Processes Grid™ Exercise

Please take out a blank piece of paper, set a timer for no more than 3 minutes, and see how much of the grid you can reproduce from memory. To make the most of this Agile PM Processes Grid™ exercise, please simulate being in the testing environment. Close your book and all your notes. Visualize the Proctor handing you the blank sheets of paper and taking your seat in the testing site. Begin by drawing the grid, 6 columns and 8 rows, and then fill in everything you can. After the 3 minutes ends, use your book and notes to complete the grid. Study it as you do so.

Terminology Matching Exercise

In the blank column to the left of the Term, fill in the letter that identifies the correct definition or description.

	Term		Definition / Description
	1. Active listening	A	Defines specific metrics or acceptance criteria for each user story
	2. Cone of uncertainty	B	Have whatever graphic images and narrative content is necessary to convey its purpose
	3. Pre-assignment	C	Capture a project's objectives in a minimalist document
	4. Business Case	D	Is the philosophy that advocates doing only what is necessary to achieve success
	5. Definition of done	E	Intentionally focuses on who is speaking in order to understand what is said and what is meant
	6. Product backlog	F	Describes an environment where team members may both innovate and come to friendly disagreements
	7. Product vision boxes	G	Is the "most obvious secret" to success that is commonly overlooked
	8. Participatory decision making	H	Describes how customers must traverse through an ambiguous process from sub-optimal solutions to finding optimal solutions
	9. Barely sufficient	I	Is necessary when the project is dependent on specific expertise and that expertise is in short supply
	10. Listing stakeholders	J	Establish norms and expectation for team member's treatment of one another
	11. Project data sheets	K	A creative process where ownership of decisions belongs to the team
	12. Scanning	L	A written document that explains how the use of resources is aligned with the accomplishment of a goal
	13. Rules of engagement	M	A simple tool that helps the customer/proxy clarify how to handle the unavoidable tradeoffs that may arise
	14. Flexibility matrix	N	Represents the vision for the entire product as decided by the customer/proxy
	15. Personal safety	O	The art of looking ahead to learn the unknown and reduce uncertainty as quickly as possible

Crossword Puzzle

Hints:

ACROSS
2 Describes when the team has finalized their analysis and agreed they can succeed.
4 Focus on who is speaking in order to understand what is said and what is meant.
7 The "most obvious secret" to success that is commonly overlooked.
9 Explains how resources are aligned with the accomplishment of a goal.
10 Where team members may both innovate and come to friendly disagreements.
11 Advocates doing only what is necessary to achieve success.
13 Represents the vision for the entire product as decided by the customer/proxy.
14 Looking ahead to learn the unknown and reduce uncertainty as quickly as possible.
15 Skills and techniques aimed at developing and facilitating the agile project team.

DOWN
1 Captures a project's objectives in a minimalist document.
3 Defines specific metrics or acceptance criteria for each user story.
5 Customers must traverse through an ambiguous process to find the optimal solution.
6 Has whatever graphic images and narrative content is necessary to convey its purpose.
8 Tool that clarifies how to handle unavoidable tradeoffs in the future.
12 Principle that delivering a product at regular intervals is a motivating reward.

Word Search

Word Search - 15 Words to find:

- ACTIVE LISTENING
- SCANNING
- DEFINITION OF DONE
- PRODUCT VISION BOXES
- SERVANT LEADERSHIP
- BUSINESS CASE
- SMALL WINS
- FLEXIBILITY MATRIX
- PRODUCT BACKLOG
- ADAPTIVE PLANNING
- PERSONAL SAFETY
- CONE OF UNCERTAINTY
- LISTING STAKEHOLDERS
- PROJECT DATA SHEET
- BARELY SUFFICIENT

```
S _ P S E R V A N T _ L E A D E R S H I P I T N R P A P N I
M S R D P S A _ B _ C C O N E _ O F _ U N C E R T A I N L
E B O T H R A Y O U E T F L E X I B I L I T Y _ M A T R S T
R I D D _ T O I E R S A D A P T I V E _ P L A N N S S R I H
P N U P B F _ D O E _ I U _ N A B U S I N E S S _ C A S C A
N T C E P Y L G U I C O N E _ O F _ U N C E R T A I N T Y F
B G T R M D C E V C S E P E S _ T O E V A P G _ T A A V E C
A K _ S A N X V X V T G E N S _ D I L R D N D S F D S X E O
E X B O N G C P D I O _ C L A S E E E I L N Y D A T S X K
S C A N N I N G R T B L V P R H _ N T N S E V H N P D C A X
S T C A N S F E R O G I C I S Y O C E A T E O S L T D A S T
D N K L I E E N S C J I L _ S D E T A S A _ T T T I P N M I
E A L _ F E S _ C F _ E A I _ I S _ I S E N O D O V R N A I
F _ T S M R _ P C E E T C F T I O L T S E _ _ N U E O R L T
I _ _ A G N U V R T A T O T L Y _ N A N S A L X E _ D E L E
N A _ F _ I T E T D C _ S _ _ E _ K _ S O R E G C P U A _ T
I A N L P D Y C _ N N Y E T V D X M A B R I E A E L C E W I
T R F F L T D T B O R V U I I A A E A F O V L E C A T S I _
I _ N N K N C T I R I _ T O G N D T Y T S X N T O N _ F N K
O L S C Y E B T A T H C N A S T I A A I R A E L V N B _ S S
N I B C J F I I C E A R E S S M A L L _ W I A S U I A S E O
_ S S O I N S A A _ F U _ V O A O I D H S S X M I N C V Y E
O A R L I T B V O F G C R D R I N V D N I H O E U G K L I D
F P I F S L I S T I N G _ S T A K E H O L D E L M P L N O J
_ I E I A P E R S O N A L _ S A F E T Y N S E E I E O N D G
D D J A I R S V O F L A O E E N M _ A T E _ E K T I G T E G
O E I O L I S T I N G _ S T A K E H O L D E R S T N S E _ A
N D E _ A I X U M I I F N _ A B A R E L Y _ S U F F I C I A
A _ I L D _ X R B A R E L Y _ S U F F I C I E N T S P A G S
D I U O Y _ S T I N I M I E A I _ M I E A E S E D _ A N E N
```

Chapter Practice Test

1. Initiating a project in an agile environment requires getting input from stakeholders and setting priorities according to their values. The output of collecting, refining, and prioritizing input from stakeholders, customers, end users, and the team produces a(n) _____.

    A. Product backlog
    B. Team velocity
    C. User story
    D. Iteration plan

2. The primary responsibility for creating the product backlog belongs to the _____.

    A. Customer
    B. Product Owner and is done in collaboration with the agile team
    C. Customer and senior management
    D. Customer and the project team

3. The team makes a _____ to a specific set of features to be included in the iteration backlog based on their initial understanding of what needs to be done.

    A. Hard commitment
    B. Soft Commitment
    C. Velocity commitment
    D. Preliminary schedule commitment

4. Once the team has finalized their analysis and agreed they can succeed, they make a _____ to the specific set of features that will be delivered to the Product Owner at the end of the iteration.

    A. Hard commitment
    B. Soft Commitment
    C. Velocity commitment
    D. Preliminary schedule commitment

5. The _____ signals that the iteration has been initiated.

    A. Soft commitment
    B. Daily Scrum
    C. Hard commitment
    D. Retrospective

6. Sometimes when using a traditional project management approach, an inordinate amount of time is spent on planning or estimating future tasks of which few details are known. This practice tends to use up valuable resources and results in plans having _____.

    A. Progressive elaboration
    B. Scope creep
    C. Hard commitments
    D. False precision

7. The practice of waiting to create detailed estimates of stories planned far in the future until more information about the stories is known is referred to as _____.

   A. Deferred commitment
   B. Iteration planning
   C. Soft commitment
   D. False Precision

8. The most effective mode of communication is _____.

   A. Formal written documentation
   B. Email
   C. Face to face
   D. Phone or IM chat

9. Weick's principle of _____ states that delivering a quality product at regular intervals – even if the project scope is small – is a motivating reward for the project team.

   A. Small wins
   B. Barely sufficient
   C. Minimally marketable feature
   D. Short stories

10. An agile term for looking ahead to learn the unknown and reduce uncertainty as quickly as possible is known as _____.

    A. Product review
    B. Scanning
    C. Forecasting
    D. Risk management

11. The purpose of the _____ process is to help stakeholders clarify and articulate their values and priorities early in the project management process.

    A. Risk management
    B. Value-driven delivery
    C. Forecasting
    D. Scanning

12. An agile technique that was developed in the Lean manufacturing field to analyze, and potentially redesign, the flow of materials and information required to deliver a product or service to the customer is referred to as _____.

    A. Scanning
    B. Value-driven delivery
    C. Forecasting
    D. Value stream mapping

13. A particular product or service group, family or category where improvement can provide strategic and competitive advantage is referred to as a _____.

    A. Value stream target
    B. Value-driven delivery
    C. Minimally marketable feature
    D. User story

14. A minimalist document (typically one page) that captures the project's key objectives, capabilities, and information needed to understand the purpose and progress of the project is referred to as a _____.

    A. Value stream target
    B. Project data sheet (PDS)
    C. Elevator statement
    D. Product vision sheet

15. A(n) _____ is an uncomplicated way to define the product vision in a short statement, using language everyone can understand.

    A. Elevator statement
    B. Project data sheet (PDS)
    C. Value stream target
    D. Product vision statement

16. A single timebox during which specific agreed upon deliverables will be constructed and then demonstrated to the stakeholders is referred to as a(n) _____.

    A. User story
    B. Release
    C. Value stream target
    D. Iteration or sprint

17. Iteration length should be chosen to _____.

    A. Be as long as possible
    B. Be as short as possible
    C. Optimize the amount, frequency, and timeliness of feedback shared by the agile team and the product owner
    D. Be the length that is determined optimal by the customer/proxy

18. A(n) _____ is composed of release plans and is most similar to a program plan in traditional project management.

    A. Sprint
    B. Retrospective
    C. Roadmap
    D. Iteration

19. The _____ defines the smallest set of functionality that provides satisfactory customer value.

   A. User story

   B. Minimally marketable feature (MMF)
   C. Value stream target
   D. Iteration

20. Facilitating, and not controlling team meetings, is characteristic of _____.

   A. Traditional project management
   B. Servant leadership
   C. Adaptive leadership
   D. Scrum leadership

Answers – Terminology Matching

1:E, 2:H, 3:I, 4:L, 5:A, 6:N, 7:B, 8:K, 9:D , 10:G , 11:C , 12:O , 13:J ,14:M , 15:F

Answers – Crossword Puzzle

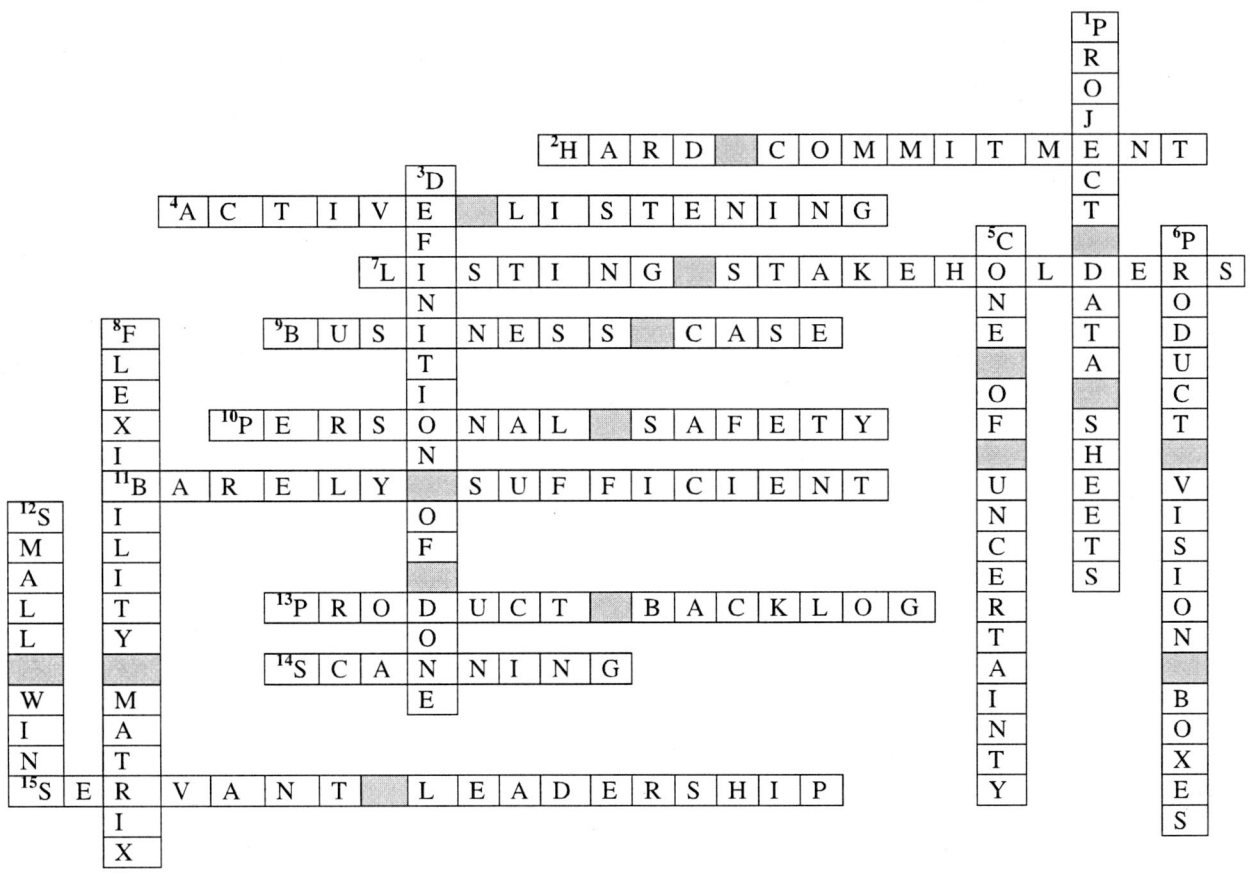

Answers – Word Search

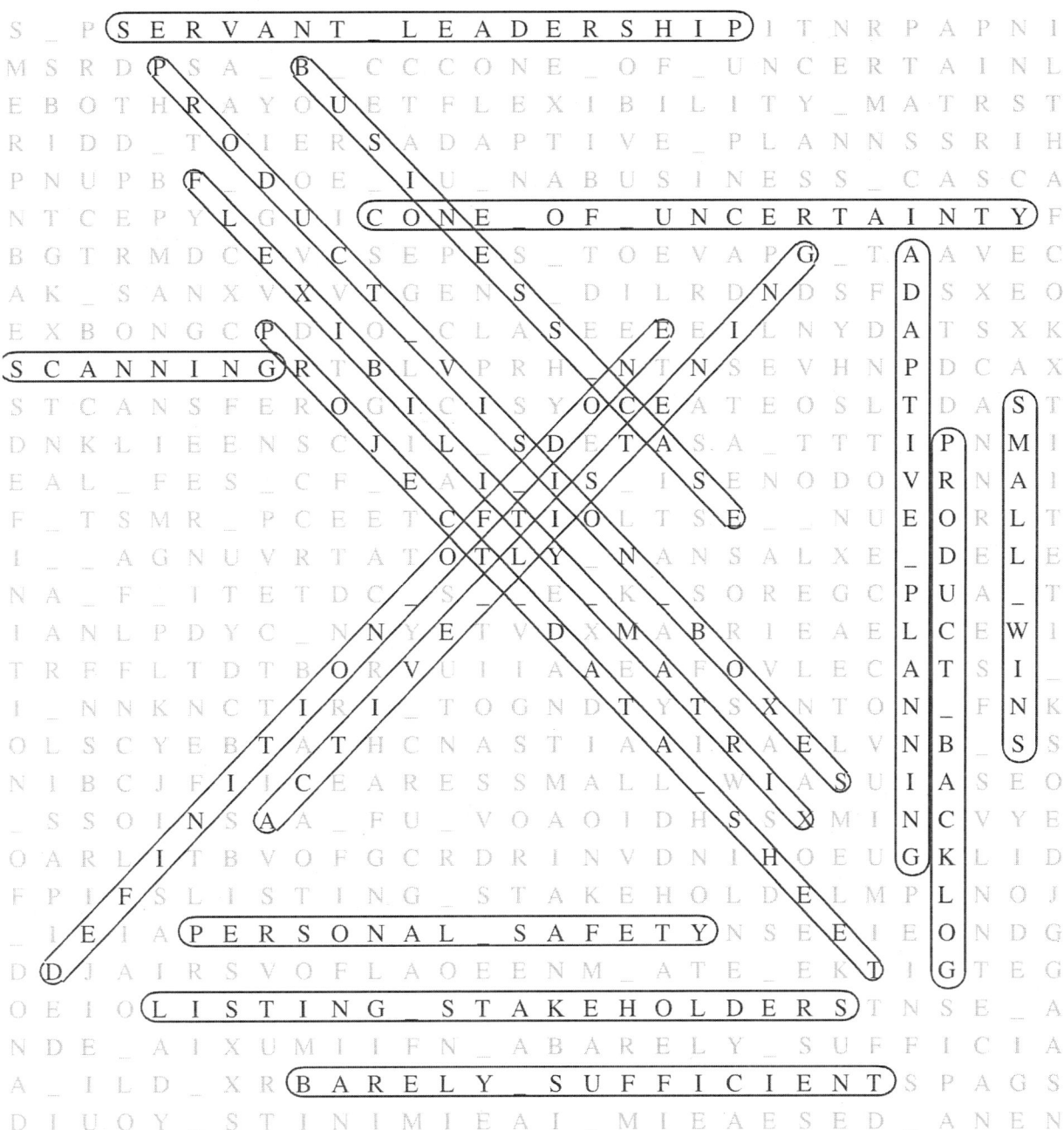

Answers – Practice Test

1. **A.** The process requires taking input from stakeholders and setting priorities according to their values. In order to do that successfully, the agile framework recognizes and responds to the demand to engage stakeholders in structured, meaningful discussions that help them clarify and articulate their values and priorities. The output of collecting, refining, and prioritizing input from stakeholders, customers, end users, and the team produces a product backlog.

2. **B.** Although primary responsibility for creating the product backlog belongs to the product owner it is done in collaboration with the agile team. The product backlog represents the vision for the entire product as decided by the customer/proxy.

3. **B.** Based on the mutual understanding that has been established, the team makes a ***soft commitment*** to a specific set of features for the iteration backlog. Directly following the soft commitment, while the product owner is still immediately available to clarify any unexpected additional questions, the team discusses the approach they will use to create the deliverables, decomposes the user stories into tasks, and does detailed estimating of each task. Once the team has finalized their analysis and agreed they can succeed, they make a ***hard commitment*** to the specific set of features that will be delivered to the Product Owner at the end of the iteration.

4. **A.** Directly following the soft commitment, while the product owner is still immediately available to clarify any unexpected additional questions, the team discusses the approach they will use to create the deliverables, decomposes the user stories into tasks, and does detailed estimating of each task. Once the team has finalized their analysis and agreed they can succeed, they make a ***hard commitment*** to the specific set of features that will be delivered to the Product Owner at the end of the iteration.

5. **C.** Once the team has finalized their analysis and agreed they can succeed, they make a ***hard commitment*** to the specific set of features that will be delivered to the Product Owner at the end of the iteration. The hard commitment signals that the iteration has been initiated.

6. **D.** A third advantage is that user stories align with the Lean principle of deferred commitments. Because the team and customer/proxy know a placeholder exists – and their concern won't get forgotten – they are encouraged to defer spending precious time and expensive resources discussing details too early. This technique avoids the mistake of "false precision," uses resources wisely in time-constrained projects, and enables the team to very quickly get focused on high priority stories and developing them.

7. **A.** The practice of not doing a detailed estimate of stories to be done far in the future employs the Lean principle of deferred commitments. Because the team and customer/proxy know a placeholder exists – and their concern won't get forgotten – they are encouraged to defer spending precious time and expensive resources discussing details too early.

8. **C.** Face-to-face (F2F) communication is more effective and thus preferable to the agile team than are other modes of communication. This preference must be balanced against Cockburn's barely sufficient philosophy, which advocates doing only what is necessary to

achieve success. If a stakeholder cannot be present physically at a retrospective meeting for face-to-face communication, then the next best mode of communication (i.e., a teleconference) must be sufficient.

9. **A.** Building trust occurs when an agile team delivers a quality product according to schedule. Weick's principle of small wins tells us that delivering a quality product at regular intervals – even if the project scope is small – is a motivating reward for the project team. Just as importantly, it inspires confidence in stakeholders.

10. **B.** In agile, the art of looking ahead to learn the unknown and reduce uncertainty as quickly as possible is known as scanning. Scanning reduces risk by proactively gathering information early enough in the process to make desirable changes while it is still inexpensive to do so. Scanning, of course, entails active listening.

11. **B.** The purpose of the value-driven delivery process is to help stakeholders clarify and articulate their values and priorities early in the project management process. A second purpose is to identify for the team which components of the solution are most important and to create a documenting mechanism to manage the follow-up conversations that will be required to define and direct the work efforts of the team.

12. **D.** Value stream mapping is a technique that was developed in the Lean manufacturing field to analyze, and potentially redesign, the flow of materials and information required to deliver a product or service to the customer. It documents the value stream using icons or pictures then analyzes the stream for waste. The focus is on reducing the total time from beginning to end of the entire stream, without taking shortcuts now at the expense of opportunities in the future.

13. **A.** The value stream target is a particular product or service, or sometimes a product or service group, family or category where improvement can provide strategic and competitive advantage.

14. **B.** The project data sheet (PDS) captures a project's objectives in a minimalist document that is typically one page long and contains the key objectives, capabilities, and information needed to understand the purpose and progress of the project.

15. **A.** An elevator statement is an uncomplicated way to define the product vision in a short statement, using language everyone can understand.

16. **D.** Adaptive planning, as commonly practiced, entails incremental delivery cycles, which are referred to by various names such as iterations or sprints. Each iteration is a single timebox during which specific agreed upon deliverables will be constructed and then demonstrated to the stakeholders.

17. **C.** Iteration length should be chosen to optimize the amount, frequency, and timeliness of feedback shared by the agile team and the product owner. Because the feedback loop is a key control that limits the risk of the team spending time and effort incorrectly developing a product or service due to a misunderstanding of the Product Owner's vision, shorter iterations may save a significant amount of rework.

18. **C.** The roadmap is most equivalent to program level planning and it is decomposed into release plans, which are most equivalent to project schedules in traditional project management.

19. **B.** The MMF is the smallest set of functionality that provides satisfactory customer value.

20. **B.** Servant leadership includes a number of skills and techniques, all aimed at developing and facilitating the agile project team including facilitating (and not controlling) team meetings, such as release planning, daily stand-ups, demonstrations, reflection workshops, reviews, and retrospectives.

Chapter End Notes

[1] Highsmith, J. (2010). *Agile project management creating innovative products, Second edition.* Upper Saddle River, NJ: Pearson Education.

[2] Ibid.

[3] Sliger, M., & Broderick, S. (2008). *The software project manager's bridge to agility.* Upper Saddle River, NJ: Addison-Wesley.

[4] Cockburn, A. (2007). *Agile software development: The cooperative game, Second edition.* Upper Saddle River, NJ: Addison-Wesley.

[5] Weick, K. E. (1979). *The social psychology of organizing (Topics in social psychology), Second edition.* New York: McGraw-Hill

[6] Ibid.

[7] Cohn, M. (2006). *Agile estimating and planning.* Upper Saddle River, NJ: Pearson Education.

[8] Benefield, G. (2008). *Rolling out agile at a large enterprise.* HICSS'41, Hawaii International Conference on Software Systems, Big Island, Hawaii.

[9] Sliger, M., & Broderick, S. (2008). *The software project manager's bridge to agility.* Upper Saddle River, NJ: Addison-Wesley.

[10] Cockburn, A. (2007). *Agile software development: The cooperative game, Second edition.* Upper Saddle River, NJ: Addison-Wesley.

[11] The Fibonacci sequence was introduced Western European mathematics by Leonardo of Pisa, also known as Fibonacci, in his book Liber Abaci in 1202, although the sequence had been described earlier in Indian mathematics. It is a non-linear sequence where each subsequent number is the sum of the previous two. Over the centuries it has been used in biological sciences to describe branching in trees, fruit spouts on pineapples, and uncurling of ferns. More recently its applications have included computer search algorithms, graphs of interconnecting parallel and distributed systems. In Agile Project Management it is used in the process of defining the size of user stories

[12] Highsmith, J. (2010). *Agile project management creating innovative products, Second edition.* Upper Saddle River, NJ: Pearson Education.

[13] Goleman, D. (1998, November-December). What makes a leader? *Harvard Business Review*, 76(6), 93-103.

[14] Cohn, M. (2006). *Agile estimating and planning.* Upper Saddle River, NJ: Pearson Education.

[15] Knowledge Structures, Inc., 2031 Rockwood Drive, Sacramento, CA 95864

[16] Drucker, P. F. (1999). *Management challenges for the 21st century.* New York: HarperCollins.

[17] Collins, J. (2001). *Good to great: Why some companies make the leap... and others don't.* New York: HarperCollins.

[18] Martin, R. (2007). *The opposable mind: How successful leaders win through integrative thinking.* Boston: Harvard Business School Press.

CHAPTER 4

Planning Projects – Part 1

Chapter Highlights

Let's reflect on where we are in the Agile PM Processes Grid™ *(See Figure 2.16)*. We covered the Initiate process in Chapter 3 and will review agile planning in Chapters 4 through 6. In Chapter 4, we examine External Stakeholders Management and Value-Driven Delivery in their entirety and begin Adaptive Planning. Here, we focus on agile as a process-centric framework, where the goals are to create stakeholder engagement and value-driven delivery cycles. In striving to build agile products, we need adaptive teams that include the customer/proxy and apply a participatory decision-making model.

Understanding Agile Planning

When using traditional project management, oft-quoted maxim is that on a successful project, approximately 25% of the effort is spent on planning – and that such planning is the most difficult part of the project! When employing agile methods, project planning is just as complex and time-consuming. However, utilizing agile methods has positive implications, both for planning and customer satisfaction:

• Not all product features have to be planned in detail before starting the project – just those highest in priority to the customer/proxy.

• The use of short iterations means valuable features are delivered sooner – and the customer/proxy gets to appraise product functionality development.

• Since additional planning (i.e., re-grooming and re-prioritizing of the product backlog) occurs **between** iterations, the customer/proxy can add features and alter priorities based on changing business needs.

These benefits for planning are considered *organic*, as they result inherently from using agile practices. If specific planning strategies beyond routine agile practices are employed, they would be considered *overt* interventions. We'll revisit this distinction between organic and overt agile practices when we discuss risk management.

We reviewed both agile planning and roadmaps at a very high level in Chapter 2 *(See Figure 2.5)*. Here, we'll add to these concepts. In terms of planning, the agile project is characterized by several processes[1], including:

- Articulating the product vision;
- Designing the product roadmap; and
- Creating the product backlog

 Figure 4.1 presents a high-level view of the agile project lifecycle. Here we see that the triumvirate of agile planning consists of the product vision, the product roadmap, and product backlog. Together, these elements guide the team in subsequent agile product development activities. The vision and roadmap serve as inputs to the product backlog prior to release planning, and the product backlog may be revisited by the customer/proxy and project team during inter-iteration planning meetings. We'll consider this in greater detail later in this chapter when we discuss prioritizing stories.

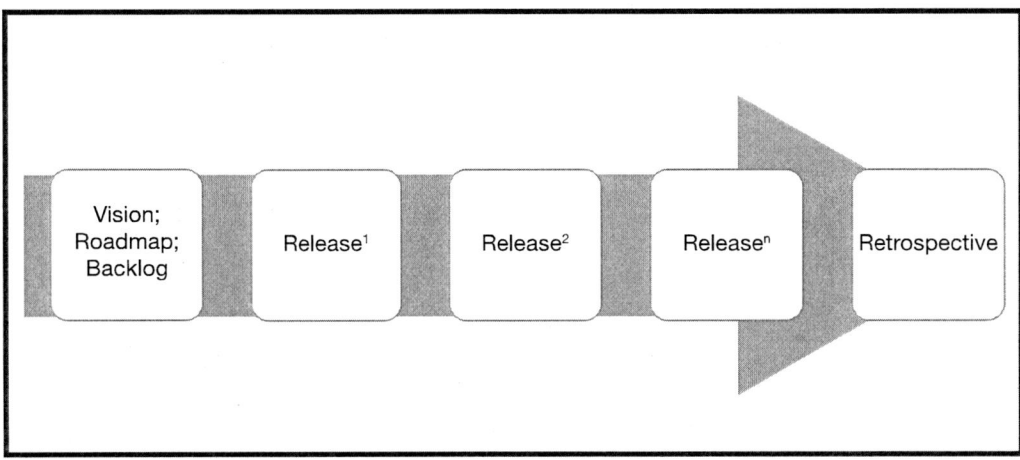

Figure 4.1. High Level View of the Agile Project Lifecycle.

External Stakeholders Engagement

In some agile methods, as in Extreme Programming (XP), the primary stakeholder is the customer/proxy, who is considered part of the project team and is directly responsible for writing and prioritizing stories. In Scrum, it is the Product Owner who represents the "voice of the customer" and thus translates the external stakeholder's vision for the project team. In either case, within the agile Plan process, there are several facets to engaging the stakeholder. They include:

- Designing the product roadmap
- Identifying minimal marketable features (MMF)
- Prioritizing stories for the project team

Designing the Product Roadmap

One of the key stakeholder responsibilities is to help the agile project team design the product roadmap. Thus, one way the stakeholder remains engaged is by operationalizing the product vision for the team. In traditional project management, this effort may be called product specifications, a preliminary scope statement, or a requirements document. In the agile world, we refer to it as the product roadmap, as shown in Figure 4.2.

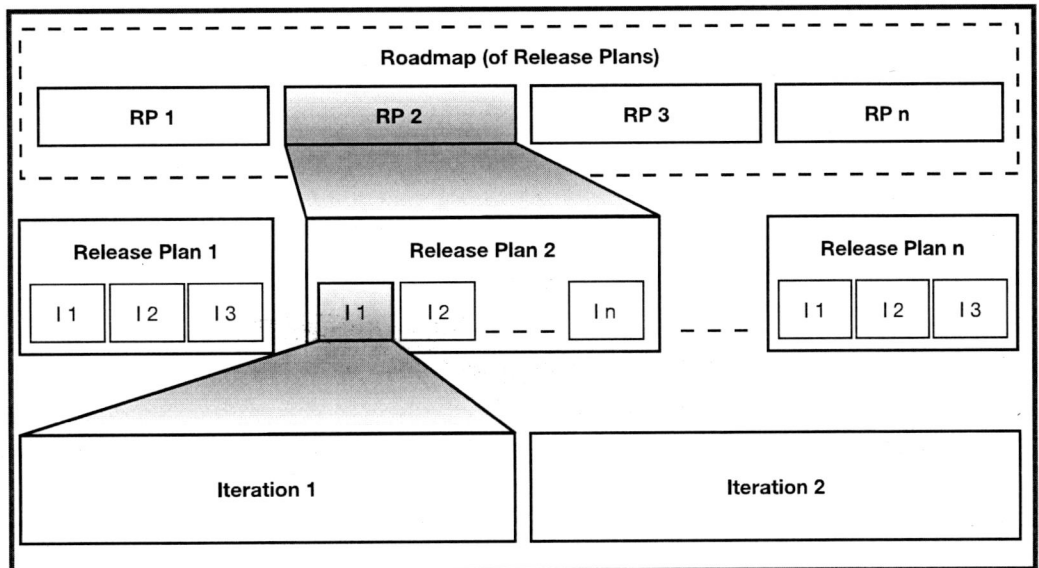

Figure 4.2. The Product Roadmap Shown with its Component Elements.

The product roadmap's component elements are the release and iteration plans.

 The **_product roadmap_** is an artifact, which shows how the product is intended to evolve over time. It specifies the contents of each release and maps delivery timelines.[2] As shown in both Figures 4.1 and 4.2, the product roadmap is equivalent to program planning in the traditional world and consists of multiple releases.

For Agile Project Management to succeed, it must use timeboxes intelligently and well. When organizations transition to an agile framework they still need - and demand - to accurately predict planned release dates. Customers simply won't accept anything less. So planning roadmaps, releases, and iterations is part of a bigger process goal. The goal is to transform a product vision into a product backlog of features that can be estimated and then measured against a reliable productivity rate (referred to as team velocity) to quantify predictable points in time for delivering releases. We'll discuss team velocity in more detail in subsequent chapters on the Iterate and Control processes.

There are two major approaches to the agile planning process - planning by date or planning by scope. It is good to note the "or" in the prior sentence is not an "and" because many project failures have been induced by management who thought they could control both!

 When a project must be completed by a certain date, such as to comply with an SEC or FDA regulation, it is called **_planning by date_** (also known as a **_timeboxed plan_**). Here, the release date is defined in advance, but the specific features of the release are negotiable. Thus, timeboxed plans require specific functionality to be delivered at the prescribed time. Once the scope of work has been sized, using team velocity, we can perform a quick calculation and **determine the probability** of meeting that given **release date**.

For example, if the team will need to develop features with a total size of 750 story points and we know that the mean value of their best three iterations was 100 points, the mean for their last 10 iterations was 75 points, and the mean of their worst three iterations was 50 points, then we can do a quick analysis. The probability that they will be done in five iterations, as management wants, is very low because 750/100 is 7.5 or 50 percent greater than five iterations at the team's highest productivity rate. The probability that they will be done in 10 iterations, as the team forecasts, is high because 750/75 is exactly 10 iterations with team productivity at the mean for the last 10 iterations. And the probability that they will need 15 iterations, as the accounting department is betting, is very low because 750/50 is 15, or 50 percent below the team's worst productivity rate.

Identifying Minimal Marketable Features (MMF)

Another aspect of engaging stakeholders is delivering a product that has value to them. Ultimately, the agile team must rely on stakeholders – typically in the form of the external customer or a customer/proxy – to define what features are valuable to the business. Even given its shorter iterations (as compared to traditional project management), without appropriate input from stakeholders, the agile project remains at risk of committing the sin of delivering an unwanted product. Agile teams avoid this when they plan by scope.

> ***Planning by scope*** (also known as a scopeboxed plan) involves first defining the key product features that need to be built into the release before committing to a release date. These key features are called the ***minimal marketable features (MMF),*** which comprise the smallest set of functionality that provides satisfactory customer value.[3] Typically, the goal of planning by scope is to create a competitive distinction as a first mover, thereby capturing market share, generating premium margins, and possibly enjoying cost savings.

Once the MMF has been defined and sized, the same team velocity calculation explained above can be used to determine the probability of meeting any given release date. If the release date is not soon enough, the MMF can be reassessed to see what features could be modified or eliminated to achieve the desired market timetable.

Prioritizing Stories for the Project Team

Prioritizing stories for the agile project team is the third facet of engaging the stakeholder. As noted earlier, once the product vision and roadmap are defined, they serve as inputs to the product backlog. Prior to performing release planning, the product backlog must be prioritized and estimated.

In traditional project management, one of the challenges in planning (requirements gathering, in particular) is disagreement among stakeholders. Such disagreements, whether over the relative importance of specific features or how the product looks to end users, may paralyze the project until a resolution occurs. In agile, this situation is largely alleviated by designating the customer/proxy[4] as the one who directs "what the product should do, what the product should look like, and how it should perform."[5] Thus, in agile, the customer/proxy is responsible for prioritizing stories in the product backlog while the project team is responsible for providing work and time estimates.

For the agile process to be successful, prioritization requires cooperation from multiple stakeholders. When prioritizing stories, the customer/proxy must accurately portray the needs of the business and of other stakeholders (e.g., end users) to the project team. Similarly, the project team must give the customer/proxy accurate information (about risks, assumptions, constraints, and estimates) so that effective decisions about prioritizing stories can be made.

Finally, story prioritization is iterative, first occurring when the product backlog is prioritized and estimated and then again after each successive iteration. This is one of the strengths of employing agile methods. Between iterations, the product backlog is groomed – features may be added, deleted, and/or reprioritized based on the current needs of the organization. This fosters consistent customer/proxy engagement throughout the project.

Summary

On agile projects, stakeholder engagement emerges through several key organic processes – most notably designing the project backlog, identifying minimal marketable features (MMF), and prioritizing user stories. Regardless of which flavor of agile is being practiced, stakeholder disagreement is minimized by selecting a single voice (that of the customer/proxy) to convey the organization's needs to the project team. If this level of customer/proxy participation is not forthcoming, it signifies a dysfunction in the agile process and represents a significant project risk. In the event that such breakdowns occur, retrospectives and team reflective sessions are appropriate forums where agile teams may initiate corrective action.

Value-Driven Delivery

Agile methods are value-driven in that they emphasize delivering features that have the highest customer value and defining the values and working agreements which govern the process of how the team works.[6]

Global agile values originate from documents such as the Agile Manifesto and the Declaration of Interdependence (DOI)[7], which have received much treatment elsewhere.[8] Team-level values are affirmed in working agreements.

A ***working agreement*** is a standard that an agile team applies to its work. The team usually identifies its working agreements at the start of a project and may add to them based on retrospectives and team reflective workshops. Frequently, the team posts its working agreements in an information radiator where everyone can see them. Here are some examples:

"Always remember that the customer/proxy is part of the working team."
"We are not done until the use cases are written and tested."
"If the build is broken then everyone stops to fix it."
"We resolve to be on time for the daily stand-up meeting!"

In Chapter 2, we introduced several points of the agile feedback cycle, including the daily stand-up meeting, the iteration review meeting, and the retrospective meeting. An optional feedback point is the ***team reflective workshop.*** The reflective workshop is process-oriented and may occur at any time when the team deems necessary. Thus, the reflective workshop is an appropriate forum to correct flawed agile processes, introduce new ones, or augment working agreements *during* an iteration. The obvious implication is that the reflective workshop is a way for the agile team to be proactive and initiate corrective action in its agile processes prior to the end of an iteration.

As we examine value-driven delivery, we will focus on the following:

- Release/Iteration Plans
- Planning Activities
- Decomposition and Progressive Elaboration
- Story Maps

Release/Iteration Plans

We introduced the concepts of timeboxes, release plans, and iteration plans in Chapter 2. Figure 4.3 illustrates a further drill-down of the product roadmap, from the release plan to the story level.

In review, the product roadmap serves as the customer/proxy's vision for the product. The release plan is the equivalent of the project schedule, being, in turn, comprised of short iterations. The iteration is not only a timebox unto itself, but it also contains work effort descriptions called user stories.

As we proceed, we'll consider some of the preparation work for release planning before delving into more detail.

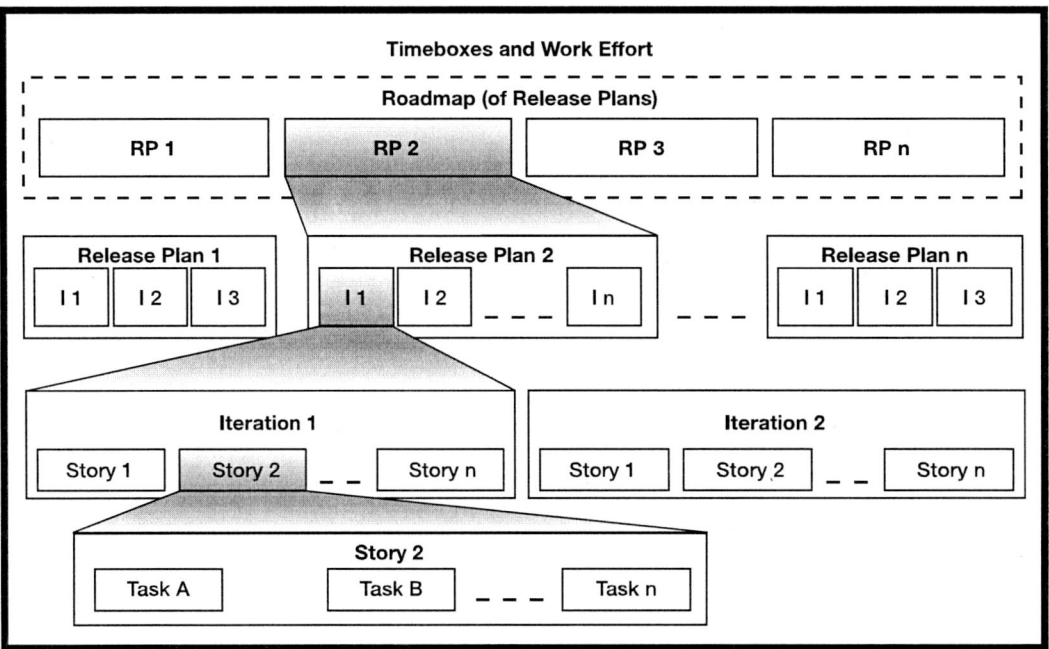

Figure 4.3. A Product Roadmap Drilldown.

Getting Started: Building a Central Feature List

Prior to release and iteration planning, the agile team should construct a central feature list. While the customer/proxy typically is responsible for communicating and prioritizing features for the team, feature requests may originate from a variety of sources. End users, functional business units, internal and external stakeholders, requests for proposals (RFPs), development team members, senior management, competitors, and government regulations all may be sources of product features. The project team should enact some controls to prevent duplicate items, impossible features, and overly vague requests from appearing on the central feature list. The team should be encouraged, however, to enter new features as they identify them, so that they may be included in the prioritization and planning process.

The *central feature list* may be a rough sketch, a superset, to be used as an input for planning the release and first iteration. It represents the current potential of what the product could become, perhaps over several releases. You need not wait until all features are defined before getting started delivering the product. Moreover, you need not adhere senselessly to the original list, original descriptions, or original priorities. One of the main points of agile development is that this list is dynamic and evolving, iteration by iteration.

Let's pretend that a rough feature list is constructed, a release plan and iteration plan are drawn up, and the first iteration is completed... THEN a few more critical features are identified by the customer/proxy. What happens now? These features simply get folded into the evolving release plan and a later iteration, being delivered as soon as possible. But meanwhile, time is not wasted. The team starts delivering value as soon as possible, and creates the infrastructure to allow the project to adapt over time to new priorities, information, and strategic business goals.

Release Plans

The *release plan* is a timebox equivalent to a project or sub-project schedule in the traditional project management world. Release plans identify specific feature sets that represent **a recognizable, logical component of the overall solution.** Frequently, release plans represent the point at which deliverables can be used or implemented by customers. Release plans are composed of iteration plans. The size of the timebox represented by a release plan is the sum of the iterations within that release.

How long does a release planning session take? Small projects (i.e., three months or less) may be done in a day. Larger projects may take several days. During the session, the team has to constantly remember that it is being driven by two forces:

- *Creating value for the customer.* The focus is not on building the product; it is on increasing the value of the product created to those who will use it. The product is a means to an end, but it is not the value itself.
- *Getting to market quickly.* Develop plans around minimum marketable features (MMFs). View features from the MMF perspective: What is required to develop and release them?

Iteration Plans

The iteration plan is unique because it combines the timebox with detailed work effort descriptions *(See Figure 4.3)*. Thus, each iteration contains the user stories, which describe the work effort for specific features or components that will be created by the agile team. Within iteration plans, user stories are decomposed into tasks, which can be estimated for the amount of work required to complete them. Iteration plans define the work that will be done in that specific timebox and are rolled up into release plans. (We will discuss user stories in more detail under Adaptive Planning.)

By definition, the size of the timebox for an iteration is stable. Based on organizational norms or rules, an iteration timebox will typically be defined as either two, three, or four weeks. Once the timebox for iterations has been defined, it remains fixed because rhythm helps the team increase speed, while stability helps the team improve quality over time.

Although variations exist between different agile methods, iteration planning typically occurs in two parts. During the first part, the customer/proxy presents a select list of the highest priority stories tentatively slated for the iteration. The customer/proxy presents these stories, related acceptance criteria, and then fields questions from the team about the stories.

Example: Release Planning Session
Typical release planning sessions often follow a sequence like this:

- Introductions and specify meeting ground rules. (Project Manager)
- Review product vision and theme for the release. (Customer/Proxy)
- Identify features needed for the release. (Customer/Proxy)
- Prioritize features. (Customer/Proxy)
- Split features using the minimum-marketable-feature (MMF) perspective. (Customer/Team)
- Estimate the value and cost of the features. (Customer/Team)
- State known assumptions, constraints, and risks. (Team)
- Elaborate further by writing stories for features, repeating until you have reasonable clarity on what the features are and how valuable they are to the customer. (Customer/Proxy's Team)
- Create a specific release plan by date or by scope. ("What is the release date?" and "How many iterations comprise this release?") (Team)
- Estimate team velocity or capacity. (Team)
- Discuss remaining issues and concerns. (Team)
- Commit to the release as a team, given the information known right now. (Team)
- Close meeting, including make agile process observations and facilitate action items. (Project Manager)

During the second part of the meeting, the team may decompose the stories into the various tasks required to meet the customer/proxy's acceptance criteria. The result will be a set of sufficiently small stories to be included in the iteration and their related subtasks – otherwise known as the iteration backlog. (We'll talk more about decomposition and the iteration backlog later in this chapter.) The goal of iteration planning is to identify the activities (i.e., stories and their subtasks) that the team can commit to finishing within the iteration timebox.

Types of Iterations

Just as there are various flavors of agile, there are different types of iterations. While all agile methods employ the standard iteration as a matter of practice, some methods (e.g., Scrum) are more flexible and have adopted specific types of iterations as described below.

Traditional (Standard): While often associated with software development, the traditional iteration may be applied to many types of projects, including business process improvement, event planning, construction, and manufacturing. Figure 4.4 summarizes the various inputs for the standard iteration.

Level	Inputs
Product	• Product Vision • Product Roadmap • Product Backlog
Release	• Release Plan • Team Velocity (Or Capacity)
Iteration	• Iteration Plan • Iteration Backlog • Working Agreements

Figure 4.4 Standard Iteration Inputs by Level.

The standard iteration is also characterized by the following:
- New development work
- QA (i.e., internal QA and user acceptance testing)
- Miscellaneous items and defect repairs
- Demonstration for customer/proxy and key stakeholders
- Retrospective

Planning ("Iteration 0"): Here, the focus of the entire iteration is on planning rather than on executing new development work. The planning iteration may be referred to as "Iteration 0" because customer deliverables begin in Iteration 1. Typically, a planning iteration is followed by a series of standard iterations. Planning iterations are useful when:

- Ramping up an agile methodology for the first time in an organization
- Building up the product backlog
- Launching a complex project
- Starting a unique or never-before attempted project

Hardening (Release, or "Iteration H"): Some large or complex projects may require a hardening (release) iteration at the end of a release cycle. While the team strives for a potentially shippable product each iteration, the hardening iteration may be run every few iterations for "sanity testing" of the product.[9] One advantage of the hardening iteration is that (on software development projects), it may allow for manual testing that would be prohibitively expensive to perform during each standard iteration. Note that the length of the hardening iteration is independent of the number of preceding iterations. That is, whether there are five or ten two-week standard iterations, you may have just one three-week hardening iteration.

Handoff: A handoff iteration may be used to prepare the formal documentation and other deliverables that production requires, including attending final approval meetings. Handoff iterations may be utilized to transition a new product from one business unit to another (i.e., from development to maintenance) or to prepare a submission to an external agency (e.g., submit a new drug application to the FDA).

QA/Testing: Ideally, QA and testing are included as part of a standard iteration. However, an organization may conduct a specialized QA/Testing iteration if it wants to refine these functions occasionally.

Defect Repair: The defect repair iterations devoted exclusively to fixing product errors. Product defects (e.g., software bugs) may be treated as any other group of stories – placed in the product backlog and addressed within an iteration.

Hybrid: The hybrid iteration has most characteristics of the standard iteration, except that a significant percentage of the story points are reserved for non-development work. Examples include:

- 50% Development/50% Unplanned Items
- 33% Development/33% Defect Repair/33% Unplanned Items
- 50% Development/25% QA/Testing/25% Unplanned Items

For most organizations, repeated use of the hybrid iteration signifies a breakdown in agile processes. If it becomes the norm, both organizational commitment to agile and the adequacy of resources must be questioned.

Christensen's concept of **heavyweight teams,** which asserts that innovation is fostered by splitting teams into those devoted to new development versus those focused on maintenance, has applications in the agile world.[10] Especially when ramping up agile in an organization, teams are more likely to succeed when they are devoted solely to the iteration at hand (i.e., performing new development) rather than being **fractionally assigned** to multiple projects or to concurrent project and operational work. The specialized iterations discussed above may be viewed as extensions of heavyweight teams, where specialization is expected to encourage innovation.

Planning Activities

Activities are structured, interactive processes that help the agile team generate insights about the work to be done. They are optional and may be used in a variety of contexts, including during planning meetings and retrospectives. Activities aid the team in honing their ideas about the project and have several benefits as opposed to unstructured discussion, such as: 1) Directing the conversation to the goal at hand; 2) Encouraging participation from all team members; and 3) Generating "outside the box" thinking.[11] Activities are intended to be fun and energizing to the team, but if you find that they aren't adding value to the planning session, do not use them!

While not an exhaustive list, here are some common activities that may be used during planning meetings and retrospectives:

 Brainstorming: During brainstorming, the team generates ideas and then applies them to the project at hand. Three permutations of brainstorming[12] are:

- *Free-for-all:* Everyone in the room participates and shouts out ideas. The meeting facilitator (i.e., project manager) or a designated scribe writes down the ideas for subsequent discussion.
- *Round-robin:* Go around the room and each team member may speak in turn.
- *Silent generation of ideas:* Each team member has a finite time period (e.g., 5 minutes) to write down ideas on index cards. Upon completion, all ideas are submitted to the meeting facilitator for subsequent discussion.

 Fishbone (Ishikawa) Diagram: In this activity, the team identifies a problem, draws a fishbone diagram, and labels the "head" of the fish with the problem and the "bones" of the fish with categories. This is a type of root cause analysis, with the fishbone diagram leading the team to a solution. Figure 4.5 presents an example.

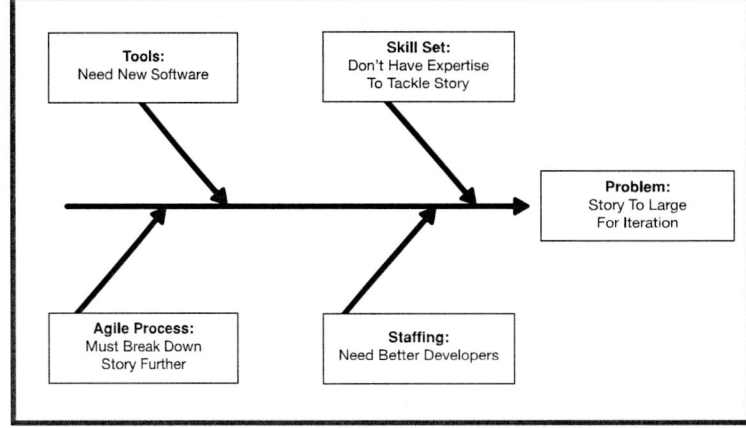

Figure 4.5 Using a Fishbone Diagram Helps a Team Ascertain a Problem's Root Cause.

Force Field Analysis: The force field analysis allows the team to examine factors in an organization that will drive or hinder a proposed change. For the activity, the team splits into two groups, one which lists things that might drive the change and the other which lists potentially hindering factors. In the example shown (Figure 4.6), the issue at hand is "Customer/Proxy Unavailability" and the desired state is "Daily F2F Access to the Customer." Force field analysis helps the team look at factors that affect a proposed change.

Once factors on both sides are identified, the agile team analyzes which factors they can influence and which are beyond their control, in an attempt to find a way to influence the desired change in the organization.

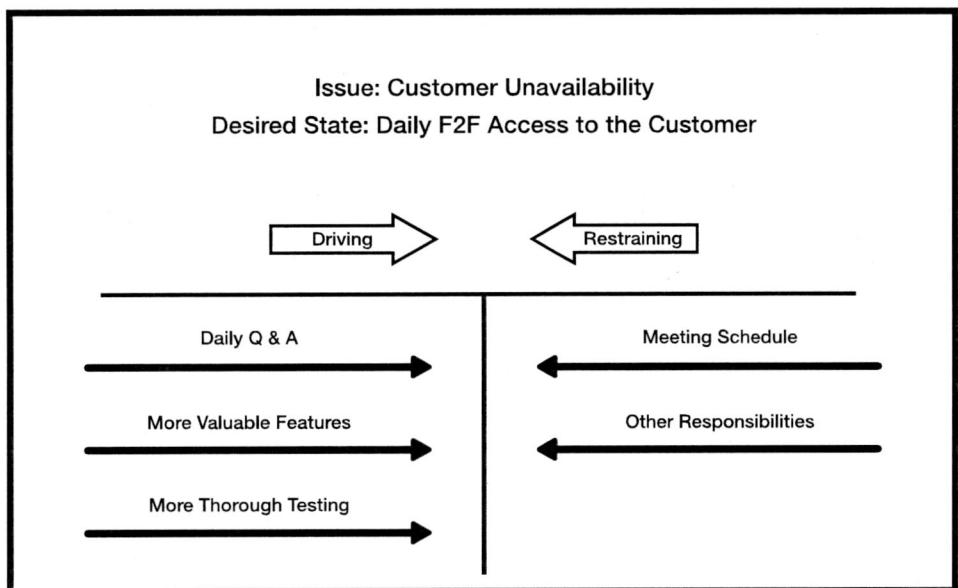

Figure 4.6 A force field analysis of factors that affect a proposed change.

 Prioritize with Dots: Prioritizing with dots helps a team narrow down a long list of items. For example, this activity may be used to prioritize stories from the product backlog in the absence of overriding stakeholder preferences. Each team member gets ten colored sticky dots and may vote for up to four stories to be included in the iteration. There are several permutations of how the ten dots may be allocated. One method is to allow team members to vote any number of dots per story until their ten dots have been spent. A more structured method is:

- Priority #1 = 4 dots
- Priority #2 = 3 dots
- Priority #3 = 2 dots
- Priority #4 = 1 dots

If the first team vote does not resolve the prioritization issue, some stories may be eliminated from contention and the process repeated until the iteration backlog is populated. Figure 4.7 shows members of a project team voting with dots.

Figure 4.7 Members of a project team using the Prioritizing with Dots activity.

 Learning Matrix: The learning matrix is an activity used to generate ideas and gather feedback about the meeting, particularly about agile process issues. In this activity, we divide a flipchart or white board into quadrants that represent four perspectives on the meeting:

- Things done well
- Things needing change
- New ideas generated
- Appreciations to acknowledge

Figure 4.8 shows an example of a learning matrix stemming from an iteration planning meeting. Outcomes from the learning matrix may be process changes in future meetings, action items for team members, or updates to the team working agreement. The learning matrix allows the team to brainstorm quickly based on four set perspectives.

This is a simple activity that works well when time is tight, and one that is used often to close retrospectives.

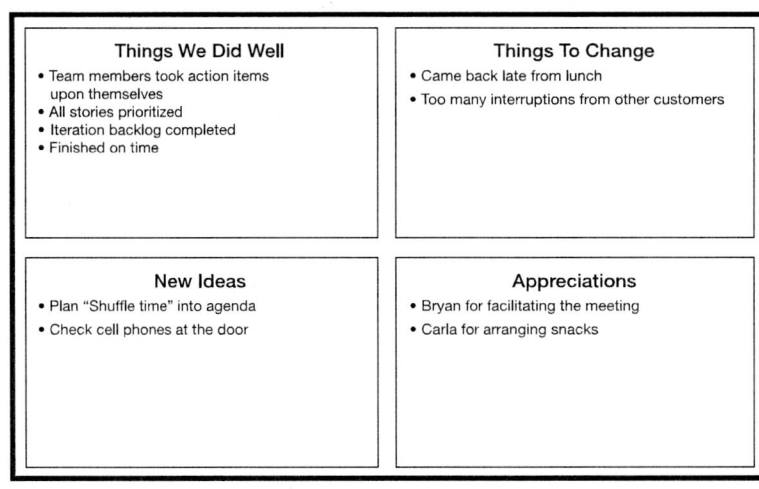

Figure 4.8 A Learning Matrix.

Decomposition and Progressive Elaboration

 Decomposition and progressive elaboration, terms common to traditional project management, have somewhat different connotations in the agile world. **Decomposition** involves breaking large items (i.e., features) into smaller ones (i.e., stories and tasks). Since organizations employing agile methods typically have high flux environments, the agile approach is to decompose items as needed.

Think of release planning as just-in-time (JIT) *progressive elaboration* on the product vision – focusing on those features of greatest priority to the business and eliminating unnecessary work on requirements that may never be needed. This approach to decomposition uses JIT methods to prevent wasted effort on lower-priority or unneeded features. The agile team expands on features only to the extent that it needs to, according to the customer/proxy's defined priority of which deliver the most value.

For the product backlog, features are estimated at the 50,000 foot level, without specific tasks being defined or resources assigned to them. During iteration planning, the features designated for that iteration – and not for the entire product backlog – are then elaborated into tasks, with resources being applied during the iteration.

Story Boards

 The *story board* shows the status of user stories. The story board may be a physical board (See Figure 4.9) on a wall or white board or it may be a virtual table in one of many available commercial software applications.

Figure 4.9. The Story Board.

Observe that this board portrays columns for stories from *(L to R)* Product Backlog, Sprint Backlog (i.e., Not Started), In Progress, and Done.

At the iteration level, the board may contain the decomposed tasks underneath the user story. Generally, the story board will contain several categories that indicate the item's progress towards completion. As items move forward towards completion, they are moved from left to right on the board (See Figure 4.9).

There are several permutations on story board categories, but most versions align with Not Started, In Progress, Ready for Testing, and Done. Figure 4.9 shows a board where stories from the product backlog are seen on the far left, followed by iteration backlog items in various states of completion (Not Started, In Progress, and Done). Sophisticated story boards (particularly electronic versions) also may show dependencies between tasks.

When we discuss the Manage process in the Agile PM Processes Grid™ *(See Figure 2.16)*, we'll go into detail about how the agile team updates the board each day.

Summary

Value-driven delivery stresses delivering features with the highest value to customers as well as defining the values which govern the agile process.

Global agile values are defined in documents such as the Agile Manifesto and the Declaration of Interdependence. Team-level values are publicized in the form of working agreements.

Release planning involves just-in-time (JIT) progressive elaboration of the product vision. This allows the project team to concentrate on those features of greatest priority to the business and avoid wasting effort on lower-priority or unneeded features.

Some agile methods have adopted specific types of iterations to help in delivering value to customers. Iteration types include standard, planning, hardening, handoff, QA/testing, defect repair, and hybrid.

Planning activities are structured, interactive processes that help the agile team generate insights about the work to be done. They are optional, intended to be fun, and often enhance planning meetings and retrospectives. They should be used only when they add value to the agile planning process.

Adaptive Planning

Adaptive planning, as commonly practiced, entails use of incremental delivery cycles or iterations. We have already described how decomposition and progressive elaboration work in an agile environment.

The process or "struggle" of agile involves a balancing act between environmental flux and discipline. When presented with change, ***agility*** is the project team's ability to adapt to the business's needs (as voiced by the customer/proxy) while ***discipline*** is the team's capacity to adhere to the methodological dogma to get the work done.[13] Adaptive planning, as described in the remainder of this chapter and in Chapter 5, is how agile teams balance flux and discipline – from the agile method chosen to delivering product to the customer.
Key elements of adaptive planning include User Stories, Iteration Backlog, and the Definition of Done, which we will explore now.

User Stories

A ***user story*** is a description of a product feature that is written from the perspective of the end user. The customer/proxy is primarily responsible for writing user stories and prioritizing them for the project team. The team is responsible for estimating the work involved (i.e., the size) and for deciding *how* to accomplish the work.

As illustrated in Figure 4.10, stories usually follow the format:

As a: *<Role>*
I want: *<Function>*
So that: *<Desired Goal>*

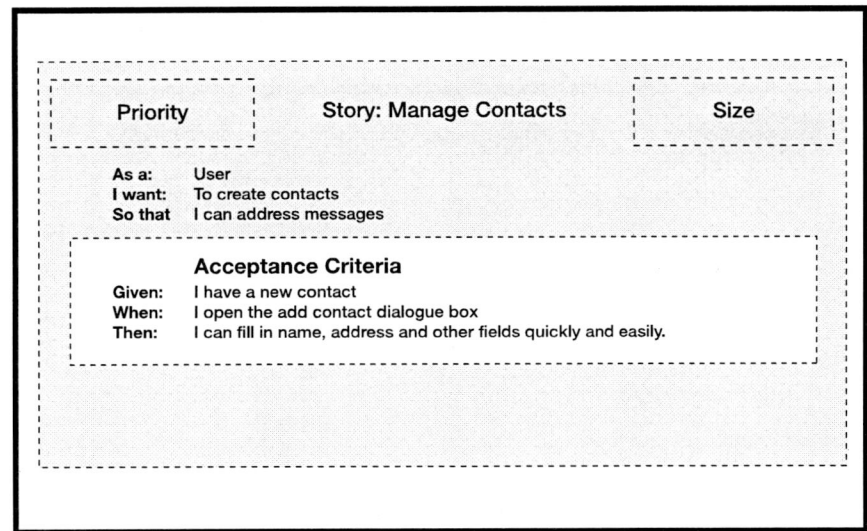

Figure 4.10 A User Story, Which Includes the Story's Acceptance Criteria.

This example of a user story on an index card contains the story, the acceptance criteria, and places for priority and size to be entered. The customer/proxy also has provided acceptance criteria, or guidance about how to test the feature. Acceptance criteria follow the format:

Given: *<Function Input or Data>*
When: *<Operational Functionality Trigger>*
Then: *<Criteria to Achieve Desired Goal>*

As noted previously, stories are often written on sticky notes or index cards, and arranged on a wall or white board. The purpose of organizing stories in this fashion is to foster discussion and planning focused on the end user's view of the feature. In fact, one of the most important benefits of using note cards this way is that it practically requires everyone to participate in the process.

By comparison, if tasks are being projected on a screen and someone is typing them into mind-mapping software, the typist has unintentionally been granted the power to control the input and outcome. All conversations are forced to pass through the typist, who may change what gets recorded, disempowering the team.

Each user story is a description for planning, a placeholder for any needed clarifications and a repository for the tests and acceptance criteria that determine when it is done. An incredible amount of discussion, even vigorous debate, goes into them. This participatory decision making approach has many advantages for the team.

First, user stories emphasize face-to-face (F2F) verbal communication, which (as you'll remember from the Communications Effectiveness Pyramid in Chapter 3) reduces the time and cost of idea transfer. Remember that the user stories are documented on index cards, which allows the customer/proxy and team to revisit them when needed for clarification.

A second advantage of user stories is their contribution to continuously re-planning the product backlog, accommodating discussion during the planning process. While the thousands of requirements and inter-relationships between them are considered, the inherent need for flexibility to re-prioritize them is obvious.

The third advantage is the alignment of user stories with the Lean principle of deferred commitments. Because the customer/proxy and team know that a placeholder exists – and their concern won't be forgotten – they are encouraged to defer spending precious time and expensive resources discussing details too early. This technique avoids the mistake of "false precision," uses resources wisely in time-constrained projects, and enables the team to concentrate on developing high-priority stories.

At its core, participatory decision making is action-oriented and so are user stories. That is why they are such a good tool in supporting participatory decision making.

We'll continue this conversation about user stories in Chapter 5 when we discuss estimating, sizing, and story points.

Iteration Backlog

When conducting iteration planning, the goal is to identify the activities that the agile team will complete by the end of the iteration. The iteration backlog is the prioritized, detailed story list for the current iteration that the agile team commits to delivering. (Figure 4.9 captures a real story board showing a project's iteration backlog.)

A **reciprocal commitment** exists when the team commits to delivering to specified functionality and the business commits to not changing priorities during the iteration. Thus, the team has the latitude to "freeze the build" during the ongoing iteration to prevent scope creep. However, at any time in between iterations, the customer/proxy may introduce change, which the project team embraces.

Definition of Done

Let's examine what "done" means to the agile project team. First, let's review a global definition and then consider how it may be impacted by the choice of agile discipline and iteration-specific inputs.

The expression *"done-done"* represents an agile state of being, akin to achieving Nirvana for the agile project team. It occurs when the product feature is complete, tested, defect-free, and may be put into production (i.e., released to the customer). For a high discipline agile framework such as Extreme Programming (XP), this is really the only definition of done, as evidenced by XP's quality standard of being able to pass unit tests at a 100 percent level at all times.

Some agile practitioners following Cockburn's barely sufficient philosophy[14] may adapt methods such as Scrum and have less rigorous, intermediate definitions of done where all aspects of testing (e.g., user acceptance testing) may not be included.

Iteration-specific definitions of done may include the following inputs:

- The acceptance criteria specified by the customer/proxy as part of the user story
- The agile team's definition of done, which may be clarified in its working agreements

It's critical that the definition of done is publicized (i.e., in an information radiator) and a shared understanding exists between the agile team, the customer/proxy, and key stakeholders.

Summary

Adaptive planning is how agile teams balance flux and discipline – from the agile method chosen to delivering product to the customer. In practice, it utilizes incremental delivery cycles or iterations to accomplish this work.

Key elements of adaptive planning include:

- User stories
- Iteration backlog
- Definition of done

A user story is a description of a product feature that is written from the perspective of the end user. Typically, user stories are written on index cards using a specific template that include not only a feature description, but also acceptance criteria used in testing.

The iteration backlog is the prioritized, detailed task list for the current iteration the agile team commits to delivering. A story or task board is used to manage the iteration backlog, with common categories of progress being Not Started, In Progress, In Testing, and Done.

"Done" represents an agile state of being when the product feature is complete, tested, defect-free, and may be put into production (i.e., released to the customer). Some agile methods are more flexible in the definition of done, usually by lowering the testing requirements.

Chapter Close-Out

Agile PM Processes Grid™ Exercise

Please take out a blank piece of paper, set a timer for no more than 3 minutes, and see how much of the grid you can reproduce from memory. To make the most of this Agile PM Processes Grid™ exercise, please simulate being in the testing environment. Close your book and all your notes. Visualize the Proctor handing you the blank sheets of paper and taking your seat in the testing site. Begin by drawing the grid, 6 columns and 8 rows, and then fill in everything you can. After the 3 minutes ends, use your book and notes to complete the grid. Study it as you do so.

Terminology Matching Exercise

In the blank column to the left of the Term, fill in the letter that identifies the correct definition or description.

	Term		Definition / Description
	1. Force Field Analysis	A	An artifact showing how the product is intended to evolve over time.
	2. Iteration plan	B	Has a release date defined in advance with the specific features being negotiable.
	3. Team reflective workshop	C	Key features that comprise the smallest set of functionality providing satisfactory customer value.
	4. Done-Done	D	A standard that an agile team applies to its work.
	5. Product roadmap	E	A process-oriented forum during an iteration to correct flawed agile processes or introduce new ones.
	6. Iteration backlog	F	A rough sketch or superset used for planning the first iteration and release.
	7. User story	G	A timebox equivalent to a traditional project schedule.
	8. Timeboxed plan	H	Combines a timebox with detailed work effort descriptions.
	9. Working agreement	I	Used to examine factors that will drive or hinder a proposed change.
	10. Release plan	J	Involves breaking large features into smaller stories and tasks.
	11. Minimal marketable features	K	A product feature description written from the perspective of the end user.
	12. Scopeboxed plan	L	The prioritized, detailed task list for the current iteration the agile team commits to delivering.
	13. Decomposition	M	Exists when the team commits to delivering specified functionality and the business commits to not changing priorities during the iteration.
	14. Reciprocal commitment	N	An agile state occurring when the product feature is complete, tested, defect-free, and put into production.
	15. Central feature list	O	Has defining key product features that must be built before committing to a release date.

Crossword Puzzle

Hints:

ACROSS
- 3 Involves breaking large features into smaller stories and tasks.
- 4 Has a release date defined in advance with the specific features being negotiable.
- 9 An artifact showing how the product is intended to evolve over time.
- 12 Exists when the team commits to delivering specified functionality and the business commits to not changing priorities during the iteration.
- 14 Combines a timebox with detailed work effort descriptions.
- 15 A product feature description written from the perspective of the end user.

DOWN
- 1 The smallest set of key feature functionality that provides satisfactory customer value.
- 2 A standard that an agile team applies to its work.
- 5 Defining key product features must be built before committing to a release date.
- 6 A process-oriented forum during an iteration to correct flawed agile processes.
- 7 Used to examine factors that will drive and hinder a proposed change.
- 8 A rough sketch or a superset used for planning the first iteration and release.
- 10 When the product feature is complete, tested, defect-free, and put into production.
- 11 A timebox equivalent to a traditional project schedule.
- 13 The prioritized, detailed task list that the agile team commits to delivering.

CHAPTER 4: Planning Projects – Part 1

Word Search

Word Search - 15 Words to find:

- DECOMPOSITION
- ITERATIONPLAN
- FORCE FIELD ANALYSIS
- RELEASE PLAN
- WORKINGAGREEMENT
- DONE-DONE
- PRODUCT ROADMAP
- RECIPROCAL COMMITMENT
- SCOPEBOXEDPLAN
- MINIMAL MARKETABLEFEATURES
- ITERATIONBACKLOG
- CENTRAL FEATURELIST
- REFLECTIVE WORKSHOP
- TIMEBOXED PLAN
- USER STORY

```
G R N C _ T N _ K R E F L E C T I V E _ W O R K S H O P N E
F M I N I M A L _ M A R K E T A B L E _ F E A T U R E S E R
W O R K I N G _ A G R E E M E N T E _ R _ I _ A B P _ O M R
S O O X F _ H S T S A N N P I O S M Y A N T E U E K _ T Y T
T E I W O R E C I P R O C A L _ C O M M I T M E A L C I E A
F O F O R O A K M G N I I R _ P R O D U C T _ R O A D M A P
F L O R C R G C E N T R A L _ F E A T U R E _ L I S T E F A
A P R K E _ E O B F D E O R L E D L _ T O T O D E F D B T D
E T C I _ O T N O L S E T M E _ T T E U I U K A A R I O I T
_ N E N F O O O X C N T C M I L D U D M S R V _ P M E X E I
L D _ G I O I E E D L M N O S I E D N R P E O F K E M E O L
I E F _ E A _ A D E F I K U M _ L A N R O O R E E E C D P T
D T I A L R D E _ _ A S D X M P L T S G A C E _ A L _ _ A L
E E E G D S E U P O N D I T _ P O K R E E A T M S C E P A P
C C L R _ M M T L O - N K A _ R E S P R _ L M O N T E R I B
O O D E A E E R A T L O D N M L D R I _ A P L A M U O _ G _
M E _ E N T U O N D A _ O E A P T C T T C L L A M R S R R A
P E A M A S I E A O E I T F M T O K T N I E N A T _ R D Y R
O P N E L M N O I R T A A O S D N E E V I T T T N O O C E R
S R A I Y T L D N A R I A _ S C O P E B O X E D _ P L A N E
I E L E S A L C R _ _ E R C E N T R A L _ F E A T U R E _ L
T T Y T R T V E B G B E R E F L E C T I V E _ W O R K S E R
I O S E A P T K F C S A T I T E R A T I O N _ B A C K L C _
O _ I A A I B A L U E F C L I I R U A C R _ O H N W _ S F O
N O S O T M V E O S _ C R K L E S C O P E B O X E D _ P L A
L N A D O N E - D O N E D E L E R E L E A S E _ P L A E N R
E S O E O I N O M S T K D _ _ O N I T E R A T I O N _ P L M
X R C P I C T T N E I O S A I G A N F E N T P L O I G L A
L E P B R P P R E C I P R O C A L _ C O M M I T M E N T E D
E A C A R E O L D A _ N E I C R _ X L N O F O E R I E T A _
```

Chapter Practice Test

1. All of the following statements regarding project planning in an agile environment are true except _____.

   A. Not all product features have to be planned in detail before starting the project – just those highest in priority to the customer/proxy
   B. Valuable features are delivered sooner
   C. All product features are planned in detail at the beginning of the project to maximize customer value
   D. The customer/proxy can easily add features and alter priorities between iterations based on changing business needs

2. Three key elements that guide the project team in agile product development are _____, _____, and _____.

   A. Customer, Product Owner, Scrum Master
   B. Product vision, product roadmap, product backlog
   C. Iteration, release plan, product backlog
   D. Requirements, specifications, test plan

3. The _____ is an artifact which shows how the product is intended to evolve over time.

   A. Product data sheet (PDS)
   B. Retrospective
   C. Vision statement
   D. Product roadmap

4. The effort of developing a scopeboxed plan is characterized by which of the following?

   A. The product release date is well defined, but the features to be developed are undefined
   B. The plan is based on the project scope statement
   C. The team defines the key product features to be built into the release before committing to a release date.
   D. The customer/proxy defines the product scope and release date.

5. When we say that between iterations the product backlog is groomed, the action taking place can best be described as _____.

   A. Features may be added, deleted, and/or reprioritized based on the current needs of the organization
   B. The backlog is reduced so that only important features remain
   C. The backlog is edited so that all the work is described clearly.
   D. Features are added to fill out the release plan

6. Which of the following best describes the primary participants in a release planning session?

   A. The customer/proxy and senior management
   B. The customer/proxy, project manager, and project team
   C. The customer/proxy and project manager
   D. Only the project team members are involved in release planning

7. Work to prepare the formal documentation and other deliverables that production requires, including attendance at final approval meetings, is typically accomplished during the _____ iteration.

   A. Handoff
   B. Hardening
   C. Hybrid
   D. Planning

8. A description of a product feature as seen from the perspective of the end user and written and prioritized primarily by the customer/proxy is best described as a _____.

   A. Sprint
   B. Product data sheet
   C. Feature plan
   D. User story

9. A prioritized, detailed task list describing work that the agile team has committed to accomplish during the current iteration is referred to as a(n) _____.

   A. Product roadmap
   B. User story
   C. Iteration backlog
   D. Product task list

10. When the agile team commits to delivering a specified functionality and management agrees to not change the team's priorities during the iteration a condition of _____ is said to exist.

    A. Flexibility
    B. Reciprocal commitment
    C. Agreed goals
    D. Agile agreement

11. The term _____ describes the condition where the product feature is complete, tested, defect-free, and may be put into production.

    A. Done-done
    B. Agile complete
    C. Re-factored
    D. Production ready

12. Agile teams utilize _____ to balance flux and discipline by applying incremental delivery cycles or iterations to accomplish project work

    A. Progressive elaboration
    B. Adaptive planning
    C. Iteration retrospectives
    D. Test driven development (TDD)

13. The effort of developing a timeboxed plan is characterized by which of the following?

    A. The team defines the key product features to be built into the release before committing to a release date.
    B. The plan is based on the project scope statement
    C. The product release date is well defined but the features to be developed are undefined
    D. The customer/proxy defines the product scope and release date.

14. A standard that an agile team applies to its method of work is described as a _____.

    A. Agile agreement
    B. Reciprocal commitment
    C. Standard of practice
    D. Working agreement

15. When launching a complex project, building up a product backlog or implementing agile methodologies for the first time, a _____ iteration can be very useful.

    A. Planning
    B. Hybrid
    C. Hardening
    D. Handoff

16. When agile project team members are assigned to multiple projects or have both project and operational support responsibilities they are said to be _____.

    A. Multitasked
    B. Fractionally assigned
    C. Matrixed
    D. Re-factored

17. When a team examines factors in an organization that will drive or hinder a proposed change they are performing a _____.

    A. Retrospective
    B. Brainstorming session
    C. Force field analysis
    D. Review meeting

18. Agile project teams will often use a _____ to show the status of user stories.

    A. Working agreement
    B. Retrospective
    C. Roadmap
    D. Story map

19. The application of just-in-time (JIT) progressive elaboration to the product vision during release planning allows the agile project team to _____.

    A. Both B and D
    B. Concentrate on those features of greatest priority
    C. Ensure that the project completes on schedule and on budget
    D. Avoid wasting effort on unneeded features.

20. An agile project team may conduct a _____ as a way to initiate corrective action to its processes prior to the end of an iteration.

    A. Force field analysis
    B. Team reflective workshop
    C. Working agreement
    D. User story

Answers – Terminology Matching

1:I, 2:H, 3:E, 4:N, 5:A, 6:L, 7:K, 8:B, 9:D, 10:G , 11:C , 12:O , 13:J ,14:M , 15:F

Answers – Crossword Puzzle

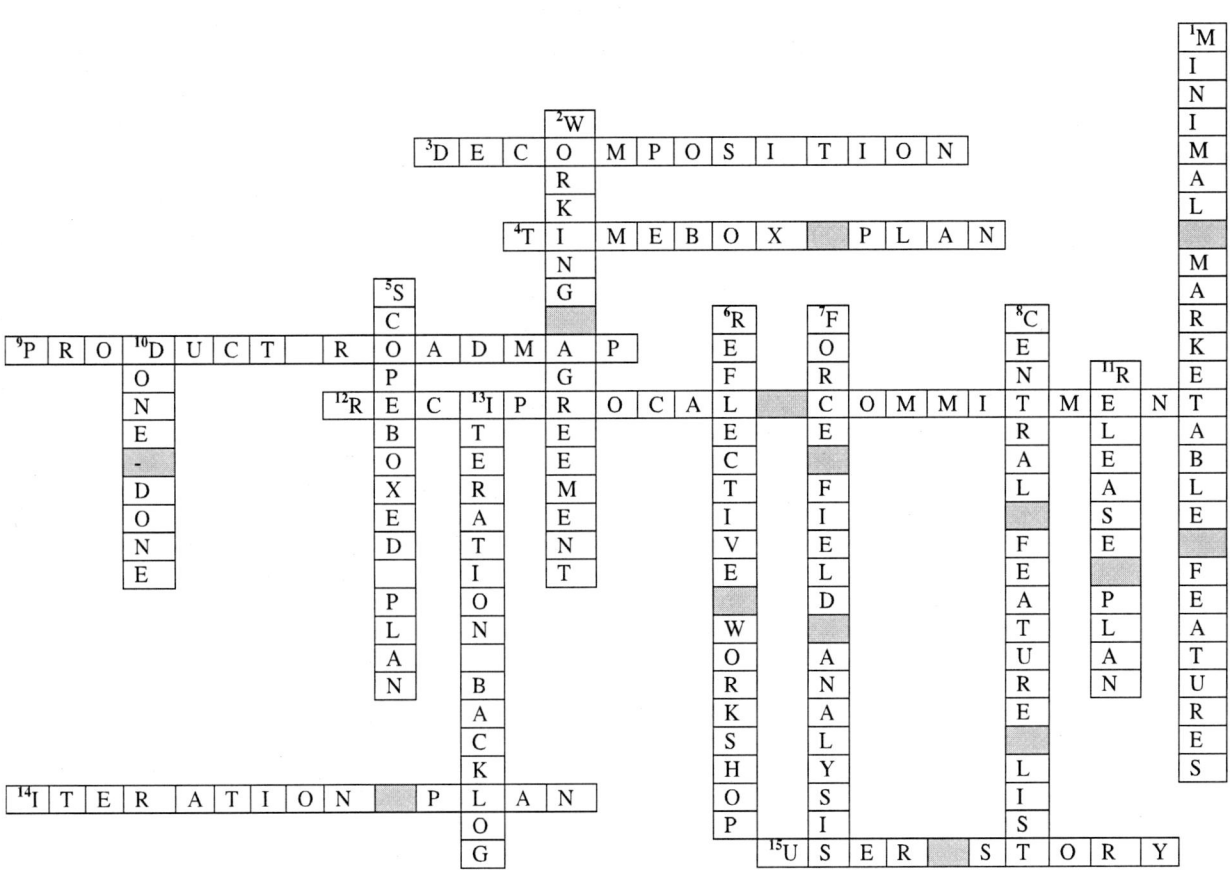

CHAPTER 4: Planning Projects – Part 1

Answers – Word Search

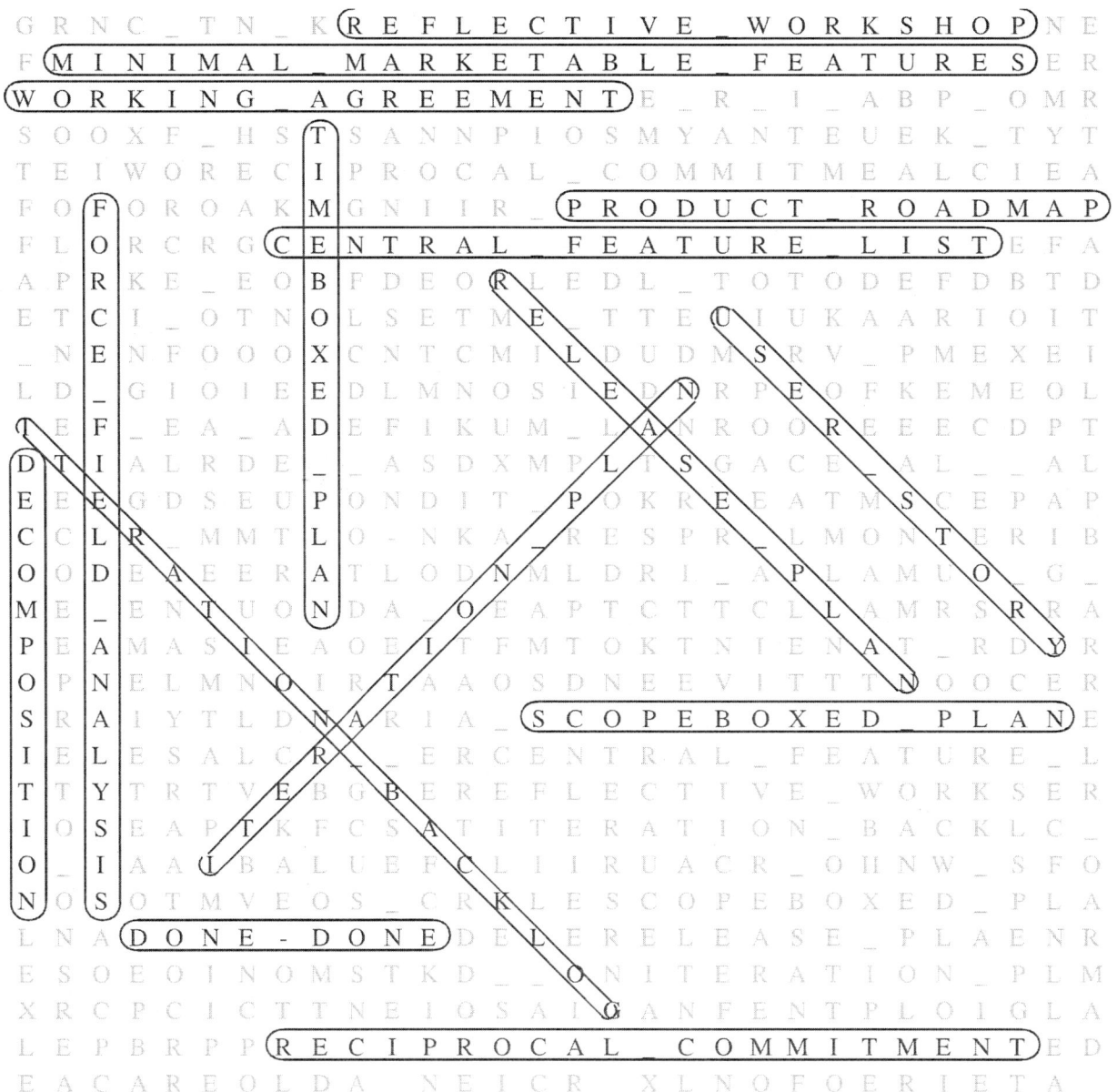

Answers – Practice Test

1. **C.** The agile philosophy suggests planning in sufficient detail only to accomplish the work of the immediate iteration. By taking this approach, the agile team can spend more effort on doing work (creating customer value) and less time planning work that may not be fully understood or that may change making the planning effort wasted. Frequent, short iterations allow the customer/proxy to make changes to features and priorities with minimal disruption to project work. This approach also allows the team to deliver valuable features sooner and more often.

2. **B.** The *triumvirate of agile planning* consists of the product vision, the product roadmap, and product backlog. Together, these elements guide the team in subsequent agile product development activities. The vision and roadmap serve as inputs to the product backlog prior to release planning, and the product backlog may be revisited by the customer/proxy and project team during inter-iteration planning meetings.

3. **D.** The *product roadmap* is an artifact which shows how the product is intended to evolve over time. It specifies the contents of each release and maps delivery timelines. The product roadmap is equivalent to program planning in the traditional world and consists of multiple releases.

4. **C.** *Planning by scope* (also known as a scopeboxed plan) involves first defining the key product features that need to be built into the release before committing to a release date. These key features are called the *minimal marketable features (MMF)*, which comprise the smallest set of functionality that provides satisfactory customer value.

5. **A.** Story prioritization is iterative, first occurring when the product backlog is prioritized and estimated before release planning and then again after each successive iteration. This is one of the strengths of employing agile methods. Between iterations, the product backlog is groomed – features may be added, deleted, and/or reprioritized based on the *current* needs of the organization. This fosters consistent customer/proxy engagement throughout the project.

6. **B.** The customer/proxy, project manager, and project team members are all participants in release planning. The customer/proxy reviews product vision and theme as well as drives product features and feature priority. The project manager facilitates the meeting while the team contributes to cost and schedule estimating as well as defining assumptions, constraints, and risks.

7. **A.** A handoff iteration may be used to prepare the formal documentation and other deliverables that production requires, including attendance at final approval meetings. Handoff iterations may be utilized to transition a new product from one business unit to another (i.e., from development to maintenance) or to prepare a submission to an external agency (e.g., submit a new drug application to the FDA).

8. **D.** A *user story* is a description of a product feature that is written from the perspective of the end user. The customer/proxy is primarily responsible for writing user stories and for prioritizing them for the project team. The team is responsible for estimating the work involved (i.e., the size) and for deciding how to accomplish the work.

9. **C.** When conducting iteration planning, the goal is to identify the activities (i.e., stories and related tasks) that the agile team will complete by the end of the iteration. The ***iteration (or sprint) backlog*** is the prioritized, detailed task list for the current iteration that the agile team commits to delivering.

10. **B.** A reciprocal commitment exists when the team commits to delivering to specified functionality and the business commits to not changing priorities during the iteration. Thus, the team has the latitude to "freeze the build" during the ongoing iteration to prevent scope creep. However, at any time in between iterations, the customer/proxy may introduce (and the project team embraces) change.

11. **A.** The expression ***"done-done"*** represents an agile state of being, akin to achieving Nirvana for the agile project team. It occurs when the product feature is complete, tested, defect-free, and may be put into production (i.e., released to the customer).

12. **B.** Adaptive planning is how agile teams balance flux and discipline – from the agile method chosen to delivering product to the customer. In practice, adaptive planning utilizes incremental delivery cycles or iterations to accomplish this work.

13. **C.** When a project must be completed by a certain date, such as to comply with an SEC or FDA regulation, it is called ***planning by date*** (also known as a ***timeboxed*** plan). Here, the release date is defined in advance, but the specific features of the release are negotiable. Thus, timeboxed plans require specific functionality to be delivered at the prescribed time. Once the scope of work has been sized, using team velocity, we can perform a quick calculation and determine the probability of meeting that given release date.

14. **D.** A working agreement is a standard that an agile team applies to its work. The team usually identifies its working agreements at the start of a project and may add to them based on retrospectives and team reflective workshops.

15. **A.** Typically, a planning iteration is followed by a series of standard iterations. Planning iterations are useful when: Ramping up an agile methodology for the first time in an organization, building up the product backlog, launching a complex project, or starting a unique or never-before attempted project.

16. **B.** Teams are more likely to succeed when they are devoted solely to the iteration at hand (i.e., performing new development) rather than being fractionally assigned to multiple projects or to concurrent project and operational work.

17. **C.** The force field analysis allows the team to examine factors in an organization that will drive and hinder a proposed change. For the activity, the team splits into two groups, one which lists things that might drive the change and the other which lists potentially hindering factors.

18. **D.** The story map or story board shows the status of user stories. The story board may be a physical board (See Figure 4.7) on a wall or white board or it may be a virtual table in one of many available commercial software applications.

19. **A.** Release planning involves just-in-time (JIT) progressive elaboration on the product vision. This allows the project team to concentrate on those features of greatest priority (i.e., value) to the business and to avoid wasting effort on lower-priority or unneeded features.

20. **B.** An optional feedback point is the ***team reflective workshop.*** The reflective workshop is process-oriented and may occur at any time when the team deems it necessary. Thus, the reflective workshop is an appropriate forum to correct flawed agile processes, to introduce new ones, or to augment working agreements *during* an iteration. The obvious implication is that the reflective workshop is a way for the agile team to be proactive and initiate corrective action in its agile processes prior to the end of an iteration.

Chapter End Notes

[1] Sliger, M., & Broderick, S (2008). *The software project manager's bridge to agility.* Upper Saddle River, NJ: Addison-Wesley.

[2] Ibid.

[3] Denne, M., & Cleland-Huang, J. (2003). *Software by numbers: Low-risk, high-return development.* Upper Saddle River, NJ: Prentice-Hall.

[4] In Extreme Programming (XP), an onsite customer prioritizes stories and grooms the backlog. In Scrum, the Product Owner serves this role.

[5] Sliger, M., & Broderick, S (2008). *The software project manager's bridge to agility.* Upper Saddle River, NJ: Addison-Wesley.

[6] Ibid.

[7] The DOI can be found at http://pmdoi.org. ©2005 David Anderson, Sanjiv Augustine, Christopher Avery, Alistair Cockburn, Mike Cohn, Doug DeCarlo, Donna Fitzgerald, Jim Highsmith, Ole Jepsen, Lowell Lindstrom, Todd Little, Kent McDonald, Pollyanna Pixton, Preston Smith and Robert Wysocki.

[8] Cockburn, A. (2007). *Agile software development: The cooperative game, Second edition.* Upper Saddle River, NJ: Addison-Wesley.

[9] Cohn, M. (2007, June 27). Correct use of the release sprint. Retrieved November 1, 2011, from http://blog.mountaingoatsoftware.com/correct-use-of-a-release-sprint.

[10] Christensen, C. M., & Overdorf, M. (2000, March-April). *Meeting the challenge of disruptive change.* Harvard Business Review, 78(2), 66-76.

[11] Derby, E., & Larsen, D. (2006). *Agile retrospectives: Making good teams great.* Raleigh, NC: The Pragmatic Bookshelf.

[12] Ibid.

[13] Marcus, A. (2005). *Big winners and big losers: The 4 secrets of long-term business success and failure.* Upper Saddle River, NJ: Wharton School Publishing.

[14] Cockburn, A. (2007). *Agile software development: The cooperative game, Second edition.* Upper Saddle River, NJ: Addison-Wesley.

CHAPTER 5

Agile Estimating

Chapter Highlights

Our review of agile estimating is really a continuation of the Plan process. In Chapter 4, we began our discussion of adaptive planning, including the following key points:

- User Stories
- Iteration Backlog
- Definition of Done

To perform adaptive planning, agile teams employ incremental delivery cycles as they strive to balance flux in the work environment and discipline in their chosen agile method.

In Chapter 5, we explain how planning with stories aligns with the agile estimating approach to improve accuracy and optimize resource usage. We also describe how to apply the tools and techniques of agile estimating.

As we proceed, let's take a moment to review the remainder of the Adaptive Planning knowledge area in the Agile PM Processes Grid™ *(See Figure 2.16)* to see the topics that we'll cover:

- Estimation
  - Sizing
    - Wideband Delphi
    - Planning Poker
    - Story Points
    - Ideal Days
    - Affinity Estimates

CHAPTER 5: Agile Estimating 125

Estimation and Sizing

Estimates are, by definition, inaccurate because they tend to be based on ever-changing assumptions. However, the desire for accurate estimating is driven by a need to know "When will it be done?" and "What will it cost?" Trying to answer those two vital questions has been a challenge since the dawn of project management. Unfortunately, neither question has a particularly easy answer due to the high complexity – bordering on chaos – in most modern projects.

The problem is compounded further by two factors. First, over- and under-estimating do not occur symmetrically. Second, as shown in Figure 5.1, the variability of the estimate correlates with how far in the future the work occurs. As you can see, the risk of the activity being under-estimated is always greater than the risk that it has been over-estimated. In fact, chronic under-estimation is frequently revealed as work moves into the current time horizon and is decomposed into smaller tasks that are better understood. Compared to the estimate, the amount of work required seems to grow, but seldom shrinks. While this conundrum isn't new, due to the high complexity of today's projects, the reliability and usefulness of estimates has sunk lower and lower over the decades.

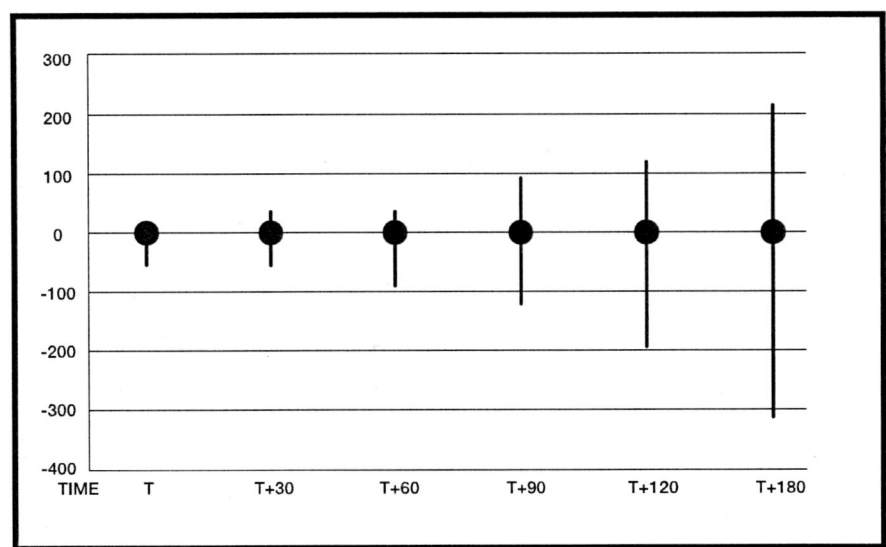

Figure 5.1 Estimation Variance Over Time.

 These insights about the science of estimation have emerged from the *law of large numbers (LLN)*, which is used by major businesses – as diverse as insurance and casinos – to manage earnings within reliable percentages. The LLN "guarantees" stable long-term results for random events by acknowledging the impact of variability. Based on the LLN, estimating accuracy is now understood to be inextricably linked to time in an inverse proportion. This means that the further ahead you try to estimate, the more the estimate decreases in accuracy.

 Taking this into account, agile estimating spends resources in direct proportion to the accuracy they produce. That means minimizing cost when the probable accuracy is low, and investing more when the probable accuracy is higher. This pattern was established in planning where user stories on the longer-term time horizon were treated as placeholders with minimal, high-level details and stories on the near-term horizon had greater detail and even included acceptance criteria.

Previously, we introduced the idea of a **cone of uncertainty** that impacts estimating *(See Figure 3.3)*. For many who are new to agile frameworks, this notion is a major paradigm shift. Our experience has shown that understanding the cone model requires clarity about stability and flexibility. Organizations need stability, but agile teams need flexibility and those positions are perceived to be in conflict. The key to unlocking that dilemma is two-fold. First there is the variable of "what-versus-how," and second is the variable of time, specifically timeboxes and time scales.

When it comes to defining what is being developed, organizations need stability or reliability, so they can plan and manage the myriad of marketing, operations, and other business functions affected by the solution being developed. Luckily, that is not in conflict with the agile team's need for flexibility in defining how the solution will be developed. So the variable of What-versus-How is actually in alignment, despite first appearances of being in conflict.

When we analyze the variable of time, we see that organizations need flexibility on the long-term scale, but can support stability on the short-term scale. Flexibility is provided with the roadmap and release plan timeboxes *(and product backlog grooming)*. At the same time, stability is provided with the iteration timebox (and committed iteration backlog).

A key principle in Scrum (one shared by other agile frameworks) is that during a project, customers need to be able to change their minds about requirements, and the best way to meet those emerging needs is a combination of short-term stability (during the sprint) and long-term flexibility (outside the sprint). This notion is operationalized in agile through the reciprocal commitment between the agile team and the customer/proxy to postpone changes until the end of a given iteration.

Thus, agile frameworks accept that complex problems cannot be fully defined in advance. They use the scientifically validated empirical process control approach – transparency, inspection, and adaptation – to focus the team on quickly delivering results that move through the cone of uncertainty towards a solution in the midst of emerging requirements.

Sizing is another technique that enables the agile team to act as participatory decision makers. The goal of sizing is to give the team and the customer/proxy a quick, relative measure of the effort involved with delivering a particular user story. The process, at a high level, is to assess how big, complex, and risky a story is compared to other stories and then assign it a value.

An iteration's duration becomes more accurate due to the detailed discussion regarding the size and value of each story. Since all projects begin with incomplete requirements, the traditional practice of devoting huge amounts of time (and expensive resources) to create detailed estimates only produces false precision. This creates a false sense of security and ultimately, bad results. In contrast, sizing allows for adequate and appropriate planning, focusing the team on identifying what is needed to accurately estimate high priority components on a time horizon that is near enough to be accurately understood and applied.

The process of sizing melds team ideas about stories, subjects them to energetic discussion, analyzes them according to the customer/proxy's vision, and begins to align them with time and other constraints. The result is not simply team consensus, it is a deeper level of voluntary, discretionary, decision-making authority that is unlocked by dedicated participation. This balances agility in decision making with ownership and accountability, a hallmark of participatory decision making.

The objective of participatory decision making is to provide a framework for project decisions by extracting pertinent information while limiting individual biases. Team participation in the agile process thus produces sustainable, effective, efficient decisions that can be implemented.

During detailed planning, agile development favors a *feature breakdown structure (FBS)* approach instead of the work breakdown structure (WBS) used in waterfall development approaches. The FBS is a useful tool for the agile team in that it establishes:

- Business value as the customer/proxy's overriding criterion for prioritizing work
- A common language – specifically, user stories and related tasks – for planning discussions between the customer/proxy and the project team
- A basis for performing a variance analysis between estimated and actual business value delivered (See Figure 6.10 for a real world example!)

It is acceptable – and even customary – to start with large features (called epics in Scrum lexicon) and then break them out into smaller ones (i.e., stories and related subtasks) over time. This allows the customer/proxy to keep from diving into too much detail until that detail is needed to help facilitate actual design and delivery.

In the remainder of Chapter 5, we'll first consider units of story value and then we'll discuss specific sizing activities used by agile teams.

Story Points Versus Ideal Days

There are various measures of size that agile teams may utilize.

An *actual day* is just that – a standard working day in the given work environment. For example, if a team's standard work day runs from 8:00 am to 5:00 pm with an hour for lunch, the actual day would be eight hours. Using the actual day as measure of size is fraught with problems, most notably in that it erroneously assumes that all time during the actual day is productive time, devoted solely to work on the current iteration. Since we all know from experience that this is rarely (if ever) true, the actual day is not a useful measure, albeit one sometimes used by teams transitioning from traditional to agile development methods.

Another unit that the agile team may utilize in estimating stories is the *ideal day.* An ideal day is the amount of time per day that a team member would spend on a story if working full speed without any interruptions, meetings, vacations, or other competition for his time. Using the ideal day rectifies many of the aforementioned difficulties associated with the actual day. Ideal days are used by many successful agile teams, most effectively when all team members are senior developers with equivalent skills.

The most commonly used measure of size is *story points.* Story points are an estimate of story complexity that uses numbers to provide a high-level indicator of how difficult the story is in relation to others. When estimating user stories with story points, the team typically establishes a midpoint ("We think that developing a new software user interface will be 13 story points.") and then proceeds to estimate the other stories in the iteration backlog relative to the agreed-upon standard. In estimating stories, teams may employ the Fibonacci sequence or exponential number series to assign points. Experienced teams may customize a generic story point number series for a given work environment. When a team can estimate accurately how many story points it can complete in one iteration (i.e., forecast its velocity), it can also project the number of iterations it will take to implement the complete product backlog.

The *Fibonacci sequence* is a number series (1, 2, 3, 5, 8, 13, 21, 34, 55, etc.) where the next number is derived by adding the previous two. (Mathematically, it is defined by the non-linear equation Fn = Fn-1 + Fn-2.) The Fibonacci sequence is used by Scrum teams when providing value point estimates for stories during planning poker.

So, which are better – story points or ideal days? Based on our experience, there are several advantages that favor the use of story points.

Ideal days are not universal, either between or within team members. All team members are not equal. The experienced developer may be able to accomplish in two ideal days what may take the newly-hired developer five or seven ideal days. Moreover, as someone gains experience during a project (or even an iteration), the original estimate of four ideal days during iteration planning may turn out to be two ideal days by the time the developer starts working on the story.

Story points promote more participatory decision-making and cross-functional behavior. Since a story point estimate is a single number representing the entirety of the team's work on the story, it fosters discussion about all aspects of completing the story (e.g., design, programming, internal QA, and user acceptance testing). It thus focuses the team on the project as a whole rather than on the aforementioned areas of specialization.

Story points are a better measure of pure size than are ideal days.[1] Story points estimate the size of the story relative to the others considered, whereas ideal days are more dependent on the experience and skill sets of individual team members. When using ideal days as a measure when performing estimates, teams tend to dwell on making the distinction between ideal and actual days instead of focusing on story size. Stakeholders, too, regardless of their level of agile education, tend to hold teams to an unrealistic standard of making an ideal day equal to an actual day.

We prefer using story points for sizing stories, except in those rare situations when we have a uniformly skilled, experienced agile team. In the real world, this is an often unattainable luxury.

Estimation and Sizing Risks

At this juncture, we want to highlight some specific risks associated with estimation and sizing. Regardless of which sizing activity is used, within some teams there may be conformity pressure to "vote with the team." Conducting individual, silent votes – revealed simultaneously by each team member – after group discussion on a story is an effective way of avoiding such scenarios.

Divergence in experience or competency between team members may be another source of risk. The impact of productivity variation between team members may be mitigated by using team velocity measures to cap the amount of work a team can commit to for an iteration. Moreover, having senior developers mentor junior ones may not only reduce such a productivity gap, but may foster better story estimates and enhance cross-functionality.

There is no "one size fits all" for estimation and sizing activities.

Next, we will review some of the common sizing activities.

Wideband Delphi

The **Wideband Delphi** method is a consensus-based technique for estimating work effort; the variant used in the agile world today is a derivative of the Delphi method that originated at the Rand Corporation in the 1940s as a forecasting tool.[2] Boehm and Farquhar, who popularized the method in the 1970s, affixed the "Wideband" moniker because they believed it reflected the greater communication and interaction among participants performing the estimates.[3]

For estimating agile user stories, Wideband Delphi is applied as follows:

- *Kickoff meeting:* The facilitator (i.e., project manager) presents the backlog of stories. The customer/proxy is available to answer questions from the team, who discuss the stories as well as any assumptions, constraints, and risks, and select the unit for sizing stories.
- *Individual estimates:* Following the kickoff meeting, each team member individually estimates the stories.
- *Estimation meeting:* The facilitator records the individual story estimates on the white board so that the team may view the range of estimates. Following discussion, each team member votes silently and provides a revised estimate to the facilitator. The process continues in an iterative fashion until consensus is reached for each story.
- *Compose task list:* The facilitator organizes the stories, estimates, and any related subtasks and assumptions.
- *Present results:* The facilitator reviews the finalized iteration backlog – stories, subtasks, estimates, risks, and assumptions – with the agile team.

Planning Poker

Planning poker is a consensus-based game where team members individually estimate user stories using of numbered cards, followed by iterative discussions, until consensus is achieved. It is a variation of the Wideband Delphi method, used to estimate the relative size of tasks in software development, particularly with Scrum or Extreme Programming (XP) methods. By having team members play their estimate cards face down prior to any discussion, planning poker minimizes **anchoring** – exerting undue influence on the team by individual voters who are outliers, who are strong-willed, or who have specific agendas.[4]

Story estimates may be done in actual days, ideal days, or story points. Typically, all team members have identical card decks (either commercial or homemade) containing the Fibonacci sequence (1, 2, 3, 5, 8, 13, 21, 34, 55, etc.).

The process of a planning poker session is:

- The meeting is led by a facilitator (often a Product Owner or Scrum Master from another team) who does not play.
- For each story, the team asks questions of the Product Owner and discusses assumptions, constraints, and risks.
- To vote, each team member plays a card face down that represents his story estimate. This is followed by discussion, during which no mention of the unrevealed number estimate is made. Then all players simultaneously reveal their cards by turning them over.
- Outliers (i.e., players with highest and lowest estimates) are given an opportunity to explain their estimates to the team.
- The process continues in an iterative fashion until consensus is reached for each story.
- If stories are deemed too large to be included in the iteration, they may be divided or deferred to a later iteration.

If teams are not colocated, some electronic tools exist which can simulate the planning poker session.

Affinity Estimates

 Affinity estimating is a technique some agile teams employ to quickly and easily estimate a large number of user stories. It's particularly helpful when starting a new project that has a large backlog that has not been estimated. Figure 5.2 shows an affinity estimate in progress on a white board.

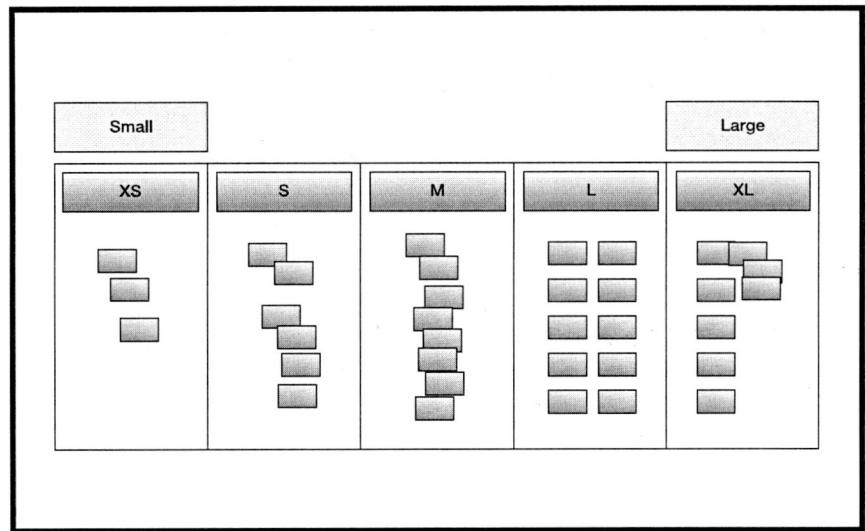

Figure 5.2 Affinity Estimating on a White Board.

The basic flow of affinity estimating is as follows:

- A facilitator reads all user stories under consideration to the team. A brief question-and-answer session between customer/proxy and team may occur to clarify any uncertainties.
- The team, working together but not talking, arrange the stories in size order. Story point numbers can also be used.
- After discussing the initial estimate, the team is given another opportunity to make silent adjustments to the board.

Work-in-Process (WIP) Limits

Work-in-Process (WIP) limits are not strictly speaking a type of user story sizing activity. Rather, WIP limits are an example of how agilists have borrowed techniques from Lean thinking to improve the value stream of product development.

 A project at any point in time may be considered as a type of *work-in-process (WIP)*. While a project user story is in process, the business does not realize value from it. Expediting the completion of a story means that the business derives value from it sooner. Rather than managing the flow of value through short iterations, use of WIP limits strives to manage an agile team's workflow (or throughput) by limiting the amount of WIP at each step in the process – creating and estimating the backlog, performing new development work, and testing. In other words, enacting WIP limits reduces bottlenecks by limiting the number of stories. Fewer stories must be "done," but those that are generate value for the business.

Figure 5.3 illustrates a **Kanban board** where WIP limits for a project are displayed. In the example shown, the Backlog (Not Started) limit is ten stories, the In Process limit is seven stories, and the Testing limit is five stories.

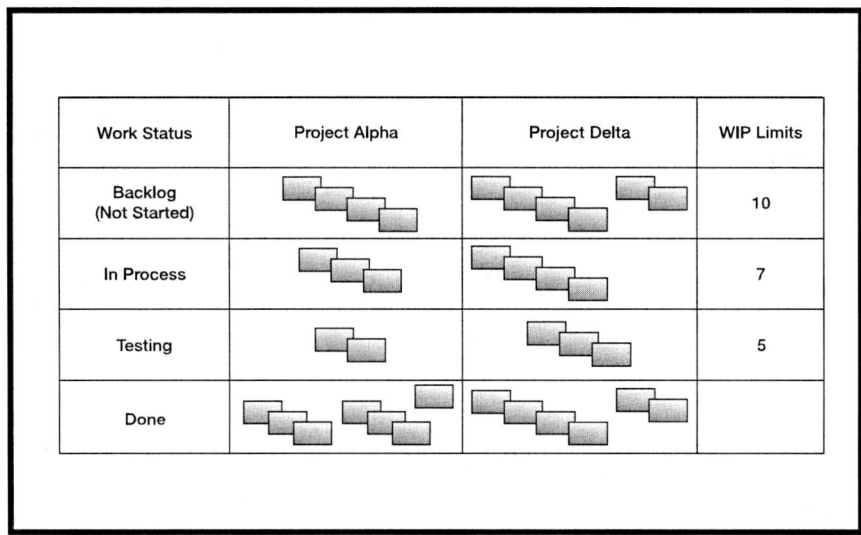

Figure 5.3 Kanban Board Showing Work-in-Process (WIP) Limits.

This Kanban board serves as a transparent window to the iteration, where the current status of each story may be viewed. It is an ideal information radiator. (We'll discuss these in more detail in Chapter 6.) If bottlenecks occur at a particular point (testing is a bottleneck in many software development shops), then the agile team and management can work to improve the process – perhaps by adding more resources.

Some ambitious organizations have adapted hybrid Agile/Lean methods, where they strive to deliver value by using both short iterations and WIP limits.

Summary

Project estimates, whether in the traditional or agile world, are to be inaccurate because they are based on ever-changing assumptions. Moreover, the further ahead you attempt to estimate, the more the accuracy of the estimates decrease. We've already seen that a hallmark of agile – working in short iterations – makes long-term, inaccurate estimates a moot point.

The goal of sizing is to give the agile organization a quick, relative measure of the effort involved with delivering user stories. It helps the team provide the business with an idea of how much value it can deliver during an iteration, thus bolstering the short-term stability (i.e., within the iteration) that the agile team needs to balance the long-term flux that the business demands.

Common units of size include actual days, ideal days, and story points. **We recommend using story points for sizing stories,** except in those rare situations when we have a uniformly skilled, experienced agile team. In those cases, ideal days may be utilized.

Sizing activities reviewed include Wideband Delphi, planning poker, and affinity estimate. Some ambitious organizations have adapted hybrid Agile/Lean methods, where they strive to deliver value by using both short iterations and work-in-process (WIP) limits.

Chapter Close-Out

Agile PM Processes Grid™ Exercise

Please take out a blank piece of paper, set a timer for no more than 3 minutes, and see how much of the grid you can reproduce from memory. To make the most of this Agile PM Processes Grid™ exercise, please simulate being in the testing environment. Close your book and all your notes. Visualize the Proctor handing you the blank sheets of paper and taking your seat in the testing site. Begin by drawing the grid, 6 columns and 8 rows, and then fill in everything you can. After the 3 minutes ends, use your book and notes to complete the grid. Study it as you do so.

Terminology Matching Exercise

In the blank column to the left of the Term, fill in the letter that identifies the correct definition or description.

	Term		Definition / Description
	1. Anchoring	A	An estimating technique that defines the relative effort involved with delivering a particular user story.
	2. Planning poker	B	Depicts the backlog and enhances communication by avoiding techno-jargon.
	3. Story points	C	A standard working day in a specific work environment.
	4. Actual day	D	The time per day a team member would spend working without any interruptions, like meetings.
	5. Sizing	E	Quantify work effort to provide a high-level indicator of how difficult development will be.
	6. Information radiator	F	A non-linear number series where the next number is derived by adding the previous two.
	7. Work-in-process	G	A consensus-based estimating technique derived from Rand forecasting tool.
	8. Feature breakdown structure	H	An estimating technique where team members individually decide then discuss user stories until consensus is achieved.
	9. Ideal day	I	Undue influence exerted by a single strong-willed member, often because of an undisclosed agenda.
	10. Wideband Delphi	J	A technique employed to quickly and easily estimate a large number of user stories.
	11. Affinity estimating	K	The set of unfinished items being developed which produce no business value.
	12. Law of large numbers	L	A visual display that concentrates important project information where anyone can see and evaluate it.
	13. Backlog grooming	M	A visual display of the scheduling process and the work that is being "pulled" through development.
	14. Kanban board	N	Preparing the next iteration planning meeting by adding stories, refining, and estimating stories as needed.
	15. Fibonacci sequence	O	Concept that larger samples transform unpredictable individual outcomes into stable cases for groups.

Crossword Puzzle

Hints:

ACROSS

2. Sequence is a non-linear numbers.
3. Undue influence exerted on a team by a single strong-willed member.
6. Consensus-based technique for estimating work effort derived from Rand Corporation forecasting tool.
11. Visual display in the project workspace that concentrates important project information where anyone can see and evaluate it.
12. Standard working day in a specific work environment.
13. Display of the scheduling process, the limits set on WIP, and new work that is being "pulled" through the development system.
14. Depicts the backlog planning in a way that enhances communication by avoiding techno-jargon.
15. Estimating technique where team members individually decide the size of user stories, and then discuss it.

DOWN

1. Employed to quickly and easily estimate a large number of user stories.
4. Statistical concept that larger samples of observations predict the behavior.
5. Unfinished items being developed which produce no business value until finished.
7. Time per day that a team member would spend working without any interruptions.
8. Preparing for the next iteration planning meeting by adding stories, refining existing stories, and estimating stories as needed.
9. Estimating technique that defines the relative effort involved with delivering a particular user story.
10. High-level indicator of work effort and complexity relative to other stories.

Word Search

Word Search - 15 Words to find:

- ACTUAL DAY
- ANCHORING
- BACKLOG GROOMING
- INFORMATION RADIATOR
- WIP
- IDEAL DAY
- KANBAN BOARD
- WIDEBAND DELPHI
- FIBONACCI
- LLN
- STORY POINTS
- PLANNING POKER
- AFFINITY ESTIMATING
- FBS
- SIZING

```
N A Y F D A A F Y S T O R Y _ P O I D K E
I M R D R I C O I I D E A L _ D A Y B N B
N N I N D G F T A B G I N E N P L M E S D
A A F N R S W I U C O I I I P E Z S T W A
F _ D O P D G A O A T N T F _ I D R G B E
F _ _ N R W B I A B L U A O S N _ O H A N
I A L W P M T A S A R _ A C N R Y K I N H
N L A I S N A C C C O E D L C W I P E O L
I N P D T K W T B K F B S A _ I B R D Y N
T I L E O A I A I L L D L R Y D O D R O F
Y O A B R N D I U O G O I N I C A B L N I
_ O N A Y B E E N G N L G O T D G I I O G
E N N N _ A B N O _ S _ F _ S I Z I N G R
S B I D P N A G N G G _ R I G I O P I O S
T W N _ O _ N A N R S T I A B R N N A N N
I K G D I B D O N O O E S A D O O T A O O
M D _ E N O _ N A O A N F R Y I N O D F D
A I P L T A D A I M O I G I T N A A M O _
T A O P S R E C N I L I A P A E T T C I T
I A K T _ D L E D N M A N C H O R D O C B
N A E L L N P Y T G K I D E A L _ D I R C
G S R O A I H A N C H O R I N G I N A H I
S I N O L M I B H N _ G A E K W T U E U D
```

CHAPTER 5: Agile Estimating 135

Chapter Practice Test

1. In general, the accuracy of estimates is higher for work that _____.

   A. Is to be completed far into the future because those tasks are closer to the final completion date of the project
   B. Is to be completed in the near term because those tasks are better understood
   C. Consists of more complex tasks because those tasks are better understood
   D. Consists of less complex tasks because those tasks are better understood

2. In general, estimates are more likely to be _____.

   A. Higher than what is actually required because teams tend to be conservative in their estimates
   B. Very accurate because project teams consist of experienced subject matter experts
   C. Lower than what is actually required to complete the work
   D. Either higher or lower than actual, one is not more prevalent than the other

3. In an agile estimating environment, project teams strive to minimize cost when the probable accuracy is low, and invest more when the probable accuracy is higher. Given that, an agile project team would be expected to _____.

   A. Estimate stories on the near term horizon in great detail while doing high level estimates on stories that are farther out
   B. Estimate all stories in great detail to maximize the accuracy of the estimates
   C. Focus their time on developing accurate estimates for more complex tasks
   D. Spend as little time as possible on developing estimates

4. When we compare the needs of organizations with those of agile teams we see that organizations require a degree of long term flexibility while agile teams require a certain amount of stability during the product development process. Long term flexibility for agile organizations is provided by the _____.

   A. Iteration plan timebox
   B. Roadmap and release plan timeboxes
   C. User stories
   D. Version control process

5. A key principle in Scrum (and in Agile in general) is that the project team be able to easily accommodate changes to requirements during product development. This is accomplished through the application of "reciprocal commitment" which requires that _____.

   A. The product owner and customer/proxy agree to implement all changes upon request
   B. Senior management and the customer/proxy agree on all changes
   C. The product owner approve all changes
   D. The customer/proxy postpone changes until the end of the current iteration

6. In order to address the fact that complex problems cannot be fully defined in advance, agile practitioners apply the concept of the empirical process control approach defined by the three principles of _____, _____, and _____.

   A. Transparency, inspection, and adaptation
   B. Planning, execution, delivery
   C. Transparency, execution, test
   D. Test, execution, test

7. Agile teams "size" user stories by comparing effort, complexity, and risk of a story compared to others and then assigning that story a value. All of the following are units of value used in this process except _____.

   A. Actual days
   B. Story points
   C. Timeboxes
   D. Ideal days

8. Agile practitioners use a _____ to account for project work rather than the work breakdown structure (WBS) approach used in traditional project management.

   A. Retrospective
   B. Task breakdown structure (TBS)
   C. Thematic structure
   D. Feature breakdown structure (FBS)

9. A typical work day that begins at 0800 and ends at 1700 with a one hour lunch break is best described as a(n) _____.

   A. Ideal day
   B. Actual day
   C. Agile work day
   D. Story point group

10. The amount of time in a work day that a team member would spend working on a story without interruptions of any kind is referred to as a(n) _____.

    A. Actual day
    B. Ideal day
    C. Story point group
    D. Agile work day

11. _____ are used to estimate the complexity and difficulty of a story in relation to other stories.

    A. Story points
    B. Agile days
    C. Retrospectives
    D. Product data sheets

12. A series of numbers where each number equals the sum of the two preceding numbers is defined as a _____.

    A. Story point group
    B. Da Vinci code
    C. Fibonacci sequence
    D. Prime series

13. Which of the following is true regarding the use of story points during agile estimating?

    A. Story points discourage detailed discussion about all aspects of completing the story
    B. Story points promote more participatory decision-making and cross-functional behavior
    C. Story points focus the discussion on areas of specialization
    D. Story points tend to be less accurate than actual or ideal days

14. Which of the following is true regarding the use of ideal days during agile estimating?

    A. Ideal days are the same as actual days
    B. Ideal days do not require a uniformly skilled, experienced team in order to work well
    C. Ideal days produce more accurate estimates than story points
    D. Ideal days are more dependent on the experience and skill sets of individual team members

15. An activity where team members individually estimate user stories through use of numbered cards, followed by discussion, until consensus is achieved is best described as _____.

    A. Ideal estimating
    B. Fibonacci estimating
    C. Wideband Delphi method
    D. Planning poker

16. During story estimating, the exertion of undue influence on voters by individuals who are strong willed or who have separate agendas is referred to as _____.

    A. Anchoring
    B. Refactoring
    C. Coaching
    D. Scrumming

17. _____ is best described as a technique employed to quickly and easily estimate a large number of user stories.

    A. Wideband Delphi
    B. Backlog grooming
    C. Affinity estimating
    D. Anchoring

18. The goal of sizing is to _____.

    A. Provide an accurate cost estimate for the iteration
    B. Give the team and the customer/proxy a quick, relative measure of the effort involved with delivering a particular user story
    C. Optimize the size of each user story
    D. Produce a detailed schedule for the customer/proxy

19. Which of the following is not a part of the basic flow of affinity estimating?

    A. After the initial estimate is done, the team is given another opportunity to make silent adjustments to the board
    B. The team, working together but not talking, arranges the stories in order of size
    C. The customer/proxy and product owner review and approve the story sizes
    D. A facilitator reads all user stories under consideration to the team

20. The set of unfinished items being developed which produce no business value can best be described as _____.

    A. Work-in-process
    B. Story point group
    C. Feature breakdown structure (FBS)
    D. Work breakdown structure (WBS)

Answers – Terminology Matching

1:I, 2:H, 3:E, 4:C, 5:A, 6:L, 7:K, 8:B, 9:D, 10:G , 11:J , 12:O , 13:N ,14:M , 15:F

Answers – Crossword Puzzle

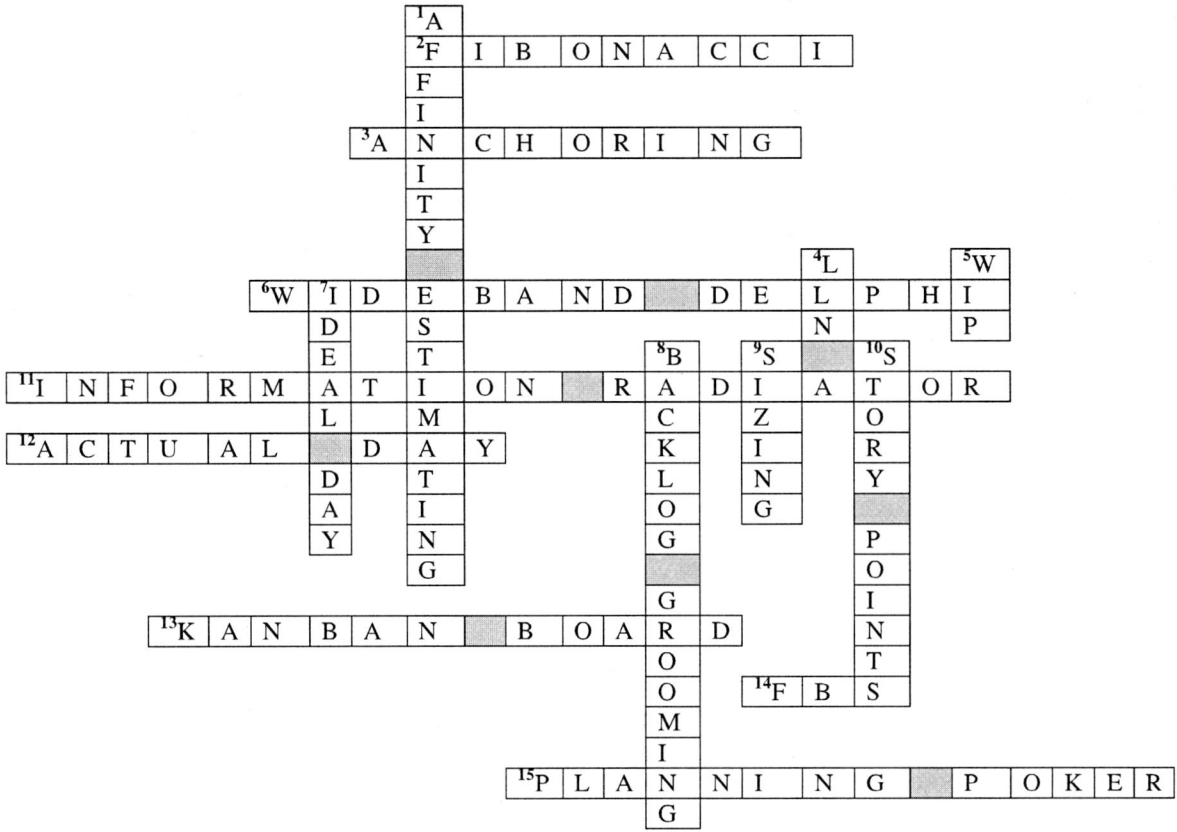

Answers – Word Search

Word Search - 15 Words to find:

- ACTUAL DAY
- ANCHORING
- BACKLOG GROOMING
- INFORMATION RADIATOR
- WIP
- IDEAL DAY
- KANBAN BOARD
- WIDEBAND DELPHI
- FIBONACCI
- LLN
- STORY POINTS
- PLANNING POKER
- AFFINITY ESTIMATING
- FBS
- SIZING

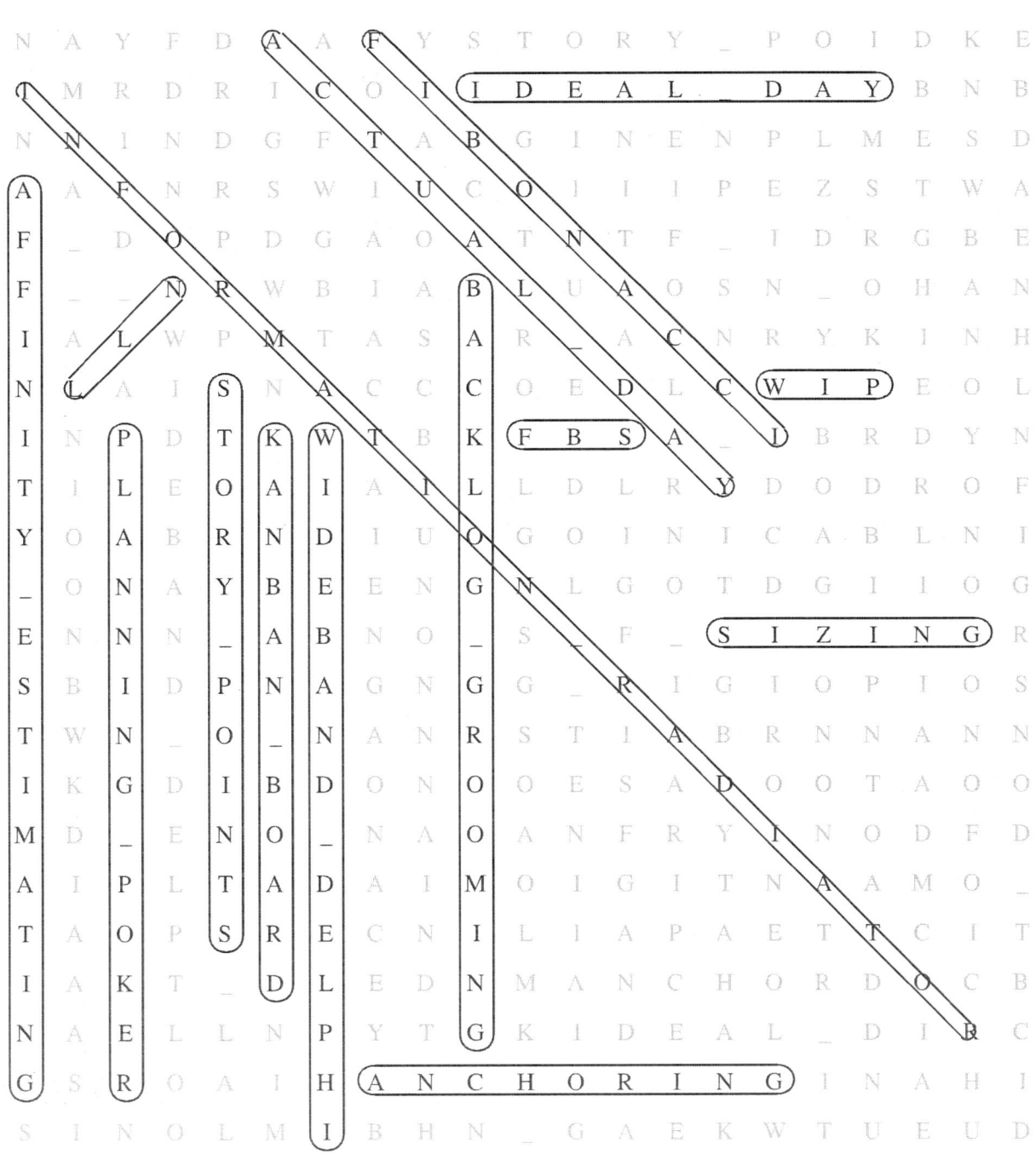

CHAPTER 5: Agile Estimating

Answers – Practice Test

1. **B.** The variability of the estimate is correlated to how far in the future the work occurs. As you can see (refer to figure 5.1 in the text), the risk of the activity being under-estimated is always greater than the risk that it has been over-estimated. In fact, chronic under-estimation is frequently revealed as work moves into the current time horizon and is decomposed into smaller tasks that are better understood.

2. **C.** The risk of the activity being under-estimated is always greater than the risk that it has been over-estimated. In fact, chronic under-estimation is frequently revealed as work moves into the current time horizon and is decomposed into smaller tasks that are better understood.

3. **A.** Estimating accuracy is now understood to be inextricably linked to time in an inverse proportion. This means that the further ahead you try to estimate, the estimate decreases in accuracy. Taking this into account, agile estimating spends resources in direct proportion to the accuracy they produce. That means minimizing cost when the probable accuracy is low, and investing more when the probable accuracy is higher. This pattern was established in planning where user stories on the longer-term time horizon were treated as placeholders with minimal, high-level details and stories on the near-term horizon had greater detail and even included acceptance criteria.

4. **B.** When we analyze the variable of time, we see that organizations need flexibility on the long-term scale but can support stability on the short-term scale. Flexibility is provided with the roadmap and release plan timeboxes (and ***product backlog grooming***). At the same time, stability is provided with the iteration timebox (and committed iteration backlog).

5. **D.** A key principle in Scrum (one shared by other agile frameworks) is that during a project, customers need to be able to change their minds about requirements, and that the best way to meet those emerging needs is a combination of short-term stability (during the sprint) and long-term flexibility (outside the sprint). This notion is operationalized in agile through the reciprocal commitment (presented in Chapter 4) between the agile team and the customer/proxy to postpone changes until the end of a given iteration.

6. **A.** Agile frameworks accept that complex problems cannot be fully defined in advance. They use the scientifically validated empirical process control approach – transparency, inspection, and adaptation – to focus the team on quickly delivering results that move through the cone of uncertainty towards a solution in the midst of emerging requirements.

7. **C.** The goal of sizing is to give the team and the customer/proxy a quick, relative measure of the effort involved with delivering a particular user story. The process, at a high level, is to assess how big, complex, and risky a story is compared to other stories and then assign it a value. When assigning a value to stories, the units employed vary, but most agile teams use: 1) Actual days; 2) Ideal days; or 3) Story points.

8. **D.** During detailed planning, agile development favors a ***feature breakdown structure (FBS)*** approach instead of the work breakdown structure (WBS) used in waterfall development approaches. Feature breakdown structures are advantageous in that they foster communication between the customer/proxy and the development team. In addition the FBS encourages the customer/proxy to prioritize the team's work based on business value and permits tracking of work against the actual business value produced.

9. **B.** An actual day is just that – a standard working day in the given work environment. For example, if a team's standard work day runs from 8:00 am to 5:00 pm with an hour for lunch, the actual day would be eight hours.

10. **B.** An *ideal day* is the amount of time per day that a team member would spend on a story if working full speed without any interruptions, meetings, vacations, or other competition for his time.

11. **A.** *Story points* are an estimate of story complexity that uses numbers to provide a high-level indicator of how difficult the story is relation to others.

12. **C.** The *Fibonacci sequence* is a number series (1, 2, 3, 5, 8, 13, 21, 34, 55, etc.) where the next number is derived by adding the previous two. (Mathematically, it is defined by the non-linear equation $F_n = F_{n-1} + F_{n-2}$.) The Fibonacci sequence is used by Scrum teams during planning poker when providing value point estimates for stories.

13. **B.** Story points *promote more participatory decision-making and cross-functional behavior.* Since a story point estimate is a single number representing the entirety of the team's work on the story, it fosters discussion about all aspects of completing the story (e.g., design, programming, internal QA, and user acceptance testing). It thus focuses the team on the project as a whole rather than on the aforementioned areas of specialization.

14. **D.** Story points estimate the size of the story relative to the others considered whereas ideal days are more dependent on the experience and skill sets of individual team members. When using ideal days as a measure when performing estimates, teams tend to dwell on making the distinction between ideal and actual days instead of focusing on story size. Stakeholders, too, regardless of their level of agile education, tend to hold teams to an unrealistic standard of making an ideal day equal an actual day.

15. **D.** Planning poker is a consensus-based game where team members individually estimate user stories through use of numbered cards, followed by discussion, until consensus is achieved. It is a variation of the Wideband Delphi method, used to estimate the relative size of tasks in software development, particularly with Scrum or Extreme Programming (XP) methods.

16. **A.** Planning poker minimizes anchoring – exerting undue influence on the team by individual voters who are outliers, who are strong-willed, or who have specific agendas – by having team members play their estimate cards face down prior to any discussion.

17. **C.** Affinity estimating is a technique that some agile teams employ to quickly and easily estimate a large number of user stories. It's particularly helpful when starting a new project that has a large backlog that has not been estimated.

18. **B.** Sizing is another technique that enables the agile team to act as participatory decision makers. The goal of sizing is to give the team and the customer/proxy a quick, relative measure of the effort involved with delivering a particular user story. The process, at a high level, is to assess how big, complex, and risky a story is compared to other stories and then assign it a value.

19. **C.** The basic flow of affinity estimating is as follows:

> A facilitator reads all user stories under consideration to the team. A brief question-and-answer session between customer/proxy and team may occur to clarify any uncertainties The team, working together but not talking, arranges the stories in order of size. In the example presented in Figure 5.2, we see that the largest stories are on the left and the smallest ones are on the right. Also observe that note cards may serve as relative size anchors (i.e., XL, L, M, S, and XS). In lieu of the size categories employed here, story point numbers often are used
>
> After the initial estimate is done, the team is given another opportunity to make silent adjustments to the board

20. **A.** Work-in-process is defined as the set of unfinished items being developed which produce no business value.

Chapter End Notes

[1] Cohn, M. (2006). *Agile estimating and planning*. Upper Saddle River, NJ: Pearson Education, Inc.
[2] Boehm, B. (1981). *Software engineering economics*. Upper Saddle River, NJ: Prentice-Hall, Inc.
[3] Ibid.
[4] Grenning, J. (2002, April). *Planning poker*. Renaissance Software Consultin105

CHAPTER

6

Planning Projects – Part 2

Chapter Highlights

In Chapter 6, we complete our discourse on the Plan process, as we cover the Team Performance, Risk Management, Communication, and Continuous Improvement knowledge areas. Before we start, remember to scan the Agile PM Processes Grid™ *(See Figure 2.16)* for a high-level content overview!

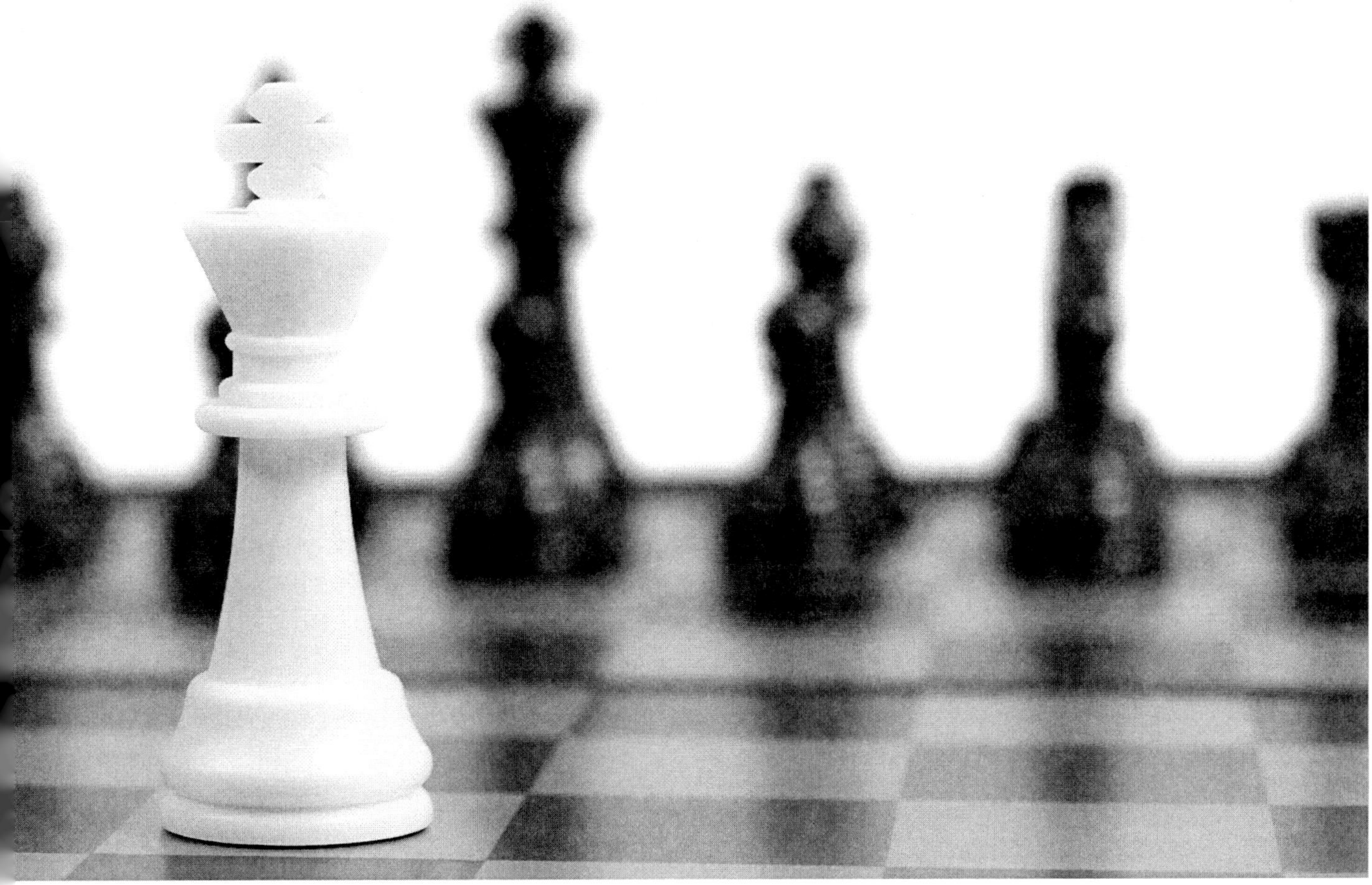

Team Performance

Coaching/Facilitation

Traditional project managers tend to take a command-and-control approach while agilists focus more on coaching and facilitating the team.

It can be quite challenging for the traditional project manager to "cross the road" and begin facilitating projects using agile methods. Just as the technical expert tends to fall back into that comfort zone when assigned to manage a project, the traditional project manager may lapse into command-and-control mode on agile projects. *Self-regulating questions* ("What am I feeling?" and "Are my biases interfering with the team's goals or the agile process?") help you make this transition.

We have found through experience that there are several keys to succeeding in the facilitator role:

- ***Removing obstacles:*** Regardless of which agile method you're using (but especially important in Scrum), one of your responsibilities is to keep the team moving forward. Sometimes, this involves removing roadblocks that are preventing the team from getting work done. One of your challenges may be in ascertaining when the team can solve the problem on their own and when you must intervene on their behalf.

- ***Focusing on the goals and not the tasks:*** This goes back to relinquishing the command-and-control approach. There are times during any project when you may have to "get your hands dirty," but make it the exception and not the rule. The facilitator is a liaison between the team and everyone else. Thus, ensure you understand the product vision and customer/proxy's priorities and are able to translate them when necessary.

- ***Running meetings:*** Facilitating meetings doesn't come naturally to many, particularly those who have logged time as technical experts. How can you improve? Observe other agile coaches and facilitators. You cannot adopt another's personality or style, but you can take experiences you've learned from watching others to hone your own skill set. One way to get practice is by volunteering to facilitate meetings for other teams. If you want to learn more about activities to use during planning meetings, we recommend that you read Derby and Larson's Agile Retrospectives, Making Good Teams Great.[1]

The specific situations in which the team may benefit from formal coaching are when:

- ***Employing certain agile methods.*** Extreme Programming (XP) is considered a high discipline agile method and its advocates recommend using a coach to enforce methodological doctrines such as paired programming, always having a viable build, and being able to pass unit tests at 100% at all times.

- ***Ramping up agile in an organization.*** It's one thing to embark on a bottom-up innovation such as when a group of developers decides to adopt Scrum as their methodology of choice. There's a big difference, however, between reading a book or attending a Certified Scrum Master class and being a successful agile practitioner. Some of the greatest lessons are those learned from mistakes, but we recommend bringing in an external coach to educate both management and team when onboarding agile. Having that external viewpoint is a good reality check on whether you're using best practices, too.

- ***Non-agilists are attending your meetings.*** If functional managers, senior management, or customers naïve to agile, intend to join a retrospective, you may want to coach these attendees prior to the meeting. Educate them on agile vernacular, processes, and their appropriate roles and levels of participation for the meeting. This preparation may prevent someone high in organizational power or status from derailing the meeting.

- **Conducting release and project retrospectives.** For iteration perspectives, the team lead or internal coach may lead the meeting. However, for release and project retrospectives, it's wise to bring in a coach external to the team to conduct the meeting, so everyone on the team can then contribute their experiences.

> **TIP: When to Step Out of the Facilitator Role**
>
> When serving as an agile coach or project leader, your primary role is that of a facilitator – to ensure the success of the team by encouraging self-organization, fostering adherence to agile principles, and removing obstacles. At various times during a project, particularly when it comes to problem-solving, you may be "chomping at the bit" to jump in and get your hands dirty.
>
> So, when is it appropriate for you to relinquish the facilitator role? ***Only when you have important content to offer that no one else on the team has.*** Whether it stems from subject-matter expertise or simply from experience gained on previous projects, in these situations, you need to step out of the facilitator role and provide your input for the benefit of the team.
>
> Let's say that you are leading an agile retrospective or a team reflective workshop and such a situation arises. What do you do? Tell the team that you are leaving the facilitator role temporarily to contribute to the discussion. Hand your marker to another team member to symbolize that you are not in the facilitator role while you participate. (Just make sure you get the marker – and your role – back.)

Collaboration/Negotiation

As you may have gleaned from our review of agile assumptions *(See Figure 2.4)* and of iteration planning in Chapter 3, perhaps the most important negotiation that occurs in the agile process is negotiation of scope. In contrast to traditional project management, where scope is typically defined in large form at project onset with a lengthy requirements document, agile project scope is negotiated during a series of iteration planning meetings.

During iteration planning, the customer/proxy identifies features having the highest business value and prioritizes them for the team. A portion of the product backlog is selected for the iteration backlog through a negotiated process where the agile team and the customer/proxy hone their mutual understanding of what will be delivered at the end of the iteration.

At the end of each iteration, scope is revisited. If the agile team meets its commitments and delivers the expected business value (i.e., story points), the customer/proxy and team reconvene to identify the next set of features with the highest priority. If the team falls behind, a renegotiation of scope must occur to decide what features in the product backlog might have to be postponed to ensure delivery of other more desirable features.

We address aspects of contract negotiation specific to agile in Chapter 10.

Motivation/Empowerment

For the agile team, an overriding motivating factor is that of delivering value as defined by the customer/proxy and the organization. In terms of metrics, we, as agile practitioners, often focus on measuring what business value (in story points, etc.) is being delivered.

Cockburn presents a succinct framework that describes pride-related factors, which influence the intrinsic motivation of agile teams - pride in work, pride in accomplishment, and pride in contribution.[2]

- *Pride in work:* Team members want to believe their work is valuable to themselves, the team, and the customer. Just delivering on time is not sufficient. Delivering a quality product is important.

- *Pride in accomplishment:* Weick's principle of small wins[3] tells us that delivering a quality product at regular intervals - even if the project scope is small - is a motivating reward for the project team. Moreover, such success builds trust within the team and establishes the team's credibility with the customer/proxy and with management.

- *Pride in contribution:* The agile team is a community and individual members, particularly those on experienced teams, will sacrifice individual accolades to support the team goals.

A tenet of agile is that the customer/proxy defines business value and priorities, but that the agile team has the latitude to decide *how* the work is done. This notion of allowing the team to solve its own problems, while apprising management of impediments beyond its control is an empowering one. It encourages a partnership between the team, the customer/proxy, and management to overcome such hurdles. Giving the team this power over the "how" also promotes a learning environment - sometimes, the team has to research the best possible solution and propose options to the customer/proxy.

Risk Management

Risk-Adjusted Backlog and Regulatory Compliance

As we noted in Chapter 3 under Regulatory Discovery, organizations must perform due diligence to adhere to their industry's specific legal and regulatory requirements. A product feature might have little apparent business value to the organization, the customer, or to end users, but there might be a regulation that mandates its early inclusion in the product. In the healthcare industry, a classic example is that databases storing patient electronic health records (EHR) must be designed to capture audit trails of anyone who accesses, views, or alters patient data.

Features in the product backlog thus may be weighted to accommodate governmental regulations. A *risk-adjusted backlog* occurs when the customer/proxy and key stakeholders (e.g., corporate medical or regulatory officer) provide the agile team with feature priorities that take such regulatory requirements into consideration. The risk-adjustments are not limited to formal external regulations, but may also be influenced by industry best practices (e.g., Six Sigma metrics for controlling manufacturing process defect rates.)

Other aspects of regulatory compliance include project auditing and documentation. If the agile team is apprised of audit needs at project onset, then it can modify generic agile processes to more rigorous standards. Protocols may be created to document user stories and track test plans to comply with Sarbanes-Oxley regulations or to appease agencies such as the Food and Drug Administration (FDA).

As we observed, handoff iterations may be used to prepare a submission to an external agency (e.g., submit a new drug application to the FDA).

Overt agile risk management practices may be employed to address regulatory concerns. Figure 6.2 shows a risk board that can be used for such purposes.

Communication

Communication Protocols

In Chapter 4, we made the distinction between organic and overt agile practices in the context of risk management. Having the daily stand-up meeting is considered organic risk management – risks (or impediments) are reviewed each day as a natural by-product of using agile methods.

Similarly, agile methods have a variety of organic communication protocols, the most noteworthy of which is the emphasis on face-to-face (F2F) communication. Another embedded communication protocol is planning meetings, including those pertaining to:

- Product vision
- Release planning
- Iteration planning
- Daily stand-ups
- Retrospectives

Optional meetings include the team reflective workshop and the **open space meeting**, a self-organized meeting where the attendees define the topic and the agenda. (Typically, an open space meeting is a team "subcommittee" meeting aimed at removing an impediment or solving a technical problem.)

Rather than having a direct-and-control project manager, most agile methods have someone who acts as a coach or facilitator for many meetings. In Scrum, an external Product Owner or Scrum Master may be brought in to facilitate a retrospective meeting so that the team's Scrum Master may participate fully. The Scrum team may also have a protocol to allow the Scrum Master to step outside of the role by taking off a hat or handing over a marker to symbolize relinquishment of the facilitator role. (See **TIP: When to Relinquish the Facilitator Role**)

As shown in Figure 6.3, the agile team may document some of its communication protocols in its team working agreements.

The agile team should define its preferred method of real time communication. In most cases, this will be a face-to-face convocation of the interested parties, although texting, wikis, and other tools may suffice. Moreover, when some team members cannot be present at typical F2F meetings, a backup plan (i.e., "the next best thing") needs to be arranged in advance.

When we discuss Team Space, we'll see that proximity of team members may be considered a communication protocol.

Information Radiators

An **information radiator** displays project-related information in a place where passersby can see it.[4] Many agile methods (particularly Scrum) employ information radiators as a concise way of updating the agile team, stakeholders, and management on product development status.

Common information radiators used in Scrum environments include the following:

- Product vision
- Product backlog/release plan
- Iteration backlog
- Burn-down and burn-up charts
- Risk/impediment board
- Team work agreements

These are often organized on a team project board, a kind of "super" information radiator. To help you visualize what some of these information radiators look like, the following figures present examples of a burn-down chart (Figure 6.1), a risk board (Figure 6.2), and team working agreements (Figure 6.3).

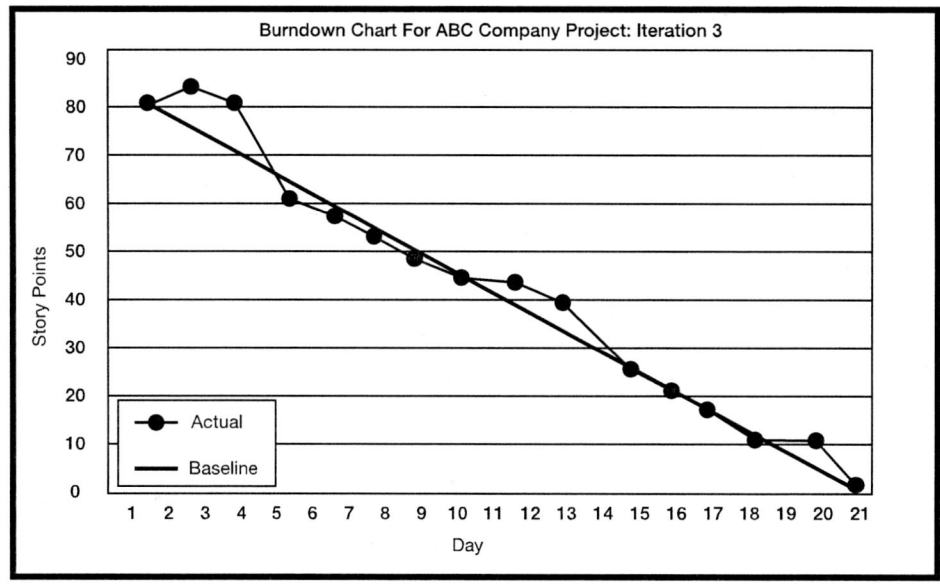

Figure 6.1 A Burn-Down Chart.

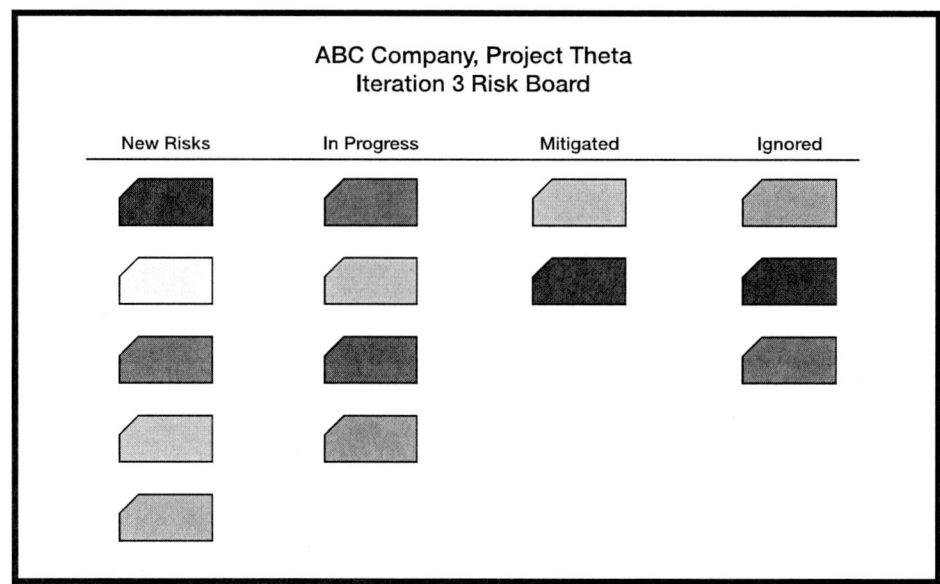

Figure 6.2 A Risk Board, Used for Overt Risk Management.

```
ABC Company, Project Iteration 3
Team Working Agreements

1) If the build is broken then the entire team stops to fix it.
2) We resolve to be on time for team meetings.
3) Always remember that the customer is part of the working team.
4) We are not done until the cases are written and tested.
```

Figure 6.3 Team Working Agreements Radiator.

When using information radiators, agile practitioners incorporate tools from the Lean manufacturing world. Information radiators are really a specialized type of ***visual control***. In Lean environments, visual controls are used to make it easier to control an activity or process through a variety of visual signals or cues.[5] In this context, the visual control:

- Conveys its information visually
- Mirrors (at least some part of) the process the team is using
- Describes the state of the work-in-process
- Is used to control the work-in-process
- Can be viewed by anyone

We advocate using the term visual control (over information radiator) because it communicates more effectively the desired attitude and behavior we want from the agile team. "Information radiator" indicates a one-way direction of information from the team to passersby, including management. It subtly reflects a belief that some agile practitioners hold (incorrectly) that the team needs to provide only information about results to management, but does not need to provide management with information about how they work. Such an attitude hinders implementing agile methods at the enterprise level when such information is needed.

In Lean thinking, "visual control" is more inclusive. In addition to communicating information to all passersby (so that they don't have to ask for status reports, which are disruptive to generate), it also reflects the intent that management is a participant in the team's processes. Visual controls invite management to help detect early when there are problems impeding progress toward the team's goals. That is exactly when the team needs to be interrupted – so that they can stop and adjust while it still matters. Visual controls thus increase the likelihood that management's "interruptions" actually add value to the process.

Team Space

In Chapter 2, we highlighted several things that lowered the cost of idea transfer:

- Face-to-face (F2F) communication
- Osmotic communication
- Colocation of teams

Proximity of team members is paramount. Colocation of agile teams fosters both F2F and osmotic communication. As a result, questions get answered faster and there tend to be fewer unasked questions.

Having a "caves and commons" arrangement gives the agile team the best of both worlds – the luxury of being colocated and the latitude to retreat to a private area when the situation warrants it.

Ideally, the customer/proxy is included when team space is being planned. Some high discipline agile methods (e.g., Extreme Programming) require an on-site customer/proxy.

Particularly when ramping up agile, an organization must consider the costs of colocating teams versus the potentially high costs of idea maintaining transfer for distributed teams.

Agile Tooling

The Agile Project Manager's toolbox should contain those tools and techniques which help him fulfill the product vision and nurture the agile team. Such tools may not be exclusive to agile methods. For example, the planning activities described in Chapter 4 (i.e., brainstorming, fishbone diagrams, force field analysis, prioritizing with dots, and learning matrix) are often used in traditional project management. In Chapter 3, we introduced several artifacts used to hone the product vision. Here, we'll focus on the same ones as being critical to the Agile Project Manager's arsenal:

- Product vision box
- Elevator statement
- Flexibility matrix
- Project data sheet

The ***product vision box*** may be thought of as the product box on a store shelf. It contains whatever graphic images and narrative content are needed to convey the product vision to the customer. Significantly, it is in end user language and not techno-jargon. Constructing and demonstrating a product vision box is a useful exercise for the team to see if they truly understand the customer's vision and stated priorities for the product. Figure 6.4 illustrates an example of a product vision box.

Figure 6.4 Product Vision Box Example.

The notion of an ***elevator statement*** (or elevator test statement) was popularized by Geoffrey Moore in his book ***Crossing the Chasm.***[6] Similar in concept to the product vision box, devising an elevator statement is a challenge for the agile team – that of quickly explaining the product vision to someone "in an elevator," in one minute or less. It is thus an uncomplicated way to define the product vision in a short statement, using language everyone can understand. The generic format of the elevator statement is:

FOR <a customer>, WHO <statement of need>, THE <product name>, IS A <type of product>, THAT <has this compelling reason to buy/use>, UNLIKE <competitive products>, OUR PRODUCT <is differentiated in these ways>.

Figure 6.5 presents an elevator statement, using our same fictitious iPetOwner 1.0 product.

> **Elevator Statement:**
> **For** pet owners who need to manage the health of their chronically ill or geriatric pets, **iPetOwner 1.0** is an "iDevice" compatible software application **that** tracks and reports feedings, medication administration and laboratory values. **Unlike** all competitors **iPetOwner 1.0 our product** is both unique to the "iDevice" portable market and is easy to use.

6.5 An Elevator Statement.

Creating either a product vision box or an elevator statement allows the agile team and the customer/proxy to establish a common understanding of the product vision and project deliverables. Such exercises create value by revealing misunderstood or missing pieces of information about the product. They have the added value of inspiring the team and all stakeholders to focus their incongruent views into a concise product description.

 A *flexibility (or tradeoff) matrix* is a simple tool that helps the customer/proxy clarify how to handle the unavoidable tradeoffs that may arise in the future and communicate that perspective to the team. The matrix clarifies which constraints are flexible and which are not, hence the name. This grid shows the relative importance of project constraints (i.e., scope, schedule, cost, and quality) in terms of Fixed, Firm, or Flexible; only **one** constraint may be Fixed. It thus allows the customer/proxy to establish a top-level decision tool for making tradeoff decisions when the usual resource, time, or cost conflicts arise during project execution. The flexibility matrix and the elevator statement are typical components of the project data sheet, as we'll see.

Scrum practitioners often utilize the flexibility matrix. When used in Scrum, the Product Owner is responsible for gathering information from the customer on tradeoffs and documenting the results in the matrix. Because the matrix will be used throughout the project to adjudicate tradeoffs, getting it settled early is key to avoiding subsequent difficult or impossible negotiations. Once people decide their position on a specific tradeoff, the effort to get cooperation becomes much more difficult without a flexibility matrix. Figure 6.6 portrays a flexibility matrix.

Flexibility (Tradeoff) Matrix				
	Fixed	Firm	Flexible	Target
Scope		X		60 Points
Schedule	X			4 Weeks
Cost			X	$150,000
Quality		X		Pass Unit tests at 100%

Figure 6.6 A Flexibility Matrix Showing Project Schedule as the one Fixed Constraint.

 A **project data sheet(PDS)** captures a project's objectives in a minimalist document.[7] While not quite equivalent to a project charter from the traditional project management world, it is one-page summary of the key objectives, capabilities, and information needed to understand the purpose and progress of the project.

While there is no universal standard for project data sheets, common elements include:

- Project Start Date
- Projected End Date
- Project Manager/Scrum Master/Team Facilitator
- Primary Customer/proxy or Product Owner
- Elevator Statement
- Customer Attributes
- Customer Benefits
- Key Product Performance Attributes
- Key Product Features
- Flexibility Matrix
- Milestones and Deliverables
- Comments

Figure 6.7 exemplifies a project data sheet for our fictitious iPetOwner 1.0, a Scrum software development project. While this particular example focuses on a single sprint, project data sheets may be published as part of release planning and revised during iteration planning.

Sprint Start Date: 10/01/2010					Projected Finish Date: 10/29/2010	
Scrum Master: Brooks Bookbinder					**Product Owner:** T. Kernan Blackstone	
Elevator Statement: **For** pet owners **who** need to manage the health of their chronically ill or geriatric pets, the iPetOwner 1.0 **is an** iPhone and iPad compatible software application **that** tracks and reports feedings, medication administration, and laboratory values. **Unlike all** competitors **our product** is unique to the "iDevice" portable market and is easy to use.						
Customer Attributes (Target Market): 1) Pet owners 2) Having chronically ill or geriatric pets 3) Middle to upper socioeconomic status					**Customer Benefits:** 1) Assists in maintaining pet's health 2) Centralized pet medical record 3) Transportable for veterinary review	
iPetOwner 1.0 Performance Attributes: 1) Quick access via handheld devices 2) Backup capability to remote server 3) Synchronized between multiple devices					**iPetOwner 1.0 Feature/Ability to:** 1) Maintain complete pet medical record 2) Download & store pet lab data 3) Email reports to veterinarian	
Flexibility (Tradeoff) Matrix					**Major Milestones & Deliverables**	
	Fixed	Firm	Flexible	Target	Milestone (Deliverable)	Estimated Date
Scope		•		60 points	Kickoff Meeting	10/01/2010
Schedule	•			4 weeks	Planning Meeting A	10/04/2010
Cost			•	$150,000	Planning Meeting B	10/04/2010
Quality		•		Pass Unit Tests at 100%	Coding/Internal QA	10/05/2010
Comments:					User Acceptance Testing	10/21/2010
					Software Demonstration	10/27/2010
					User Acceptance Signoff	10/28/2010
					Software Installation	10/29/2010

Figure 6.7 A Project Data Sheet for a Scrum Software Development Project.

The great utility of the agile tools we've discussed is that they serve as inputs for subsequent project planning (i.e., release planning, iteration planning, retrospectives, etc.). They are also useful in the creation and estimation of user stories. Finally, they are artifacts which help refresh faulty memories and assist the agile team manage stakeholder expectations throughout the project.

Continuous Improvement

Agile continuous improvement is really an homage to practices borrowed from Lean manufacturing. This is apparent in value stream mapping, which focuses on improving the overall process of delivering product to the customer. It crops up again in forming cross-functional teams, a notion derived from having employees cross-trained on the manufacturing line. Finally, metric reports exemplify how visual controls may be used to add value to the project and also to appease stakeholders.

Value Stream Mapping

As we have discussed, **the agile framework is process-centric, with the process goal being to create stakeholder engagement and value-driven delivery cycles.**

Value-driven delivery cycles require understanding the product value stream that creates customer value – from project charter to final deliverables. The value stream begins with the customer's vision, which proceeds through various stages of clarification and elaboration, until the agile development team is engaged and an agile framework is applied.

Borrowed from Lean manufacturing to augment agile's strengths, value stream mapping expands the agile framework, from a focus on improving the team's performance to improving the entire development environment. This has the benefit of identifying the root cause of development delays or problems that are bigger than the team, even when it appears to be a team problem at first glance. Value stream mapping applies the Lean principle of optimizing the whole by identifying waste (i.e., rework and late detection of problems caused by multi-tasking and overloading the team), which degrades quality and delays delivery.

Value-driven deliverables may be the most recognized, differentiating, and critical success factor in Agile Project Management. For the team to produce value-driven deliverables, they must understand the "what, who and how" of the project early in the process.[8] In other words, the customer/proxy must convey to the agile team, early in the project, ***what*** is envisioned and must be delivered, ***who*** the key stakeholders are, and ***how*** the stakeholders will use the deliverables. This is especially true at the "points of interfacing," the junctures where different stakeholders must collaborate and their work products intersect.

Early in the initiating process, the team goes through an "exploring" phase to create and document product stories.[9] This early occurrence is important for two key reasons. First, it is unavoidable. Many projects that have tried to skip it ended up with great difficulty later as "undocumented features" showed up in the form of "contention" between the stakeholders and the team. Second, creating the stories cultivates an environment where a collaborative, self-organizing team can develop, while simultaneously interacting with customers, managers, and contractors.

 At Intel®, where such a process has been successfully institutionalized to create a continuous flow of innovative breakthroughs, they call it "MAPP Day." ***MAPP*** stands for ***Make A Project (or Program) Plan.*** It is so important that Intel® has dedicated facilitators who guide the MAPP Day process.[10]

Establishing Value-Driven Delivery

As experience at Intel® has demonstrated, establishing a value-driven delivery process is neither quick nor painless, but is well worth the investment. While it is not easy, it is effective when the right tools are employed and accompanied by adequate training and usage standards.

The purpose of the value-driven delivery process is to help stakeholders clarify and articulate their values and priorities early in the project management process. Another reason is to identify which components of the solution are most important and to create a documenting mechanism for the team to manage the follow-up conversations required to define and direct the team's work efforts.

One approach used to help stakeholders clarify and articulate their values is value-based analysis, which employs value stream mapping.

Value stream mapping is a technique developed in the Lean manufacturing field to analyze (and potentially redesign) the flow of materials and information required to deliver a product or service to the customer. It documents the value stream using icons or pictures then analyzes the stream for waste. The focus is on reducing the total time from beginning to end without taking shortcuts at the expense of opportunities in the future.

Value stream mapping has been adapted in many industries. Figure 6.8 presents an example where changing the process and substituting a piece of equipment reduced waste by 25%.

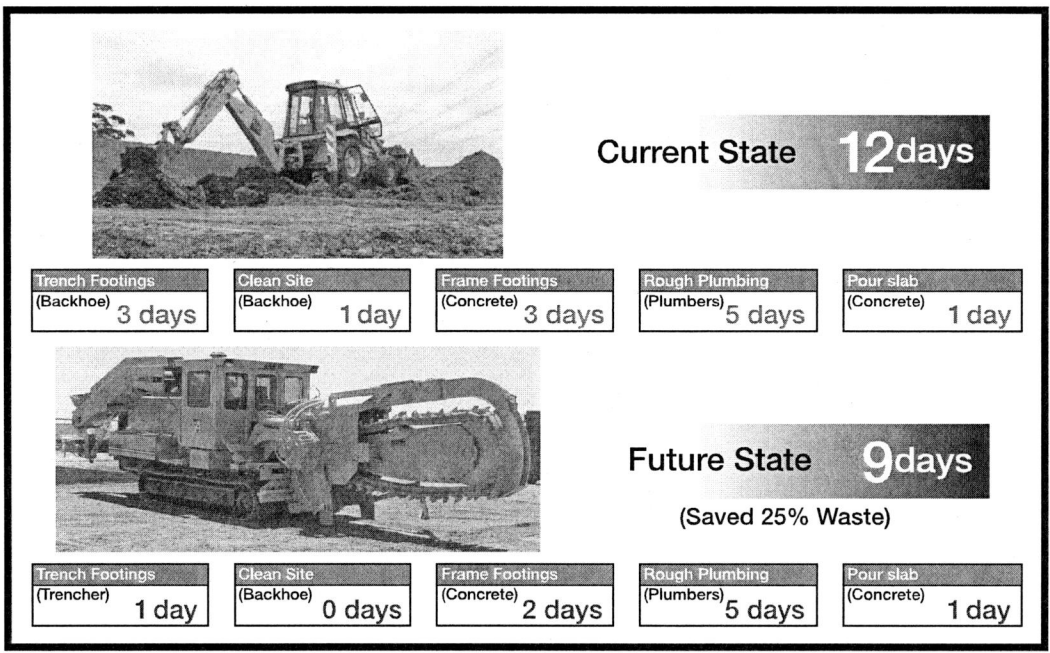

Figure 6.8 The Value Stream Map Allows the Team to Scrutinize the Stream for Waste.

The basic value stream mapping process consists of the following steps:

- ***Identify the Value Stream Target.*** The target is a particular product or service (sometimes a product or service group, family or category) where improvement can provide strategic and competitive advantage.

- ***Define the Current State.*** Identifying the current state of the value stream is accomplished by creating a "map" or diagram. The map illustrates the productive steps required to deliver the product or service. It also includes unproductive steps such as lead time, delays, queuing time, or holds. For tangible products, the flow will show everything from acquiring the raw materials to customer receipt. For intangible products, the flow will show everything from concept design to delivery of the software or launch of the service.

- ***Clarify the Current Opportunity.*** By analyzing the current-state value stream map, it is possible to identify opportunities to increase flow by eliminating waste, thereby raising customer satisfaction and enhancing competitive advantage.

- ***Depict the Desired Future State.*** Once the current state has been properly understood, the next step is to document a desired future-state value stream map. Then, that map may be used to implement a plan to transform the current workflow into the desired future state.

In most widely used forms of value stream mapping, the value-adding steps are drawn horizontally across the middle of the map and the non-value-adding steps are drawn in vertical lines perpendicular to the value stream. This has the advantage of making the value-added activities the focus of attention and the waste-type activities apparent as cross-purposed steps in the flow. It does not imply that the steps are not operationally necessary, only that if and when they can be minimized it will not have a negative impact on customer value. So in Figure 6.8, an agile team might focus on processes A1 through A4 to analyze potential waste.

Value stream mapping is part of the recognized Six Sigma methodologies. While in the past, value stream mapping was most often associated with manufacturing, it has begun to see widespread use in industries as varied as logistics, healthcare, and software development for establishing value-driven delivery processes.

Business cases, feasibility studies, and contracts are other tools used to help establish value-driven delivery focused on the key stakeholder values.

Agile project leaders need to focus on ***value determination.***[11] Value determination uses quantitative assessments, such as return on investment (ROI) divided by total cost of ownership (TCO) or the discounted cash flow (DCF) brand value created, to move beyond qualitative judgments to refine the focus on value prioritization and creation. Although the customer/proxy has primary responsibility, the entire agile team should attend to the key aspects of the project that drive value such as the cost/benefit analysis. The team plays a particularly important role in managing the value of non-customer-facing, internal features or stories by avoiding technical debt, integrating quality, and anticipating long-term needs. There are many ways the Agile Project Manager can promote a value-oriented perspective within the team using backlog management and iterative development processes.

Ultimately, the test of value-driven deliverables is whether a releasable product reflects the product vision and meets the acceptance criteria (and related metrics) defined by the customer/proxy.

Cross-Functional Team Formation

A strength of agile methods is they focus the team on group accountability to achieve results. While individual team members bring their own skill sets and subject-matter expertise to the project, agile promotes an attitude of self-organizing, cross-functional teams. What does this mean? Again, borrowing a mindset from Lean manufacturing, it means that the agile team is so committed to delivering product features, individuals will step outside of their respective areas of expertise and help in any way to ensure the team meets its goals for the iteration.

For the organization, building agile project teams of cross-functional generalists may present a human resources challenge. The traditional roles of programmer, business analyst, and QA tester become blurred on the agile project team, as members are asked to "wear multiple hats." Hiring, compensation, and personnel evaluation practices may have to be modified to accommodate the emphasis on team, rather than individual, success. Moreover, the structure of contracts (i.e., the relationship between vendor and customer) may have to be changed to foster an organization "becoming agile."

Metrics Identification

As with traditional project management, project metrics may be highly subjective. The Agile Project Manager should strive to create an integrated assemblage, or **dashboard**, of metrics that have meaning to the team, to the customer/proxy, and to key stakeholders.

Agile metrics are intended to be used as visual controls, as discussed earlier in this chapter. That is, the intent is not merely to publish information, but to drive the team towards project-level and the organization towards process-level improvements. The dashboard metrics presented here are modeled after those used on real agile projects by Berthot[12] as well as those presented in an article by Leonardo Simini.[13]

Overall Project Status: Stoplight Report

The basic stoplight report (Green: On track; Yellow: Warning – Implement corrective action or monitor performance; Red: Immediate corrective action required) is a time-honored indicator of overall status for both traditional and agile projects. Typically, the stoplight indicators are the last thing to be completed on the project dashboard, after all other data is available to the project manager. Figure 6.9 presents an example in which project constraints and overall CIO rating are color-coded.

		Status: In Progress					
Project ID	Project Title (Project Manager)	Status	Schedule	Budget	Scope	Risk	CIO Rating
1.02	Financial Accounting System	In Progress					

Figure 6.9 A Basic Stoplight Report Indicating Overall Project Status.

Product Release Burn-up Chart

The product release burn-up chart is really nothing more than an inverted burn-down chart. The appeal of this presentation lies in its simplicity – a line moving upward towards the target "shows progress" to stakeholders and senior management who might not be intimately familiar with agile. As seen in Figure 6.10, the burn-up chart also highlights the baseline project scope (i.e., Target Scope) as well as any changes to scope occurring during the project. (In this example, no scope changes occurred.) Finally, it summarizes actual work completed versus baseline estimates (i.e., a visual variance analysis) across several iterations.

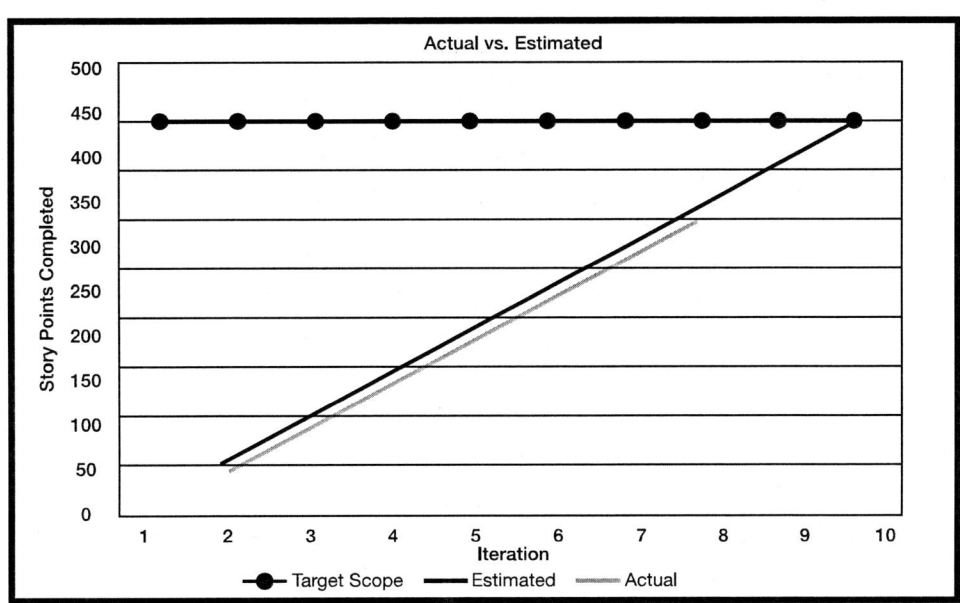

Figure 6.10 A Product Release Burn-up Chart.

Team Performance

Agile team performance is captured in the Functionality Delivered and Team Velocity graphs shown in Figure 6.11. The Functionality Delivered graph presents estimated versus delivered story points and is a good way of tracking estimate accuracy. The Team Velocity graph shows story points delivered by iteration and is a measure of team work consistency, stability, and even improvement over time.

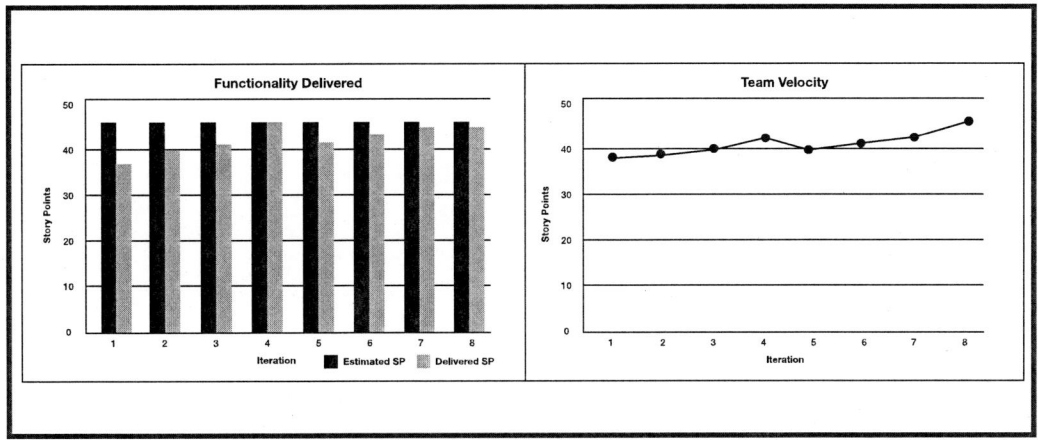

Figure 6.11 Team Performance Metrics.

Project Progress

Project progress may be summarized by percentage measures of **Business Value Delivered and Time Completed,** as seen in Figure 6.12. In the example shown, Time Completed represents the eight out of ten iterations (80%) completed to date. Business Value Delivered and Time Completed is calculated by dividing the business value per story (i.e., business value points) by the total business value points for the product backlog.[14] In this case, Business Value Delivered = 341/450 = 76%.[15] (To see where these raw numbers came from, see Iteration 8 in Figure 6.12.)

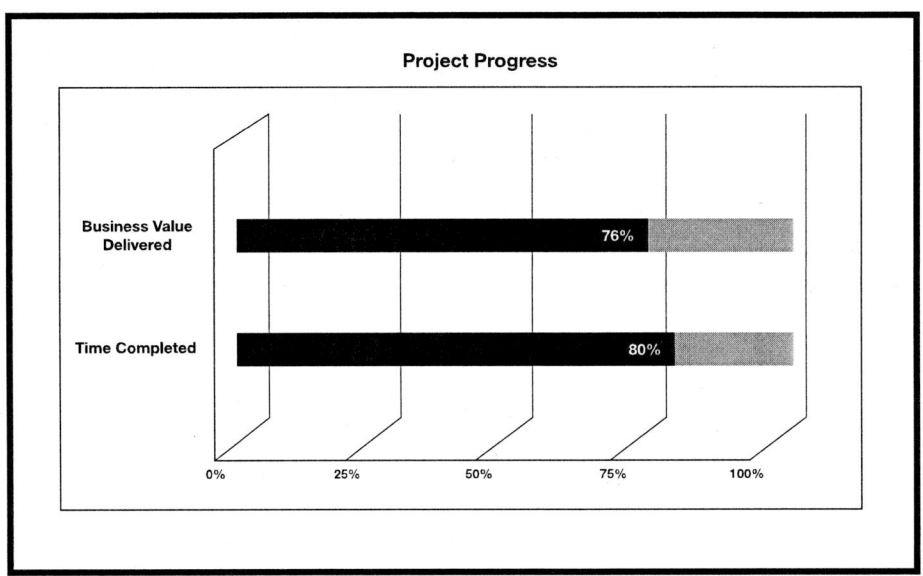

Figure 6.12 Project Progress.

Project Risk Status

If the agile team practices overt risk management, risk metrics may certainly be captured in the project dashboard. For example, in Figure 6.13, identified project risks to date are categorized both in terms of status (Newly Identified, In Progress, Resolved, and Deferred) and in terms of severity (High, Medium, and Low).

To get you thinking like an Agile Project Manager, let's interpret some of the data presented in Figure 6.13. Three risks have been newly identified (and are either unassigned to an owner or no action has been taken). Four risks are currently "In Progress" – that is, they have an owner and are being monitored or some action is ongoing. Fifteen risks have been resolved in some way. Finally, two risks – both of Low severity – have been deferred to some later date.

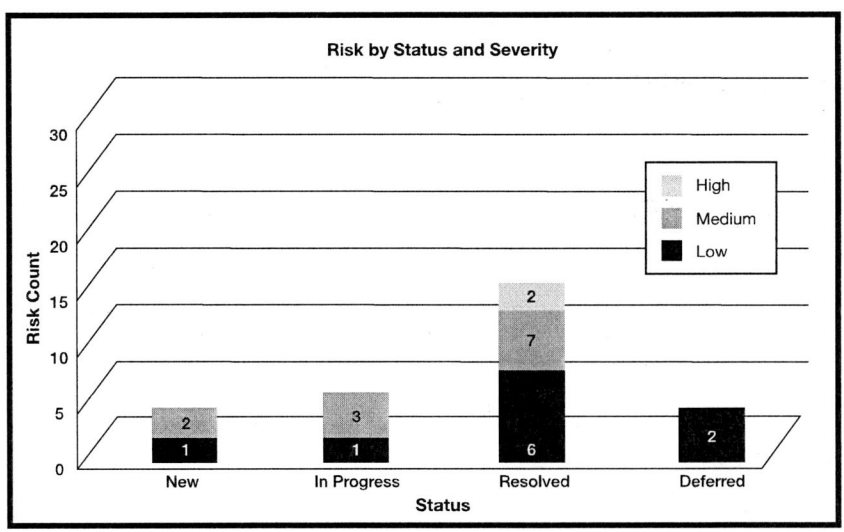

Figure 6.13. Project Risk Categorized.

Interpreting the Data

Each of the individual metrics presented above may be integrated into a comprehensive dashboard report for the team and all stakeholders. To avoid unnecessary overhead in constructing such documents, the Agile Project Manager should be guided by the question, "What value do these indicators bring to the organization?" Sometimes, the metrics stand alone as information radiators. In some situations, you may want to add some level of interpretation for the readers to allay stakeholder concerns, as shown in Figure 6.14.

Highlights
- 8/10 iterations (80%) are complete
- 341/450 business value points (76%) have been delivered

Risks
- Over the bext two iterations, we need to recoup the 4% business value that we're behind!

Action Items
- **All** 8 team members will devote 100% of their time to the next 2 iterations!

Figure 6.14 Interpretation to Metrics for Stakeholders.

Summary

For the Agile Project Manager, keys to succeeding in the facilitator role include successfully removing obstacles, focusing on goals and not low-level tasks, and running effective meetings.

The specific situations in which the team may benefit from formal coaching are when:

- Employing certain agile methods.
- Ramping up agile in an organization
- Non-agilists are attending your meetings
- Conducting release and project retrospectives

Agile methods have a variety of organic communication protocols, the most noteworthy of which is the emphasis on face-to-face (F2F) communication. Another embedded communication protocol is planning meetings.

Organizations must perform due diligence to adhere to their industry's specific legal and regulatory requirements. A product feature might have little apparent business value to the organization, the customer, or to end users, but there might be a regulation that mandates its early inclusion in the product. A risk-adjusted backlog occurs when the customer/proxy provides the agile team with feature priorities that take such regulatory requirements into consideration.

Information radiators display project-related information in places where passersby can see them. They are really a specialized type of visual control, which in Lean environments are used to make it easier to control an activity or process through a variety of visual signals or cues.

Agile tools critical to the Agile Project Manager's arsenal are: 1) Product vision box; 2) Elevator statement; 3) Flexibility matrix; and 4) Project data sheet.

Agile continuous improvement borrows much from Lean manufacturing. This is apparent in value stream mapping, which focuses on improving the overall process of delivering product to the customer. It crops up again in forming cross-functional teams, a notion derived from having employees cross-trained on the manufacturing line. Finally, metric reports exemplify how visual controls may be used to add value to the project and to appease stakeholders.

Chapter Close-Out

Agile PM Processes Grid™ Exercise

Please take out a blank piece of paper, set a timer for no more than 3 minutes, and see how much of the grid you can reproduce from memory. To make the most of this Agile PM Processes Grid™ exercise, please simulate being in the testing environment. Close your book and all your notes. Visualize the Proctor handing you the blank sheets of paper and taking your seat in the testing site. Begin by drawing the grid, 6 columns and 8 rows, and then fill in everything you can. After the 3 minutes ends, use your book and notes to complete the grid. Study it as you do so.

Terminology Matching Exercise

In the blank column to the left of the Term, fill in the letter that identifies the correct definition or description.

	Term		Definition / Description
	1. Elevator statement	A	Probes feelings and biases to help traditional project managers adapt to facilitative agile management practices.
	2. Self-regulating question	B	Factors influencing the intrinsic motivation of teams – pride in work, accomplishment, and contribution.
	3. Information radiator	C	Defines feature priorities taking into account regulatory requirements and industry best practices.
	4. Risk-adjusted backlog	D	A self-organized meeting where the attendees define the topic and the agenda.
	5. Product vision box	E	Displays project-related information in a place where passersby can see it.
	6. Value stream mapping	F	Activities or processes that communicate via a variety of visual signals or cues.
	7. Project data sheet	G	A workspace arrangement where the agile team is colocated but has private areas to use when needed.
	8. Pride-related motivation	H	Contains whatever graphic images and narrative content are needed to convey the product vision to customers.
	9. Open space meeting	I	A short uncomplicated statement of the product vision everyone can understand in one minute or less.
	10. Caves and commons	J	A tool the customer/proxy uses to clarify how to handle future unavoidable tradeoffs and communicate that perspective to the team.
	11. Flexibility matrix	K	A minimalist one-page summary of key objectives, capabilities, and information needed to understand the project objectives and progress.
	12. Value stream target	L	A technique used to analyze the flow of materials and information required to deliver products to the customer.
	13. Dashboard	M	Uses quantitative assessments to move beyond qualitative judgments to refine the focus on value prioritization and creation.
	14. Value determination	N	An integrated assembly of visual controls that move beyond publishing information and drive project-level and process-level improvements.
	15. Visual controls	O	A particular product or service where improvement can provide strategic and competitive advantage.

Crossword Puzzle

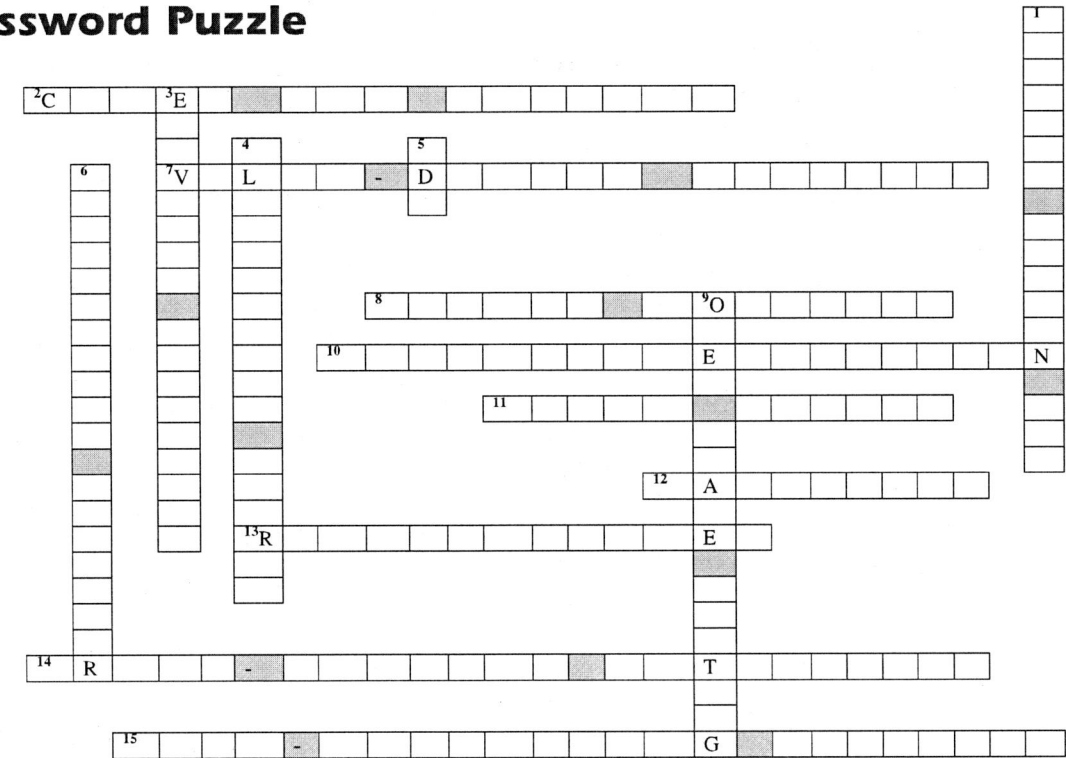

Hints:

ACROSS

2. A workspace arrangement where the agile team colocated but has private areas to use when the situation warrants it.
7. A process to help stakeholders clarify and articulate their values and priorities early in the project management process.
8. Activities or processes that communicate via a variety of visual signals or cues.
10. Quantitative assessments to move beyond qualitative judgments to refine the focus on value prioritization and creation.
11. A particular product or service where improvement can provide strategic and competitive advantage.
12. An integrated assembly of visual controls that move beyond publishing information and drive project-level and process-level improvements.
13. Defines feature priorities taking into account regulatory requirements and industry best practices.
14. Factors that influence the intrinsic motivation of agile teams – pride in work, accomplishment, and contribution.
15. Probes feelings and biases to help traditional project managers adapt to facilitative agile management practices.

DOWN

1. Contains whatever graphic images and narrative content are needed to convey the product vision to customers.
3. A short uncomplicated statement of the product vision using language everyone can understand in one minute or less.
4. A tool the customer/proxy uses to clarify how to handle future unavoidable tradeoffs and communicate that perspective to the team.
5. A minimalist one-page summary of key objectives, capabilities, and information needed to understand the project objectives and progress.
6. Displays project-related information in a place where passersby can see it.
9. A self-organized meeting where the attendees define the topic and the agenda.

Word Search

Word Search - 15 Words to find:

- ELEVATOR STATEMENT
- PRODUCT VISION BOX
- DASHBOARD
- FLEXIBILITY MATRIX
- PRIDE-RELATED MOTIVATION
- CAVES AND COMMONS
- VALUE DETERMINATION
- VALUE TARGET
- INFORMATION RADIATOR
- VALUE-DRIVEN DELIVERY
- OPEN SPACE MEETING
- PDS
- VISUAL CONTROLS
- RISK-ADJUSTED BACKLOG
- SELF-REGULATINGQUESTION

```
P P V A L U E - D R I V E N _ D E L I V E R Y A L I
R R A I N F O R M A T I O N _ R A D I A T O R H O U
I O T I T I V A L U E _ T A R G E T V A O I C R I R
D D E S E L F - R E G U L A T I N G _ Q U E S T I N
E U U U E O O P E N _ S P A C E _ M E E T _ A T _ S
- C S E L F - R E G U L A T I N G _ Q U E S T I O N
R T T J T D L P C A V E S _ A N D _ C O M M O N S I
E _ V A L U E - D R I V E N _ D E L I V J E V R N M
L V V R I S K - A D J U S T E D _ B A C K L O G O I
A I L I C I N F O R M A T I O N _ R A D I A T T N R
T S N S A I M F L E X I B I L I T Y _ M A T P O S R
E I F K V R _ O S R E - E T O A E D O N U I I S B A
D O L - E L E V A T O R _ S T A T E M E N T S G S N
_ N E A S D A S H B O A R D E Q D R M A A L N D S U
M _ X D _ _ A D _ _ E O R A V E S E A N O I P O R H
O B I J A I T T T T A R O V I O T R I R T F L I D S
T O B U N P T I A T L R C D N A S M T E M O A T E N
I X I S D R R N A I E E O I T R R N E C R M P D E E
V R L T _ S _ N M L R P L S S E O M V T A T R E A _
A A I E C T I E _ R O I _ S T C _ G N E I A U V O R
T - T D O I M _ T N O R _ E _ E P O A P T T U - T E
I R Y _ M T S L E A O P D L C E C A L _ A R D _ M V
O N _ B M F I E X T T _ A A O _ E N E T D A S H B O
N L M A O D O _ A _ E U P O L D T U _ C M E I T A O
I I A C E M O V T U S S _ A L P L A A C T A _ A R P
A O T K I A E S L I _ D U E O A A C U I S L C I L T
S C R L O L O A V N E S D A V E L E _ E I A A C M O
O _ I O E F V D E T I L R L Q E N L _ E I N U E D I
I M X S G E N P V V P R O D U C T _ V I S I O N _ O
P O G C T R O E D E A I E X A _ E A R T H A L V - S
```

CHAPTER 6: Planning Projects – Part 2

Chapter Practice Test

1. One situation where the help of a formal coach would be beneficial is _____.

   A. When the project is experiencing technical setbacks
   B. When ramping up agile in an organization
   C. When the customer is requesting numerous changes
   D. When senior management is not changing priorities during the iteration

2. In an agile environment, the role of the project manager is one of a facilitator, meaning he or she promotes the success of the team by encouraging self-organization, fostering adherence to agile principles, and removing obstacles. When is it appropriate for the project manager to step out of the facilitator role and participate actively in the project work?

   A. When the project manager has important content to offer that no one else on the team has
   B. When the project is falling behind schedule
   C. When the project is encountering technical issues
   D. When directed by senior management

3. A self-organized meeting where the attendees define the topic and the agenda is referred to as a(n) _____.

   A. Product vision meeting
   B. Daily stand-up
   C. Retrospective
   D. Open space meeting

4. A(n) _____ displays project-related information in a place where passersby can easily see it.

   A. Retrospective
   B. Scrum Master
   C. Information radiator
   D. Customer/proxy

5. In Lean environments, _____ are used to make it easier to control an activity or process through a variety of visual signals or cues.

   A. Story points
   B. Visual controls
   C. Minimal marketable features
   D. Rules of engagement

6. An item consisting of graphic images and narrative content conveying the product vision to the customer/proxy in end user language is referred to as a(n) _____.

   A. Product report
   B. Elevator statement
   C. Product vision box
   D. Product data sheet

7. When the project team creates a written statement, possibly using a template, that can quickly explain the product vision in about one minute or less they have created a(n) _____.

   A. Elevator statement
   B. Product data sheet
   C. Product vision box
   D. Feature matrix

8. A tool that can help a team manage tradeoffs and evaluate which constraints are flexible and which are not is referred to as a(n) _____.

   A. Product data sheet
   B. Feature breakdown structure
   C. Fishbone diagram
   D. Flexibility matrix

9. A one-page summary of the key objectives, capabilities, and information needed to understand the purpose of the project can best be described as a(n) _____

   A. Elevator statement
   B. Product data sheet
   C. Product report
   D. Minimal marketable feature

10. _____ may be described as an agile technique, borrowed from Lean manufacturing, that applies the Lean principle of optimizing the whole by identifying waste in the development process.

    A. Progressive elaboration
    B. Value stream mapping
    C. Daily stand-up meetings
    D. Story points

11. The purpose of the value-driven delivery process is _____.

    A. To completely define the product at the beginning of the project
    B. To help senior management identify valuable products
    C. To help stakeholders clarify and articulate their values and priorities
    D. To help the team recover when the project falls behind schedule

12. _____ is a technique developed in the Lean manufacturing field to analyze (and potentially redesign) the flow of materials and information required to deliver a product or service to the customer.

    A. Value stream mapping
    B. Progressive elaboration
    C. Daily stand-up meetings
    D. Regression analysis

13. Within the value stream mapping process, a particular product or service where improvement can provide strategic and competitive advantage is referred to as a _____.

    A. Product cost/schedule target
    B. Product vision box
    C. Minimal marketable feature
    D. Value stream target

14. Which of the following is not a part of the value stream mapping process?

    A. Clarify the current opportunity
    B. Define the current state
    C. Create the elevator statement
    D. Depict the desired future state

15. A type of information radiator referred to as a _____ would typically use green, yellow, and red color indicators to show status of specific aspects of the project.

    A. Burn up chart
    B. Dashboard
    C. Product vision box
    D. Product value stream map

16. An information radiator that shows story points both planned and completed during an iteration is referred to as a _____.

    A. Burn up chart
    B. Product value stream map
    C. Product feature breakdown structure
    D. Fishbone diagram

17. To be successful in the role of facilitator, the Agile Project Manager must do all of the following except _____.

    A. Conduct effective meetings
    B. Successfully remove roadblocks
    C. Assign specific tasks to the most appropriate individual
    D. Focus on goals rather than on low level tasks

18. Specific situations in which the team may benefit from formal coaching include all of the following except _____.

    A. When ramping up agile for the first time in an organization
    B. When conducting release retrospectives
    C. When conducting project retrospectives
    D. An experienced agile team that has worked several projects together in the past is beginning a new project

19. All of the following are critical tools for the Agile Project Manager except _____.

   A. Monthly project status reports
   B. Product vision box
   C. Elevator statement
   D. Flexibility matrix

20. In agile projects using Scrum, the _____ is responsible for gathering information from the customer on tradeoffs and documenting the results in the matrix.

   A. Scrum Master
   B. Product Owner
   C. Senior programmer
   D. Product analyst

Answers – Terminology Matching

1:I, 2:A, 3:E, 4:C, 5:H, 6:L, 7:K, 8:B, 9:D, 10:G, 11:J, 12:O, 13:N, 14:M, 15:F

Answers – Crossword Puzzle

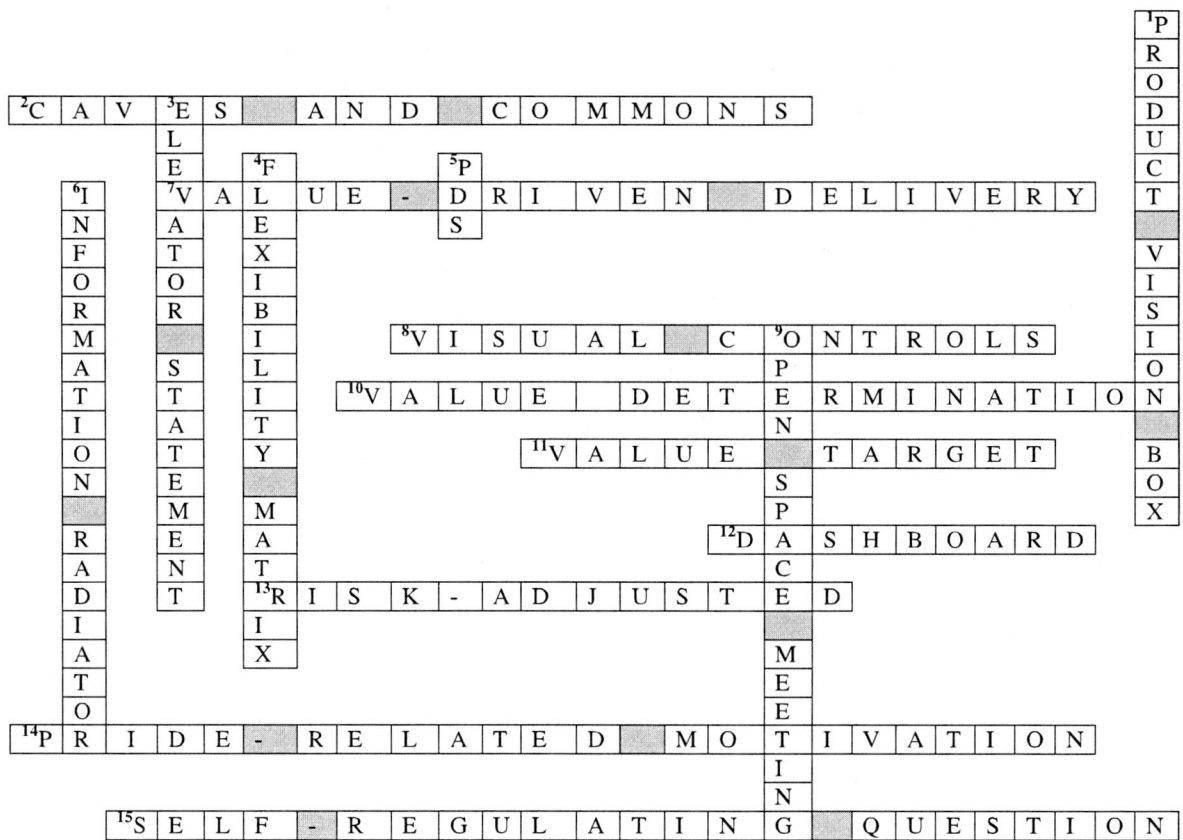

Answers – Word Search

Word Search - 15 Words to find:

ELEVATOR STATEMENT
PRODUCT VISION BOX
DASHBOARD
FLEXIBILITY MATRIX
PRIDE-RELATED MOTIVATION
CAVES AND COMMONS
VALUE DETERMINATION
VALUE TARGET
INFORMATION RADIATOR
VALUE-DRIVEN DELIVERY
OPEN SPACE MEETING
PDS
VISUAL CONTROLS
RISK-ADJUSTED BACKLOG
SELF-REGULATINGQUESTION

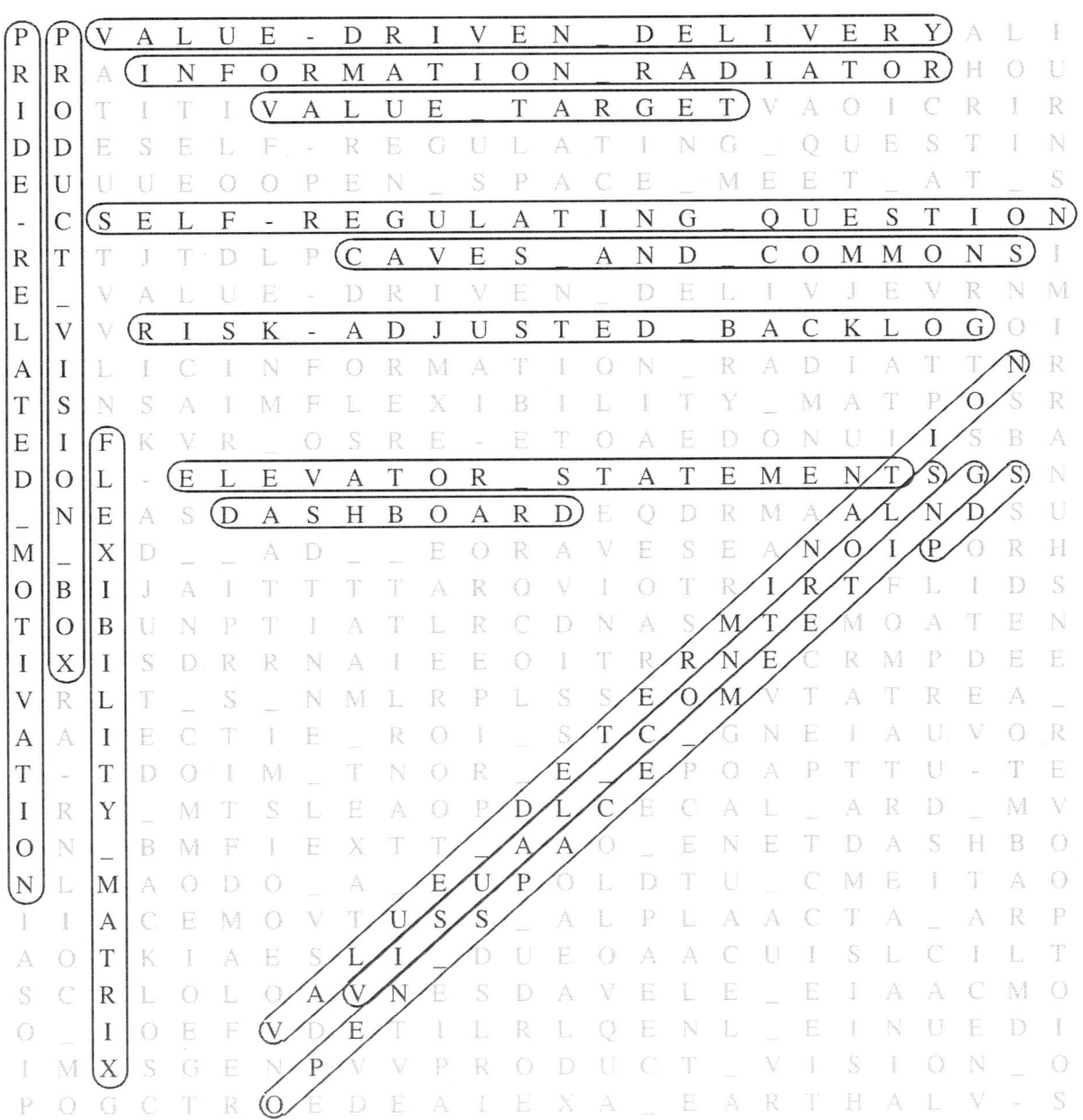

Answers – Practice Test

1. **B.** It's one thing to embark on a bottom-up innovation such as when a group of developers decides to adopt Scrum as their methodology of choice. There's a big difference, however, between reading a book or attending a Certified Scrum Master class and being a successful agile practitioner. Some of the greatest lessons are ones learned from mistakes, but we recommend bringing in an external coach to educate both management and team when on-boarding agile. Having that external viewpoint is also a good reality check on whether the team is effectively using best practices.

2. **A.** It is only appropriate for you to relinquish the facilitator role ***when you have important content to offer that no one else on the team has.*** Whether it stems from subject-matter expertise or simply from experience gained on previous projects, in these situations, you need to step out of the facilitator role and provide your input for the benefit of the team.

3. **D.** Optional meetings include the team reflective workshop and the open space meeting, a self-organized meeting where the attendees define the topic and the agenda. (Typically, an open space meeting is a team "subcommittee" meeting aimed at removing an impediment or solving a technical problem).

4. **C.** An information radiator displays project-related information in a place where passersby can see it. Many agile methods (particularly Scrum) employ information radiators as a concise way of updating the agile team, stakeholders, and management on product development status.

5. **B.** When using information radiators, agile practitioners incorporate tools from the Lean manufacturing world. Information radiators are really a specialized type of ***visual control.*** In Lean environments, visual controls are used to make it easier to control an activity or process through a variety of visual signals or cues.

6. **C.** A product vision box may be thought of as the product box on a store shelf. It contains whatever graphic images and narrative content are needed to convey the product vision to the customer. Significantly, it is in end user language and not techno-jargon. Constructing and demonstrating a product vision box is a useful exercise for the team to see if they truly understand the customer/proxy's vision and stated priorities for the product.

7. **A.** Devising an elevator statement is a challenge for the agile team – that of quickly explaining the product vision to someone "in an elevator," in one minute or less. Thus it must be an uncomplicated description of the product vision in a short statement, using language everyone can understand.

8. **D.** A ***flexibility (or tradeoff) matrix*** is a simple tool that helps the customer/proxy clarify how to handle the unavoidable tradeoffs that may arise in the future and communicate that perspective to the team. The matrix clarifies which constraints are flexible and which are not, hence the name. This grid shows the relative importance of project constraints (i.e., scope, schedule, cost, and quality) in terms of Fixed, Firm, or Flexible; only **one** constraint may be Fixed. It thus allows the customer/proxy to establish a top-level decision tool for making tradeoff decisions when the typical resource, time, or cost conflicts arise during project execution.

9. **B.** A product data sheet (PDS) captures a project's objectives in a minimalist document. While not quite equivalent to a project charter from the traditional project management world, it is one-page summary of the key objectives, capabilities, and information needed to understand the purpose and progress of the project.

10. **B.** Value stream mapping applies the Lean principle of optimizing the whole by identifying waste (i.e., rework and late detection of problems caused by multi-tasking and overloading the team), which degrades quality and delays delivery.

11. **C.** The purpose of the value-driven delivery process is to help stakeholders clarify and articulate their values and priorities early in the project management process. Another reason is to identify which components of the solution are most important and to create a documenting mechanism for the team to manage the follow-up conversations required to define and direct the team's work efforts.

12. **A.** Value stream mapping is a technique developed in the Lean manufacturing field to analyze (and potentially redesign) the flow of materials and information required to deliver a product or service to the customer. It documents the value stream using icons or pictures and then analyzes the stream for waste. The focus is on reducing the total time from beginning to end of the entire stream, without taking shortcuts at the expense of opportunities in the future.

13. **D.** The value stream target is a particular product or service (sometimes a product or service group, family or category) where improvement can provide strategic and competitive advantage.

14. **C.** The basic value stream mapping process consists of the following steps: Identify the Value Stream Target, Define the Current State, Clarify the Current Opportunity, and Depict the Desired Future State.

15. **B.** The basic stoplight scheme (Green: On track; Yellow: Warning – Implement corrective action or monitor performance; Red: Immediate corrective action required) is typical of product dashboards and is a time-honored indicator of overall status for both traditional and agile projects.

16. **A.** The burn up chart is really nothing more than an inverted burn down chart. The appeal of this presentation lies in its simplicity – a line moving upward towards the target "shows progress" to stakeholders and senior management who might not be intimately familiar with agile.

17. **C.** For the Agile Project Manager, keys to succeeding in the facilitator role include successfully removing obstacles, focusing on goals and not low-level tasks, and running effective meetings.

18. **D.** The specific situations in which the team may benefit from formal coaching are when: employing certain agile methods, ramping up agile in an organization, non-agile trained personnel are attending team meetings, and conducting release and project retrospectives.

19. **A.** Agile tools critical to the Agile Project Manager's arsenal are: 1) Product vision box; 2) Elevator statement; 3) Flexibility matrix; and 4) Project data sheet.

20. **B.** Scrum practitioners often utilize the flexibility matrix. When used in Scrum, the Product Owner is responsible for gathering information from the customer on tradeoffs and documenting the results in the matrix. Because the matrix will be used throughout the project to adjudicate tradeoffs, getting it settled early is key to avoiding subsequent difficult or impossible negotiations. Once people decide their position on a specific tradeoff the effort to get cooperation becomes much more difficult without a flexibility matrix.

Chapter End Notes

[1] Derby, E., & Larson, D. (2006). *Agile retrospectives making good teams great.* Raleigh, NC: The Pragmatic Bookshelf.

[2] Cockburn, A. (2007). *Agile software development: The cooperative game, Second edition.* Upper Saddle River, NJ: Addison-Wesley.

[3] Weick, K. E. (1979). *The social psychology of organizing (Topics in social psychology), Second Edition.* New York: Addison-Wesley.

[4] Cockburn, A. (2007). *Agile software development: The cooperative game, Second edition.* Upper Saddle River, NJ: Addison-Wesley.5

[5] Shalloway, A., Beaver, G., &Trott, J. R. (2009). *Lean-agile software development: Achieving enterpriseagility.* Boston: Pearson Education.

[6] Moore, G. A. (2002). *Crossing the chasm.* New York: Harper Paperbacks.

[7] Highsmith, J. (2004). *Agile project management creating innovative products, Second edition.* Boston: Pearson Education.

[8] Ibid.

[9] Ibid.

[10] One of the best known Intel©MAPP Day facilitators in Jeff Hodgkinson who can be found on LinkedIn©.

[11] Highsmith, J. (2004). *Agile project management creating innovative products, Second edition.* Boston: Pearson Education.

[12] Berthot, B. D. (2011). *Program dashboard.* Unpublished [Excel spreadsheet].

[13] Simini, L. (2011, July 1). *Agile project dashboards: Bringing value to stakeholders and top management.* Retrieved October 21, 2011, from www.amazon.com/Agile-Project-Dashboards-Stakeholders-ebook/dp/B005D7FE6U/ref=pd_sxp_f_pt.

[14] Ibid.

[15] For the discerning analyst, yes, this means that the agile team on this project is approximately 4% behind in terms of delivering business value - assuming that 1 Story Point = 1 Business Value Point.1

CHAPTER 7

Iterating Projects

Chapter Highlights

Once the project has been initiated, as described in Chapter 3, and planned and estimated, as described in Chapters 4 through 6, the next challenge becomes successfully guiding the Iterate process that delivers results - potentially shippable products! This chapter covers the Iterate process from backlog grooming through adaptive planning, team performance and risk management, and down to continuous improvement.

Overview of Execution

An interesting paradox in project management, regardless of whether a traditional or agile framework is used, is that the flow of time, from the present into the future, is the opposite of the flow of elaboration or planning process. The project moves from the present into the future, but to be successful it must "start with the end in mind" to paraphrase Stephen Covey and back into a plan.[1] *(See Figure 7.1.)*

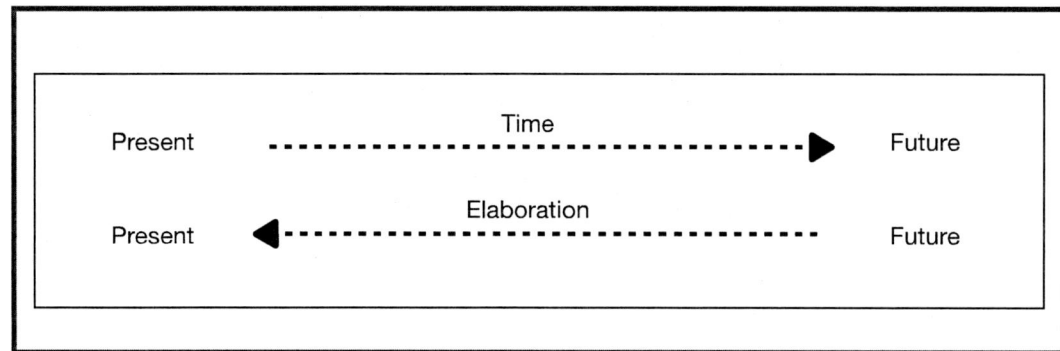

Figure 7.1 Time Flow Versus Elaboration Flow.

Expanding further, business planning flows the same direction as project elaboration because it moves from strategic objectives on the future time horizon and decomposes them into tactical objectives on the mid-term horizon and finally, details them as operational objectives on the near-term horizon. (See Figure 7.2.)

Agile frameworks use different vocabulary, but similar principles for elaborating projects. Planning starts with the business-value or strategic objective and organization leaders or a product management team who define capabilities, themes, and sometimes high-level features that must be delivered. The desired output is a product backlog and becomes a roadmap.

Planning continues with a release where a project team decomposes the capabilities and themes from the roadmap into specific, but imprecisely described epics and stories, and assigning them a size using Planning Poker or a similar technique. The desired output is one or more release plans with iteration goals described at a high-level.

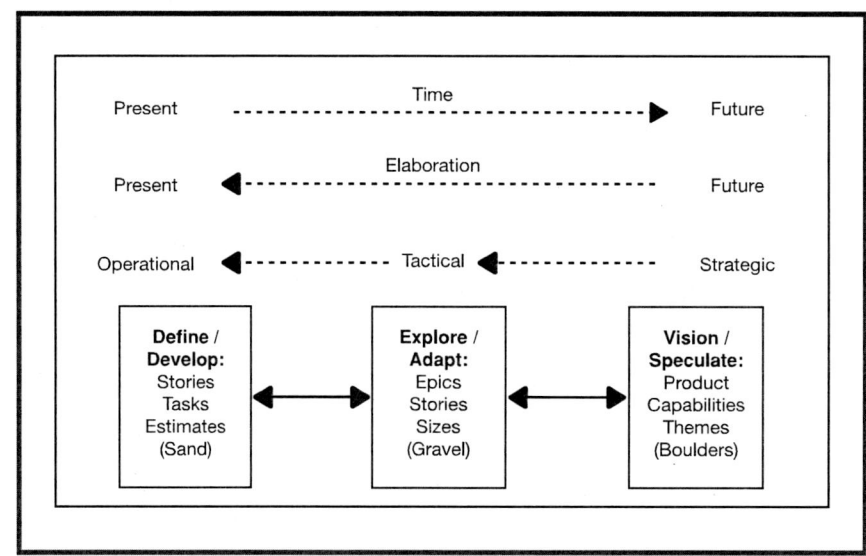

Figure 7.2 Strategic Alignment of Agile Elaboration and Backlog Grooming.

Finally, the project team decomposes each release plan into more specific iteration goals and begins iteration planning where tasks and estimates are generated. Then, work begins and flows in the direction of time moving from development to integration to delivery of the iteration goal. (See Figure 7.3)

Excellence in execution is built upon a foundation of excellence in planning. Excellence in planning is achieved through diligent grooming of the product backlog. The product backlog, on the long-term horizon, is strategic in nature and therefore imprecisely defined by design. Grooming it means prioritizing and choosing those parts of the backlog that need refining – that is additional grooming – so that they can be properly evaluated on the tactical mid-term horizon. Grooming the backlog from tactical to operational, from the mid-term to near-term horizon, means prioritizing and choosing those parts of the backlog that need refining so that the team can execute development and delivery of specific goals.

Product Backlog Grooming

In many ways, product backlog grooming is the "steering wheel" that insures the "agile truck" is headed in the right direction and stops to deliver packages at the right time and location. Quantitatively, backlog grooming also has a strong correlation to positive financial impact. Research indicates that the cost of a $250,000 IT development project can have a negative variance of as much as $130,000 to achieve target functionality. The amount of the variance correlates to the quality of grooming or the maturity of the requirements.[2]

Agile Project Managers must insure that the customer/proxy is continuously refining the business value assessment of the product and setting backlog priorities accordingly. Although responsibility for the business value assessment lies primarily with the customer/proxy, Agile Project Managers need to be capable of articulating the cost/benefit analysis in customer-facing, non-technical terms.

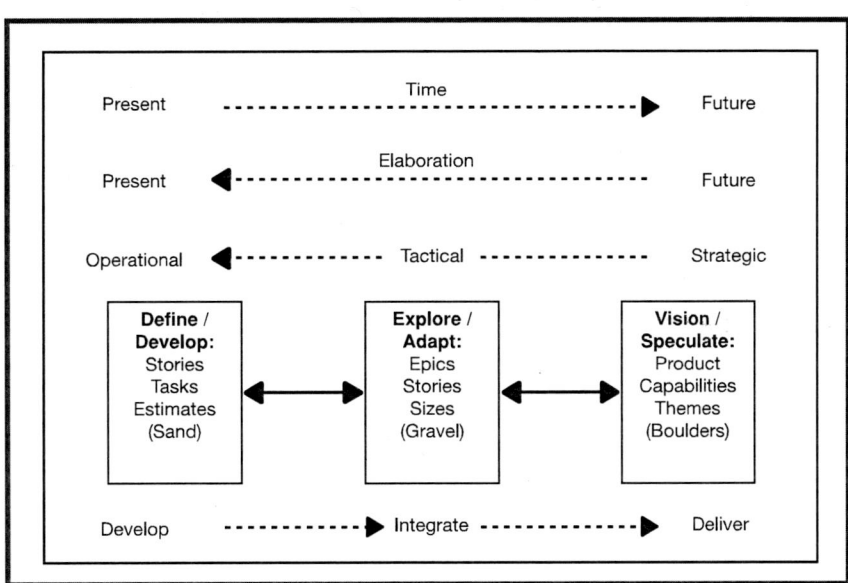

Figure 7.3 Integrated View of Elaboration, Planning, and Execution Flows.

Setting the priorities drives product backlog grooming. The customer/proxy will lead customer collaboration activities like focus groups, marketing studies, and product visioning exercises. Using those experiences, the customer/proxy will discern the timing and minimal marketable feature (MMF) sets needed to create both incremental and long-term value. The Agile Project Manager must collaborate with the customer/proxy to instill a *value-oriented perspective* within the team by communicating that understanding.

The product backlog contains the product vision and grooming it is a real-time, rolling wave, iterative process that guides the project through an evolutionary requirements elaboration process. Feature details evolve as the team creates a preliminary product breakdown structure then expand on that list by creating user stories containing descriptive estimating content.

Because there are enormous differences between developing tangible and intangible products, as well as between large capital and product-to-market projects, the process of analyzing and defining features varies widely. However, elaboration should align with a hierarchy such as product, segment, and niche, or application, capability, and story.

The lack of good release planning is rampant in parts of the agile community who seem to reject it as unnecessary. The Scrum Guide states that release planning is entirely optional, but goes on to say that starting work without its artifacts will become an impediment to resolve.[3] It seems many agile practitioners see "entirely optional" and miss the serious warning that follows it. Teams can get caught up in an iteration-plus-backlog-only mindset and not invest in the planning needed for an entire release or project.

Doing so is a mistake because then the teams can't adequately address significant business questions like, "How much will this cost?" or "Will we have a releasable product on the launch date?" This lack of sensible answers creates immense frustration for the executives subjected to this behavior by agile teams.

Product backlog grooming, also known as **product backlog management,** is a just-in-time process that prioritizes and clarifies each backlog items it moves from the outer edge of the time horizon into the mid-term then current time horizon. The information about each specific backlog item increases as it nears likely development. Grooming avoids waste by only gathering detailed information as it is needed and usable because most items will change as development progresses and the customer/proxy gains insight.

Overall a product backlog grows with time as more detailed information and new items are added. Because the quantity of backlog items, by definition, always exceeds the capacity to deliver them, the process of grooming the backlog to align development decisions to business priorities and articulate them in roadmaps and release plans, will always be significant.

As organizations mature, a common best practice is to use a roadmap and backlog at the capability level on the six month to multi-year horizon, in addition to multiple or rolling three-month release plans and one to four week iteration plans at the story level.

A best practice for identifying and defining backlog items is to have the customer/proxy discuss each of the following **elements** with the team.

- *Process:* The definition, usage, and management of procedures discussed in the Business Case and Value Analysis (from Chapter 3).

- *Organizational:* The infrastructure support from the current business practices and the support needs of the future-state practices.

- *Human:* The knowledge and skills applied by the Users in the current business practices and the additional needs for the future-state practices.

- *Risk and regulatory compliance:* What provisions are needed "just because" of the need for risk mitigation or regulatory compliance?

- *Automation and technology:* How will the organization's approach to fulfilling required value-creation processes use a different model, such as query replacing report, pull replacing push, automated replacing manual?

As explained earlier, reducing waste is a Lean principle that is imbedded in agile frameworks. That means that the frequency and level of detail in refining estimates must be tied to the business benefits of doing so. Elaboration for the sake of elaborating, or estimating for the sake of estimating, is waste. Elaborating and estimating to create insight, plan the future, and guide execution to create business value is not waste.

Improve Value-Driven Deliverables

Measuring and Using Cycle Time

One of the reasons so many organizations are pursuing agile frameworks is due to the competitive pressure to reduce how long it takes for an idea to get from vision, business case, and charter to delivered capability that customers value (and will pay for!).

 Cycle time is the time (weeks, months, or years) required to deliver capabilities. A properly implemented agile framework should minimize cycle time and increase organizational advantage with responses to market opportunities, competitive threats, or business needs. But the organization must develop a strategic competence for clustering or grouping ideas into projects in ways that allow for removing waste, optimizing flow, and decreasing cycle time.

Understanding that fact and working with the customer/proxy to achieve it is a particularly important aspect of being a professional Agile Project Manager. As Figure 7.4 shows, regardless of whether you use traditional or agile nomenclature, the potential for waiting time to increase your cycle time is a very real risk. Measuring the process cycle time and using that information to improve the process often creates significant advantages for the organization.

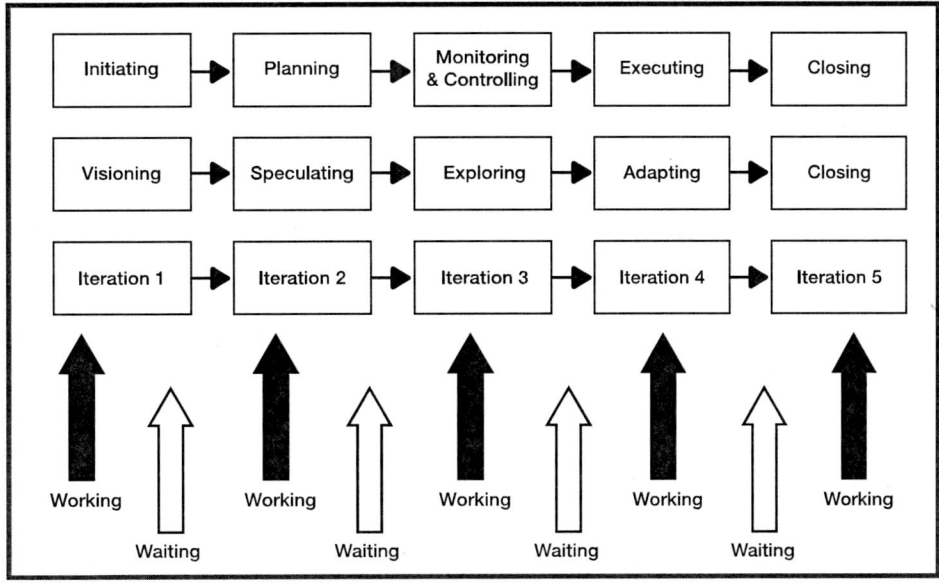

Figure 7.4 Cycle Time = Work Time + Wait Time.

CHAPTER 7: Iterating Projects

Agile borrows the drive from Lean principles to constantly improve the development process with an aim to perfect them. That drive centers the way testing is done. Testing is done very early in the process in order to find and fix errors quickly. Doing so shortens the cycle-time by fixing the errors before they delay the finish or it becomes part of something else, increasing rework.

 The definition of cycle time in an agile framework is narrower than in Lean. **Agile cycle time** is the start-to-finish time required to complete a potentially shippable increment of the solution. Cycle time is used to measure the process, not a person, because one person will post faster times than another, possibly untrained, one. The goal is to understand then improve the process so that reliable, repeatable outcomes minimize variations and the waste that accompanies them. Eliminate process variation and waste and cycle time will come down.

Cycle time in an agile environment does not measure how fast a team member develops or tests a particular story or task because that would be person-centric. **Cycle time is how fast the system can produce potentially shippable increments, or iteration goals.** A system that produces usable increments in two-week iterations offers twice as much opportunity to adapt to competitive pressures and threats than a system producing results in four-week iterations. That added flexibility also avoids the risk of waste occurring if the wrong thing is developed.

Because agile frameworks are rooted in Lean thinking, they are a type of continuous improvement method that places significant focus on time. Because the frameworks use stable time increments – two or three or four-week iterations – improving cycle time is external to the team dynamic or work process within the iteration. However, the external changes needed to improve cycle time, things like better roadmap planning, release planning, and solution architecting, enable the team dynamic to mature from a four-week focus to a three-week or even two-week focus.

Understanding that **cycle time** is a **process measure, not a person measure,** is hard for many people to do when they see a real or figurative "stopwatch" or "microscope" being used to collect data for evaluation. They have to be shown and reminded that the goal is to discover if the process that currently takes four weeks could be improved to take three.

A common fear for many people is that the work that fills up those four weeks will be expected in three. The key is to show that the quantity of time hasn't changed – six four-week iterations equal eight three-week iterations – even though the number of delivered increments has gone up. But be careful, if you add more deliverables before reducing the cycle time, then the team is being asked for more work.

If successful outcomes vary widely from iteration to iteration, it is an indication that something is wrong with the process. On occasion, a team can't seem to make it happen, but it is more probable that the process is not being followed. The roadmap may be too vague because an executive lacks clarity, the release plan is unrealistic because the customer/proxy is trying to cut corners, or some similar process violation is occurring and sabotaging the team's performance.

To improve cycle time and build the strongest possible processes, remember these guidelines:

1. ***Build the roadmap as a swarm:*** Roadmap deficiencies result most often from builds that are compiled with missing links and unknown dependencies.

     Swarming is the practice of bringing together all of the people, and their insights, needed to define a roadmap that decreases the overall time required to complete the product.

2. ***Define acceptance metrics for releases and iterations:*** This practice applies to tangible and intangible products because it requires enhancing the focus of customer/proxy conversations until they produce specific metrics that will validate the potentially shippable increment.

3. ***Select an iteration length that is sustainable:*** Cycles improve results by limiting variances and lowering waste, so it is paramount to select an iteration length that represents a sustainable pace and allows completion of potentially shippable increments.

4. ***Recalibrate and institutionalize learning:*** Continuously seek improvements to the processes that improve the team dynamic within the iteration. Refine organizational standards for acceptable complexity at the capability and feature levels and then with architecting expectations. Align the complexity and architecting standards to estimating expectations for roadmaps and release plans.

Measuring and Using Work-in-Process (WIP)

In Chapter 5 it was noted that Work-in-Process (WIP) limits are an example of how agilists have borrowed techniques from Lean thinking to improve the value stream of product development. It was also noted that at any point in time a project is a type of WIP because the business cannot realize value from user stories in process, but only from potentially shippable increments of the solution.

As we explained just above, expediting the completion of user stories only means that the business can derive value sooner if the cycle time is shortened by way of process improvements external to the team. Managing the flow of value through short iterations is external, but managing WIP is part of the internal team dynamic.

The use of WIP limits strives to improve the team's workflow (or throughput) by controlling the amount of WIP at each step in the process helping the team overcome perceived impediments and completely finishing each story. WIP limits reduce bottlenecks the same way stop lights on freeway on-ramps prevent rush hour gridlock. The total throughput of cars from entry point to exit point is increased if the maximum capacity of the freeway is not violated because the flow of cars doesn't become inhibited by the inherent complexity of drivers' needs to pursue interdependent outcomes. That is, the complexity of the interdependent need to change lanes to reach various exit points isn't compounded by a lack of run to make lane changes.

By limiting the number of stories being actively worked by the team at any single point in time, more stories actually get done despite seeming counter-intuitive to many people.

In order to manage anything it must be measured, as the well-respected management saying goes. Measuring WIP can look complicated because of the simple fact that it is a moving variable, not a constant, so the measurement at any given point in time will be different from any other point in time. Measuring it produces results like those on the left side of Figure 7.5. So, the way to measure and manage WIP is simply to start by guessing at the value of the likely maximum WIP. It does not matter whether the current maximum WIP is 15 or 20 or 25 stories.

A simple practice for estimating the current WIP level is to check the story board a few times per day and count how many stories are in the queue. Record each WIP value and then after several days of taking measurements set the likely maximum near the average of your measurements plus some allowance for comfort. There is no need for complicated formulas. If you are not sure which value to choose, make it the higher one.

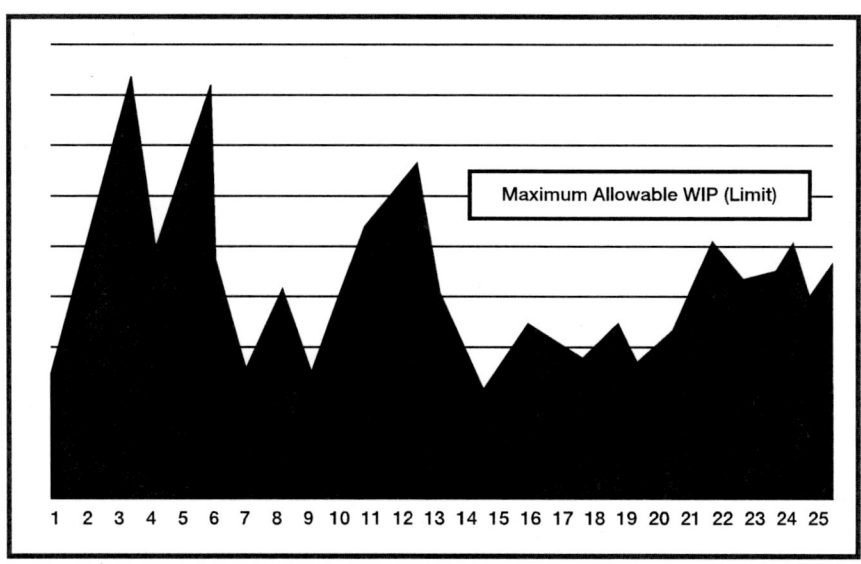

Figure 7.5 Work-in-Process (WIP) and WIP Limit.

"Guess-timate" the maximum and set it as the initial limit or the starting Maximum Allowable WIP. Over time, make periodic reductions in the limit and measure the impact on productivity. The most desirable WIP limit will emerge rather quickly and can then be used as shown on the right side of Figure 7.5.

Another thing to note about Figure 7.5 is that variations before measurement and a WIP limit were larger and that the variances became smaller following the application of a limit. This is very common and is the reason the first target should be set at a level that is very easy to achieve. The main purpose of the initial limit is to reduce variances and create a reference point for WIP measurement. Then, begin a program of periodic adjustments to lower the total WIP value.

After WIP measurement has begun, asking the following types of questions will help identify how to improve the team dynamic and reduce WIP.

- Does the iteration backlog exceed the team's capacity?
- How does the actual work process compare with a best practice process?
- Where are the most common impediments in the process?
- Have team members synchronized to avoid sub-optimization?
- Does the team use the storyboard to really help them manage workflow?
- How much are limited resources associated with the stories in WIP?

 Little's Law may be applied to the relationship between cycle time, WIP, and throughput and a production system in a steady state.[4] It is important because it correlates three significant performance measures – inventory, flow time, and throughput – in units per time period. This is very useful because risk can be identified with the amount of time represented by the user stories in inventory. For instance, if we see 200 stories of WIP for a team that produces 10 per day, a disaster probably awaits. Conversely if we see 200 stories of WIP for a team that produces 100 per day then it is extremely lean

To leverage Little's Law and improve the process, the values for inventory, flow time, and throughput should be long-term averages measured in consistent units. Once we have those values, we can use them to estimate waiting times, plan WIP levels to reduce variability, and track flow time to ensure high delivery reliability.

Because Little's Law shows that Flow Time = WIP/Throughput, it is clear that reducing WIP while holding throughput constant will reduce flow time. That is very desirable but Agile Project Manager's must resist the temptation to conclude that WIP reduction will always reduce cycle time. Reducing WIP without making required external process changes will also reduce throughput – that is, the probability that the team will reliably deliver potentially shippable increments of value. An essential part of an agile framework implementation is to reduce variability and enable the team to achieve greater throughput with less WIP.

Using Cumulative Flow Diagrams (CFDs)

 A *cumulative flow diagram* (CFD) is a tool for understanding project execution and using that insight to improve performance. It reduces risk due to workload imbalance by spreading it more evenly, creating a more effective and sustainable pace. It also provides insight into the feasibility of using shorter iterations for more flexibility, if needed.

The keys to creating a more sustainable pace are creating accurately sized and testable stories and focusing on a few stories at a time in order to finish specific work pieces more quickly. The linkage occurs between the customer/proxy driving better stories, the CFD providing more visibility, and the team driving for reduced WIP levels.

The idea of applying a CFD to agile development has been articulated by Lean thought leaders Don Reinertsen and David Anderson.[5,6] They demonstrate that WIP is a leading metric and can be tracked using CFD. That means WIP can predict lead times and delivery dates and be used to adjust for risks before they become serious problems.

For example, Figure 7.6 shows a CFD with an undesirably large WIP that contributes to an undesirably long cycle time. Having a large WIP is undesirable because the complexity of managing the relationships between multiple variables increases in a more than linear way, inducing more opportunities for errors and failure. Having a longer cycle time is undesirable because it increases the probability that the team's understanding of the customer's need will deteriorate, again, inducing more opportunities for errors and failure.

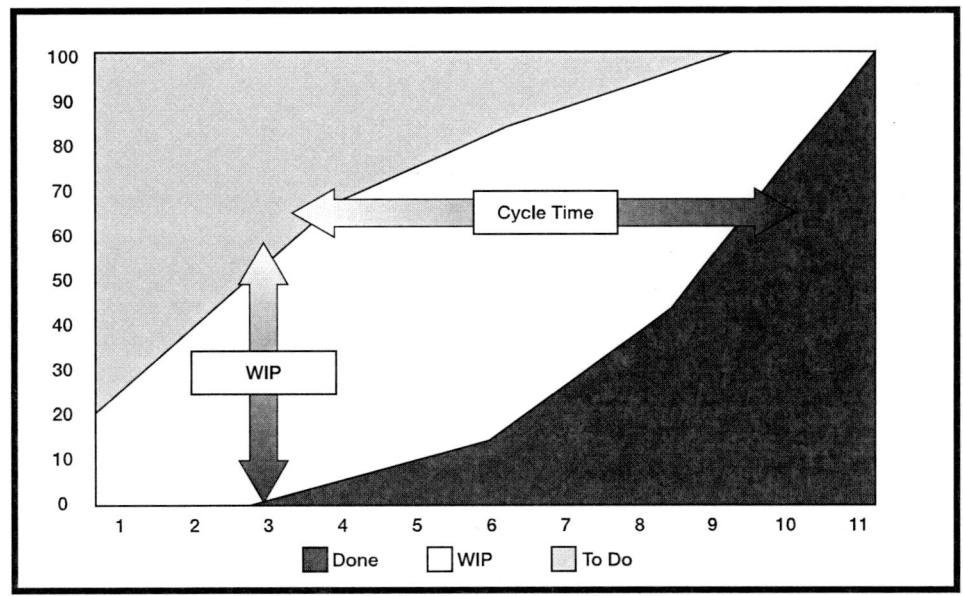

Figure 7.6 A Cumulative Flow Diagram (CFD) with Undesirable Cycle Time and WIP Levels.

By comparison, Figure 7.7 shows a CFD with a desirable WIP and cycle time. Having a smaller WIP is desirable because it minimizes complexity and reduces opportunities for errors and failure. Having a shorter cycle time is desirable because it increases the probability that the team's understanding of the customer's need will be accurate, again reducing opportunities for errors and failure.

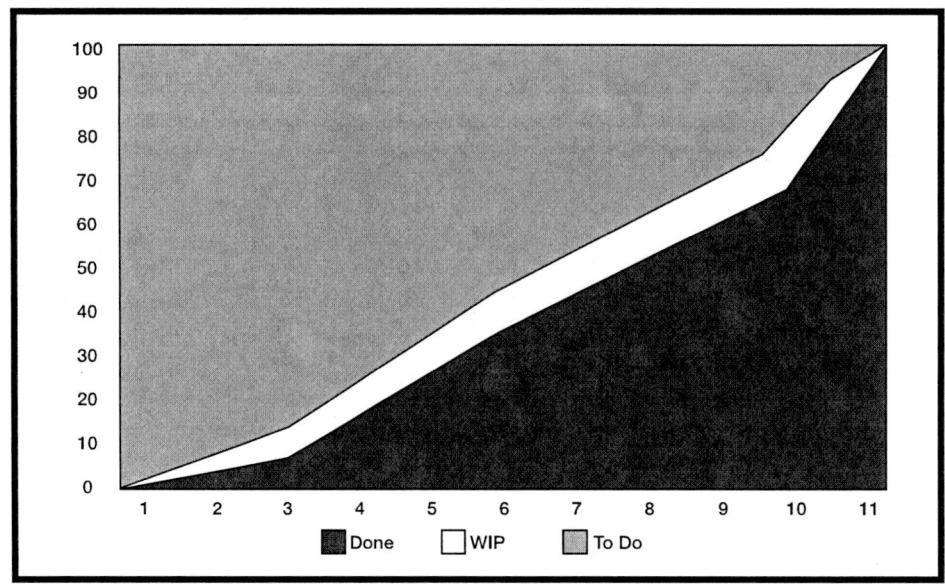

Figure 7.7 CFD with a Desirable Cycle Time and WIP levels.

It is interesting to note what a CFD for a typical, traditionally managed project looks like, as shown in Figure 7.8, and recognize that a CFD can be a valuable tool for non-agile projects also.

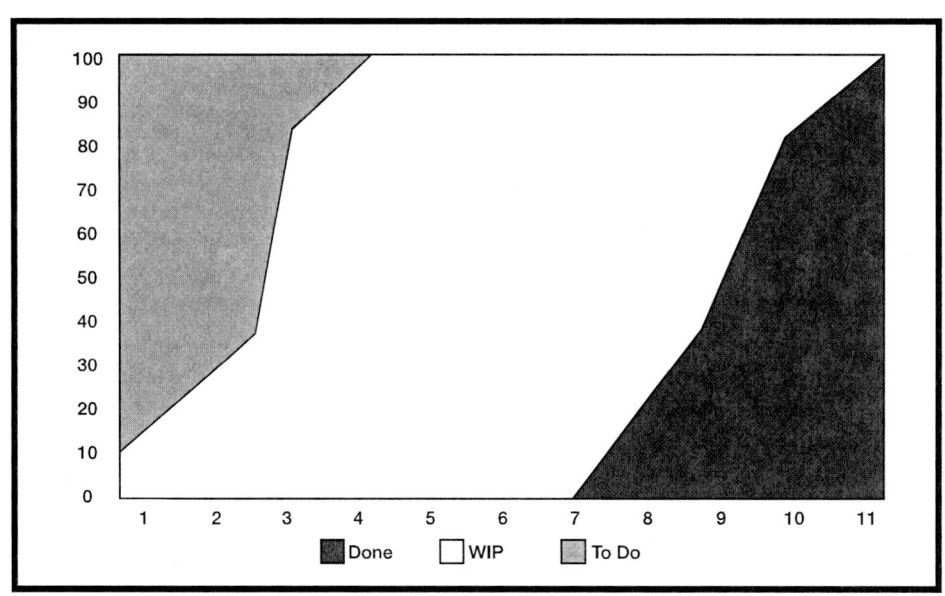

Figure 7.8 CFD for a Typical, Traditionally Managed Project.

Cumulative flow diagrams are a tool for tracking project progress in a burn-up format. For an Agile Project Manager they provide insight into the total scope and the progress of stories and tasks using an accessible, visual, proportional image of actual completeness. CFDs present the team with a simple analysis of work-in-progress and the lead time trending probability of delivery of a working solution. As a leading metric, CFDs enable Agile Project Managers and teams to act appropriately to growing problems in a transparent way.

Facilitate Adaptive Planning

Adaptive planning requires synchronization of the team internally and also between the team and customer/proxy. That synchronization happens for the team during daily stand-up meetings and with the customer/proxy during review meetings. The customer/proxy review meetings happen informally on a periodic, as needed, basis throughout the iterations and formally at the end of the iteration with the customer/proxy and all interested stakeholders.

Adaptive planning occurs during those meetings and the information is published using visual controls.

Create Visual Controls

As stated in Chapter 6, the term visual control is preferred to information radiator because it communicates more effectively the desired two-way communication that the agile team needs and provides. A two-way attitude and communication channel is needed to implement agile methods at the enterprise level. Visual controls invite management to help detect early when there are problems impeding progress toward the iteration or release goals.

Previously discussed visual controls used to display project information include product vision boxes, product backlogs, release and iteration plans, burn-down and burn-up charts, risk/impediment boards, and team work agreements.

We will now further discuss the following visual controls:

- Burn Charts
- Task Boards
- Kanban Boards

Creating Burn Charts

Burn charts come in two basic forms, burn-down and burn-up. **Burn-down charts** show the work remaining, like number of story points or ideal days, in the project or release. Burn-up charts show the work completed, again in story points or ideal days for the project or release. Burn-down charts are used most often for iterations and typically reflect the results of the team's daily meeting. Burn-up charts are used most often for releases and typically reflect features or deliverables completed.

Burn charts are rarely smooth because they reflect the team's actual progress. Because of unexpected technical challenges or breakthroughs, estimate variances, and scope changes, for example, a burn-down chart may show negative progress where the line of progress goes up instead of down during an iteration. The line radiates insight that the work the team has completed, the team's "net-net" progress, is not occurring at the expected pace, which threatens completion of the entire project scope.

The value of a burn-down chart is correlated to the length of the iteration. Because the value of the chart is seeing trend lines and adjusting the project team's approach and resources, the smaller the iteration, the smaller the value of the burn-down chart. With very short iterations, by the time the trend line is recognizable it is too late to adjust.

For iterations of two weeks and longer, burn-down charts can be very valuable. The standard iteration burn-down chart is two-dimensional and plots days on the horizontal, (X) axis. It plots hours remaining on the vertical (Y) axis, as shown in Figure 7.9.

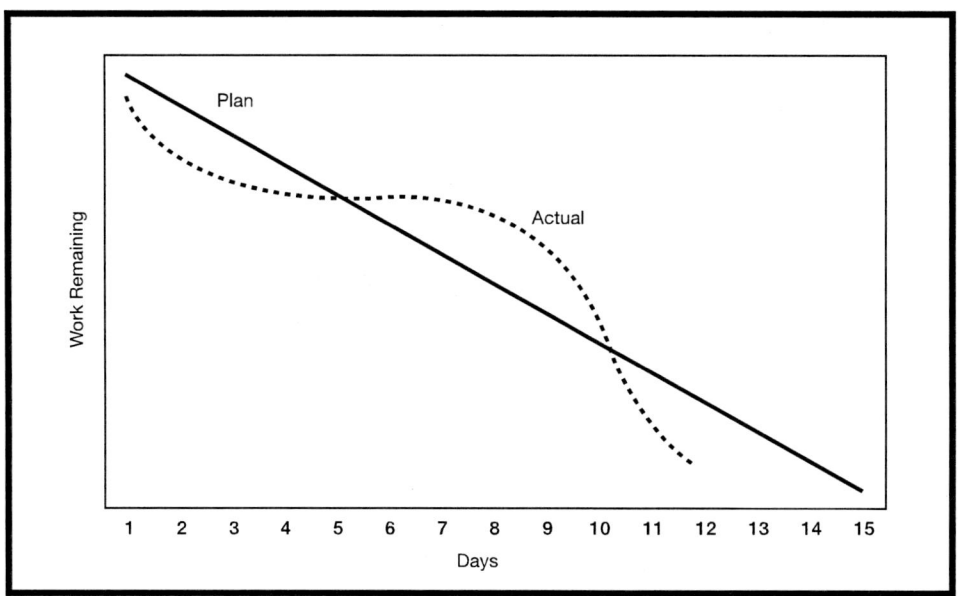

Figure 7.9 The Standard Burn-Down Chart.

The two most common ways to create and manage a burn-down chart are manually, for colocated teams, and using Excel for remote, distributed teams. The most common mistake made on burn-down charts is overcomplicating the process. A burn-down simply reports the sum of all work remaining (in hours or points) on a daily basis.

Following the team's report-out at the daily meeting, plot the work remaining on the chart. If the team identifies additional tasks or unexpected difficulty, and therefore estimates additional work time is needed, record the increase on the chart. Conversely, if they experience a break-through that substantially decreases the estimate of work remaining, record that information.

The trend line that emerges becomes a powerful visual communicator of the team's progress towards the iteration goal. The **power of this simple chart** lies in the clarity with which it articulates the project's two most important numbers – **how much work remains** and the **net-net rate of progress** against the project scope including all changes and challenges.

The burn-down chart can be used to forecast the figurative probability of completing the entire scope by the end of the iteration and the figurative probability of particular stories being completed. The term figurative probability used here means a pseudo-scientific, non-calculated visual forecast where the result bears a strong correlation to the outcome of the much more effort-intensive statistical approach. Taking a ruler or straight-edge and drawing a line that projects the current trend into future until the horizontal X-axis is crossed, allows one to see the most probable point in time for completing the entire scope. Then, if one desires to see which stories will be complete at a specific point or when a specific story will be done, plot a vertical line that intersects the trend line at the point representing that story in the prioritized iteration backlog. (See Figure 7.10.)

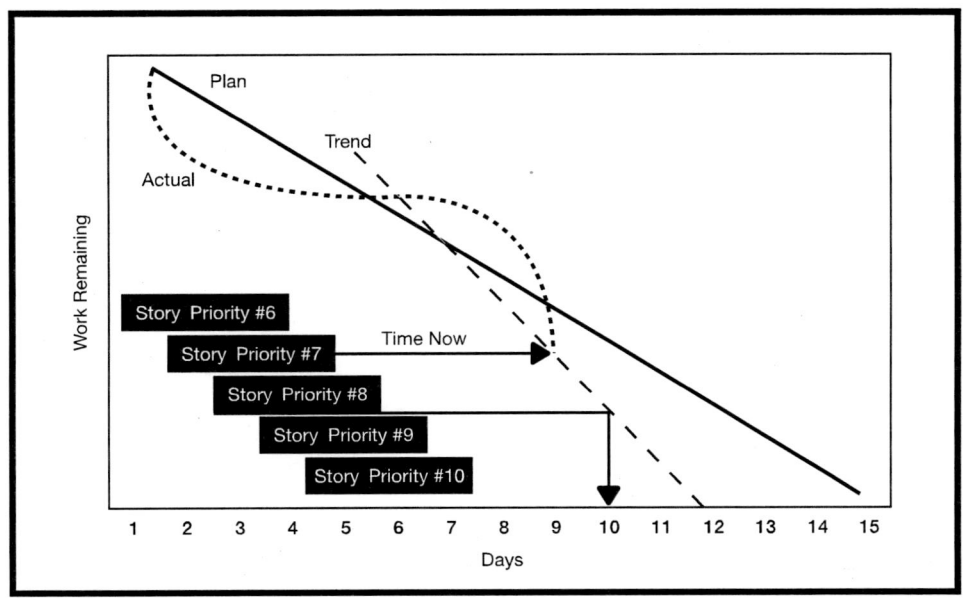

Figure 7.10 Forecasting on a Burn-Down Chart.

Figure 7.10 shows that at Time Now, the current point in time being reported, the story that was prioritized as seventh out of ten is nearly complete. We can also forecast that Story #8 will be completed on day 10 and that the whole project scope will be finished 3 days early.

Alternately, typical burn-up charts show the features or deliverables for the current release and plot the sum of completed ones using similar, simple math. They can also forecast the figurative probabilities of desired results.

Using burn charts implies the existence of a Task Board – typically a physical one for colocated teams or an electronic one for remote, distributed teams.

Creating and Using Task Boards

Task boards (or story boards) are used by teams during their daily meetings to focus their discussion on the topics needed to synchronize their work efforts. They also provide a convenient visual radiator of the project's work organization as well as how much work is left. In a sense, it is the narrative that explains the quantitative results shown on the burn chart.

Because the primary duty of the task board is to enable team synchronization, it must be designed with the flexibility to allow self-organization of their work. As the project progresses, many tasks and stories are in the backlog and, by definition, not assigned to specific individuals. When a team member finishes a task and has bandwidth available, they volunteer to do a specific task next. Typically they announce and explain their planned choice in the days before they anticipate the additional bandwidth becoming available (usually because they are finishing a task or because another project or burden has been removed). Other team members express concurrence or make alternate suggestions until a mutually agreeable decision is made. By being easily visible and flexible, the task board helps the team see which tasks are being worked and which are available to choose.

Task boards can be corkboards, whiteboards or even walls, windows, cubicle dividers or the backs of files cabinets with columns delineated using masking tape. The central design element of the task board is the column. Columns define the process steps or development stages which tasks or stories pass through from backlog to completion.

The tasks or stories are written on sticky notes or cards and they are fixed, taped or pinned in the backlog column.

Then they move, in the western or American convention, from left to right as they progress towards completion. If they encounter difficulties, they can be moved in the opposite direction and return to a prior process step for rework. Many enhancements can be added to the basic card convention, including color-coded cards to signify specific feature groups or priorities, sizing or estimate information, and prioritization information.

In Figure 7.11, a typical task board shows columns for Backlog, Development, Test & UAT, and Completed. For this team and this project, those were judged to be the categories needed to enable proper synchronization and self-organized planning. They also represent a continuum of progress that the average stakeholder can decipher to understand the state of the project and correlate it to the burn chart usually displayed nearby.

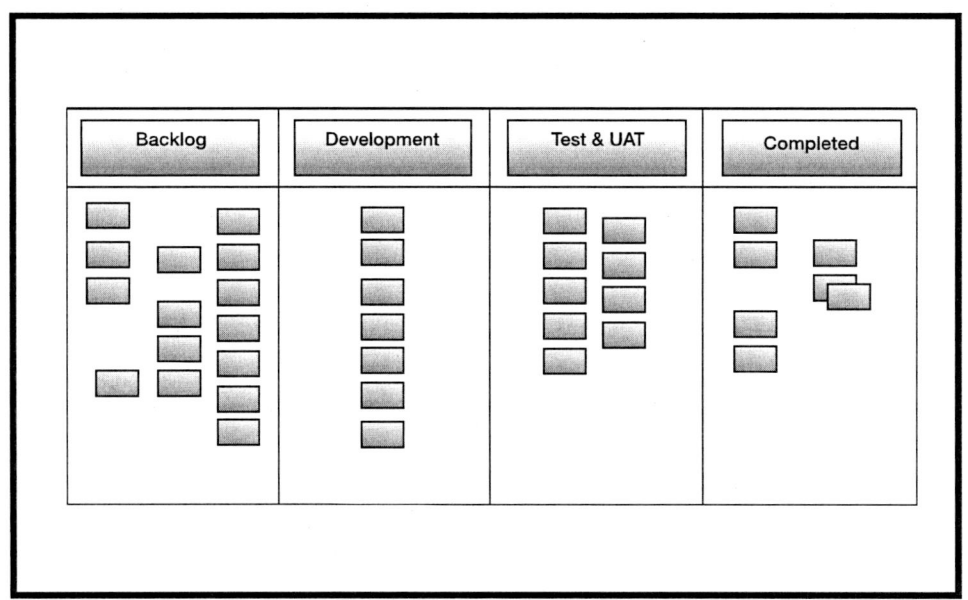

Figure 7.11 A Typical Task (or Story) Board.

Because user stories can have a one-to-many relationship with tasks, some teams will choose to have stories in the backlog, but more detailed tasks in the other columns. When they do this, some teams include numbering or color-coding to identify the task to the story or person doing the work. Other teams use nested naming conventions and initials on the in-process tasks. The key is to create visibility into work that is being finished and what has been selected to work on next.

A best practice for maintaining low WIP, good cycle time, and efficient processing is to limit each team member to no more than two cards at a time. If they hit an impediment working on any one task, they can switch to the other task until the impediment is removed, thereby maintaining *personal* efficiency. Alternately, when any other *team* member finishes a task, they have the flexibility to begin working on the next highest priority task in the queue, thereby maintaining team efficacy. At all times, team members should be encouraged to adjust estimates for work remaining on any task as new information and insight is gained. That may even mean "splitting" a task card into multiple, differentiated tasks, each with a separate estimate where the sum of the parts is greater than the previous whole.

Electronic task boards for remote, distributed teams accomplish the same purpose as their physical counterparts, and can often be facilitated using a conference call and a spreadsheet such as Excel. Typically the task list (i.e., task board) is maintained on one tab and the estimate values are summarized and graphed on a second tab. The results can then be easily published as a daily PDF, printed and posted in each remote location, and archived for future reference.

As we will discuss in the next section, Kanban boards are a specific type of task board applying additional processing disciplines.

Understanding and Using Kanban Boards

Kanban boards are one tool in the continuous improvement culture that is part of the agile ethos. We delve into continuous improvement in more detail at the end of this chapter, but here we will explain Kanban boards as part of the Adaptive Planning knowledge area. **Kanban boards are a visual management system utilizing a single-piece, pull-driven flow to limit WIP and increase throughput.** They enable a process for managing the team dynamic so the unpredictable finish times of predecessor tasks and flux of actual task durations don't needlessly impede the team's productivity and throughput.

In order to use a Kanban board, a value stream map must exist or be created. The Kanban board is organized using columns that represent the value stream. Figure 7.12 shows the **Product Backlog** column flowing into a value stream that is mapped from **Analysis & Prep** through **Deploy** and includes the respective queues where stories are held until they are pulled by a team member into the next step.

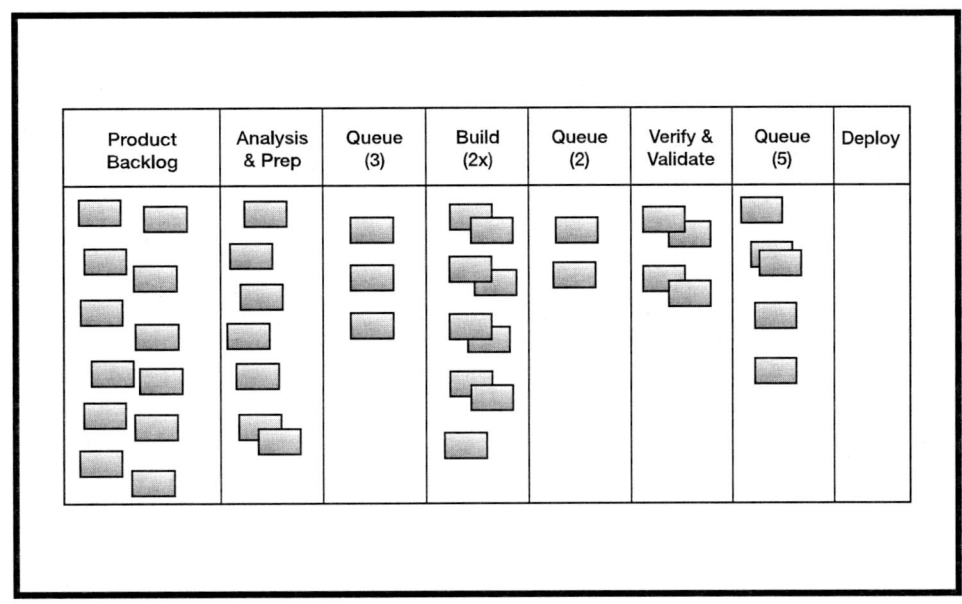

Figure 7.12 Kanban Board Based on a Value Stream Map.

Starting with the first queue, the WIP limit is denoted in parenthesis. The **Build** step notes that the WIP limit is two (2) per team member, and the stacked cards belong to a single team member so it can be seen that this team has 5 builders or developers. It can also be seen that this team has two (2) members doing the ***Verify & Validate*** work with a 2x WIP limit. The final queue has a WIP limit of five (5) and when it is reached, or a smaller group of related stories that can be deployed are available, the team identifies which members are needed for the deployment activities and deployment is done.

Kanban recognizes that teams are cross-functional by design, and Agile Project Management means that people with different skills are working together to produce potentially shippable increments of product features. They don't write unneeded specifications or build unneeded features, but they do deploy those needed features at the most responsible moment. Kanban utilizes the team's knowledge to make intelligent choices, pulling the most appropriate piece of work into the process at each step in the system. The goal is to create and apply a process allowing the team to make sequencing decisions at the last responsible moment in order to minimize risk and deliver at the lowest incremental cost.

In order to accommodate the reality of "classes of service" existing in some organizations, the Kanban process is sometimes modified or tailored to include color-coding for variables such as time, risk, or policy sensitivities. Those variables are additional elements the team considers when making intelligent decisions about pull choices.

Kanban and task boards, as well as burn charts, can be used at the release level. When being used at the release level, they typically depict information with MMF granularity.

Task boards and Test-driven Practices

Test-driven practices, which we will discuss next, are a preferred, if not required, enabler of Agile Project Management. Task and Kanban boards support this need.

Whether a value stream map underpins the board or not, one or more columns in the process will usually articulate acceptance testing needs. By defining the high-level metrics as well as the conditions that satisfy each metric of a story during iteration planning, the team has laid the groundwork for designing the needed acceptance tests. The team should be encouraged to design the acceptance tests before development or building begins.

Apply Test-driven Practices

The conditions for customer/proxy satisfaction with a user story are essentially the high-level acceptance tests. It is very beneficial for developers if they can refer to specific examples of how a business rule or product function is expected to work.

Because that is true, it is a best practice to require that the tests be specified before stories or cards are moved to the development or build column. Often times the board will include a column, such as Tests Written, as a visible reminder to the team that specifying acceptance tests are required before building begins.

Imbed Test-driven/Test-first/Acceptance Test-driven Practices

With all of the emphasis on the importance of cycle-time and WIP, you might think measuring and improving throughput was the goal. Actually, it is a means to the goal of stabilizing the system so waste can be reduced.

Drawing on its Lean roots, Agile Project Management takes the "Plan-Do-Check-Act" (PDCA) cycle and implements it using test-driven practices. PDCA requires teams to work using a defined plan of execution based on solid principles, guided by experience, and continuously refined with lessons learned. Thus, the most desirable solutions emerge from the disciplined process.

Test-driven practices support the emergent designs required by agile through inspection and adaptation using the iteration planning, execution, retrospective ceremonies. As the team sees the results their plan is producing, it enables them to validate the accuracy of their understanding of the work involved. They can then re-plan the iteration or revise the process accordingly. The test-driven mindset should become such a part of the team's work process that non-development activities, like a business analyst's interview process, become test-driven for results and gets adjusted when the acceptance criteria results do not have the usefulness expected.

One key to get TDD adopted by an organization is to identify the general and specific benefits expected from applying emergent design techniques. To paraphrase what was stated in Chapter 2, emergent design is the team's internal creative work process that delivers design artifacts, which are more than the sum of the parts. It cannot be done by rote or by accident, it must be intentional. The choice to acknowledge the reality of a cone of uncertainty and the need for a dynamic team process to move through it to find the best solutions, is a starting point for identifying the benefits of emergent design. Another source for identifying the benefits is the idea that quality assurance (QA) is responsible for preventing defects, not merely finding them leading to the use of test-driven practices in the process.

By moving QA to the front of the build process, the team eliminates many of the communication disconnects that cause delays, defects, and waste. Understanding and applying agile design patterns and test-driven practices enables the team to design change-tolerant architecture. Test-driven practices help developers recognize how their work will perform and integrate into the whole so they can insure high-quality results with minimal waste. Test-driven practices give the team the confidence to embrace needed, even aggressive, design changes when circumstances cause them to emerge because they know the architecture can support them. But, test-driven practices will also require the organization to commit to automated testing tools in order to allow the extensive verification and validation needed as changes emerge and adjustments are implemented.

Test-driven development, with its emphasis on design patterns and refactoring, enables organizations to design mock-ups against tests, refactor them against design patterns, and subject them to continuous integration tests creating an emergent design that has significantly less risk, problems and cost during the deployment and post-implementation phases. In fact, classical TDD is primarily about reducing technical risk.

With **Agile Project Management**, the new perspective of **test-driven development is to reduce both market and technical risk.** Reducing market risk is the far bigger financial driver because properly identifying the MMF and delivering it quickly can increase both margin and market share. Reducing technical risk, while not insignificant, serves the purpose of protecting brand value and reducing the costs of rework or retrenchment. Using acceptance tests to drive development reduces both risks simultaneously.

This newer perspective has led to a – dare we say, emerging – best practice where writing tests starts with the top-level acceptance test and decomposes them into unit tests, instead of starting with unit tests and assembling them into acceptance tests. Doing it the new way helps insure tests cover all the functions the solution needs to include.

Another emergent design tool is Agile Modeling.

Agile Modeling

As was noted in Chapter 2, **Agile Modeling (AM)** is a tool used in conjunction with an agile framework to create models for software development projects. It is intended to be an effective, light-weight approach that is tailored *into* a framework such as Scrum, XP, or Lean. AM creates effective models that support development of solutions using a performance-based approach.

The basic AM principle is to create multiple models in small increments, because any given model is bound to include some inaccuracies, and use them to learn and iterate so the best possible solution will emerge. The practice is to create an abstract representation of the software then prove or disprove its performance with code that actually works or does not work. Using the results or artifacts from each model, the team improves its understanding of the situation, then iterates to an improved model expecting better artifacts to emerge again. What follows is a continuous march towards a more usable solution with each cycle. Active stakeholder participation in AM is critical because the project stakeholders know what the result of a successful model will be and can provide the feedback needed to improve each one.

The principle of *applied simplicity* is used in AM to focus on only creating models that address the current facet of the problem, avoiding large, detailed, unwieldy models. The principle of open communication is practiced in AM by displaying models on walls or wikis, embracing collective ownership of artifacts, following modeling standards, and using group-based model development practices.

AM suggests doing just enough modeling to understand the scope of the problem and the architecture of possible solutions, then using development iterations to improve those models until a solution emerges that can be developed and deployed.

Wireframes

Wireframes are visual guides starting with a skeletal structure or framework, layering on additional facets of the desired solution. The concept of wireframes comes from the website development world where fast, emergent designs are a mandatory part of succeeding. They are an analogy similar to an electrical schematic or building blueprint.

A website wireframe depicts page layout and content arrangement, and may include information about user interface elements and navigational options. By definition, a wireframe usually does not include typefaces or styles, color combinations or palettes, or graphical schemes and images. The focus is functionality, behavior, and prioritization of content to be displayed. Wireframes can be delivered as drawings and sketches on a non-electronic media or produced using a broad array of free or commercial applications.

Generically, wireframes – whether for a website or a construction project – focus on:

- Categories or types of information to be communicated
- Prioritization of information and functions to be shared
- Range or variety of functional choices to be managed
- Guidelines or rules that govern what information is shared and how

Wireframes are an effective tool for rapidly prototyping partial solutions in an emergent design approach to finding the full solution. They facilitate measurement of the pragmatic, practical concerns of various design concepts in a fast and cost effect manner. Wireframes make intangible concepts tangible enough to apply clear evaluation criteria – that is acceptance tests – without the challenge of building the full solution.

Embracing these various types of adaptive planning techniques and tools requires a team to operate at a peak level. Helping the team sustain peak performance capability is also part and parcel of the Agile Project Manager's role.

Nurture Team Performance

Nurturing the team goes beyond facilitating it. To review, in Chapter 6 it was noted that several keys to succeeding in the facilitator role include:

- Removing roadblocks and obstacles to enable the team to get the work done.
- Focusing on being a liaison between the team and the goals while avoiding getting involved in the work tasks.
- Facilitating, not running, team meetings.

In the execution phase being covered, we need to recognize how metrics and performance awards can be productive or counterproductive. To use a well-recognized analogy, some companies have incentivized sales people for systems sold, only to discover when the company was losing money on the system sold, they should have been rewarding on systems installed profitably.

Agile project teams are typically composed of very bright, highly motivated individuals. Metrics or rewards focused only on part of the value stream, or on the wrong part of the value stream, are often counterproductive because the bright, motivated team will optimize the variable being rewarded. They will do so even if it sub-optimizes the organizations strategic goal. Therefore, a professional Agile Project Manager must be aware and intelligent about structuring metrics that foster and nurture the team's performance.

It is critically important to integrate individual metrics and team metrics so that team members are motivated to contribute on both levels. Metrics for the individual's contribution can include things like contributing during team meetings, communicating in constructive, non-demeaning ways, and timely high-quality work products. Metrics for the team's performance can include things like how well the team's dynamic works, team meeting effectiveness, ability to implement participatory problem-solving and decision making techniques, and delivering potentially shippable iteration goals.

It is also important to understand common challenges that cause teams to fail so that the Agile Project Manager can remain vigilant and enable the team dynamic. **Internal things** to watch out for include:

- Team members don't really commit to the iteration goals and reaching them.
- Team members can't reconcile differences or resolve interpersonal conflict.
- Team members are vague during the daily planning meetings.
- The team's daily meetings don't produce synchronization.
- Team members avoid using influence to get support from key stakeholders.

External things to watch out for include:

- Departmental or other project workload overwhelming a team member's capacity.
- Management behavior that is incongruent with agile principles and behaviors.
- Compensation incentives not aligned to both teamwork and individual work.
- Managers exerting inappropriate control over team members.
- Organizational churn causing frequent changes in the team.

Experience has shown that **at least five factors are highly correlated to team success, including:**

- On-going training – even if it is informal and done by the Agile PM acting as a team mentor – reinforcing team participation skills used to plan and achieve the iteration goals.
- Maintaining osmotic communication within the team, and visual controls with the organization so the team does not become isolated.
- Top management support as a "champion" is critical to team success because it creates a climate conducive to the team developing and maturing.
- Team member inter-accountability for measurable progress in reasonable time towards achievement of the iteration goals.
- Standards for supportive team behavior, such as cooperation, patience, participatory decision making, which are directed at work activities and goals.

There are many agile metrics that can be used depending on the processes being implemented. They include:

- *Velocity.* It is simple to measure and can be assessed, for example, as the improvement over the average of the last seven iterations, minus the highest and lowest values in the sample.
- *MMFs Delivered.* This metric would be more valuable to the business, but can be trickier to measure because it is very dependent on how the customer/proxy defines the MMF.
- *WIP Improvement.* This can be measured as change in WIP limits or total WIP. Cycle time has many more external variables, but WIP is within team control.
- *Sizing or Estimation Variance.* This may sound a little heretical and traditional, but studying the variances between estimates and actuals, and then attempting to control the variance can have many benefits.

Remember that trying to compare a team's metrics against a standard or the performance of another team is fraught with failure. The goal is to help the team understand itself and its process then enable continuous, measurable improvement. **The Agile Project Manager must be part coach, part mentor, and adept at resolving conflict.** Nothing more, nothing less will do in fulfilling the mandate to cultivate team performance.

Enhance Risk Management

As was explained in Chapter 6, risk management in an agile framework is primarily organic. That means that during project execution, the technical best practices that agile provides, such as short iterations, test-first development, and continuous integration, are simply not optional. Whether the agile framework is being used for software development, pharmaceutical discovery or aerospace engineering, it does not limit the inherent complexity of the project, with all of its nonlinear beauty. Instead, the framework rationalizes the way risk is handled, especially as project size escalates.

Enhancing risk management means taking the agile technical best practices and tailoring them to the specific project and environment where the Agile Project Manager is leading.

Simplify Problem Solving

Organic risk management begins with the *science of simplicity,* the art of maximizing the amount of work not done, by eliminating what is not needed and focusing on only what is essential. On so many levels, the ancient maxim, "Less is more!" is true. There is less risk, less cost, and less maintenance required on a project with ten functions than a project with more than ten functions. Moreover the difference, the escalation, is not linear.

Agile frameworks embrace the science and art of simplicity by helping the customer/proxy clarify what the key functions are one iteration at a time. With each iteration, the customer/proxy moves farther through the cone of uncertainty and achieves greater clarity about what is truly needed. The cost and risk associated with developing possibly unneeded functions is postponed until a need is clearly established or development is not done. If a feature isn't essential to the product, it does not get built.

Incorporate Continuous Integration

Historically, integration was infrequent during development and integration issues were discovered late in the process, raising the cost and difficulty of fixing them, often logarithmically. The risk mitigation solution is continuous integration, which is familiar in software development circles, but because it is based on the principle of testing early and often, it can be tailored for many situations.

Continuous integration in software development requires developers to continually integrate their work to verify that recent changes haven't broken the base code. Continuous integration also requires the entire team work on the same version of the base code.

The same concepts – frequently checking the effect of changes against a baseline and having the entire team working from the same set of plans – can be applied in many non-software development environments.

Integrating each and every change requires discipline, but enables the goal of technical excellence through good design and agility. Technical excellence is essential to unlock a truly agile development process. The extensible designs and architectures made possible create product with market advantage precisely because they are created in an evolutionary manner. Continuous integration is essential for agile frameworks to produce products with the assurance that they will work after each change.

In software development, continuous integration requires automated testing tools in order to ensure that refactoring can occur. In other settings, the testing tools and processes may need development and definition. But the **most significant facet of adopting continuous integration is getting the teams to see the value and agree to the discipline required to integrate on a frequent (possibly every few hours) basis.** Agreement is the key to adopting continuous integration because there's no way to force adequate compliance.

The most successful way to get agreement and commitment is to describe how much aggravation and work it will save the team. The success of continuous integration hinges on a simple truth. Reducing the scope where possible errors can "hide" is the trick to making them easy to find. Doing so, in turn, is the key to being able to quickly develop radically innovative and elegant solutions.

Consider this simple proof. If the software (or design or pump) worked five minutes ago, then only actions or changes taken in the last five minutes could be the cause of it failing now. Therefore, finding the problem is reduced to figuring out the impact of those changes made in the last five minutes.

The agile framework that most requires continuous integration is XP. A best practice is to adopt it first on brand-new projects where it will be the easiest to do. It will require the installation of a version control system during the first iteration then the new practice can begin. If XP is introduced on an existing project, a common problem is that the tests and build may not be good enough to sustain continuous integration. Because this topic has been covered extensively by other authors, we will limit our discussion of the specifics here.

If adoption of continuous integration practices is desired in other fields, the following guidelines will help with developing the environment specific practices:

- Work must be "ready to deploy," "ready to roll out" or "ready to mock-up for analysis" every few hours requiring the team to have an integration protocol that is mandatory and aligned to the correct frequency.

- Adequate infrastructure and technical resources must be available to maintain "the build" and tests at a standard of live, up-to-date, and aligned to the correct frequency. Attempting continuous integration without a version control system will be painful.

- A dedicated "sandbox" or "destructive and non-destructive" testing facility with the latest baseline must be available and maintained, even if it must be scheduled for use with restoration time required between uses.

- The team must develop a "mantra" or "esprit de corps" centered on integrating every time they make a significant change or create something the rest of the team may want right away. This may include a rule that integration, at a minimum, must occur daily before the end of the day.

- An "integration token" is a required part of the process because it manages the queue of changes to the baseline.

- Continuous integration doesn't work well with large teams because too much time is wasted waiting to integrate. Use smaller teams on independent subsets or use private branches in the version control system if the team cannot be subdivided.

Each time an integrationist done it should emulate the real environment as closely as possible. The goal is to make "Go Live!" an ordinary event, so that when the "live fire drill" occurs it is a nonevent (except for the celebration afterwards, of course).

Risk-based Spike

Usually spikes are needed when the team doesn't have enough information to adequately estimate a story or a task. The common practice is to create two story cards – a spike and a placeholder with a WAG estimate of the duration.[7] The spike helps the team learn enough to determine a rational estimate to replace the WAG.

Chapter 3 noted scanning reduced risk by proactively gathering information early enough in the process to make desirable changes while it was still inexpensive to do so. Scanning may identify assumptions, future decision points, or design questions where performing short experiments will provide the insight needed to identify the last responsible moment to make a decision as well as clarify what options are feasible.

A *spike* is a task, a short experiment, included in an iteration plan carried out to gain knowledge about a specific question. Usually the team doesn't have enough information to adequately estimate a story or a task, so two story cards are created – a spike and a placeholder with a WAG estimate of the duration.[8] The spike helps the team learn enough to determine a rational estimate to replace the WAG.

For intangible-product projects, like software, the experiments usually take the form of simple, throw-away code. For tangible-product projects, like hardware development, experiments usually take the form of engineering mock-ups, prototypes, or simulations.

In Chapter 6, we noted that overt agile risk management practices are sometimes needed to address organizational concerns where due diligence must be performed to adhere to legal and regulatory requirements. A product feature might have little apparent business value, but there may be regulations mandating its early inclusion in the product. In order to assess its impact on the project, a risk-based spike may be required.

A *risk-based spike* is an experiment specifically designed to assess the probability of an event occurring. For intangible-product projects, the experiment might test for the probability that a database will reach a certain size or that a population subset will exceed the limits set for it. For tangible-product projects, the experiment might test for the probability that the number of days it will take a human body to reject a medical device will exceed a certain time limit or that a certain level of impact will cause damage beyond a desired limit. For either type of project, defining the risk that a key person or resource will be unavailable is another common risk-based spike.

The purpose of a spike is to replace speculation with concrete data about triggering events and the need for mitigation planning so early responses can be developed as alternative project plans. They help the team know when key future decisions must be made in order for the project to adhere to the release plan or roadmap, thus maintaining its schedule.

The purpose of a risk-based spike is to identify the extent to which high risk items can be mitigated through architectural or developmental choices. It answers questions like, "How can the highest risk items be mitigated and what will trigger a response?" or "Have any of the spikes shown that the project is not feasible or won't operate within specifications using the planned architecture?" When the team doesn't know the answer, rather than speculate about it, they should conduct a spike!

The challenge, of course, is finding out how the team can use an experiment to get real data about the probability of making progress. The key is to stay focused on the risk from a practical point of view.

Remember that clearly stated technical questions with narrowly defined experiments limit the time spent speculating and increase the likelihood that the knowledge needed to build a working solution will be found. A best practice rule is to isolate specific facets of the overall risk and design experiments that test each narrowly defined issue and avoid large experiments. Avoid generic experiments and focus on answering specific (technical) questions, stopping the spike as soon as the question is answered.

Ultimately, spikes are an agile learning technique so if the results of the experiment aren't as expected, they are performing their function. The team must ask if its understanding of the risk or technology is wrong. Whether the results are due to unforeseen interactions or structural constraints? Is it possible the story or feature cannot be done at all? Decompose the risk, simplify the experiment, and adapt to the results. Use the spike to learn then clarify the team's understanding.

Risk Burn-down Charts

Burn charts were discussed earlier in this chapter as well as in Chapter 6. Chapter 6 also noted that a risk-adjusted backlog is used when the customer/proxy and key stakeholders define feature priorities with requirements for regulatory or industry best practice compliance that must be included, such as Six Sigma.

Most agile risk management is organic. However, when it is overt, a risk burn-down chart may be needed as a visual control.[9]

The data for a risk burn-down chart is derived using a traditional risk list. Each of the risks being tracked, typically the project's top ones, are assigned a probability value and an impact value. The impact value is the number of days that would be lost if the risk materializes into a problem. The two values are then multiplied to quantify the risk in a single variable – the risk exposure. A baseline, or forecast, is then plotted and each day the sum of the remaining risk exposure is plotted. The results are interpreted the same as with other burn charts. (See Figure 7.13.)

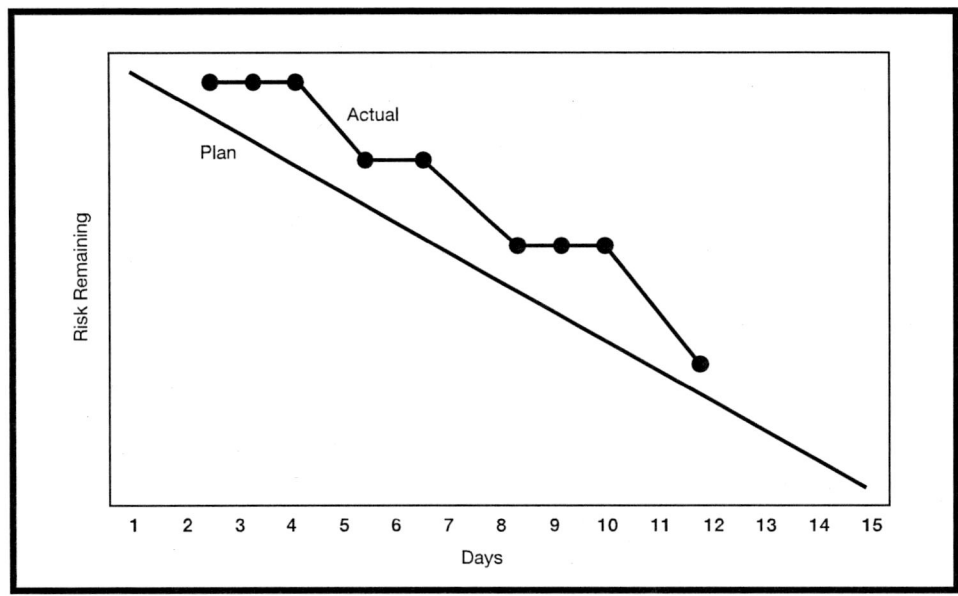

Figure 7.13 A Risk Burn-Down Chart.

Figure 7.13 shows a typical pattern where risk reduction happens in a stair-step pattern because they either exist or do not exist in a dichotomous way.

Verification and Validation

One last risk element deserves mentioning. For agile projects being executed in the government sector or healthcare industry, there is sometimes a requirement for independent validation and verification to be done at the end of the project. The team can think of it as a final user acceptance test or a final customer audit.

When such a requirement exists for the project then the team must adapt typical agile processes to include this need. The team should avoid deciding they are being forced to accept the unreasonable demands of traditional process requirements. Instead the team should integrate these requirements into tailored agile procedures and investigate ways to streamline required activities and eliminate waste so they don't hinder the project.

At some level it just boils down to adapting the what, when and how of communications.

Adapt Communications

Daily Stand-up, Iteration Review, & Team Retrospective Meetings

Daily Stand-up

 The *daily meeting* is sometimes referred to as a daily stand-up, or Scrum, meeting. It is held **primarily to synchronize** the team members' activities. Secondarily, it also provides information for documenting work progress against the iteration plan. The team's daily meeting is part of the feedback cycles that occur in the Agile Project Management process.

Because the core purpose of the meeting is to synchronize the team members' activities, the meeting has a lightweight framework and a few rules, but allows the team to adapt the content exchange to meet their needs.

First of all, it is called a "stand up" meeting because of the practice of having the team stand around the task board for the discussion. The belief is that standing up helps maintain brevity and keep the meeting short and focused.

The framework for the meeting is that it is time-boxed to 15 minutes, facilitated by the Agile Project Manager or Scrum Master, and occurs at the same time and place every day. It is mandatory that every team member attend and participate. Although others can attend and observe, they may not participate.

Second, the pattern of the daily meeting is having the team gather, facing each other, and address remarks on three topics to the rest of the team. Three questions are used to prompt and guide the remarks. They are:

- What have I done since the last daily meeting?
- What will I do between now and the next daily meeting?
- What obstacles are impeding my work performance?

Teams employ a variety of methods to decide who speaks first. Some common ones include 911 (i.e., "I have an emergency/impediment!"), Last In First Up, Round Robin, Pass the Token, Draw Cards, and Walk the Board. Using a variety keeps things from going rote and losing focus.

Lastly, the meeting dynamic is going well when the team is staying focused on the work and not personalities, everyone is arriving on time, and the meeting begins and ends on time. The dynamic is not going well when team members are being vague about their work results, the discussion sidetracks into problem solving, and obstacles aren't be addressed during and removed between the meetings.

Iteration Review Meeting

 The team's iteration review meeting is also part of the Agile Project Management feedback cycle. The *iteration review meeting* occurs at the end of each iteration and is product-centric. The agile team presents the most recently completed work products to all interested stakeholders so they can give feedback on how well it meets their needs and expectations. It provides transparency between the stakeholders' needs and the agile team's work, allowing adaptations to occur when needed.

The iteration review is a collaborative, collective decision-making forum, as well as a review of project metrics and iteration progress. The review meeting requires minimal preparation because only products that have been completed, tested, and meet the acceptance criteria set forth as the iteration goal are demonstrated. No smoke, no mirrors, no PowerPoint presentations about what it will do – just working, potentially shippable solutions.

The meeting begins with the team providing a walkthrough of the completed work, as well as disclosure of expected work that was not completed during the iteration. Optionally, the team may present a review of iteration performance metrics, such as burn charts, velocity metrics, and testing results. This would only be done to help the stakeholders and attendees get a clearer picture of the state of the project.

Then, the attendees ask questions and interact with the work products. That interaction leads to the meeting results. Those results include product feedback, potential updates to the product backlog, and sometimes updates to the release plan.

Team Retrospective Meeting

The team's retrospective occurs at the end of each iteration, like the review meeting, but it process-centric. The agile team worked together to deliver potentially shippable products, but along the way they each saw different things, had different experiences, and ended up with different perspectives of the same iteration. **The retrospective allows them to create a shared understanding of how they worked together and how it affected what they delivered.**

In order for the retrospective to avoid the pitfall of each person staking out their territory to defend, it is critical that the meeting start with the best available facts. Notice that it is the best available, not perfect, data about the iteration metrics. How many features or stories completed versus how many were committed to? What was the team's velocity and how did it compare to the average? Were there changes in team membership? Were any new technologies tested or deployed? Was daily meeting attendance 100%? 100% on time? 100% participation? What do the burn charts show? Other company or industry specific data like software defect counts or the amount of code refactored can be included as well. The point is to encourage the team to refer to artifacts and add to the picture.

Use the data to create visual radiator of the iteration so it is easier for the team to see any patterns and identify linkages. Then, ask the team to do the serious lifting of interpreting the picture. How did the event pattern impact their ability to strive for hyper-productivity or not? What feelings were elicited – both positive and negative – by specific aspects of the pattern? How did that unite the team in productive ways or divide them in unproductive ways? When was the iteration just a job versus exciting as hell versus being caught in hell?

The observations are usually recorded in a three column format. Some of the more common configurations are:

- What Went Well – What To Improve – What We Need To Find Out
- Try – Keep – Stop
- Fears – Hopes – Expectations
- Do the Same – Do More – Do Less
- Enjoyable – Frustrating – Puzzling

The iteration retrospectives a cooperative, concerted effort to create a forum to identify opportunities for significant, incremental progress. Saying significant, incremental progress sounds like an oxymoron, but it is the key to the power of the retrospective. The meeting is an invitation to experiment with changes during the next iteration that can achieve a figurative 1% goal. One percent is definitely incremental, but when it is compounded every 2 or 3 or 4 weeks, it becomes an immensely significant return on investment!

As an Agile Project Manager it is critical that mastery of the science and art of retrospectives be achieved. A best practice is to have a Scrum Master or Product Owner, who is not part of the team, act as facilitator so everyone can participate. The worst possible outcome is the "Ho Hum Nothing New" event. The basic structure of the Retrospective is solid and predictable, but the delivery of the event has to be refreshed often enough to keep the team engaged.

The Agile Project Management feedback cycle occurring during these meetings relies on the core concept of osmotic communication.

Osmotic Communication

The agile ethos recognizes that teams must be cross-functional, trusted, and should be colocated, in order to optimize the chance to identify risks and reduce errors. The team's osmotic communication about risks will dramatically affect the success of the project. Unfortunately, this type of good communication does not occur automatically, it must be cultivated.

Osmotic communication happens when team members pick up pieces of conversations occurring in a common area and link them to vital insights, thereby making a meaningful contribution to the discussion.

Face-to-face (F2F) communication is widely recognized as the most effective channel available and therefore is a core element of Agile Project Management. The idea of osmotic communication builds on this truth by suggesting that projects benefit when people with a high need to communicate are in close proximity where they can overhear communications between all parties. This heightens awareness of issues that are current and important so they can be responded to quickly.

The key implication is that team members should be colocated to take advantage of the improved information flow. There is an opportunity cost associated with team members not asking questions. When a team is colocated their very proximity leads them to ask more questions and discover unexpected answers. Direct communication actually lowers the cost of information transfer and ultimately saves time!

Osmotic communication and colocation are not without some limitations however. Foremost among those limits is team size. Both concepts work best with relatively small teams which can be a problem if a large project is involved. The next limitation is personal needs and preferences when doing tasks that require serious unbroken concentration. A best practice for mitigating this challenge is the concept of workspace layout called caves and common room (which was described in Chapter 2). Lastly is the need for occasional privacy to handle personal affairs and the need to sometimes just get away from "the noise." Caves and commons can help, but sometimes a private office is needed.

The forgoing does not mean that agile denies the reality that many projects redelivered by distributed teams. In prior chapters, the challenges to high trust levels fostered by colocation were discussed along with practices for curbing the deterioration experienced by distributed teams. The Agile Project Manager must keep them in mind in order to help distributed teams achieve the best level of communication possible.

That communication becomes a key element in the drive to implement continuous improvement.

Implement Continuous Improvement

 By definition ***continuous improvement*** requires investing the effort and resources required to change from a baseline to a higher or more desirable level of functioning. It can be applied to products, services, or processes. Continuous improvement can seek incremental change over time, which is the agile best practice, or breakthrough change, as is the case in other settings. The technique is to measure processes and improve the customer value delivered by raising effectiveness, efficiency, or flexibility, or a combination of those factors. In order to improve, first it must be measured.

In the Agile Project Management frameworks, backlog grooming is a business-level continuous improvement process while retrospective meetings are continuous improvement at the team dynamic level. In order to improve either, first they must be measured. That means metrics must be defined and tracked.

Track Metrics

Suggested metrics were described previously and some ideas for measurement were implied. The point is that identifying metrics then not tracking them is a recipe for failure. The Agile Project Manager has to have the wisdom to help the team define the metrics, the discipline to track performance against those metrics, and the skill to help the team understand, evaluate and apply that information in order to create a pattern of continuous improvement.

Chapter Close-Out

Agile PM Processes Grid™ Exercise

 Please take out a blank piece of paper, set a timer for no more than 3 minutes, and see how much of the grid you can reproduce from memory. To make the most of this Agile PM Processes Grid™ exercise, please simulate being in the testing environment. Close your book and all your notes. Visualize the Proctor handing you the blank sheets of paper and taking your seat in the testing site. Begin by drawing the grid, 6 columns and 8 rows, and then fill in everything you can. After the 3 minutes ends, use your book and notes to complete the grid. Study it as you do so.

Terminology Matching Exercise

In the blank column to the left of the Term, fill in the letter that identifies the correct definition or description.

	Term		Definition / Description
	1. Spike	A	The start-to-finish time required to complete a potentially shippable increment of the solution.
	2. Agile cycle time	B	The practice of bringing together all of the people, and their insights, needed to define a roadmap that decreases the overall time required to complete the product.
	3. Burn-down charts	C	Proves the relationship between cycle time, WIP, and throughput and a production system in a steady state.
	4. Little's Law	D	A tool that reduces risk due to workload imbalance by spreading it to a more effective and sustainable pace.
	5. Wireframes	E	Shows the work remaining, like number of story points or ideal days, in the project or release.
	6. Kanban boards	F	is a tool used in conjunction with an agile framework to create models for software development projects.
	7. Daily meeting	G	The principle used in agile modeling to focus on only creating models that address the current facet of the problem, avoiding large, detailed, unwieldy models.
	8. Swarming	H	Visual guides starting with a skeletal framework, layering on additional facets of the desired solution.
	9. Cumulative flow diagrams	I	A short experiment, to gain knowledge about a specific question the team needs more information about.
	10. Applied simplicity	J	Visual radiators used by teams during their daily meetings to focus their discussion on the topics needed to synchronize their work efforts.
	11. Task boards	K	Held primarily to synchronize the team members' activities.
	12. Burn-up charts	L	Visual management system utilizing a single-piece, pull-driven flow to limit WIP and increase throughput.
	13. Risk-based spike	M	When team members pick up pieces of conversations occurring in a common area and link them to vital insights, thereby making a meaningful contribution.
	14. Osmotic communication	N	is an experiment specifically designed to assess the probability of an event occurring.
	15. Agile Modeling	O	Shows the work completed, in story points or ideal days for the project or release.

Crossword Puzzle

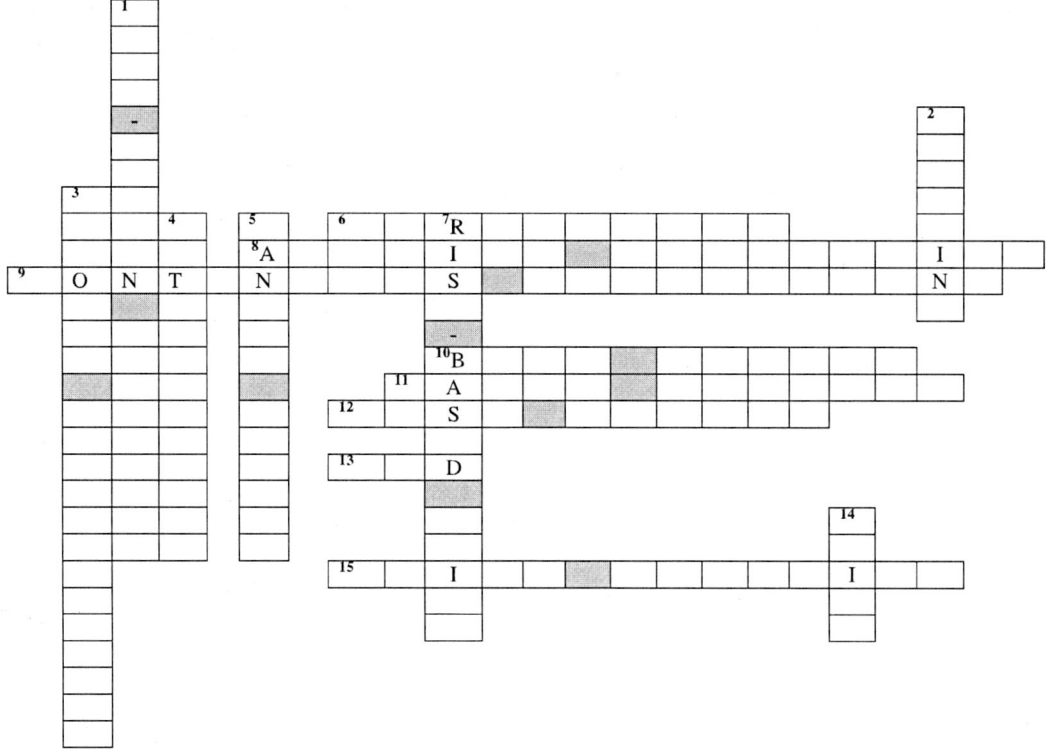

Hints:

ACROSS
- 6 Visual guides starting with skeletal structure or framework, layering on additional facets of the desired solution.
- 8 The principle used in agile modeling to focus on only creating models that address the current facet of the problem, avoiding large, detailed, unwieldy models.
- 9 A technique used to measure processes and improve the customer value delivered by raising effectiveness, efficiency, or flexibility, or combination of those factors.
- 10 Show the work remaining or completed, like number of story points or ideal days, in the project or release.
- 11 Held primarily to synchronize the team members' activities.
- 12 Visual radiators used by teams during their daily meetings to focus their discussion on the topics needed to synchronize their work efforts.
- 13 A tool that reduces risk duet workload imbalance by spreading it more evenly, creating a more effective and sustainable pace.
- 15 A tool used in conjunction with an agile framework to create models for software development projects.

DOWN
- 1 Supports the emergent designs required by agile through inspection and adaptation using the iteration planning, execution, retrospective ceremonies.
- 2 The practice of bringing together all of the people, and their insights, needed to define a roadmap that decreases the overall time required to complete the product.
- 3 Happens when team members pick up pieces of conversations occurring in common area and link them to vital insights.
- 4 Occurs at the end of each iteration, is process-centric, and enables the team to create a shared understanding.
- 5 A visual management system utilizing single-piece, pull-driven flow to limit WIP and increase throughput.
- 7 An experiment specifically designed to assess the probability of an event occurring.
- 14 A short experiment, included in an iteration plan carried out to gain knowledge about a specific question.

Word Search

Word Search - 15 Words to find:

- CFD
- WIREFRAMES
- APPLIED SIMPLICITY
- CONTINUOUS IMPROVEMENT
- DAILYMEETING
- SPIKE
- TASKBOARDS
- TEST-DRIVEN PRACTICES
- BURNCHARTS
- KANBANBOARDS
- SWARMING
- RISK-BASED SPIKE
- OSMOTIC COMMUNICATION
- RETROSPECTIVE
- AGILE MODELING

```
S S E R B I O U N O L S S R I S K - B A S E D _ S P _ I P D
O E S R A D D M A T A S W I R E F R A M E S V A A - A E P C
N T N N E G T G - A M S W A R M I N A L Y _ N B N E T L C N
D S A I N _ I C B S E I E P D T C M _ T C O T S K T B P O O
A A P G K R A E U K D N S _ S N S N I C D A T I S M O C G A
I O R I L G M I A _ T E O I N I A C S W A R M I N G N A P C
L D E C B A O I A B _ M E _ N S I I O O A S A S A O E S A K
Y W T T A S K _ B O A R N N U L N A D H V O E I I R N L C -
_ I R S B R V C E A L V I R P I C D C A _ C B T A A I M U A
M R O A U I O K C R C F D M L O T _ R - I B A H T S S A _ I
E E S K R O T A A D I T I E R C N T D T T C C N I M O B O E
E F P A N I G C K S _ S D V F R G _ C M I _ P T N I V O D A
T R E N _ I F D I P _ O L D U W D A A N N E C D S O U - G R
I A C B C _ S U A D M E O B E I R C U R K A K _ I S S S R L
N M T A H E _ - E _ S E T D T P U M U I R F S D A N R M K E
G E I N A C L I E N E S S O _ C M B P P B T U D E A I O _ C
T S V _ R _ L L C O N T I N U O U S _ I M P R O V E M E N T
G O E B N P I N P I D M E V C I _ N P S Y I A E K R O T P E
T K T O P G I T M C Y V E _ I D E H B I T T E A E S E N N T
I C G A A E P N U S I N C U E V R V I D I S I I I R E P S E
A S R R N I V N D R C I E S I _ I V M N E A S C E K S I P C
Y E C D I O W E D T T W A R D A I L Y _ M E E T L D I I I V
C N T S O S L - T O S B D A G I L E _ M O D E L I N G R K D
E D I R V _ T A M A - - T D K A N B A N _ B O A P O T M E R
E M S _ K S T S T K T F P C I E I C T F K C L N D N O S T E
E L B I E M O P S S O S M O T I C _ C O M M U N I C A T I E
S E O T I K I I E S _ I R A M T _ D R E D F E _ B M A D R O
N E S E A G R T N O P R L H T _ R R E T R O S P E C T I V V
G T E V I T S S I S U M R N T Y S C S G W C N A D P E S K D
C U E Y A N C A _ E D A P L I I G S _ C N V E _ S I E I I O
```

Chapter Practice Test

1. According to "The Scrum Guide," release planning is _____.

   A. Required
   B. Optional
   C. Of minimal impact on project success
   D. Only necessary on larger projects

2. In the agile environment, _____ is defined as the start-to-finish time required to complete a potentially shippable increment of the solution.

   A. Cycle time
   B. A roadmap
   C. Refactoring
   D. A theme

3. All of the following are guidelines to improving cycle time and building the strongest possible processes except _____.

   A. Building the roadmap as a swarm
   B. Defining acceptance metrics for releases and iterations
   C. Involving senior management at the beginning of the planning process
   D. Selecting an iteration length that is sustainable

4. The following are all examples of visual controls except a _____.

   A. Task board
   B. Burn chart
   C. Kanban board
   D. Selection board

5. A task board can best be described as an information radiator that _____.

   A. Shows the highest priority features planned for the product
   B. Shows the tasks or stories that remain to be completed versus time
   C. Defines the process steps or development stages which tasks or stories pass through from backlog to completion
   D. Shows the tasks or stories that have been completed versus time

6. _____ can be described as a tool used in conjunction with an agile framework to create models for software development projects.

   A. Agile modeling
   B. Refactoring
   C. Skirting
   D. Force field analysis

7. One risk mitigation technique used in the agile environment is _____ which requires developers to continually integrate their work to verify that recent changes haven't broken the base code.

   A. Refactoring
   B. Continuous integration
   C. WIP limits
   D. The task board

8. A task or short experiment included in an iteration plan carried out to gain knowledge about a specific question can best be described as a _____.

   A. Burn chart
   B. Value target
   C. Story point
   D. Spike

9. _____ is a meeting that can best be described as being held primarily and foremost to synchronize the team members' activities.

   A. Team retrospective
   B. Iteration review
   C. Daily stand up
   D. Monthly project review

10. A meeting that is product-centric, presents the team's most recently completed work products, and provides transparency between the stakeholders' needs and the agile team's work can best be described as a(n) _____.

    A. Monthly project review
    B. Team retrospective
    C. Iteration review
    D. Daily stand up

11. A meeting that is process-centric and allows the team to create a shared understanding of how they worked together and how it affected what they delivered can best be described as a(n) _____.

    A. Daily stand up
    B. Team retrospective
    C. Monthly project review
    D. Iteration review

12. When co-located team members pick up pieces of conversations occurring in a common area and then link them to vital insights thereby making a meaningful contribution to the discussion, we can say that _____ is taking place.

    A. Osmotic communication
    B. Face to Face (F2F) communication
    C. Bi-directional communication
    D. Refactoring

13. _____ is widely recognized as the most effective channels of communication available and is a core element of agile project management.

   A. Refactoring
   B. Osmotic communication
   C. Bi-directional communication
   D. Face to Face (F2F) communication

14. _____ is (are) an example of continuous improvement in an agile environment.

   A. Team retrospectives
   B. Osmotic communication
   C. Release planning
   D. Burn charts

15. When employing the technique of agile modeling, the principle of _____ is used to focus on only creating models that address the current facet of the problem thereby avoiding large, detailed, unwieldy models.

   A. Osmotic communication
   B. Applied simplicity
   C. Refactoring
   D. Progressive elaboration

16. A burn-up chart can best be described as an information radiator that _____.

   A. Shows the highest priority features planned for the product
   B. Shows the tasks or stories that remain to be completed versus time
   C. Defines the process steps or development stages which tasks or stories pass through from backlog to completion
   D. Shows the tasks or stories that have been completed versus time

17. An experiment or task specifically designed to assess the probability of an event occurring is best described as a(n) _____.

   A. Spike
   B. Sprint
   C. Risk based spike
   D. Retrospective

18. A burn-down chart can best be described as an information radiator that _____.

   A. Shows the highest priority features planned for the product
   B. Shows the tasks or stories that remain to be completed versus time
   C. Defines the process steps or development stages which tasks or stories pass through from backlog to completion
   D. Shows the tasks or stories that have been completed versus time

19. _____ is the process of reviewing, adding, deleting, and re-prioritizing stories such that resources are expended only on stories that are considered of high value to the customer.

   A. Backlog grooming
   B. Refactoring
   C. Review meeting
   D. Osmotic communication

20. In an agile framework, the definition of _____ is the start-to-finish time required to complete a potentially shippable increment of the solution.

   A. Theme
   B. Cycle time
   C. Timebox
   D. Scope box

Answers – Terminology Matching

1:I, 2:A, 3:E, 4:C, 5:H, 6:L, 7:K, 8:B, 9:D, 10:G , 11:J , 12:O , 13:N ,14:M , 15:F

Answers – Crossword Puzzle

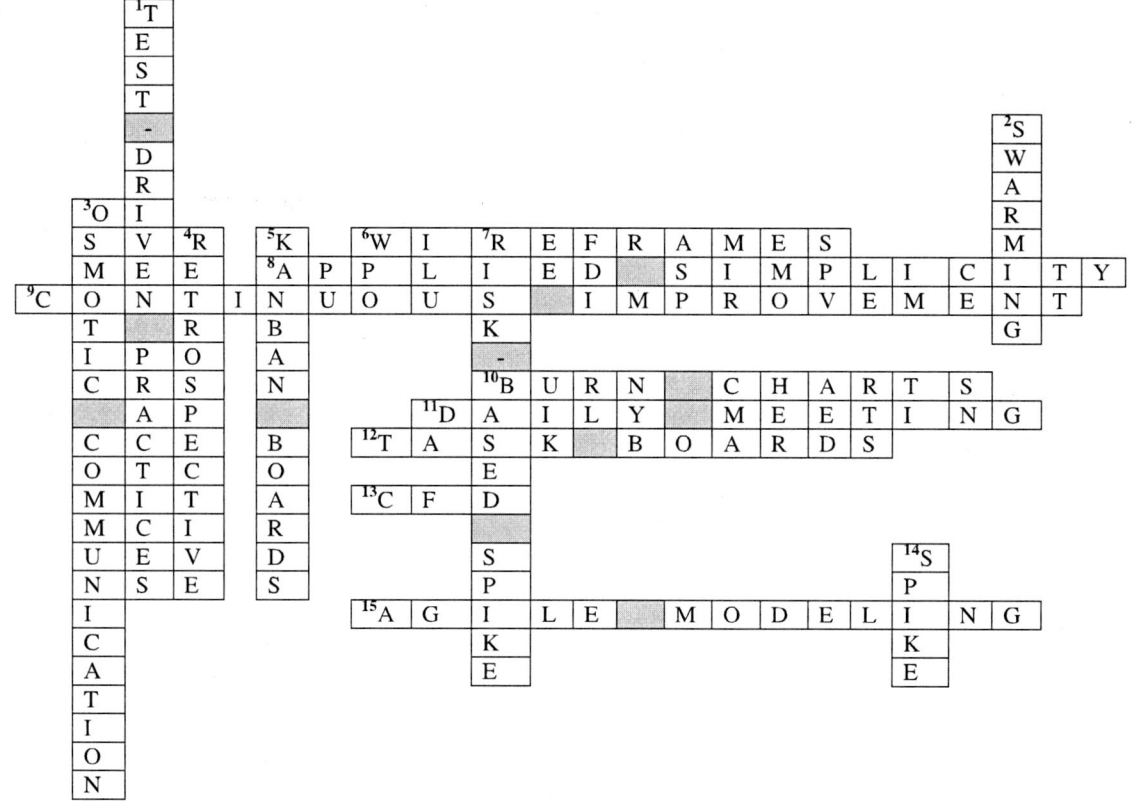

Answers – Word Search

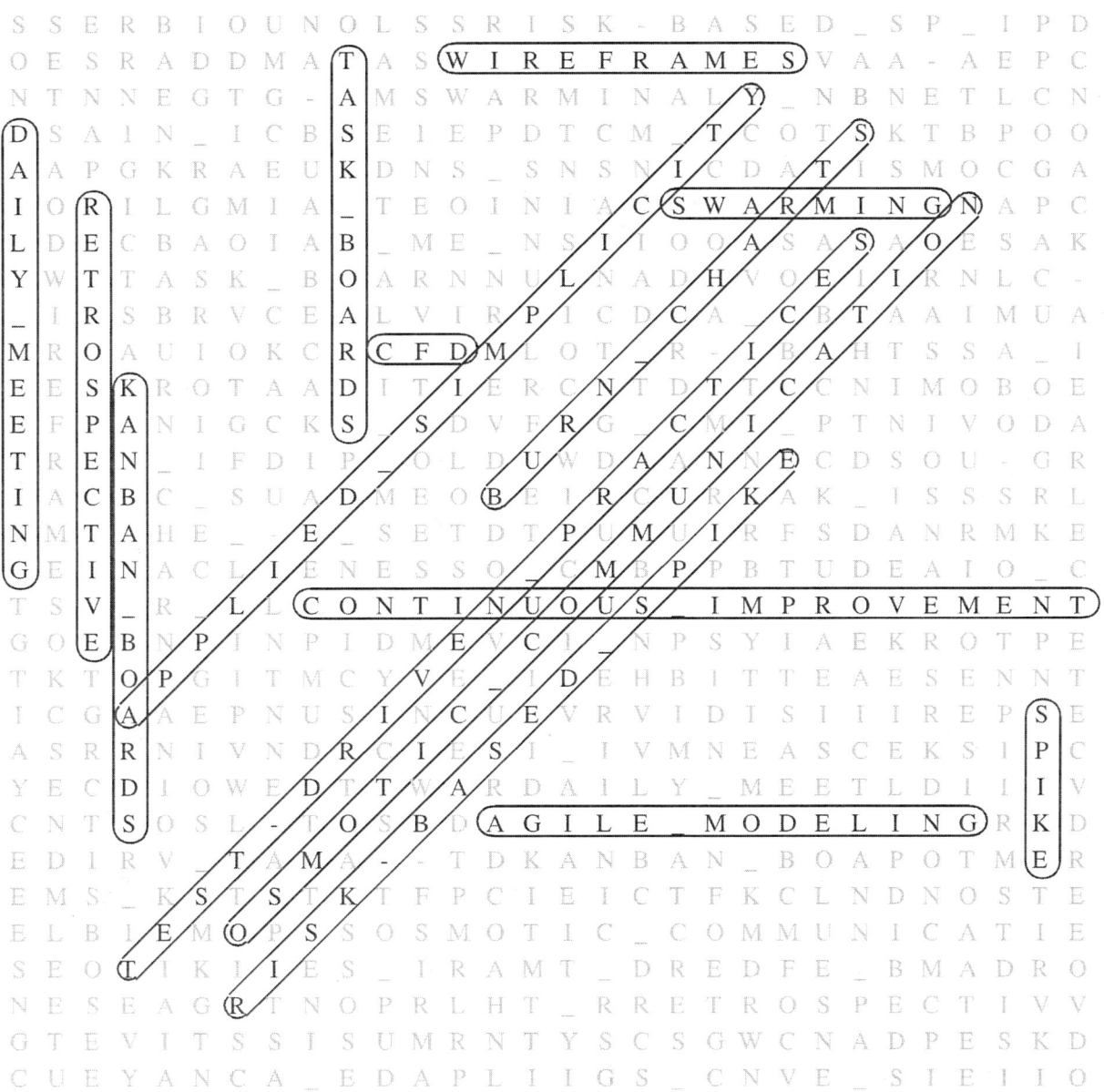

Answers – Practice Test

1. **B.** The lack of good release planning is rampant in parts of the agile community who seem to reject it as unnecessary. The Scrum Guide states that release planning is entirely optional but then goes on to say that starting work without its artifacts will become an impediment to resolve. It seems many agile practitioners see "entirely optional" and miss the serious warning that follows it. Teams can get caught up in an iteration-plus-backlog-only mindset and not invest in the planning needed for an entire release or project.

2. **A.** The definition of cycle time in an agile framework is narrower than in Lean. For agile, *cycle time* is the start-to-finish time required to complete a potentially shippable increment of the solution.

3. **C.** To improve cycle time and build the strongest possible processes remember these guidelines: Build the roadmap as a swarm, define acceptance metrics for releases and iterations, and select an iteration length that is sustainable.

4. **D.** Visual controls invite management to help detect early when there are problems impeding progress toward the iteration or release goals. Visual controls used to display project information include product vision boxes, product backlogs, task boards, release and iteration plans, burn charts, risk/impediment boards, Kanban boards, and team work agreements.

5. **C.** Task boards can be corkboards, whiteboards or even walls, windows, cubicle dividers or the backs of files cabinets with columns delineated using masking tape. The central design element of the task board is the column. Columns define the process steps or development stages which tasks or stories pass through from backlog to completion. The tasks or stories are written on sticky notes or cards and they are fixed, taped or pinned in the backlog column.

6. **A.** Agile Modeling is a tool used in conjunction with an agile framework to create models for software development projects. It is intended to be an effective, light-weight approach that is tailored *into* a framework such as Scrum, XP, or Lean. AM creates effective models that support development of solutions using a performance-based approach.

7. **B.** Historically integration was infrequent during development and integration issues were discovered late in the process, raising the cost and difficulty of fixing them, often logarithmically. The risk mitigation solution is continuous integration, which is familiar in software development circles, but because it is based on the principle of testing early and often it can be tailored for many situations. Continuous integration in software development requires developers to continually integrate their work to verify that recent changes haven't broken the base code.

8. **D.** A spike is a task, a short experiment, included in an iteration plan carried out to gain knowledge about a specific question. Usually the team doesn't have enough information to adequately estimate a story or a task, so two story cards are created – a spike and a placeholder with a WAG estimate of the duration. The spike helps the team learn enough to determine a rational estimate to replace the WAG.

9. **C.** The team's daily meeting is part of the feedback cycles that occur in the agile project management process. The daily meeting is sometimes referred to as a stand-up, or a Scrum, meeting. It is held primarily and foremost to synchronize the team members' activities. Secondarily it also provides information for documenting work progress against the iteration plan.

10. **C.** The iteration review meeting which occurs at the end of each iteration and is product-centric. The agile team presents the most recently completed work products to all interested stakeholders so they can give feedback on how well it meets their needs and expectations. It provides transparency between the stakeholders' needs and the agile team's work, allowing adaptations to occur when needed.

11. **B.** The team's retrospective occurs at the end of each iteration, like the review meeting, but it process-centric. The agile team worked together to deliver potentially shippable products, but along the way they each saw different things, had different experiences, and ended up with different perspectives of the same iteration. The retrospective allows them to create a shared understanding of how they worked together and how it affected what they delivered.

12. **A.** Osmotic communication happens when team members pick up pieces of conversations occurring in a common area and then link them to vital insights thereby making a meaningful contribution to the discussion.

13. **D.** Face-to-face (F2F) communication is widely recognized as the most effective channel available and therefore it is a core element of Agile Project Management. The idea of osmotic communication builds on this truth by suggesting that projects benefit when people with a high need to communicate are in close proximity where they can overhear communications between all parties.

14. **A.** By definition continuous improvement requires investing the effort and resources required to change from a baseline to a higher or more desirable level of functioning. It can be applied to products, services, or processes. In the agile project management frameworks, backlog grooming is a business-level continuous improvement process and retrospective meetings are continuous improvement at the team dynamic level.

15. **B.** The principle of *applied simplicity* is used in AM to focus on only creating models that address the current facet of the problem thereby avoiding large, detailed, unwieldy models. The principle of open communication is practiced in AM by displaying models on walls or wikis, embracing collective ownership of artifacts, following modeling standards, and using group-based model development practices.

16. **D.** Burn charts come in two basic forms, burn-down and burn-up. *Burn-down charts* show the work remaining, like number of story points or ideal days, in the project or release. *Burn-up charts* show the work completed, again in story points or ideal days for the project or release. Burn-down charts are used most often for iterations and typically reflect the results of the team's daily meeting. Burn-up charts are used most often for releases and typically reflect features or deliverables completed.

17. **C.** A ***risk-based spike*** is an experiment specifically designed to assess the probability of an event occurring. For intangible-product projects the experiment might test for the probability that a database will reach a certain size or that a population subset will exceed the limits set for it. For tangible-product projects the experiment might test for the probability that the number of days it will take a human body to reject a medical device will exceed a certain time limit or that a certain level of impact will cause damage beyond a desired limit. For either type of project defining the risk that a key person or resource will be unavailable is another common risk-based spike.

18. **B.** Burn charts come in two basic forms, burn-down and burn-up. ***Burn-down charts*** show the work remaining, like number of story points or ideal days, in the project or release. ***Burn-up charts*** show the work completed, again in story points or ideal days for the project or release. Burn-down charts are used most often for iterations and typically reflect the results of the team's daily meeting. Burn-up charts are used most often for releases and typically reflect features or deliverables completed.

19. **A.** Product backlog grooming, also known as product backlog management, is a just-in-time process that prioritizes and clarifies each backlog item as it moves from the outer edge of the time horizon into the mid-term and then current time horizon. The information about each specific backlog item increases as it nears likely development. Grooming avoids waste by only gathering detailed information as it is needed and usable because most items will change as development progresses and the customer/proxy gains insight.

20. **B.** The definition of cycle time in an agile framework is narrower than in Lean. For agile, ***cycle time*** is the start-to-finish time required to complete a potentially shippable increment of the solution. Cycle time is used to measure the process, not a person, because one person will post faster times than another, possibly untrained, one. The goal is to understand and then improve the process so that reliable, repeatable outcomes minimize variations and the waste that accompanies variances.

Chapter End Notes

[1] In Stephen Covey's book, *7 Habits of Highly Effective People*, Habit 2 is "Begin with the End in Mind."

[2] Source: 2009 Business Analysis Benchmark Report, IAG Consulting, 42 Reads Way, New Castle, DE

[3] The Scrum Guide documents the Scrum framework and is maintained by Scrum's creators, Ken Schwaber and Jeff Sutherland at http://www.Scrum.org/Scrumguides.

[4] Little's Law is a restatement of the work of Danish mathematician Agner Krarup Erlang (1878 – 1929) and named for John Little, an Institute Professor at the Massachusetts Institute of Technology, although he was at Case Western Reserve University when he published the first proof was published in 1961.

[5] Reinertsen, D. G. (2009). *The principles of product development flow: Second generation lean product development*. Celeritas Publishing.

[6] Anderson, D. (2010). *Kanban: Successful evolutionary change for your technology business*. Sequim, WA: Blue Hole Press.

[7] In common parlance, a WAG is short-hand for a Wild Ass Guess while a SWAG is the "scientific" version of a WAG sometimes created by executives on a whiteboard or the back of a napkin.

[8] In common parlance, a WAG is short-hand for a Wild Ass Guess while a SWAG is the "scientific" version of a WAG sometimes created by executives on a whiteboard or the back of a napkin.

[9] Cohn, M. (2010, April 8). *Managing risk on agile projects with the risk burndown chart*. Retrieved from http://blog.mountaingoatsoftware.com/managing-risk-on-agile-projects-with-the-risk-burndown-chart.

CHAPTER 8

Controlling Projects

Chapter Highlights

In Chapter 8, we present the Control process. In doing so, we cover each of the Knowledge and Skills Areas shown in the Agile PM Processes Grid™ (See Figure 2.16).

Because we believe they are so important, two topics that fall within the Control process – Accounting and Contracting Control and Agile Earned Value Management (EVM) – are presented separately in Chapter 9.

External Stakeholders Engagement

Product Demonstration

The ***product demonstration*** is the meeting where the agile team demonstrates working features to the customer/proxy, key stakeholders, and selected end users. The demonstration (or "demo") is actually one segment of three meetings that occur at the end of the iteration – the demo, the iteration review, and the retrospective. The demo is open to all, while the iteration review and the retrospective are restricted to the team. Facilitated by the Agile Project Manager (e.g., Scrum Master), the demo typically covers the following points:[1]

- Meeting participation ground rules
- Features in iteration backlog (i.e., features the team committed to delivering)
- Features completed
- Features not completed *(if any)*
- Additional features added *(if any)*
- Product demonstration of features completed in the *current* iteration

In terms of stakeholder engagement, the demo fosters trust building between the project team and the stakeholders. The agile team gains confidence in delivering a quality product according to schedule. The demo also serves the purpose of keeping the team focused on its deliverables.

For stakeholders, seeing their product vision being realized motivates them to increase their participation in the project. In a sense, the demo may be considered the best project status report the team can provide. Stakeholders become more engaged once they see the commitment of the project team.

In addition to its impact on stakeholder engagement, the product demo has several implications for general project control:

1. The demo is a critical part of agile quality assurance, as scope verification occurs during the meeting.
2. The demo may serve as an inspection point for contractually bound milestone payments.
3. Change requests may result from discussions that occur during the product demo.

Value-Driven Delivery

Product Feedback

In addition to the feedback provided by stakeholders during the product demonstration, there are other venues for ascertaining the value delivered in the iteration.

Let's start with the iteration review and retrospective meetings, both of which are limited to the agile team. During the iteration review, the team focuses on product-centric issues. Typically, project metrics (See Chapter 6) are reviewed and the team spends time interpreting and sharing lessons learned about these metrics. Thus, metrics such as functionality delivered and team velocity *(See Figure 6.11)* provide the team with insight about value delivered and team performance. Finally, the team considers whether additional metrics should be added.

During the iteration retrospective, the team addresses agile process issues and incorporates lessons learned into their practice of agile methods. As previously noted, the learning matrix activity *(See Figure 4.8)* is ideal for closing retrospectives. If changes in agile practice are recommended, measures of success are defined and action items are listed.

Adaptive Planning

Information Radiator Monitoring

As we reviewed in Chapter 6, agile approaches rely upon visual controls, often referred to as information radiators, to communicate the complex, adaptive dependencies that undergird success.

The most common approach to creating visual control boards has been to arrange rows of sized, and sometimes estimated, features into potential iterations derived from the team's velocity. Using these visual representations provides greater clarity in seeing the proposed sequence and facilitates useful discussions between multiple, interdependent teams, typically involved in solution development in large enterprises.

At an enterprise level, visual representations can also be adapted to illustrate technical dependencies across various teams throughout the enterprise so project managers can allocate the incremental deliverables into iterations leading to an optimized release plan. As unsophisticated as this type of simple visual control is, the amount of insight it provides to the organization is impressive. The traceability of shared dependencies through multiple release plans clarifies what is required to make each planned release.

Thus, information radiators may be used to affect control both at the project and enterprise levels.

By providing visibility with enough lead time to support dependency management, the agile portfolio, with its road maps and release plans, can successfully adapt and integrate the work efforts needed to provide the deliverables envisioned by the organization.

Team Performance

Task Board/Burn-down Chart Updates

We have already devoted much attention to story boards *(See Figure 2.9)* and burn-down charts *(See Figure 6.1)*. In this context, we need to reiterate that these tools not only assist the agile team in tracking progress on the current iteration, but also provide a means for planning future iterations and evaluating team performance.

Since the task board and the burn-down chart data feed into calculations of team performance, it is critical the team provides real-time updates so measures of functionality delivered and team velocity may be used to make decisions about subsequent iterations.

Even if they are not explicitly identified by team members during the stand-up meeting, the transparency of the burn-down chart may reveal obstacles. For example, a flat burn down chart means either an obstacle is hindering progress or the team is not updating its remaining work. In this case, the Agile Project Manager needs to facilitate progress by asking pointed questions of the team.

Velocity

Although we have alluded to velocity frequently, let's review some formal definitions. **Velocity** is the number of story points a team can complete in an iteration. There are three ways of estimating velocity: 1) Using historical values; 2) Running an iteration; and 3) Forecasting.[2]

Forecasted velocity is an estimate of team velocity when it is either impossible or impractical for the team to run an iteration and they do not yet have any historical observations. Typically, forecasts are based on the *capacity* of the team, a number based on the estimated productive hours per week that each team member can devote to the project.

 Velocity-driven iteration planning occurs as the team estimates how many story points should be planned into the current iteration based on its actual velocity during recent iterations. Figure 8.1 shows a run chart of team velocity over a series of iterations.

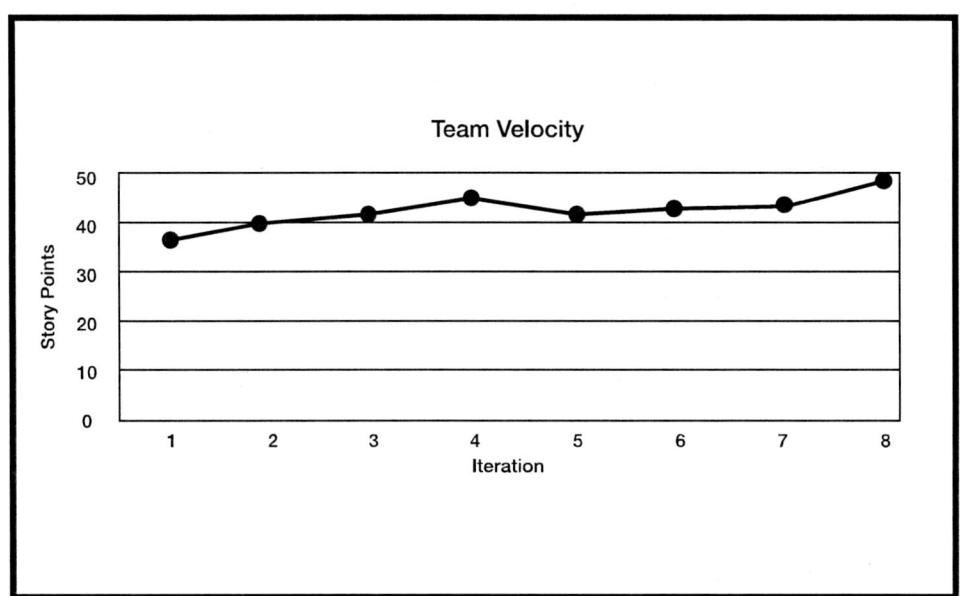

Figure 8.1 Team Velocity by Iteration.

Thus, with each completed iteration, the team acquires more data on how much work it can expect to accomplish in the next iteration. This data is used in subsequent iteration planning.

In our discussion of agile metrics in Chapter 6, we noted that the burn-up chart (Figure 6.10) and indicators of team performance (Figure 6.11; Functionality Delivered and Team Velocity) must be monitored not only to see if the team meets its estimates, but to ascertain what adjustments to future iterations must be made if all estimated work is not completed.

Risk Management

Obstacle Removal

 An obstacle, or impediment, is a situation or event blocking the progress of work during an iteration. For example, an agile team may have functional managers interrupting them constantly and thus preventing them from working on tasks in the ongoing iteration. Since such obstacles threaten the team's commitment to delivering the iteration backlog on time, in Agile Project Management we equate removing obstacles with reducing project risk.

Figure 8.2 presents some common obstacles – sources of risk – during an agile project.

Source	Examples
People	Functional managers, stakeholders, vendors, etc
Process	Breakdowns in the agile process, communications or customer / proxy input
Resources	Insufficient or removal of funding; Instability or inadequacy of team
Technology	Failures in computer hardware or software; Upgrades or changes in technology standards
Organizational	Changes in organizational priorities or strategic busines goals
Legal / Regulatory	Changes in laws or regulations
Enviromental	Geographic distribution of team members increases time and cost of idea transfer; Adverse weather conditions
External Factors	Client changes mind about product or project; Natural disasters

Figure 8.2 Agile Project Obstacles.

In terms of risk management, obstacle removal occurs at two levels – organic and overt. At an organic level, risks are addressed in the daily stand-up meetings, where the agile project manager is responsible for helping to remove obstacles the team cannot negotiate themselves.

Other meetings – release and iteration planning meetings, product demonstrations, reviews, retrospectives, team reflective workshops, and open space meetings – are all appropriate venues for risk management activities on an agile project. Retrospectives and team reflective workshops may reveal problems in the agile process while open space meetings give the team a forum for problem-solving and overcoming obstacles on their own.

During our discussion of information radiators, we presented examples of overt risk management practices. The team starts the risk board *(See Figure 6.2)* during iteration planning and updates it throughout the iteration. Each identified risk is assigned an owner and the risk's status is updated in real-time on the board. A summary risk status report *(See Figure 6.13)* may be included in a project dashboard visual control, so everyone may observe trends, a topic that we will discuss in more detail in the next section.

Variance and Trend Analysis

Variance and trend analysis are considered overt risk management interventions. The goal of employing such techniques is to increase throughput, or work accomplished, by reducing or mitigating potential obstacles. The value returned from utilizing these techniques must be balanced against the administrative overhead incurred. Ultimately, if the information provided helps the team complete more work and answers stakeholder questions, then a good balance has been achieved.

A *variance analysis* involves comparing actual data versus estimated or planned expenditures of a specified measure. Time, cost, and resource constraints are the focus of traditional variance analyses. The goal of a variance analysis is to ascertain the causes of the observed variances and their impact on the project.

A *trend analysis* utilizes historical data to evaluate patterns or trends in the data over time. It uses mathematical techniques to quantify the difference between estimated and actual data and predict future outcomes based on historical results. Trend analyses often make use of run charts (i.e., line or bar charts over time) to show patterns in variation or process over time. Selecting measures both estimable and quantifiable is key when performing a trend analysis. In the agile world, story points and team velocity are such measures.

When a difference between estimated and actual data emerges – for example, when a project goes over budget – corrective action should be taken to bring the divergent numbers "back into control." Such action may be based on an analysis of the causes of the variance as well as on historical trends in the data.

On agile projects, the burn-down chart *(See Figure 6.1)* is the team's ideal opportunity to compare actual work delivered versus their estimates. Similarly, team performance metrics (e.g., Functionality Delivered and Team Velocity, as presented in Figure 6.11) typically provide appropriate data for performing trend analyses.

We will present agile earned value management, a particular type of trend analysis, in Chapter 10.

Escaped Defects

 Escaped defects are product defects that go undiscovered by (or "escaped from") the agile project team during the development and quality assurance (QA/testing process). Tracking escaped defects is both an example of overt risk management and a metric of quality control on software development projects. Typically, escaped defects are found by end users after product release. Occasionally, defects discovered during iteration demonstrations may be counted as escaped defects until fixed. In some environments, "software bugs" and "product issues" are other monikers for escaped defects.

Escaped defects may be included in project dashboard reports as described in our discussion of agile metrics in Chapter 6. Figure 8.3 shows an example where escaped defects are used as a visual control of product quality. To make escaped defects useful as a QA metric, you must have a defect tracking system capable of linking defects to a particular point in time (i.e., iteration, release, version, etc.).

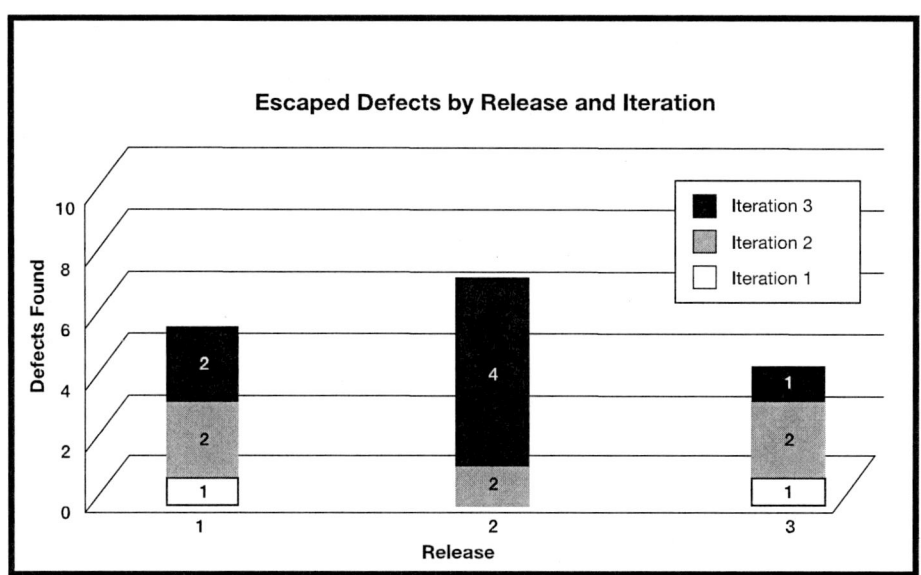

Figure 8.3 Escaped Defects Found, Categorized by Release and Iteration.

From a risk management perspective, the significance of tracking escaped defects is that it focuses the team on improving product quality. This metric may be monitored throughout the project, with the goal being to reduce the number of escaped defects *during the course of the project*. On some projects, teams may even want to apply Six Sigma controls to keep defect frequency within specified parameters.

Communication

Knowledge Sharing

We will concentrate on four aspects of knowledge sharing that enhance project control. They are: 1) Sharing of tacit knowledge; 2) Cross-training among team members; 3) Sharing knowledge learned during the project; and 4) Changing human resource practices to accommodate the agile organization.[3,4]

Sharing of Tacit Knowledge

On any project, regardless of project management methodology, much information is undocumented and thus conveyed through informal or "word of mouth" channels. ***Tacit knowledge*** is this undocumented knowledge that people retain in their heads about the project and the organization. Such knowledge may be technical, historical, or procedural. For example, experienced team members may have agile process information about the team that new hires do not, such as which activities to anticipate during retrospectives.

Tacit knowledge may be exchanged in a number of ways, ranging from informal, non-verbal communications to formal, written communications:

- Osmotic communication
- Observing team meetings
- Face-to-face conversations
- Rotations through different team roles
- Information radiators
- Formal, written documentation

To foster the exchange of tacit information, we have had great success in constructing formal mentorships between senior and junior team members.

The emphasis here is to create an environment where all team members operate from the same knowledge base.[5] Some beneficial effects for the team include a shared understanding of accepted agile practices, a (mostly) interchangeable skill set, and fewer outliers during story estimates.

Cross-Training Among Team Members

The ideal agile team is self-organizing, comprised of equally experienced, competent members working together on projects until they become high-achievers. Due to economic realities, in most workplaces the agile team has a divergence of experience, competency, and skill sets. Thus, an investment in cross-training – across skill sets and from senior to junior team members – adds another layer of control to projects.[6] It creates the "safe" working environment, allowing team members to venture into other roles to help their team meets its commitments.

Cross-training may be accomplished in several ways, including having team members learn from experts outside the team, participate in team-based peer apprenticeships, and attend hands-on courses where they can practice project-critical skills.[7]

Sharing Knowledge Learned During the Project

Knowledge acquired during project execution may be project-centric or process-centric. Let's look at examples of each and consider how such information may be communicated to the team and the organization.

Project-centric

Sometimes, the agile team must tackle a new technical challenge in order to meet customer needs. An exploratory spike may be utilized to seek and test solutions. Another approach may be for the team to call an open space meeting to brainstorm about possible solutions. In either case, the solution finders have an obligation to educate the rest of the team (and the customer/proxy) on available options and recommend a solution. The open space meeting and the retrospective are appropriate forums for communicating this information back to the team.

Process-centric

Not all knowledge acquired on agile projects is technical or solution-based. In some cases, the team learns something about the agile process itself, either pertaining to what works for the team or to what works in the organization as a whole. The team reflective workshop is an ideal forum for presenting such information. Outputs may be changes or additions to team working agreements, which in turn get posted in information radiators.

Knowledge gained on individual projects may have implications for the organization as a whole (i.e., at an enterprise-wide level). How can such critical lessons learned be communicated to the organization? The project dashboard report is one way of briefing senior management, using one of the narrative fields *(See Figure 6.14)*. We also recommend online knowledge bases and regular inter-project meetings (similar to the "Scrum of Scrums") so that an organization's Agile Project Managers can exchange information about their respective projects.

Changing Human Resource Practices

As agile team members are expected to go beyond their job description roles to help the team meet its commitments, there are several implications from a human resources (HR) perspective. We have already discussed cross-training as a means of facilitating highly productive, self-organizing teams. Hiring practices and performance incentives may also have to be adjusted in the agile organization. To hire the cross-functional employees needed on the agile team, job descriptions may have to be revised accordingly. Moreover, the agile team – and not a functional or HR manager – must be entrusted to make the final call on hiring decisions. Finally, incentive packages need to emphasize team accomplishments. This is one area where the team performance agile metrics described in Chapter 6 may be used.

Continuous Improvement

Process Analysis

On agile projects, the team's primary liaison between them and the business is the customer/proxy. As such, the customer/proxy is charged with identifying critical features and prioritizing them for the team. This highlights the customer/proxy's engagement in the project, not only from the agile team's perspective, but also from that of the business. The team is reliant on the customer/proxy's understanding of organizational processes, for having performed adequate process analysis, and for understanding the implications of how the product itself might impact these processes.[8] During demonstrations and retrospectives, the customer/proxy and team have the opportunity to communicate some of the potential process changes back to the organization.

There are a variety of approaches to business process analysis. We'll not delve into the specific process analysis techniques, but we'll focus on aspects of interest to Agile Project Managers.

Highsmith opines that several elements are important to understanding the process analysis.[9] These include:

- Identifying the roles involved in the business process
- Specifying the functions performed within these roles
- Decomposing these functions into stories

When the customer/proxy (ostensibly aided by subject-matter experts, with input on vision from senior management) has this level of mastery of the business process, the stories she identifies for the team will be valuable to the business.

With each product delivery, the customer/proxy and agile team need to revisit the business process to ascertain how it has changed and, conversely, how the product development may contribute to improving it.

Summary

The **product demonstration** is where the agile team demonstrates working features to the customer/proxy, key stakeholders, and selected end users. The demo is actually **one segment** or meeting occurring at the end of the iteration – the demo, the review, and the retrospective. The demo is open to all, while the review is for key stakeholders and the retrospective are restricted to the team.

In terms of stakeholder engagement, the demo fosters trust building between the project team and the stakeholders. The agile team gains confidence in delivering a quality product according to schedule. The demo also serves the purpose of keeping the team focused on its deliverables.

In addition to the feedback provided by stakeholders during the product demonstration, other venues for ascertaining the value delivered in the iteration are the iteration review and the retrospective. During the **iteration review**, the team focuses on product-centric issues such as performance metrics, while the **retrospective** focuses on process-centric issues focused on improving how the team practices agile methods.

Since the task board and the burn-down chart data feed into calculations of team performance, it is critical the team provides real-time updates so measures of functionality delivered and team velocity may be used to make decisions about subsequent iterations.

Velocity is the number of story points a team can complete in an iteration. There are three ways of estimating velocity: 1) Using historical values; 2) Running an iteration; and 3) Forecasting.

An obstacle, or impediment, is a situation or event blocking the progress of work during an iteration. Since such obstacles threaten the team's commitment to delivering the iteration backlog on time, in Agile Project Management we equate removing obstacles with reducing project risk. In terms of risk management, obstacle removal occurs at two levels – organic and overt.

Variance and trend analysis are considered overt risk management interventions. The goal of employing such techniques is to increase throughput, or work accomplished, by reducing or mitigating potential obstacles. A variance analysis involves comparing actual data versus estimated or planned expenditures of a specified measure. The goal of a variance analysis is to ascertain the causes of the observed variances and their impact on the project. A trend analysis utilizes historical data to evaluate patterns or trends in the data over time. It uses mathematical techniques to quantify the difference between estimated and actual data and predict future outcomes based on historical results.

Escaped defects are product defects that go undiscovered by (or "escaped from") the agile project team during the development and QA/testing process. The significance of tracking escaped defects is that it focuses the team on improving product quality.

Knowledge sharing enhances project control in four key areas. They are: 1) Sharing of tacit knowledge; 2) Cross-training among team members; 3) Sharing knowledge learned during the project; and 4) Changing human resource practices to accommodate the agile organization.

From an agile perspective, several elements are important to understanding the business process analysis: 1) Identifying the roles involved in the business process; 2) Specifying the functions performed within these roles; and 3) Decomposing these functions into stories.

Chapter Close-Out

Agile PM Processes Grid™ Exercise

Please take out a blank piece of paper, set a timer for no more than 3 minutes, and see how much of the grid you can reproduce from memory. To make the most of this Agile PM Processes Grid™ exercise, please simulate being in the testing environment. Close your book and all your notes. Visualize the Proctor handing you the blank sheets of paper and taking your seat in the testing site. Begin by drawing the grid, 6 columns and 8 rows, and then fill in everything you can. After the 3 minutes ends, use your book and notes to complete the grid. Study it as you do so.

Terminology Matching Exercise

In the blank column to the left of the Term, fill in the letter that identifies the correct definition or description.

	Term		Definition / Description
	1. Project-centric knowledge	A	Meeting where the agile team demonstrates working features to the customer/proxy, key stakeholders, and selected end users.
	2. Product demonstration	B	The number of story points a team can complete in an iteration.
	3. Impediment	C	Estimate of team velocity when there are no historical observations available.
	4. Forecast velocity	D	The sum of estimated productive hours per week that each team member can devote to the project.
	5. Escaped defects	E	An obstacle, situation or event blocking the progress of work during an iteration.
	6. Variance analysis	F	A comparison of actual data versus estimated or planned expenditures of a specified measure.
	7. Tacit knowledge	G	Utilizes historical data to evaluate patterns or trends in the data over time.
	8. Velocity	H	Product defects that go undiscovered by the team during the development and quality assurance/testing process.
	9. Capacity	I	Undocumented knowledge that people remember about the project and the organization.
	10. Trend analysis	J	Technical or solutions-based information related specifically to the work of the project.

Crossword Puzzle

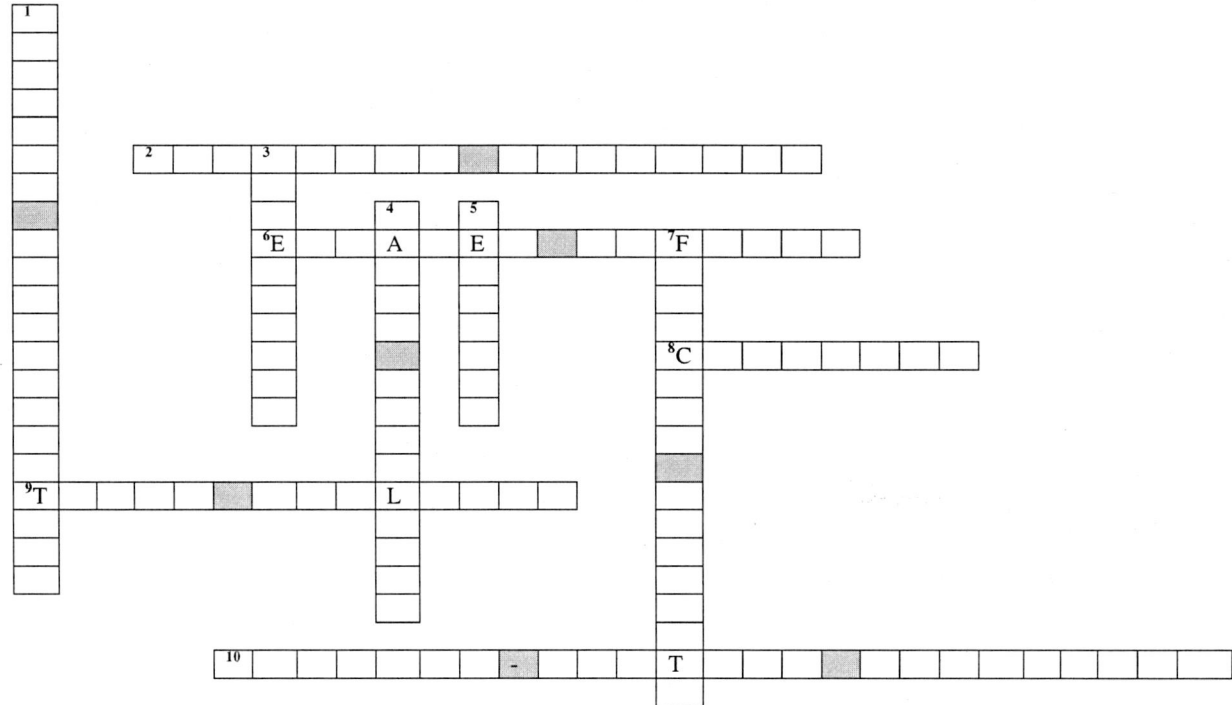

Hints:

ACROSS

2. Comparison of actual data versus estimated or planned expenditures of a specified measure.
6. Product defects that go undiscovered by the agile project team during the development and quality assurance/testing process.
8. The sum of estimated productive hours per week that each team member can devote to the project.
9. Utilizes historical data to evaluate patterns or trends in the data over time.
10. Technical or solutions-based information related specifically to the work of the project.

DOWN

1. Meeting where the agile team demonstrates working features to the customer/proxy, key stakeholders, and selected end users.
3. Obstacle, situation or event blocking the progress of work during an iteration.
4. Undocumented knowledge that people remember about the project and the organization.
5. The number of story points a team can complete in an iteration.
7. An estimate of team velocity when there are no historical observations available.

Word Search

Word Search - 10 Words to find:

ESCAPEDDEFECTS TACIT KNOWLEDGE FORECASTVELOCITY
VELOCITY CAPACITY IMPEDIMENT
TREND ANALYSIS VARIANCEANALYSIS PRODUCT DEMONSTRATION
PROJECT-CENTRICKNOWLEDGE

```
D P Y P I F O R E C A S T _ V E L O C T
F O R E C A S T _ V E L O C I T Y S N A
C V D S E S C A P E D _ D E F E T L N V
L E _ _ O C A A W E E S F C T S E S S E
R L T F T C _ D Y D D P Y A I G T F I P
A O A C E F V M T S O T S S D C T Y E T
T C S N C A P A C I T Y E E N A L D _
P I A T I T P _ A Y P L L F M A C E R _
S T A O M Y E C I C A W E I E L I O V M
C Y O E P E S D N N O D D S E V T O E _
K I R E E L C S A N _ E T I T I _ T L A
C V N T D A I _ K D P N C A K E K M O E
C A E _ I E D _ E M T O A L T E N E C L
A C C Y M N T P I C L D T I T L O W I E
P O L D E I A E I E W S M P E O W F T _
A E F R C C R F V T S N T E N P L N Y M
C E T A S I M P E D I M E N T N E C R E
C O T E N D I A _ I T K W I R I D L T S
V M T R E N D _ A N A L Y Y E I W E A V
R P _ A K C P E S O E T E F N E Y T Y I
```

Chapter Practice Test

1. The _____ is the meeting where the agile team demonstrates working features to the customer/proxy, key stakeholders, and selected end users.

   A. Project review
   B. Product demonstration
   C. Retrospective
   D. Daily stand up

2. To arrange rows of sized, and sometimes estimated, features into potential iterations derived from the team's velocity results in what can best be described as a _____.

   A. Visual control board
   B. Burn up chart
   C. Burn down chart
   D. Retrospective

3. Which of the following statements is true regarding task boards and burn down charts?

   A. They measure the effectiveness of the agile project manager
   B. They highlight individual team member performance
   C. They assist the agile team in tracking progress on the current iteration and provide a means for planning future iterations and evaluating team performance
   D. They provide the customer with a measure of feature value

4. _____ is formally defined as the number of story points a team can complete in an iteration.

   A. Continuous integration
   B. Osmotic communication
   C. Refactor rate
   D. Velocity

5. An obstacle, impediment, or roadblock is a situation or event that blocks the progress of work during an iteration. In agile project management, the removal of an obstacle is most generally equated with _____.

   A. Removing project risk
   B. Increasing project cost
   C. Increasing project risk
   D. Reducing velocity

6. Variance and trend analysis are considered _____ risk management interventions.

   A. Reactive
   B. Overt
   C. Secondary
   D. Organic

7. The effort of comparing actual data versus estimated or planned expenditures of a specified measure with the intent of determining the causes of observed differences can best be described as performing _____.

   A. Monthly project review
   B. Trend analysis
   C. Force field analysis
   D. Variance analysis

8. The effort of comparing historical data to evaluate patterns or trends in the data over time with the goal of quantifying the difference between estimated and actual data to predict future outcomes based on historical results can best be described as performing _____.

   A. Variance analysis
   B. Force field analysis
   C. Trend analysis
   D. Monthly project review

9. Product defects that go undiscovered by the agile project team during the development and quality assurance process are referred to as _____.

   A. Escaped defects
   B. Secondary defects
   C. Bonus features
   D. Organic defects

10. Technical, historical, or procedural information that is undocumented and thus conveyed through informal or "word of mouth" channels is referred to as _____.

    A. Controlled information
    B. Tacit knowledge
    C. Unreleased information
    D. Confidential information

11. Knowledge gained by addressing a new technical challenge by means of an exploratory spike or an open space brainstorming meeting is an example of _____ knowledge.

    A. Project-centric
    B. Osmotic
    C. Process-centric
    D. Secondary

12. Knowledge gained when the team learns something about the agile process itself, either pertaining to what works for the team or to what works in the organization as a whole is an example of _____ knowledge.

    A. Primary
    B. Project-centric
    C. Osmotic
    D. Process-centric

13. In terms of stakeholder engagement, which of the following can be said to foster trust building between the project team and the stakeholders?

    A. Daily stand up
    B. Iteration retrospective
    C. Product demonstration
    D. Monthly project review

14. An estimate of team velocity developed when it is either impossible or impractical for the team to run an iteration, and they do not yet have any historical observations is referred to as _____.

    A. Refactored velocity
    B. Forecasted velocity
    C. Progressive velocity
    D. Agile velocity

15. Which of the following is not considered one of the preferred ways of estimating team velocity?

    A. Velocity estimates by experienced functional managers
    B. Using historical values
    C. Running an iteration
    D. Forecasting

Answers – Terminology Matching

1:J, 2:A, 3:E, 4:C, 5:H, 6:F, 7:I, 8:B, 9:D, 10:G

Answers – Crossword Puzzle

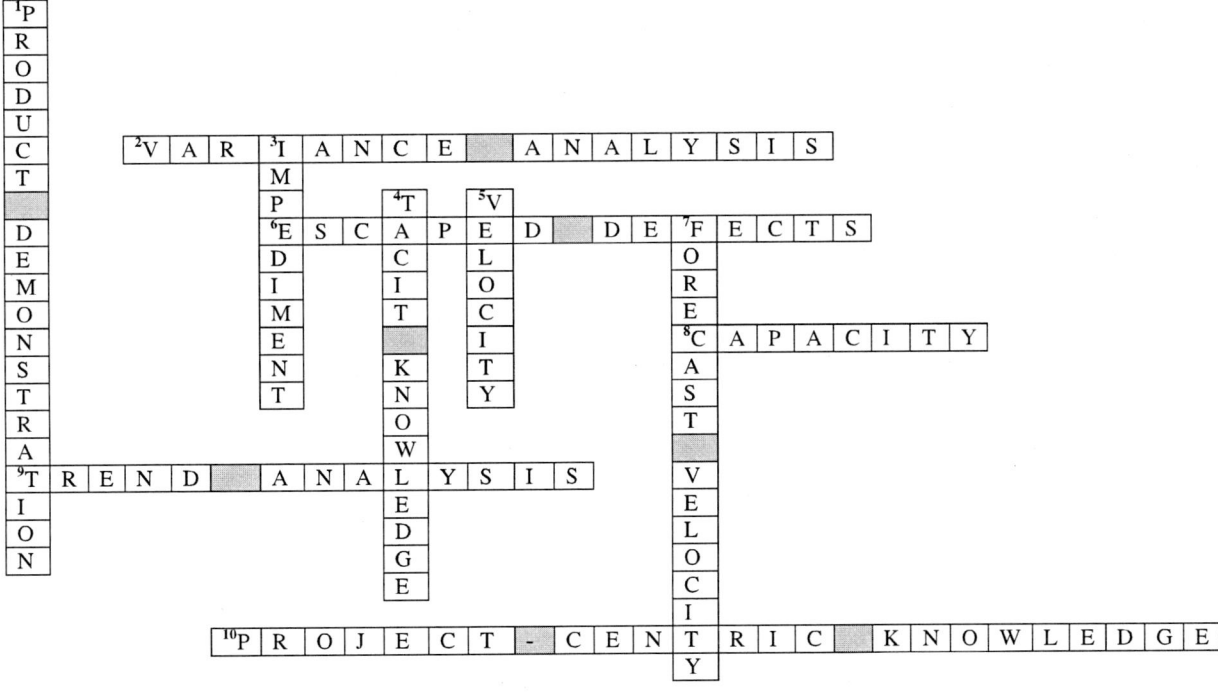

Answers – Word Search

Word Search - 10 Words to find:

ESCAPEDDEFECTS
VELOCITY
TREND ANALYSIS
PROJECT-CENTRICKNOWLEDGE

TACIT KNOWLEDGE
CAPACITY
VARIANCEANALYSIS

FORECASTVELOCITY
IMPEDIMENT
PRODUCT DEMONSTRATION

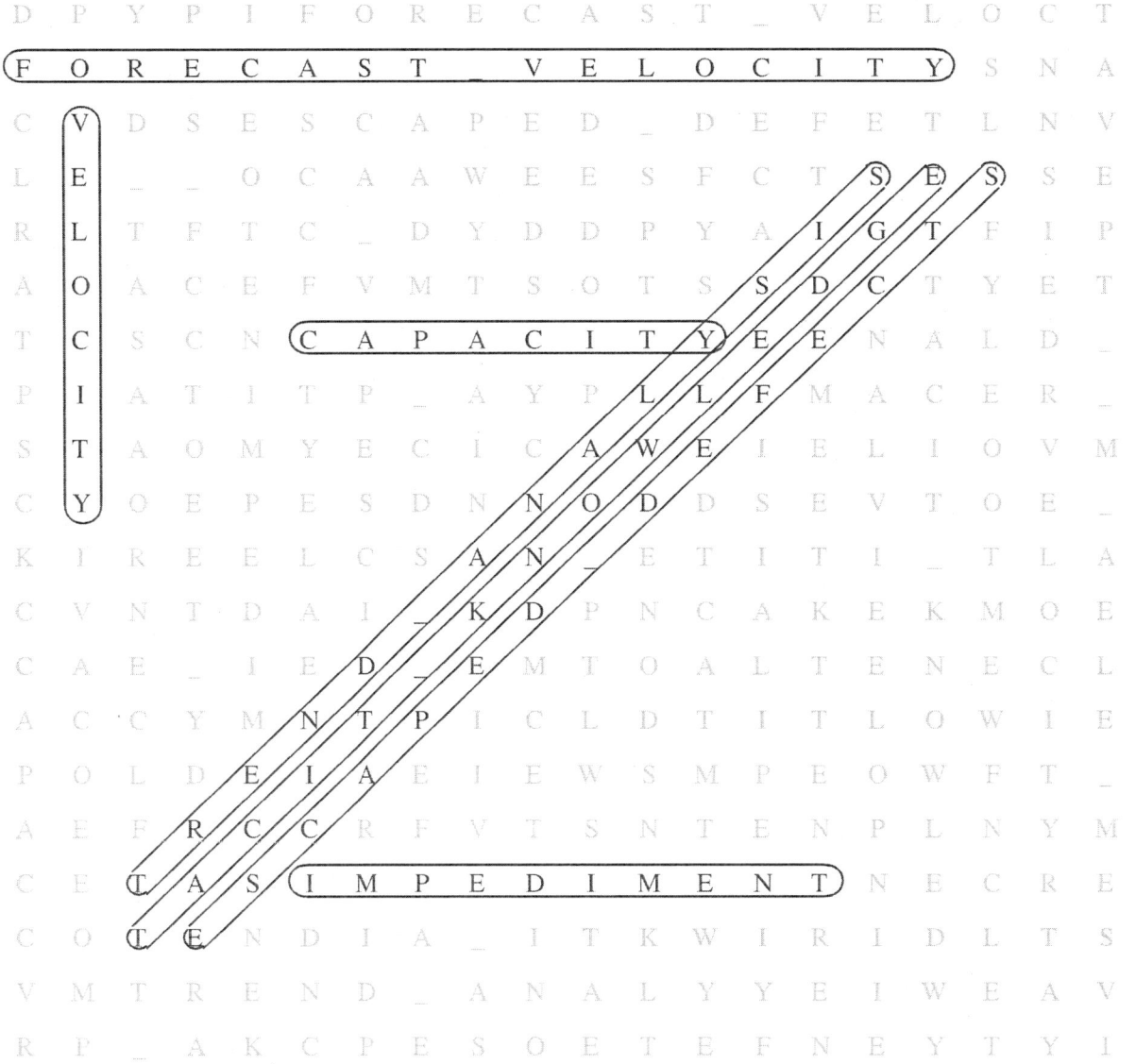

Answers – Practice Test

1. **B.** The product demonstration is the meeting where the agile team demonstrates working features to the customer/proxy, key stakeholders, and selected end users. The demonstration (or "demo") is actually one segment of three meetings that occur at the end of the iteration – the demo, the iteration review, and the retrospective. The demo is open to all, while the iteration review and the retrospective are restricted to the team.

2. **A.** The most common approach to creating visual control boards has been to arrange rows of sized, and sometimes estimated, features into potential iterations derived from the team's velocity. Using these visual representations provides greater clarity in seeing the proposed sequence and facilitates useful discussions between multiple interdependent teams typically involved in solution development in large enterprises.

3. **C.** Task boards and burn down charts assist the agile team in tracking progress on the current iteration and also provide a means for planning future iterations and evaluating team performance.

4. **D.** Velocity is the number of story points a team can complete in an iteration. There are three ways of estimating velocity: 1) Using historical values; 2) Running an iteration; and 3) Forecasting.

5. **A.** An obstacle, or impediment, is a situation or event that blocks the progress of work during an iteration. For example, an agile team may have functional managers that interrupt them constantly and thus prevent them from working on tasks in the ongoing iteration. Since such obstacles threaten the team's commitment to delivering the iteration backlog on time, in Agile Project Management we equate removing obstacles with reducing project risk.

6. **B.** Variance and trend analysis are considered overt risk management interventions. The goal of employing such techniques is to increase throughput, or work accomplished, by reducing or mitigating potential obstacles.

7. **D.** A variance analysis involves comparing actual data versus estimated or planned expenditures of a specified measure. Time, cost, and resource constraints are the focus of traditional variance analyses. The goal of a variance analysis is to ascertain the causes of the observed variances and their impact on the project.

8. **C.** A trend analysis utilizes historical data to evaluate patterns or trends in the data over time. It uses mathematical techniques to quantify the difference between estimated and actual data and to predict future outcomes based on historical results. Trend analyses often make use of run charts (i.e., line or bar charts over time) to show patterns in variation or process over time. A key in performing a trend analysis is that the measures selected must be both estimable and quantifiable. In the agile world, story points and team velocity are such measures.

9. **A.** Escaped defects are product defects that go undiscovered by (or "escaped from") the agile project team during the development and quality assurance (QA)/testing process. Tracking escaped defects is both: 1) an example of overt risk management; and 2) a metric of quality control on software development projects. Typically, escaped defects are found by end users after product release.

10. **B.** On any project, regardless of project management methodology, much information is undocumented and thus conveyed through informal or "word of mouth" channels. ***Tacit knowledge*** is this undocumented knowledge that people retain in their heads about the project and the organization. Such knowledge may be technical, historical, or procedural. For example, experienced team members may have agile process information about the team that new hires do not, such as which activities to anticipate during retrospectives.

11. **A.** Knowledge acquired during project execution may be project-centric or process-centric. An example of project-centric knowledge might be where the agile team must tackle a new technical challenge in order to meet customer needs. An exploratory spike may be utilized to seek and test solutions. Another approach may be for the team to call an open space meeting to brainstorm about possible solutions. In either case, the solution finders have an obligation to educate the rest of the team (and the customer/proxy) on available options and to recommend a solution.

12. **D.** Not all knowledge acquired on agile projects is technical or solution-based and may be considered process-centric. In some cases, the team learns something about the agile process itself, either pertaining to what works for the team or to what works in the organization as a whole. The team reflective workshop is an ideal forum for presenting such information. Outputs may be changes or additions to team working agreements, which in turn get posted in information radiators.

13. **C.** In terms of stakeholder engagement, the demo fosters trust building between the project team and the stakeholders. The agile team gains confidence in delivering a quality product according to schedule. The demo also serves the purpose of keeping the team focused on its deliverables.

14. **B.** Forecasted velocity is an estimate of team velocity when it is either impossible or impractical for the team to run an iteration, and they do not yet have any historical observations. Typically, forecasts are based on the capacity of the team, a number based on the estimated productive hours per week that each team member can devote to the project.

15. **A.** Velocity is the number of story points a team can complete in an iteration. There are three ways of estimating velocity: 1) Using historical values; 2) Running an iteration; and 3) Forecasting.

Chapter End Notes

[1] Sliger, M., & Broderick, S. (2008). The software project manager's bridge to agility. Upper Saddle River, NJ: Addison-Wesley.
[2] Cohn, M. (2006). Agile estimating and planning. Upper Saddle River, NJ: Pearson Education.
[3] Highsmith, J. (2010). Agile project management: Creating innovative products, Second edition. Upper Saddle River, NJ: Addison-Wesley.
[4] Sliger, M., & Broderick, S. (2008). The software project manager's bridge to agility. Upper Saddle River, NJ: Addison-Wesley.
[5] Cockburn, A. (2007). Agile software development: The cooperative game, Second edition. Upper Saddle River, NJ: Addison-Wesley.
[6] Sliger, M., & Broderick, S. (2008). The software project manager's bridge to agility. Upper Saddle River, NJ: Addison-Wesley.
[7] Cockburn, A. (2007). Agile software development: The cooperative game, Second edition. Upper Saddle River, NJ: Addison-Wesley.
[8] Highsmith, J. (2010). Agile project management: Creating innovative products, Second edition. Upper Saddle River, NJ: Addison-Wesley.
[9] Ibid.

CHAPTER 9

Contracting and Accounting Control

Chapter Highlights

In this chapter we will discuss contracting and accounting controls as they are practiced and applied in agile environments. We will briefly introduce Earned Value Management (EVM) use EVM basics as a bridge to an in-depth explanation of Agile Earned Value Management (A-EVM).

Contracting Control

The Agile Manifesto was spot on when it stated, "Customer collaboration over contract negotiation." Contract negotiation is fundamentally important for a successful project and must be done. But it should be done with the perspective that a vibrant working relationship between the parties must be a result that is more important than the contract.

Chapter 3 noted that at the beginning of a project there is too much at stake to work without a contract, which is just a way to define the rules for working together and communicating. So the best practice is to decide which contract best conforms to the needs of the project.

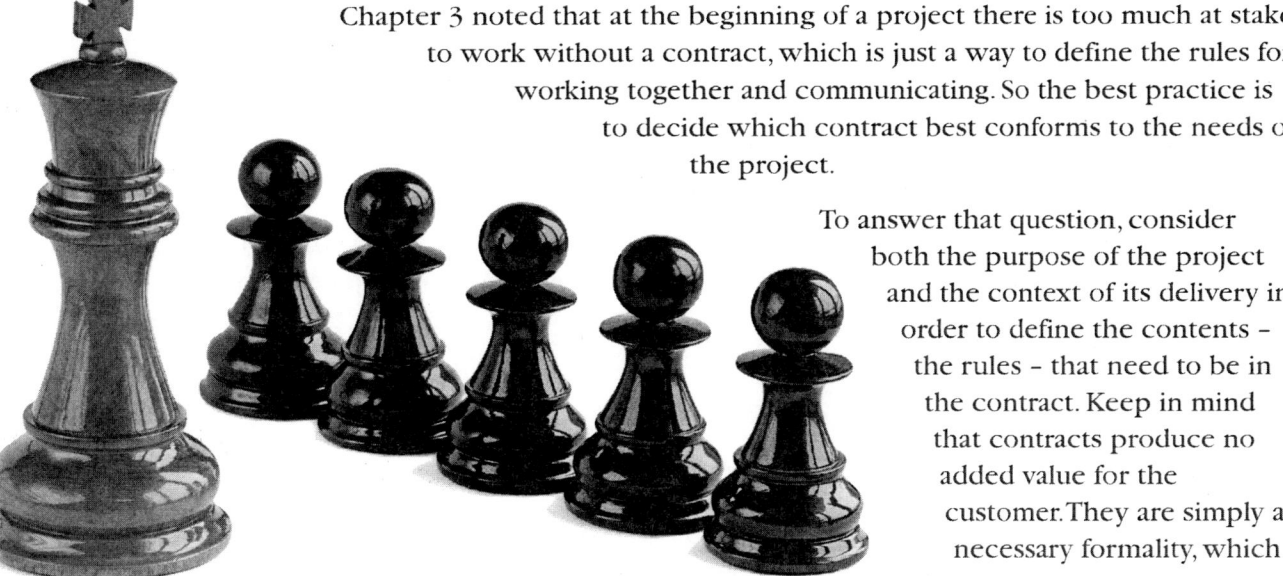

To answer that question, consider both the purpose of the project and the context of its delivery in order to define the contents – the rules – that need to be in the contract. Keep in mind that contracts produce no added value for the customer. They are simply a necessary formality, which can be used to create a win-win relationship with customers through good communication. But, by definition, contracts are a waste product, so any time spent negotiating and writing them should be optimized to improve communication and reduce cost.

Also keep in mind that a contract divides shared risk and defines trust points between the parties. Who pays how much if things are more difficult than expected and who benefits how much if the project goes well both hinge on those trust points and must be articulated well. An inequitable contract leads to compromised quality and aggravation for both parties.

Contracts should include:

- Well defined project objectives.
- Key roles and responsibilities, defined to foster cooperation.
- How scope delivery is defined, and how it is linked to invoicing and payment.
- How risks and rewards, incentives and penalties, are divided between customer and provider.

Possible contract types include:

Agile Iteration: Agile Iteration contracts are based on the team delivering agreed upon features to defined quality standards by iteration end, and the customer/proxy not changing the iteration backlog before iteration end.

Time and Materials: Time and Materials contracts allow the customer to end the project and stop paying when they don't see added value.

Phased Development: Phased Development contracts are typically funded on a quarterly basis and additional funding is approved following each successful release. Knowing another release will occur, or not, next quarter guides feature selection for the timebox.

A best practice for creating good contract content, regardless of which type of contract vehicle is chosen, is an extension of the user story development process described in Chapter 4. *(See Figure 4.10 for an illustration of a user story and acceptance criteria.)*

The best practice extension is to define a small number of high level user stories that include the acceptance criteria that are the conditions of satisfaction for each story. Discussing the conditions of satisfaction can help identify user story assumptions so that development risk can be more confidently covered in an agreement. For example, deciding to use a preview button instead of having a WYSIWYG (What You See Is What You Get) editor can save the customer money, if it meets their needs, and so might need to be discussed. Likewise, determining that very simple formatting, not elaborate font styles, sizes, and colors, for example, are all that is required can avoid a potential future conflict and money-losing project.

Admittedly, defining the conditions of satisfaction can be arduous and time-consuming, but far less so than the time and cost of mitigating the undefined requirements later. The team should strive to sufficiently eliminate uncertainty so that both parties can understand the amount of risk they are assuming. Luckily, doing so may only be required on the first contract or two while both parties are learning how to work together and establishing a trusted relationship.

Examples of customer questions the team should ask during discussions to understand the details of the high-level user stories include:

- How will the team know when the feature is done?
- During the demo what would you need to see to know the feature does what's expected?
- Are there security concerns or the need for group-based privileges?

Remember, good contracting should also align with a solid approach to estimating, and both contracting and estimating should reciprocate support with accounting control so that the likelihood of a satisfied customer and a profitable project are both high.

Accounting Control

Few things in project management – traditional or agile – are more abhorred by most project managers than accounting control, in particular creating a cost baseline and measuring performance against it. Yet few things are more fundamental to project success than proper financial performance. That means that a professional Agile Project Manager must understand accounting control well enough to effectively manage the resources required to accomplish it.

Once a release plan has been created, the forecast cost per iteration can be established and a cost baseline created. In the same way that the product backlog is groomed between iterations, the cost baseline should be reviewed before each iteration and recalculated based on changes to the backlog and release plan. Variances should be noted and analyzed for use in forecasting expected future performance.

Adjusting the cost baseline does not reduce the responsibility of the Agile Project Manager and team to prevent misdirected development, careless resource usage, and unauthorized changes from being included in the cost baseline analysis. When the team discovers a mistaken estimate or misdirected activity it has the responsibility to alert the customer/proxy and discuss the implications so the customer/proxy can make the proper decisions. Once the committed iteration plan has been defined within the approved cost baseline, any changes must be negotiated with, and approved by, the customer/proxy. Doing otherwise will quickly disrupt the team's discipline in planning and committing.

Using the team's average velocity and accounting control processes also allows the Agile Project Manager to analyze whether the probability that the forecast number of iterations is improving or deteriorating. Creating customer/proxy awareness of a deteriorating probability is a difficult message to convey, but if the value of reliable information for making timely, informed decisions is stressed it can be done. Discussing that information with the customer/proxy provides needed visibility so scope changes can be negotiated and authorized within the context of strengthening relationship trust.

Sometimes that may even mean that the Agile Project Manager and customer/proxy decide it would be beneficial to outsource a particular feature set in order to realign project costs with the cost baseline. Or it may drive a make versus buy decision where buying is less costly than building, so the customer/proxy chooses the lower-cost alternative. Remember that giving the customer/proxy the ability to lower costs also allows her to spend the savings on other features. It is not necessarily a zero sum game.

It is important for the Agile Project Manager to recognize that organizations are not indifferent to variances in the cost baseline. In order to set expectations and build a foundation for a trust-centric relationship it is important to discuss the customer/proxy's needs. The ideal level to manage the cost baseline in an agile framework is the iteration.

For most organizations, managing it at the release level is not granular enough even though it is less costly. Once they see the cost – benefit ratio, most organizations can set a standard for iteration length that allows them to have the needed granularity and control of the cost baseline. However, before they reach that desired level of maturity it is often necessary to define and manage the cost baseline at the story level (which is equivalent to the work package level in traditional project management) or even at the activity or task level.

A best practice is to analyze variances and formally evaluate them on an end-of-iteration basis, even if the cost information is captured and recorded at a lower, more granular level. Regardless of the timing and process used, validating and verifying cost baseline performance against organizational budget and funding standards must be done. And that leads to a discussion of a specific type of accounting control called Earned Value Management (EVM).

Earned Value Management (EVM)

In this section EVM (Earned Value Management) and A-EVM (Agile Earned Value Management) will be explained. Because EVM has been discussed by a great many authors elsewhere, we will provide a cursory explanation here as a bridge to its agile counterpart. Our two-fold purpose is to provide enough information and structure to insure adequate ACP exam preparation as well as a foundation for the student's continued learning when A-EVM is needed in the workplace.

One question that deserves to be addressed immediately is, **"Why is EVM or A-EVM even necessary?"** The answer is that Agile Project Management frameworks do not articulate how to identify, track and manage costs. Analyzing and evaluating Return on Investment (ROI) against the product vision is a fundamental business need, and therefore a customer need. One benefit of using EVM is seeing how effectively project funding is being managed against the metric of expected ROI. Evaluating project ROI allows the customer/proxy to determine if a specific release plan has sufficient value related to its costs or if the release needs to be re-planned with features added or removed. Also, as a program management tool that integrates the technical, cost, and schedule parameters of a contract, EVM may even prove to be the missing link that enables Agile Project Management to fully function at the enterprise level.

It is important to note that EVM is commonly discussed as if it is a monolithic tool, but that is inaccurate. There are two variations of EVM. The more commonly discussed one is used for level of effort (LOE) projects where no discrete deliverables are defined. The second type is used for projects where discrete effort delivers discrete results. Because agile iterations conclude with discrete results – potentially shippable products – the second type of EVM is easily aligned and tailored to an agile framework.

During the project planning process, EVM can be used to create an integrated baseline with time phased budgets for resources and deliverables. In EVM, as work is performed and measured against the baseline, the corresponding budget value is "earned" when discrete deliverables are completed, hence the term Earned Value (EV). For agile, that would typically be at the end of the iteration, but it could be associated with specific features or stories.

For the Agile Project Manager, A-EVM provides a reasonable measurement process that can be integrated with any agile framework and provide the additional insight the business and customer need. A-EVM's ability to provide an early forecast of final costs offers an early warning tool that signals whether required funding to finish the project is available. It does so with enough clarity and reliability to make adjustments in a timely fashion.

 Agile Earned Value Management (A-EVM) is understood, or defined, as an adaptation of the widely recognized and used EVM toolset. It uses a set of earned value calculations tailored to Agile Project Management. In practice A-EVM uses the project's release date and iteration cycle, derived from the estimates and team average velocity, to generate results from the tailored equations.

EVM Basics

EVM has been in use since the 1960s in traditional project management environments, particularly on defense and construction projects. EVM is a widely recognized program management technique that is included in *"A Guide to the Project Management Body of Knowledge"* published by PMI. EVM is also recognized by many other organizations including the American National Standards Institute (ANSI), the International Performance Management Council (IPMC) and the Advancement of Cost Engineering International (AACEi).

Earned Value Management (EVM) is a program management technique that integrates scope, schedule, and resource consumption information in order to measure project performance against planned cost metrics. It provides quantitative, objective data to supplement qualitative, subjective judgments.

In a guidance memorandum issued August 2011, the U.S. Department of Defense (DoD) described EVM as one of DoD's and industry's most powerful program management tools.[1] It stated that EVM is primarily a program management planning tool, which is also used by government and industry program managers to track program execution as they navigate the day-to-day constraints and risks that all DoD programs face. It continued, EVM is considered by many in the project management community to be the best option currently available for holding all parties accountable for the effective management of large and complex projects. EVM provides a disciplined approach to managing projects successfully through the use of an integrated system to plan and control authorized work to achieve cost, schedule, and performance objectives.

EVM's fundamental premise is that as work is *completed*, the corresponding budget value is *earned*, hence the term Earned Value (EV). In EVM for discrete deliverables that paradigm of value only being earned for completed work aligns at the most basic level with Agile Project Management. Agile frameworks can measure completed work at the story, feature or iteration level and EVM calculations can be applied.

The general EVM process can be described in the following six steps:

1. Define project scope
2. Assemble team
3. Decompose work
4. Outline project schedule
5. Estimate work package budgets
6. Specify time-phased budget

Using Earned Value (EV) as a variable, EVM calculates cost and schedule variances with equations that include Planned Value (PV) and Actual Cost (AC). By analyzing those variances, the project manager can identify the drivers that enable or hinder project progress, forecast future cost and schedule performance issues, and define appropriate corrective actions to improve the probability of project success. EVM creates insight into the current status of the project as well as what actions can be taken to improve it.

Agile Earned Value Management (A-EVM)

The challenge of applying A-EVM is not at the theoretical or mathematical level, it occurs at the practical management level. The process similarities between EVM and A-EVM can be seen as follows (Figure 9.1):

EVM	A–EVM
1) Define Project Scope	1) Create Roadmap & Release Plans
2) Assemble Team	2) Assemble Team
3) Decompose Work	3) Document Stories
4) Outline Project Schedule	4) Define Releases & Iterations
5) Estimate Work Package Budgets	5) Estimate Story / Feature Budgets
6) Specify Time–Phased Budget	6) Specify Iteration Budgets

Figure 9.1 Process Similarities Between EVM and A-EVM

A-EVM can leverage many elements that are part of all agile frameworks and processes in order to implement EVM. For example, because project progress can be measured as completed stories, features, or iterations, EVM charts share significant similarities with agile burn-up charts. *(See Figure 9.2.)*

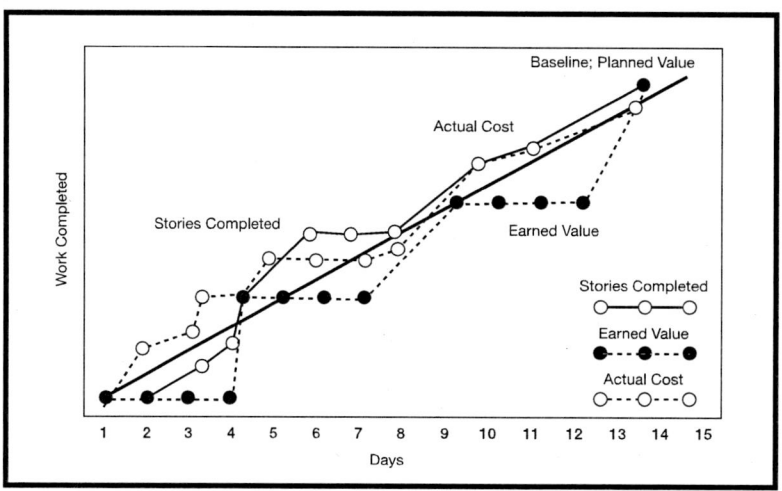

Figure 9.2 EVM and Burn-up Chart.

In Figure 9.2 there are four lines. The agile project baseline, which is equivalent to the EVM planned value, runs diagonally from the lower left to the upper right. Then the line for Stories Completed is shown rising as each story is completed. For this example, we assumed that value was only earned when a feature was complete. So the EV line rises in a stair-step pattern after the four stories in each feature are completed. Last is the AC line, which rises faster than the other lines until story completion and value earned catch up. The final point recorded shows that stories completed and EV have intersected above the cost line so value earned has exceeded costs.

Although A-EVM can leverage many agile elements, in order to implement A-EVM the organization must define standards for data collection, analysis and reporting. The standards should define the most desirable cost-benefit ratio and that is where the challenge occurs. The organization must decide how much reporting detail they require because as the need for more detailed or granular reporting increases the time and effort required to produce it increases.

There are two basic ways to increase the granularity of reporting – shorten the iteration or estimate the PV at a lower level.

Shortening the iteration requires additional work for the customer/proxy and team to define the planned values, and that increase is likely to be nonlinear. The effort required to architect and design a solution that can be measured with discrete deliverables at the end of two-week iterations can be significantly more than the effort required for deliverables at the end of three-week iterations. Moreover, the effort required to conduct three-week iterations can be significantly more than that required for four-week iterations. So there will be a **direct correlation between the level of detail required for reporting and the cost of collecting that data.**

Estimating PV at a lower level can require additional work depending on organizational standards. As explained earlier in this book, for many agile projects, sizing is used as a quick, inexpensive way to organize a roadmap and release plans. Then, detailed estimating is only done for features that end up in a near-term backlog, like the next three iterations, where the additional detail is needed. So if the organization's A-EVM standards required detailed estimating of all stories or features, the burden could be significant. Alternately, the A-EVM standard could be to use estimates for the next three iterations and base A-EVM metrics for the longer term on calculations using numerical story points, iteration length, and team velocity.

In practice, four basic scenarios exist for defining PV. They are based on whether the customer/proxy knows, or does not know, the business value of specific stories, features or iterations and whether the team knows, or does not know, the effort required for building those specific stories or features. The scenario descriptions above assume that architecting and designing are part of what the team knows or does not know. The scenario where neither knows will require the most effort to define PV, while the scenario where both know will require the least. The remaining two situations, where only one or the other knows, will require an effort best described as the median. (See Figure 9.3.)

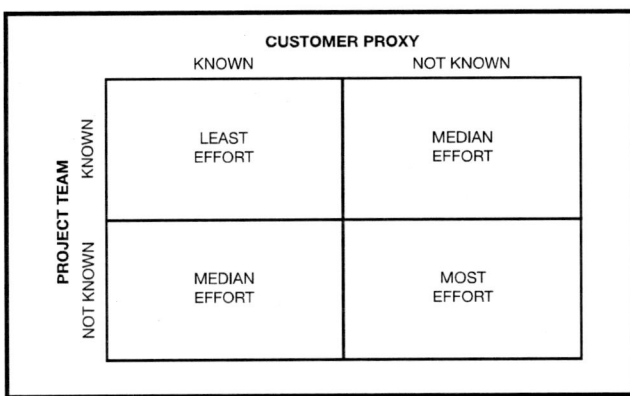

Figure 9.3 Effort Required to Define Planned Value (PV).

So the process begins in the standard agile way with the customer/proxy and team discussing features and stories in order to create a roadmap and release plan. As the release plan is decomposed into iterations and stories are estimated or sized the PV can be determined. Additionally, as the team's velocity and the total cost per iteration stabilize, the iterations on the longer-term horizon – where only sizing has occurred – can be assigned a PV, if needed. As the longer-term iterations move into the current time horizon, estimates are made so the PV can be determined. Once the PV is defined, the application of the equations becomes quite straightforward because the PV becomes the EV when the work – which can be defined at the story, feature or iteration level – is completed.

Mathematically EVM is quite compatible with agile frameworks. Comparing the standard definitions of the three core EVM variables EV, PV and AC shows that tailoring them for A-EVM is not difficult. (See Figure 9.4.)

Term	EVM Definition	A–EVM Definition
Planned Value (PV)	The budgeted cost of work planned for a **specific time period**	The budgeted cost of work planned for an **iteration**
Earned Value (EV)	The budgeted cost of work completed during a **specific time period**	The budgeted cost of work completed during an **iteration**
Actual Cost (AC)	The actual cost of work completed during a **specific time period**	The actual cost of work completed during an **iteration**

Figure 9.4 A Comparison of EVM and A-EVM Terminology.

Although there are 13 formulas associated with EVM, for ACP exam preparation and 80% of work environment situations, only four of them are commonly used. We will cover those four formulas and their equations. (See Figure 9.5.) However, we will not cover the other nine formulas because we find it is distracting and counter-productive for exam preparation.

Formula	Equation
Schedule Variance (SV)	SV = EV – PV
Schedule Performance Index (SPI)	SPI = EV / PV
Cost Variance (CV)	CV = EV – AC
Cost Performance Index (CPI)	CPI = EV / AC

Figure 9.5 Four Core EVM Equations.

As can be seen, once the PV has been established, the calculations become quite routine. If the work has been completed, the PV becomes the EV. Also, as the work is completed, the AC can be provided from the cost accounting system.

In addition to the calculations being routine, interpreting their meaning is very straightforward. **For both the SV and CV, a negative variance is undesirable and indicates the project is *behind* schedule or *over* budget or both. For both the SPI and the CPI a variance less than 1 or 100% is undesirable and indicates the project is *behind* schedule or *over* budget or both.**

Since the calculations and their interpretations are both quite simple, it is easy to wonder why EVM has received so little positive attention from project managers. Our experience teaching EVM over many years has given us two key insights. The first and most obvious one is that it takes a lot of work to create the PV estimates and once they are created the metrics they provide are very concrete. Those concrete metrics make it very difficult to avoid drawing conclusions about performance that the project manager may have wanted to escape.

The second, less obvious reason that EVM was avoided by project managers is confusion about a single core concept. When we teach EVM, we ask the students whether work completed has actual cost or planned cost. Invariably they understand and state that completed work has actual cost. That is the subtle point where project managers have confusion about EVM, but often don't recognize it. The question we ask is, in a way, a trick question. We ask it as an either/or question, but the answer is both/and. Completed work has both a planned value and an actual cost. Just because the actual cost is known does not mean that the planned value is lost. So before the work is completed, it has only a PV, but once it is completed it has an AC and an EV, which is a form of its original PV. Completed work obviously has an actual cost associated with it, so it is counter-intuitive to think of it as still having a PV expressed as an EV, but completed work has both!

It is counter-intuitive to think of a PV for completed work and that is probably the most misunderstood part of EVM. Because EVM for level of effort type projects uses a percent complete calculation it is possible for EV to vary from its PV counterpart. But in EVM for discrete projects, which is the basis for A-EVM, the EV should always equal the PV for completed work. In both types the AC will vary because it is an actual value.

In preparing for the ACP exam, we recommend students master a memorization trick regarding the four core formulas and use it in the same way as the Agile PM Processes GridTM before beginning the exam.

The memorization trick is to write the formulas in a grid instead of as a sentence or line. So in the first column, write **Schedule, Schedule, Cost, Cost** on four lines or rows. In the second column write **Variance, Index, Variance, Index** in each row. In the third column write an equal sign (=) in each row. Then remember that all four calculations begin with EV and write EV in each row in the fourth column. In the fifth column write the symbol for **Minus, Divide, Minus, Divide** in each row. And in the sixth column write **PV, PV, AC, AC** in each row. When it is completed the grid looks like (Figure 9.6):

Schedule	Variance	=	EV	–	PV
Schedule	Index	=	EV	/	PV
Cost	Variance	=	EV	–	AC
Cost	Index	=	EV	/	AC

Figure 9.6 Memorization Grid

It is good exam preparation to practice chanting (out loud to yourself) the following "lyrics" until they are committed to memory:

- Schedule, Schedule, Cost, Cost
- Variance, Index, Variance, Index
- EV is always first
- Minus, Divide, Minus, Divide
- PV, PV, AC, AC

Closing Comments on A-EVM

For projects with very short release cycles, A-EVM is typically not as useful as it is for projects longer release cycles because there is not enough time to make adjustments based on the information A-EVM provides.

A recommended practice is for the team to size any new features, or resize any significant feature changes, between iterations to determine the impact on how many iterations will be required to complete the product build. Then the baseline can be analyzed by multiplying the number of iterations times the average cost per iteration, for example $55,500. The customer/proxy can then approve or reject the entire group of changes so the additional budget and features become part of the baseline and backlog.

Alternately, using the team's average velocity and the average cost per iteration, the team can estimate the cost of specific features based on their size. Then the customer/proxy can decide on feature by feature changes, reprioritize the backlog, and adjust the current cost baseline.

In both EVM and A-EVM values are tracked and reported in cumulative amounts. Doing so facilitates project planning and control and is the reason EVM and burn-up charts align so easily.

An in-depth discussion of A-EVM, including the mathematical proofs for its accuracy, efficacy and usefulness for agile projects, was published as part of the Agile Conference in 2006 by Tamara Sulaiman, Brent Barton, and Thomas Blackburn.[2] They advocate using the following assumptions when employing A-EVM:[3,4]

- Progress should be measured at the release level (not at the iteration on product level)
- A-EVM calculations may be done at the end of each iteration, when actual iteration velocity and costs are known
- Assume that functionality is done at the end of each iteration (i.e., that each iteration delivers value based on customer acceptance whether or not a formal release occurs)

They also offer a new set of earned value definitions customized for use with agile, including the following measures.[5] We have provided them in Figure 9.7 so that you may see how they may be captured in agile projects.

Measure	EVM Definition	Formula
Performance Measure Baseline (PMB)	Total number of story points planned for a release (S_p)	$PMB = S_p$
Schedule Baseline (SB)	Total number of planned iterations (I_p) multiplied by iteration length (L)	$SB = I_p * L$
Planned Percent Complete (PPC)	The number of the current iteration (i) divided by the total number of planned iterations (I_p)	$PPC = i/I_p$
Actual Percent Complete (APC)	The number of iteration story points completed (s) divided by the total number of story points planned (S_p)	$APC = s/S_p$

Figure 9.7 Selected Agile EVM Measures, Definitions, and Formulas.

While this work is considered cutting-edge, it remains unclear the extent to which these A-EVM measures have been adopted by the agile community. We suggest that agile teams consider piloting their usage as project metrics. Note that the list provided is a partial one and that interested readers should consult Sulaiman et al. as well as Sliger & Broderick for a more thorough treatment of the topic.[6,7]

Chapter Close-Out

Agile PM Processes Grid™ Exercise

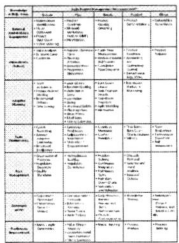

Please take out a blank piece of paper, set a timer for no more than 3 minutes, and see how much of the grid you can reproduce from memory. To make the most of this Agile PM Processes Grid™ exercise, please simulate being in the testing environment. Close your book and all your notes. Visualize the Proctor handing you the blank sheets of paper and taking your seat in the testing site. Begin by drawing the grid, 6 columns and 8 rows, and then fill in everything you can. After the 3 minutes ends, use your book and notes to complete the grid. Study it as you do so.

Terminology Matching Exercise

In the blank column to the left of the Term, fill in the letter that identifies the correct definition or description.

	Term		Definition / Description
	1. EVM	A	Projects are those where no discrete deliverables are defined and the customer pays for the "level of effort" expended.
	2. LOE	B	The budgeted cost of work planned for an iteration.
	3. Performance Measurement Baseline	C	The budgeted cost of work completed for an iteration.
	4. Earned Value	D	The cost of work completed and paid for in an iteration.
	5. A-EVM	E	Total number of story points planned for a release.
	6. Schedule Baseline	F	The total number of planned iterations multiplied by sprint length.
	7. Phased Development Contracts	G	The contractor bills the customer and allows the customer to end the project and stop paying when they don't see added value.
	8. Planned Value	H	Typically funded on a quarterly basis and additional funding is approved following each successful release.
	9. Actual Cost	I	An adaptation of EVM calculations tailored to Agile Project Management.
	10. Time and Materials Contracts	J	A program management technique that integrates scope, schedule, and resource consumption information in order to measure project performance against planned cost metrics.

Crossword Puzzle

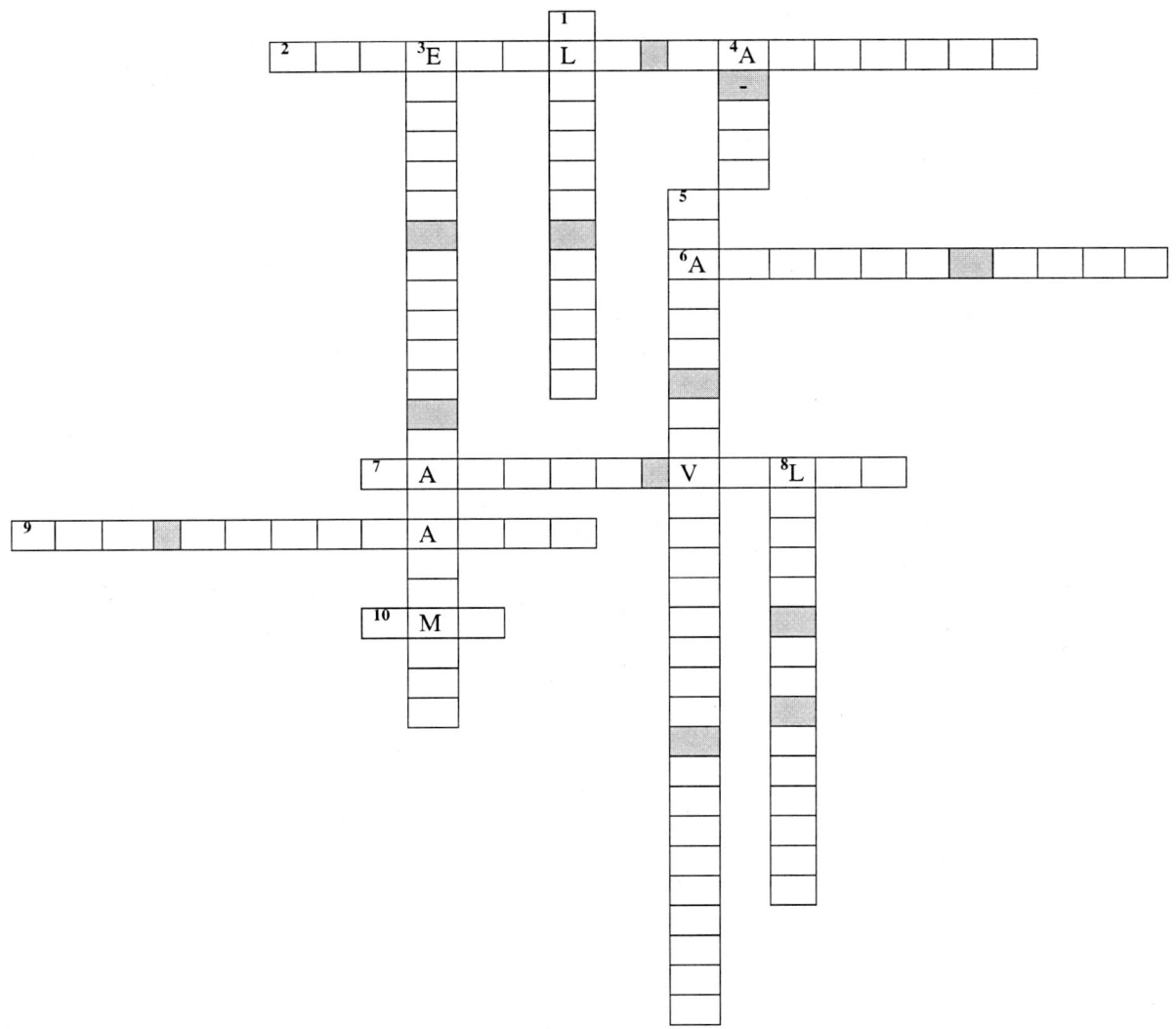

Hints:

ACROSS
2. The total number of planned iterations multiplied by sprint length.
6. The cost of work completed and paid for in an iteration.
7. The budgeted cost of work completed for an iteration.
9. The contractor bills the customer and allows the customer to end the project and stop paying when they don't see added value.
10. Total number of story points planned for a release.

DOWN
1. The budgeted cost of work planned for an iteration.
3. A program management technique that integrates scope, schedule, and resource consumption information in order to measure project performance.
4. An adaptation of the widely recognized and used EVM toolset.
5. Funded on a quarterly basis and additional funding is approved following each successful release.
8. Projects where no discrete deliverables are defined and the customer pays for the work expended

Word Search

Word Search - 10 Words to find:

- PLANNEDVALUE
- PMB
- EARNED VALUE
- PHASEDDEVELOPMENTCONTRACTS
- T&MCONTRACTS
- A-EVM
- SCHEDULE BASELINE
- LEVELOFEFFORT
- ACTUALCOST
- EARNED VALUEMANAGEMENT

```
_ M A C L U E E F A T P N V S C H E D U L E _ B A S E L I E
P H A S E D _ D E V E L O P M E N T _ C O N T R A C O T D B
_ V U A C T U A L _ C O S T V G E _ N E V P _ D E T N V C F
B F E C T L E D C U N R B N D S P T R V A P E O E T B T M
_ A A U A M C E A A A _ E E A _ C T A & N - S T M D R O & L
E - L A E O L A B U _ T N N A V T E T D N T O E A O P O M R
T _ _ A E R T E C _ D A C E T M O V F N R H G F F T N N _ M
& E A E L L D _ A E L & C G E M E V E O T A U F E N L A C E
M - - A A E N _ _ R O _ A O B _ G A F R N T E U U A C & O B
_ N E D V F P U T N N I S A E C E F C A S _ L S V G N V N V
C S V _ C S N M S L R E D F N _ E U M T F E _ U O M T D T _
O P M A C D _ P E U T O D A L _ V _ _ O U P T T N M V - R A
N L _ E - M D E E _ E U A _ F A E L _ L T A A V R E C A A M
T A - A F - E E N V C _ E O V U U L T V B N L _ V E D N C P
R N D S R P R _ M T _ B _ H L A E M F E E L T _ _ F H C T D
A N U L H S U A N T A L E A E V L N E _ C R E A C U A D S M
C E P L N V _ E A T E S V U E T D U N P P D E M N O E N C L
V D A A N E T A _ V V _ L L L E U O E O I D V C T E S L E H
U _ D L A N _ N E U D A S C H E D U L E _ B A S E L I N E E
_ V _ A T L H L O E V A A F C E E A C E A E P _ V _ E _ E E
U A E E R L A T N _ U S T L A R L T A E A R N E D _ V A E N
T L E S O _ H R D E T U M D U T T L E R T T U A L S E U L L
F U E A L L A E R A C F M P O A E H D A C T V _ N U _ S F C
T E T A T E N F D A A _ U A _ E _ E D T N O E A E E M L L A
L F L N T N A E A R N E D _ V A L U E _ M A N A G E M O R V
O R E L A T E & N N A P V N P A R O E C N P A U V U P _ N B
M N M L T U L T D E E M M L V _ E _ E - V _ P L R T L C P B
R H P M N A V S D _ C B U E E V - R T E _ E L B E U E U N _
L _ P H A S E D _ D E V E L O P M E N T _ C O N T R A C T S
A C C R A T _ T E N F P R A N H T _ N R U N - E V U L A _ _
```

Chapter Practice Test

1. Which of the following would be the least preferred contract type for an agile project?

   A. Agile iteration contract
   B. Firm fixed price
   C. Phased development
   D. Time and materials

2. A contract based on the team delivering agreed upon features to defined quality standards by iteration end with the understanding that the iteration backlog is not changed during the iteration is best described as a(n) _____ contract.

   A. Agile iteration
   B. Phased development
   C. Firm fixed price
   D. Time and materials

3. Which of the following is true regarding proposed changes to the committed iteration plan that impact the approved cost baseline?

   A. There is no approved cost baseline in an agile project
   B. Changes can be made with the unanimous approval of the team
   C. Any changes must be negotiated with, and approved by, the customer/proxy
   D. Changes can be made at the discretion of the product owner

4. One of the benefits of using Agile Earned Value Management (A-EVM) on your agile project is _____.

   A. Iteration and release planning is made much easier
   B. The customer is always assured of an adequate return on investment (ROI)
   C. Cost overruns are eliminated
   D. Visibility into how effectively project funding is being managed against the metric of expected return on investment (ROI).

5. _____ is a program management technique that integrates scope, schedule, and resource consumption information in order to measure project performance against planned cost metrics.

   A. Earned Value Management (EVM)
   B. Agile Project Management Model (APM)
   C. Extreme Programming (XP)
   D. Configuration Management (CM)

6. A contract type that is typically funded on a quarterly basis with additional funding approved following each successful release is best described as a(n) _____ contract.

   A. Agile iteration
   B. Phased development
   C. Firm fixed price
   D. Time and materials

7. The fundamental premise of Earned Value Management (EVM) is _____.

   A. Allocated budget and actual cost for specific work are completely unrelated
   B. Work cannot take longer than the amount of time scheduled for that work
   C. Work cannot cost more than the amount of funding budgeted for that work
   D. As work is completed the corresponding budget value is earned

8. In an A-EVM environment, the budgeted cost for the work performed in an iteration is best described by the term _____.

   A. Earned Value Management (EVM)
   B. Earned Value (EV)
   C. Planned Value (PV)
   D. Actual Cost (AC)

9. A contract type that is accounts for labor and material consumed to date and allows the customer to end the project and stop paying when they don't see added value is best described as a(n) _____ contract.

   A. Time and materials
   B. Agile iteration
   C. Phased development
   D. Firm fixed price

10. In an A-EVM environment, the cost of work completed during an iteration is best described by the term _____.

    A. Refactored Value (RV)
    B. Earned Value (EV)
    C. Actual Cost (AC)
    D. Planned Value (PV)

11. In an A-EVM environment, the planned value of work actually completed during an iteration is best described by the term _____.

    A. Actual Cost (AC)
    B. Earned Value (EV)
    C. Planned Value (PV)
    D. Refactored Value (RV)

12. Cost Variance (CV) and Schedule Variance (SV) are two principle terms used both in EVM and A-EVM. A negative value for CV and SV indicates _____.

    A. The project will finish under budget and late
    B. The project is currently running under budget, but more information is needed to determine schedule status
    C. The project is currently running under budget and is ahead of schedule
    D. The project is currently running over budget and behind schedule

13. Cost Performance Index (CPI) and Schedule Performance Index (SPI) are two principle terms used both in EVM and A-EVM. A value of less than one for CPI and SPI indicates _____.

    A. The project is currently running over budget and behind schedule
    B. The project is currently running under budget and is ahead of schedule
    C. The project is currently running under budget, but more information is needed to determine schedule status
    D. The project will finish under budget and late

14. The difference between Earned Value (EV) and Actual Cost (AC) is best expressed by the term _____.

    A. Cost Performance Index (CPI)
    B. Cost Variance (CV)
    C. Schedule Performance Index (SPI)
    D. Refactored Value (RV)

15. The ratio of Earned Value (EV) divided by Actual Cost (AC) is best expressed by the term _____.

    A. Schedule Performance Index (SPI)
    B. Refactored Value (RV)
    C. Cost Performance Index (CPI)
    D. Cost Variance (CV)

Answers – Terminology Matching

1:J, 2:A, 3:E, 4:C, 5:I, 6:F, 7:H, 8:B, 9:D, 10:G

Answers – Crossword Puzzle

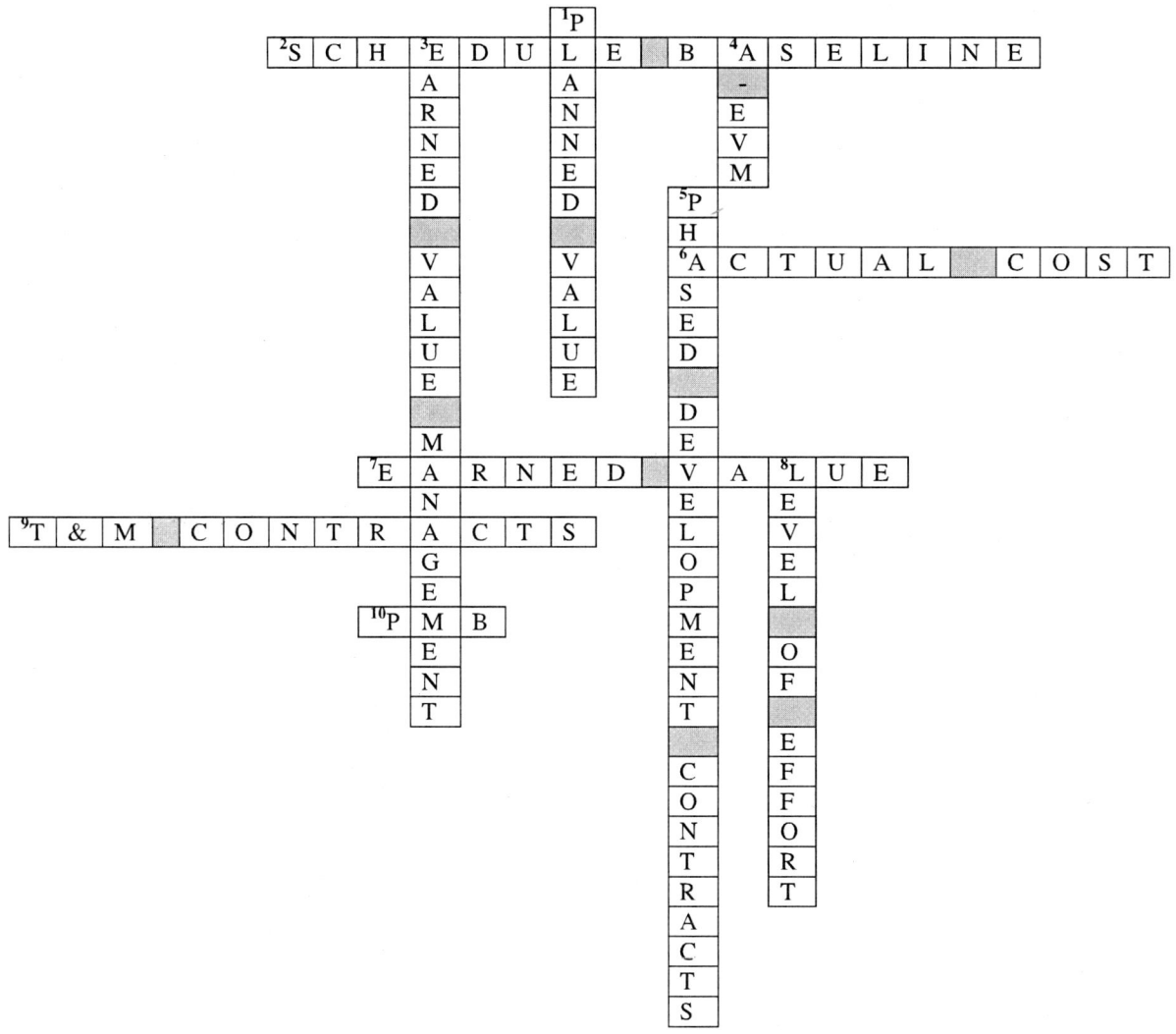

Answers – Word Search

Word Search - 10 Words to find:

PLANNEDVALUE T&MCONTRACTS LEVELOFEFFORT
PMB A-EVM ACTUALCOST
EARNED VALUE SCHEDULE BASELINE EARNED
VALUEMANAGEMENT PHASEDDEVELOPMENTCONTRACTS

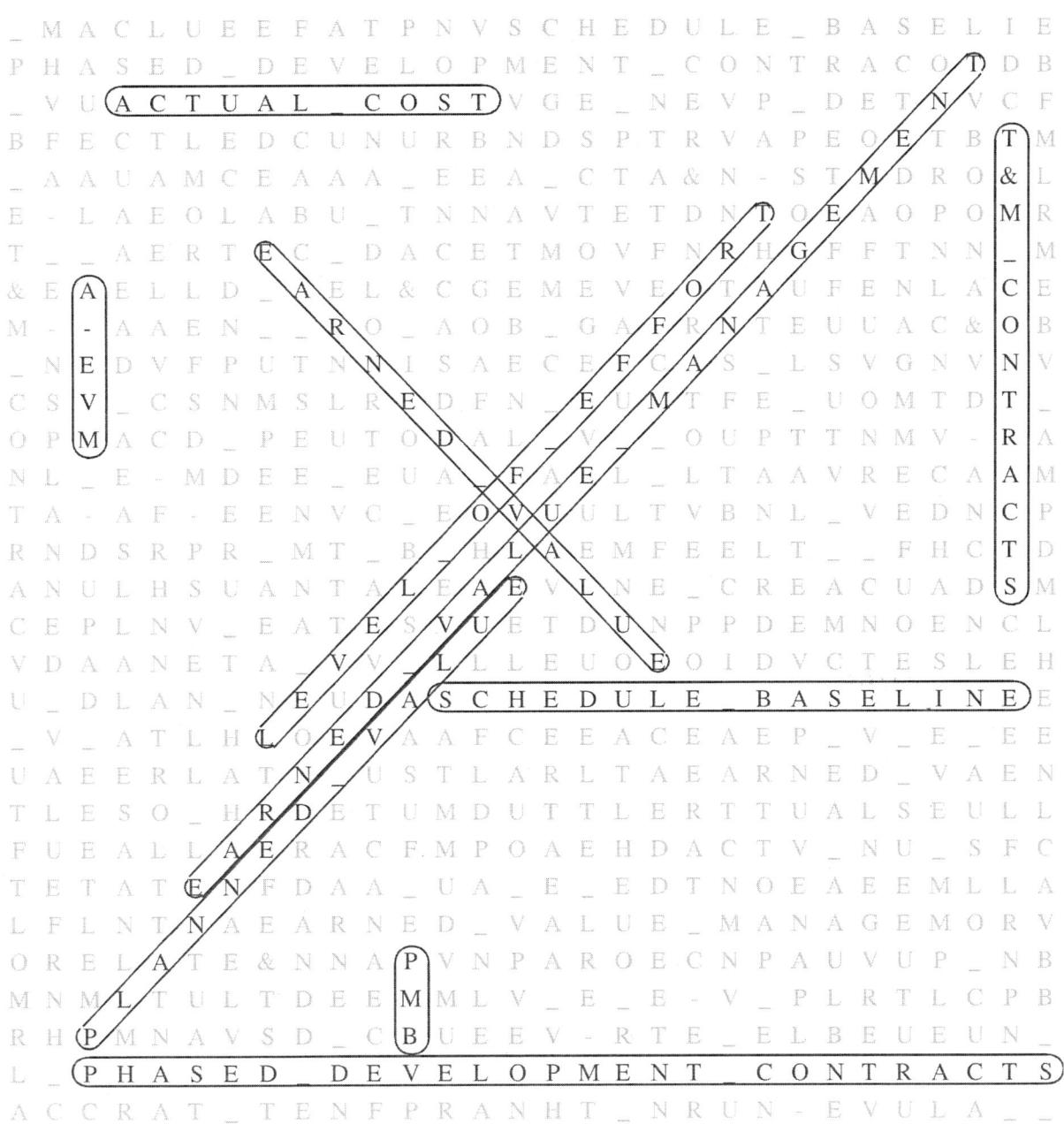

Answers – Practice Test

1. **B.** The firm fixed price contract would be the least desirable choice as it would be the contract type that would likely have the most trouble accommodating frequent changes.

2. **A.** Agile iteration contracts are based on the team delivering agreed upon features to defined quality standards by iteration end, and the Product Owner not changing the iteration backlog before iteration end.

3. **C.** Once the committed iteration plan has been defined within the approved cost baseline, any changes must be negotiated with, and approved by, the customer/proxy. Doing otherwise will quickly disrupt the team's discipline in planning and committing.

4. **D.** Agile Project Management frameworks do not articulate how to identify, track and manage costs. Analyzing and evaluating Return on Investment (ROI) against the product vision is a fundamental business, and therefore customer, need. One benefit of using EVM is seeing how effectively project funding is being managed against the metric of expected ROI.

5. **A.** Earned Value Management (EVM) is a program management technique that integrates scope, schedule, and resource consumption information in order to measure project performance against planned cost metrics. It provides quantitative, objective data to supplement qualitative, subjective judgments.

6. **B.** Phased Development contracts are typically funded on a quarterly basis and additional funding is approved following each successful release. Knowing another release will occur, or not, next quarter guides feature selection for the timebox.

7. **D.** Earned Value Management's fundamental premise is that as work is *completed* the corresponding budget value is *earned*, hence the term Earned Value (EV). In EVM for discrete deliverables that paradigm of value only being earned for completed work aligns at the most basic level with Agile Project Management.

8. **C.** Planned Value (PV) in the A-EVM environment is defined as the budgeted cost of work planned for an iteration. In the traditional project management environment applying EVM, the definition of PV is slightly different and is defined as the budgeted cost of work planned for a ***specific time period.***

9. **A.** Time and Materials contracts account for the labor hours and material consumed to date and allow the customer to end the project and stop paying when they don't see added value.

10. **C.** Actual Cost (AC) in the A-EVM environment is defined as the actual cost of work planned for an iteration. In the traditional project management environment applying EVM, the definition of AC is slightly different and is defined as the actual cost of work planned for a specific time period.

11. **B.** Earned Value (EV) in the A-EVM environment is defined as the planned value of work actually completed in an iteration. In the traditional project management environment applying EVM, the definition of EV is slightly different and is defined as the planned value of work actually completed for a ***specific time period.***

12. **D.** For both the SV and CV, a negative variance is undesirable and indicates the project is behind schedule (negative SV) or over budget (negative CV). A positive SV indicates that the project is ahead of schedule and a positive CV indicates the project is currently under budget.

13. **A.** For both the SPI and CPI, a value less than one is undesirable and indicates the project is behind schedule (SPI less than one) or over budget (CPI less than one). An SPI greater than one indicates that the project is ahead of schedule and a CPI greater than one indicates the project is currently under budget.

14. **B.** Cost Variance is defined by the equation CV = EV − AC where EV is earned value and AC represents the actual cost of work completed.

15. **C.** Cost Performance Index (CPI) is defined by the equation CPI = EV / AC where EV is earned value and AC represents the actual cost of work completed.

Chapter End Notes

[1] More information can be obtained at http://www.acq.osd.mil/evm/ or from OASD(A) / PARCA EVM, 3620 Defense Pentagon, RM 5A1082, Washington, D.C. 20301-3620, Email: parcaevm@osd.mil.

[2] Sulaiman, T., Barton, B., & Blackburn, T. (2006). AgileEVM - *Earned value management in scrum projects. AGILE 2006 (AGILE'06)*, 7-16.

[3] Ibid.

[4] Sliger, M., & Broderick, S. (2008). *The software project manager's bridge to agility.* Upper Saddle River, NJ: Addison-Wesley.

[5] Sulaiman, T., Barton, B., & Blackburn, T. (2006). *AgileEVM - Earned value management in scrum projects. AGILE 2006 (AGILE'06)*, 7-16.

[6] Ibid.

[7] Sliger, M., & Broderick, S. (2008). *The software project manager's bridge to agility.* Upper Saddle River, NJ: Addison-Wesley.

Chapter 10

Closing Projects

Chapter Highlights

While in some respects there is not a great deal of difference between agile and traditional project closure, here we highlight some of the important distinctions. Foremost is the notion that (as with most things agile) closure occurs in an iterative fashion.

External Stakeholders Engagement

Deliverables Acceptance

It is during the trio of iteration-closing meetings (i.e., demo, review, and retrospective) that the agile team gains acceptance of its deliverables. As each feature is reviewed, it is compared to both: The acceptance criteria stated as part of its user story *(See Figure 4.9)*, and The team's definition of done. Scope verification occurs as part of this customer acceptance testing and acceptance. Highsmith offers that (particularly in the software development realm) this process of acceptance should be conductedusing a series of automated testing and customer reviews.[1]

At this juncture, the team may take credit for the total story points accepted by the customer/proxy and all sticky notes may be moved to the done column on the story board.[2] In some work environments, a formal customer acceptance document is signed. In the event that some features are not accepted, they are returned to the product backlog for reevaluation during the next round of planning.

Acceptance also signifies the point where administrative aspects of project closure occur. If milestone payments and/or phase-gate decisions about the project need to be made, this is typically when they occur. For example, based on the deliverables accepted, the project may be cancelled or approved to continue.

Value-Driven Delivery

Product Release

A *release* occurs when a product is ready to use. An agile release is similar to a traditional project milestone, with the deliverable being a specified set of working features. The release may be internal to the organization or there may be formal deployment to customers and end users. Thus, an interim release may be a non-deployed set of working features that comprise a "potentially shippable product." In this context, a *project* consists of one or more releases. The end of the project is characterized by termination of funding and release of the team members to other activities (i.e.., operations or new projects).[3,4]

As we noted in Chapter 4, some agile teams will employ a hardening iteration in preparation for a product release, particularly for a project-closing release. The hardening iteration consists of specific activities to make the product ready for production, including documenting the product, marketing it, and scheduling it for production.

Team Performance

Team Evaluations, Performance Incentives, and Self-Assessment

One of the challenges in employing agile methods is effecting change on traditional human resource (HR) practices. In terms of performance evaluations and incentives, most discussions advocate two things: 1) The agile project manager should be removed from the process of doing individual performance appraisals of team members; and 2) Teams should be empowered to conduct their own performance assessments.

The main reason given for not having Agile Project Managers conduct performance evaluations of team members is that it creates role conflict.[5] The performance evaluation is viewed as a "command-and-control" responsibility by many agilists, which conflicts with the roles of facilitator and creator of a safe work environment for the agile team. If the agile project manager is charged with doing the performance evaluations, the role becomes more authoritarian than one of servant leader.

The practice of performing *self-assessments* is an empowering one for the agile team. Highsmith suggests that teams perform self-assessments at the conclusion of each iteration based on dimensions of successful performance and agile behavior.[6] On the performance dimension, the team assesses how well it did in terms of delivery. The team assessment is not just based on an objective metric (i.e., estimated versus delivered story points), but on how well the team believes it did and how it can be expected to improve in the future. The behavior dimension captures how well the team executed its agile processes. The behavior assessment really captures the questions, "How agile are we?" and "How can we improve our agility?" Figure 10.1 portrays a team self-assessment where a five-point scale was used to rate team performance and behavior.

| | Team Quicksilver–Self Assessment by Iteration ||||||
| | Behavior |||||
Performance		Far Below Standard	Below Standard	Meets Standard	Above Standard	Far Above Standard
	Far Above Standard					
	Above Standard				I$_4$	
	Meets Standard			I$_2$ I$_3$		
	Below Standard			I$_1$		
	Far Below Standard					

Figure 10.1 Team Self-Assessment Graph by Iteration (Ix).

Communication

Retrospectives (Project, Release, and Iteration Levels)
Retrospectives are really the heart of agile project closure. It is in this context that agile teams can attend to systemic process problems, discover solutions, and implement changes in a self-organizing fashion.

 Occurring at the end of each iteration, product release, and project, the agile *retrospective* is largely process-centric. The retrospective typically occurs in conjunction with two other end-of-timebox meetings, the product demo and the review meetings. The retrospective focuses on agile process improvement, and gives participants the opportunity to devise changes that produce better work products, reduce errors, or improve communications.

The retrospective is led by a meeting facilitator. At the iteration level, this may be the Agile Project Manager. At the product release and project levels, we recommend utilizing an external facilitator so that the project manager may participate actively in the retrospective. (See our Chapter 6 tip on **When to Step Out of the Facilitator Role.**) This is often accomplished by borrowing an agile coach or facilitator from another team to run the meeting.[7]

There are some other differences between the iteration retrospective and those occurring at the product release and project levels. We will address these distinctions later in this chapter.

Retrospective Structure

To derive the maximum benefits from a retrospective, a solid meeting structure and schedule should be put into place. We outline such a structure in Table 10.2, for which we are largely indebted to Derby and Larson's (2006) work.[8]

Segment	Common Elements
Establish retrospective parameters	• State retrospective goals • Establish meeting ground rules and timebox • Review team values and working agreements
Assemble data	• Review hard data: information radiators, metrics, artifacts, etc • Discuss team feelings and opinions
Develop insights	• Identify strengths, weaknesses and other issues • Interpret the data • Consider root causes
Make decisions	• Delineate potential improvements and experiments • Prioritize the list • Record action items and owners
End retrospective	• Identify learning strategies • Retain retrospective documentation • Specify additional outputs

Figure 10.2 Retrospective Meeting Structure by Segment.

The first segment involves ***establishing retrospective parameters.*** Here, it is critical for the team to identify the goals of the retrospective (e.g., "Discover ways to improve our velocity" or "How can we get the customer more engaged?"). Since you want to drive success, the ideal goals are ones that may be realistically accomplished during the retrospective. Establishing ground rules and a time frame for the retrospective helps the team focus on the work to be done. Finally, the team values and working agreements may be reviewed at this juncture. If they exist in the form of information radiators, such artifacts should be brought to the meeting.

Assembling data has two components – reviewing facts from the recently completed timebox and gathering opinions and feelings from the team about their work. The hard facts come largely from agile metrics, informatory radiators, and artifacts. All such data should be brought to the meeting for review and discussion. Soliciting opinions and gauging the feelings of the participants may be more difficult. Here, we recommend using activities aimed at eliciting feedback from the team.

Developing insights requires the team to take the data from the previous segment and to analyze it. Given the information the team has about how they are working, how can they improve? If the team is falling short in some way, what are the root causes? For example, if team velocity has dipped, have there been personnel changes, or are there other explanations? Perhaps more than in other retrospective segments, activities are helpful in evoking insights about how to improve. See the Planning Activities section in Chapter 4 for ideas on this.

After considering multiple insights, the team is then charged with ***making decisions*** to prioritize and implement them for later iterations. This includes recording action items and having participants assume ownership.

Ending the retrospective should be done in a coordinated fashion. The facilitator may restate the most important lessons learned and ask the team how they intend to use them to improve. How will the retrospective be documented? A visual record may be created using digital cameras or by archiving flip chart pages. If outputs result from the retrospective – such as new agile metrics or information radiators –this becomes an action item for someone on the team.

As with other aspects of agile methods, this generic retrospective structure may have to be tailored to meet the needs of the organization. Try experimenting with different activities; you may discard several that accomplish the same thing before discovering one that the team finds really useful!

Retrospective Activities

As we discussed in Chapter 4, activities are not limited to retrospectives. As a reminder, activities are structured, interactive processes that help the agile team focus on the work to be done. They are optional and supposed to be fun and energizing for the participants. However, if they add no value to the retrospective or if you are pressed for time, you may omit them.

Figure 10.3 presents a summary of activities commonly used in agile retrospectives, along with recommendations for where they may be used. Since it really goes beyond the scope of this book to describe all such activities in detail, we highly recommend Derby and Larson's (2006) thorough treatment of this subject.[9] Also refer to Chapter 4 and Figures 10.4 and 10.5 for more detail on select activities.

Shuffle time is the time it takes to transition from one activity to another during meetings (including retrospectives).

Example: Retrospective Schedule

As the retrospective facilitator, you should have a plan for guiding the meeting. Here's an example of how you might allot the time for a three hour retrospective:

Team Quicksilver
Iteration 4 Retrospective Schedule
Attendees: Tony B, John G, Peggy C, Joe T, Susan M, Flash G, & Bryan D

Segment	Percentage	Time (Minutes)
Establish retrospective parameters	5%	9
Assemble data	35%	63
Develop insights	20%	36
Make decisions	20%	36
End retrospective	10%	18
Shuffle time	10%	18
Totals	**100%**	**180**

The schedule percentages undoubtedly will vary in your organization, and are impacted by many factors such as the project itself, the attendees, and the agile practices that you use.

As you see, the schedule includes shuffle time, but it does not include planned breaks or lunch, so it might take four hours in real time to conduct a three hour retrospective as outlined above.

In addition to crafting a retrospective schedule, it's a good idea to choose your activities ahead of time. One clever practice is to select two equivalent activities for each segment – a long one and a short one. If you run into time constraints, opt for the shorter one!

Suggested Activity	Description
Segment : Establish Retrospective Parameters	
CheckñIn	Individual round–robin responses to questions posed by facilitator.
ESVP	Identify attitudes towards the retrospective as one of an; **E**xplorer, **S**hopper, **V**acationer or **P**risoner (ESVP). *See Figure 10.4*
Working Agreements	Group constructs working agreements for retrospective.
Segment : Assemble Data	
Color Code Dots	Post colored dots to show timeline events where emotions ran high/low.
Mad Sad Glad	Survey feelings by using sticky notes or index cards to describe points during the project when people were mad, sad or glad.
Satisfaction Histogram	Build histograms to assess individual satisfaction and teamwork on agile practices and processes. Facilitator summaries data in group histogram. *See Figure 10.5*
Timeline	Write significant events on index cards. Facilitator leads discussion of facts and feelings about the events.
Segment : Develop Insights	
Brainstorming	*See Planning Activities In Chapter 4*
Fishbone Diagram	
Force Field Analysis	
Learning Matrix	
Prioritize With Dots	
Segment : Make Decisions	
Circle of questions	Seated in a circle, participants engage in a Q & A process until consensus is achieved.
Planning game	Traditional planning game applied to retrospective. Write ideas on cards, brainstorm, elimate redundancies and fill in gaps. Used to identify workflow and decompose tasks.
SMART goals	Exercise to develop goals that are; **S**pecific, **M**easurable, **A**ttainable, **R**elevant and **T**imely (SMART).
Segment : End Retrospective	
+/Delta	Identify strengths and changes for next retrospective.
Helped, Hindered, Hypothesis	Give feedback to facilitator on retrospective on what helped, what hindered and what hypotheses you have for improvements.
Learning Matrix	*See Planning Activities In Chapter 4*
SWOT Analysis	Identify **S**trengths, **W**eaknesses, **O**pportunities and **T**hreats (SWOT).

Figure 10.3. Suggested Activities and Descriptions by Retrospective Segment.

Team Quicksilver: Iteration 4 Retrospective
ESVP Participant Types

Explorer: 4
Shopper: 3
Vacationer: 0
Prisoner: 2

Figure 10.4. Example of a Team's Summary ESVP Tally.

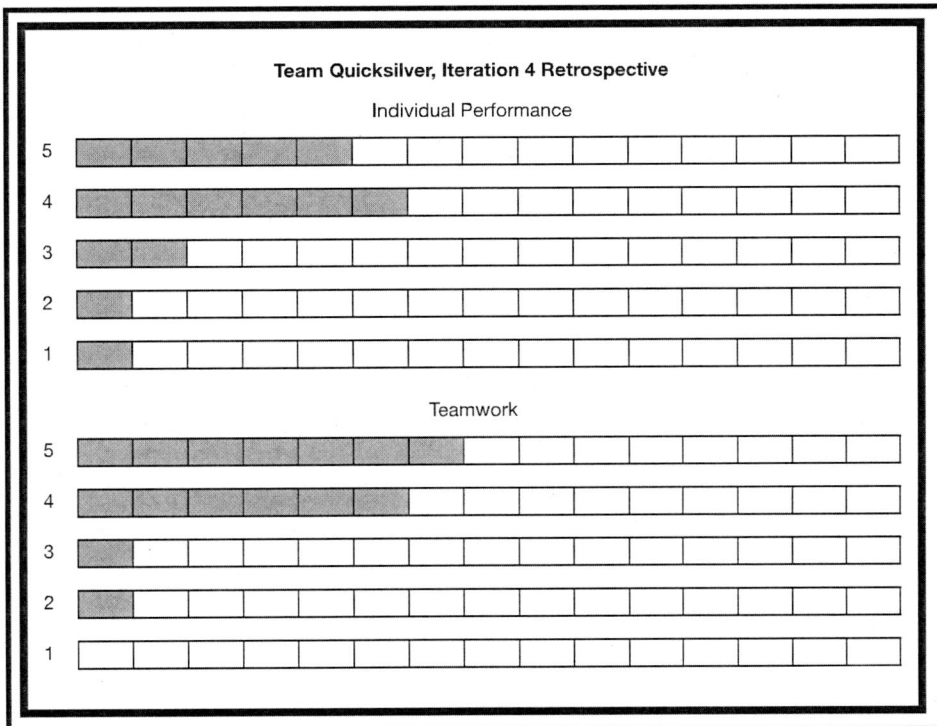

Figure 10.5. Example of a Team's Summary Satisfaction Histograms for Individual Performance and Teamwork.

Keys to Facilitating a Retrospective

The facilitator's main responsibilities during the retrospective are to:[10]

Ensure adherence to agile principles: In this sense, the facilitator fulfills the agile coach role by enforcing agile discipline, encouraging the team in its self-organizing efforts, and motivating them to strive for continuous improvement.

Foster the appropriate participation of all attendees: This does not necessarily mean that all team members participate equally, but that everyone has the *opportunity* to be heard. It also means taking action, when necessary, to "shut down" participants who are high in power or influence when their participation is at the expense of others.

Monitor for violations of team working agreements: This is one of the inevitable landmines during the retrospective. The facilitator points out such violations to the participants and makes suggestions to get them back on course.

Redirect the discussion when blaming occurs: When the focus of the discussion turns from being process oriented to blaming others, the facilitator redirects the discussion by asking questions of the parties involved, soliciting feedback from them on their feelings, and refocusing them on the retrospective goals.

Manage external invitees during release and project retrospectives: We will discuss the significance of this in more detail in the next section. The facilitator invites external participants to these retrospectives and educates them on agile conventions and meeting expectations.[11] If necessary, the facilitator meets with those new to agile and conducts training sessions.

How can the retrospective facilitator improve? Being cognizant of one's own emotional state and monitoring the room for nonverbal cues from participants are both helpful. Asking for direct feedback from the team is another way. The Helped, Hindered, Hypothesis activity *(See Figure 10.2)* is specifically oriented to eliciting such feedback. For other ways in which the facilitator can improve in running meetings, review the Coaching/Facilitation section in Chapter 6.

Release and Project Retrospectives

Throughout this book, we have focused primarily on the iteration retrospective. There are some differences between the iteration retrospective and the release and project level varieties.[37]

We have already mentioned one – for the release and project retrospectives, an external facilitator is preferred so that the Agile Project Manager may participate fully along with the rest of the team.

For the release and project retrospectives, people *from outside the team* may be invited to attend. Invitees may include external customers and key stakeholders as well as people from senior management, product support and deployment, legal/regulatory, technical support, and operations. A rule of thumb in extending invitations is that the people invited are both expected to add value to the retrospective and to abide by the agile practices of the organization.

At the iteration level, the product demo, review, and retrospective may be combined into one meeting, with non-team members being excused after the demo. However, at the release and project level, we recommend that the demo, review, and retrospective be split into three separate meetings. This decision is driven by the sheer length of time involved (i.e., potentially spanning several days if all three meetings are combined) and the fact that you may have different audiences for the respective meetings.

As compared to iteration retrospectives, additional preparation work may be needed. Such efforts may include:[13,14]

1. Arranging for an external facilitator to lead the retrospective;
2. Following up with invitees to confirm attendance and to verify that they will raise issues that they deem important;
3. Educating some attendees who are naïve to agile practices;
4. Distributing and scoring pre-retrospective questionnaires to ensure that everyone has opportunity to provide feedback;
5. Planning for a longer (i.e., full day) retrospective to allow time for cross-functional feedback; and
6. Securing a larger meeting room to accommodate the number of people.

Following the release and project retrospectives, additional documentation may be required beyond the standard information radiators.

Continuous Improvement

Process Tailoring

Process tailoring may be thought of in two ways – tailoring agile methods to the organization and tailoring organizational processes based on knowledge acquired by practicing agile. The former consists of optimizing agile methods for the organization while the latter reflects the Lean philosophy of optimizing the whole.

Tailoring Agile Methods

Cockburn opines that selecting and customizing agile methodologies should be based on what works for the organization.[15] For example, when choosing an agile methodology, an organization that struggles to adhere to (or even document) its current policies and procedures would do well to avoid a high discipline agile method such as XP. In such situations, the organization might opt for Scrum or Crystal, where the discipline requirements may be barely sufficient to get the job done.[16]

When successfully practicing an agile method over a period of time (i.e., successfully delivering valuable products to customers), a team may choose to drop some of the method's practices in favor of reducing overhead. Such an experiment epitomizes the barely sufficient philosophy – if the team can continue to deliver products of the same quality while saving a little bit of time and money previously spent adhering to agile discipline, why not try to do so?

The team does not have to wait until the end-of- timebox closing meetings to implement agile practice improvements. Team reflective workshops and open space meetings are forums which the team may employ to hone its agile methods.

An organization's efforts to optimize its product development methodology may evolve to undertaking hybrid projects. **A hybrid project is one in which agile and traditional development methodologies are combined,** or one in which multiple agile methods are combined. For an example, see the insert on *A Hybrid Project.* The decision to embark on hybrid projects is typically an enterprise-wide endeavor, and reflects an organization that has achieved a high level of process maturity.[17] For a more complete treatment of agile organizational maturity and hybrid projects, we recommend Appleby, Stenbeck, and Berthot's The Agile Maturity Model (AMM).[18]

Tailoring Organizational Processes

While the agile team's focus is the iteration deliverables, it also must consider the overall workings of the organization. Recall from our discussion of process-centric knowledge sharing in Chapter 8 that knowledge gained on individual projects may have implications for the entire organization (i.e., at an enterprise-wide level). For example, process analysis by a project team may lead to improvements in an organization's manufacturing and distribution chain. This by-product of project work thus results in optimizing the throughput of the organization. To restate, while iteration end is a natural point for implementation, it is not necessary to wait until project closure to initiate improvements.

Example: A Hybrid Project

Can both traditional and agile methodologies coexist in the same project? Yes! Let's illustrate how by examining a real case, that of a "make-or-break" enterprise software implementation for a regional US healthcare company.

ORGANIZATION: Regional healthcare company specialized in managed care and insurance claims

- 175 full-time employees (FTEs) and $100 million in annual revenues
- Very poor history of completing long-term projects

MAIN PROJECT: Baseline estimate 14 month, $2.4 million enterprise level software implementation. Standard PMBOK® methodology used to manage program of projects, including software implementation.

- Medium matrix structure with 50 FTEs reporting to a program manager (PM)
- Project sponsor: CIO with high project involvement and support for organizational process improvement
- Project charter, kickoff meeting, project plan, formal risk management, integrated change control process, lessons learned, etc.
- Tools: MS Project, project dashboard, and metrics reports

SUBPROJECTS: Scrum framework used to manage internal application development of interfaces connecting new enterprise software to 12 legacy applications (e.g., financial suite, reporting tool, document control/faxing, etc.)

- Roles: CIO = Product Owner; PM = Product Owner/Scrum Master; Senior Developer = Scrum Master; Scrum Team = 5 to 7 developers
- Product Owner maintained product and sprint backlogs
- Scrum Master maintained burn-down chart and ran meetings
- PM incorporated scrum metrics into overall project metrics reports and translated stories and tasks into the program MS Project file

OUTCOMES: *Mixed, but generally positive for this organization*

- Enterprise software implementation met budget and scope constraints
- Schedule exceeded 14 month estimate by 4 months, due to company layoffs and poor relationship with software vendor
- 10/12 (83.3%) of application development subprojects completed; 1 cancelled by senior management and 1 not completed due to insufficient resources
- 17/20 (85.0%) of sprints completed; 3 terminated abnormally due to insufficient resources or changing organizational priorities

Summary

Closure is the part of the project where we remind all agile teams to celebrate and go home!

It is during the trio of iteration-closing meetings (i.e., demo, review, and retrospective) that the agile team gains acceptance of its deliverables. As each feature is reviewed, it is compared to both: 1) The acceptance criteria stated as part of its user story; and 2) The team's definition of done. Acceptance also signifies the point where administrative aspects of project closure occur. If milestone payments and/or phase-gate decisions about the project need to be made, this is typically when they occur.

A release occurs when a product is ready to use. An agile release is similar to a traditional project milestone, with the deliverable being a specified set of working features. The release may be internal to the organization or there may be formal deployment to customers and end users. The end of the project is characterized by termination of funding and release of the team members to other activities.

In terms of performance evaluations and incentives, most discussions advocate two things: 1) The agile project manager should be removed from the process of doing individual performance appraisals of team members; and 2) Teams should be empowered to conduct their own performance assessments. The practice of performing self-assessments is an empowering one for the agile team. One way of performing team self-assessments is based on dimensions of successful performance and agile behavior.

Occurring at the end of each iteration, product release, and project, the agile retrospective typically occurs in conjunction with two other end-of-timebox meetings, the product demo and the review meetings. The retrospective focuses on agile process improvement, and gives participants the opportunity to devise changes that produce better work products, reduce errors, or improve communications.

To gain maximum benefit from a retrospective, a solid meeting structure and schedule should be established. One such structure involves dividing the retrospective into segment such as: 1) Establish parameters; 2) Assemble data; 3) Develop insights; 4) Make decisions; and 5) End retrospective.

There are some differences between the iteration retrospective and the release and project level varieties. For the release and project retrospectives, an external facilitator is preferred so that the agile project manager may participate fully along with the rest of the team. Additional preparation work and documentation may be needed for the higher-level retrospectives.

Process tailoring may be thought of in two ways – tailoring agile methods to the organization and tailoring organizationalprocesses based on knowledge acquired by practicing agile. The former consists of optimizing agile methods for the organization while the latter reflects the Lean philosophy of optimizing the whole.

Chapter Close-Out

Agile PM Processes Grid™ Exercise

Please take out a blank piece of paper, set a timer for no more than 3 minutes, and see how much of the grid you can reproduce from memory. To make the most of this Agile PM Processes Grid™ exercise, please simulate being in the testing environment. Close your book and all your notes. Visualize the Proctor handing you the blank sheets of paper and taking your seat in the testing site. Begin by drawing the grid, 6 columns and 8 rows, and then fill in everything you can. After the 3 minutes ends, use your book and notes to complete the grid. Study it as you do so.

Terminology Matching Exercise

In the blank column to the left of the Term, fill in the letter that identifies the correct definition or description.

	Term		Definition / Description
	1. Team assessment	A	A scope verification process where each feature is reviewed against acceptance criteria and the definition of done.
	2. Deliverables Acceptance	B	Occurs when a product is ready to use and may be internal, external, or interim as a non-deployed set of working features.
	3. Shuffle time	C	An empowering review of the dimensions of successful performance and agile behavior which agile teams conduct.
	4. Self-assessment	D	Defines goals and drives success by establishing ground rules and a time frame for completion.
	5. Scope verification	E	The time it takes to transition from one activity to another during meetings.
	6. Process tailoring	F	Optimizes agile methods to the organization and integrates Lean into itsprocesses.
	7. Hardening iterations	G	Combines multiple agile frameworks, or agile and traditional development methods.
	8. Product release	H	Occurs as part of customer acceptance testing and requires each feature to be compared to both the acceptance criteria and to the team's definition of done.
	9. Retrospective parameters	I	used in preparation for a product release to make the product ready for production.
	10. Hybrid projects	J	An evaluation based on how well the team believes it did and how it can be expected to improve.

Crossword Puzzle

Hints:

ACROSS
- 3 A scope verification process where each feature is reviewed against acceptance criteria and the definition of done.
- 6 The time it takes to transition from one activity to another during meetings.
- 8 Defines goals and drives success by establishing ground rules and a time frame for completion.
- 9 Part of customer acceptance testing and requires each feature to be compared to both the acceptance criteria and to the team's definition of done.
- 10 Optimizes agile methods to the organization and integrates Lean into its processes.

DOWN
- 1 Preparation for a product release to make the product ready for production.
- 2 An empowering review of the dimensions of successful performance and agile behavior which agile teams conduct.
- 4 Occurs when a product is ready to use and may be internal, external, or interim as a non-deployed set of working features.
- 5 An evaluation based on how well the team believes it did and how it can be expected to improve.
- 7 Combines multiple agile frameworks, or agile and traditional development methods.

Word Search

Word Search - 10 Words to find:

- PRODUCT RELEASE
- SHUFFLE TIME
- TEAM ASSESSMENT
- DELIVERABLES ACCEPTANCE
- PROCESS TAILORING
- HYBRID PROJECT
- HARDENING ITERATIONS
- SCOPE VERIFICATION
- SELF-ASSESSMENT
- RETROSPECTIVE PARAMETER

```
R N A T E A M _ A S S E S S M E N T M R E N H
P R O D U C T _ R E L E A S V V G E T E C N T
S C O P E _ V E R I F I C A T I O N D T L S E
E E P R O C E S S _ T A I L O R O C E R N D S
P _ P _ A F S H U F F L E _ T I M T L O O E C
A R R R C I R E L T E O _ A S T I P I S S L P
H O O E O P C U M N E A G E P R A T V P S I A
E Y E C P D I H P O A S F E N S A T E E C V E
S T B Y E A U A _ P U T M E E R S E R C O E T
E _ V R _ S _ C S T - T M E E E O H A T P R T
L C I E I E S Y T T E S O T S R _ Y B I E A N
F C C I D D S _ A _ S O I E J S L B L V _ B M
- T N F I N _ S T E R _ A U E G T R E E V L A
A S A O T D I P S A G E I _ M E A I S _ E E E
S R L S _ C E S R N I A L T N C E D _ P R S P
S E T B O _ A T I O L L A E E M F _ A A I _ I
E _ S O P - T N F E J R O B A N M P C R F A H
S I E S F T E T L A A E A R O S T R C A I C B
S S L L E D O _ R S S S C R I I E O E M C C N
M S E J R _ A O A V F S I T O N P J P E A E M
E S C A S S E N E M E M E C B R G E T T T P E
N O H G E S S H U F F L E _ T I M E A E I T E
T H A R D E N I N G _ I T E R A T I N R O A A
P I T E A M _ A S S E S S M A R R R C S A N I
```

Chapter Practice Test

1. As part of the process of deliverable acceptance on an agile project, each feature is compared to which of the following?

    A. The acceptance criteria as defined in the factory acceptance test (FAT)
    B. The acceptance criteria stated as part of its user story and the teams definition of done
    C. Acceptance criteria as defined in the quality management plan
    D. The design criteria as defined in the design requirements document

2. The Agile Project Manager should refrain from which of the following as it is viewed as a "command and control" responsibility and may inhibit the project manager's role as facilitator and creator of a safe agile team environment.

    A. Conducting individual performance appraisals of team members
    B. Participating in the iteration retrospective
    C. Leading the daily stand up
    D. Participating in backlog grooming

3. Some suggest that teams perform self-assessments at the conclusion of each iteration based on dimensions of successful performance and agile behavior. The dimension of agile behavior _____.

    A. Is based on an objective metric such as estimated versus delivered story points
    B. Is based only on the opinion of the Agile Project Manager
    C. Captures how well the team executed its agile processes
    D. Is based on how well the customer believes the team applies agile processes

4. Which of the following is not one of the meetings that typically occurs at the end of each iteration?

    A. Review meeting
    B. Product demonstration
    C. Retrospective
    D. Monthly project review

5. For the release retrospective, it is preferred to have _____ lead the meeting.

    A. The senior developer
    B. The project manager
    C. A facilitator who is not a member of the team
    D. The Scrum Master

6. Effective retrospective meetings are commonly structured by segment one of which being "establish retrospective parameters." Which of the following is not part of the "establish retrospective parameters" segment?

    A. Consider root causes
    B. State retrospective goals
    C. Establish meeting ground rules and timebox
    D. Review team values and working agreements

7. Shuffle time is defined as _____.

    A. The time it takes teams to establish a co-located work area
    B. The time required to estimate stories
    C. The time required to re-prioritize stories
    D. The time it takes to transition from one activity to another during meetings

8. In addition to examining hard data during the retrospective, the opinions and feelings from the team about their work also need to be considered. This information is gathered during which segment of the retrospective?

    A. Develop insights
    B. Assemble data
    C. Make decisions
    D. End retrospective

9. Which of the following is not one of the facilitator's main responsibilities during the retrospective?

    A. Create a detailed record of what was discussed during the retrospective
    B. Ensure adherence to agile principles
    C. Monitor for violations of team working agreements
    D. Redirect the discussion when blaming occurs

10. Which of the following is not true regarding release and project retrospectives?

    A. The Agile Project Manager participates fully in the retrospective
    B. All participants are expected to add value and to abide by the agile practices of the organization
    C. Only team members may participate in the retrospective
    D. People from outside the team may participate in the retrospective

11. A project in which agile and traditional development methodologies are combined, or one in which multiple agile methods are combined is referred to as a _____.

    A. Legacy project
    B. Green project
    C. Extreme project
    D. Hybrid project

12. Which of the following is not true regarding a release?

    A. An agile release is similar to a traditional project milestone
    B. A release typically consists of no more than one iteration
    C. The release deliverable is typically a specified set of working features
    D. The release may be internal to the organization or there may be formal deployment to customers and end users

13. Effective retrospective meetings are commonly structured by segment one of which being "develop insights." Which of the following is not part of the "develop insights" segment?

    A. Consider root causes
    B. Interpret the data
    C. Discuss team feelings and opinions
    D. Identify strengths, weaknesses, and other issues

14. At the close of an iteration, some features may not be accepted by the customer. Features that are not accepted by the customer are _____.

    A. Returned to the product backlog for reevaluation during the next round of planning
    B. Deleted from the project
    C. Delivered to the customer but not used
    D. Free to be used on other products

15. An iteration that consists of specific activities to make the product ready for production, including documenting the product, marketing it, and scheduling it for production is referred to as a _____.

    A. Supplemental iteration
    B. Hardening iteration
    C. Handoff iteration
    D. Release iteration

Answers – Terminology Matching

1:J, 2:A, 3:E, 4:C, 5:H, 6:F, 7:I, 8:B, 9:D, 10:G

Answers – Crossword Puzzle

Across:
- 3: DELIVERABLES ACCEPTANCE
- 6: SHUFFLE TIME
- 8: RETROSPECTIVE PARAMETER
- 9: SCOPE VERIFICATION
- 10: PROCESS TAILORING

Down:
- 1: HARDENING ITERATION
- 2: SELF-ASSESSMENT
- 4: PROADMUCTSRELEASE (PROADMUCTS RELEASE)
- 5: TEAMBRISDSPROJECT
- 7: HYBRID

Answers – Word Search

Word Search - 10 Words to find:

- PRODUCT RELEASE
- SHUFFLE TIME
- TEAM ASSESSMENT
- DELIVERABLES ACCEPTANCE
- PROCESS TAILORING
- HYBRID PROJECT
- HARDENING ITERATIONS
- SCOPE VERIFICATION
- SELF-ASSESSMENT
- RETROSPECTIVE PARAMETER

CHAPTER 10: Closing Projects

Answers – Practice Test

1. **B.** It is during the trio of iteration-closing meetings (i.e., demo, review, and retrospective) that the agile team gains acceptance of its deliverables. As each feature is reviewed, it is compared to both: 1) The acceptance criteria stated as part of its user story *(See Figure 4.9)*; and 2) The team's definition of done.

2. **A.** The main reason given for not having Agile Project Managers conduct performance evaluations of team members is that it creates role conflict. The performance evaluation is viewed as a "command-and-control" responsibility by many agilists, which conflicts with the roles of facilitator and creator of a safe work environment for the agile team. If the Agile Project Manager is charged with doing the performance evaluations, the role becomes more authoritarian than one of servant leader.

3. **C.** The practice of performing self-assessments is an empowering one for the agile team. On the performance dimension, the team assesses how well it did in terms of delivery. The team assessment is not just based on an objective metric (i.e., estimated versus delivered story points), but on how well the team believes it did and how it can be expected to improve in the future. The behavior dimension captures how well the team executed its agile processes. The behavior assessment really captures the questions, "How agile are we?" and "How can we improve our agility?"

4. **D.** The review meeting, product demonstration, and iteration retrospective typically occur at the end of each iteration.

5. **C.** The retrospective is led by a meeting facilitator. At the iteration level, this may be the Agile Project Manager. At the product release and project levels, we recommend utilizing an external facilitator so that the project manager may participate actively in the retrospective. This is often accomplished by borrowing an agile coach or facilitator from another team to run the meeting.

6. **A.** The first segment involves ***establishing retrospective parameters.*** Here, it is critical for the team to identify the goals of the retrospective (e.g., "Discover ways to improve our velocity" or "How can we get the customer more engaged?"). Since you want to drive success, the ideal goals are ones that may be realistically accomplished during the retrospective. Establishing ground rules and a time frame for the retrospective helps the team focus on the work to be done. Finally, the team values and working agreements may be reviewed at this juncture. If they exist in the form of information radiators, such artifacts should be brought to the meeting.

7. **D.** Shuffle time is the time it takes to transition from one activity to another during meetings (including retrospectives).

8. **B.** Assembling data has two components – reviewing facts from the recently completed timebox and gathering opinions and feelings from the team about their work. The hard facts come largely from agile metrics, informatory radiators, and artifacts. All such data should be brought to the meeting for review and discussion. Soliciting opinions and gauging the feelings of the participants may be more difficult. Here, we recommend using activities aimed at eliciting feedback from the team.

9. **A.** The main responsibilities of the facilitator during the retrospective include ensuring adherence to agile principles, fostering the appropriate participation of all attendees, monitoring for violations of team working agreements, redirecting the discussion when blaming occurs, and managing external invitees during release and project retrospectives.

10. **C.** For the release and project retrospectives, people *from outside the team* may be invited to attend. Invitees may include external customers and key stakeholders as well as people from senior management, product support and deployment, legal/regulatory, technical support, and operations. A rule of thumb in extending invitations is that the people invited are both expected to add value to the retrospective and to abide by the agile practices of the organization.

11. **D.** An organization's efforts to optimize its product development methodology may evolve to undertaking hybrid projects. *A hybrid project* is one in which agile and traditional development methodologies are combined, or one in which multiple agile methods are combined.

12. **B.** A release occurs when a product is ready to use. An agile release is similar to a traditional project milestone, with the deliverable being a specified set of working features. The release may be internal to the organization or there may be formal deployment to customers and end users. The end of the project is characterized by termination of funding and release of the team members to other activities.

13. **C.** Developing insights requires the team to take the data from the previous segment and to analyze it. Given the information the team has about how they are working, how can they improve? If the team is falling short in some way, what are the root causes? For example, if team velocity has dipped, have there been personnel changes, or are there other explanations? Perhaps more than in other retrospective segments, activities are helpful in evoking insights about how to improve.

14. **A.** In some work environments, a formal customer acceptance document is signed. In the event that some features are not accepted, they are returned to the product backlog for reevaluation during the next round of planning.

15. **B.** Some agile teams will employ a hardening iteration in preparation for a product release, particularly for a project-closing release. The hardening iteration consists of specific activities to make the product ready for production, including documenting the product, marketing it, and scheduling it for production.

Endnotes

[1] Highsmith, J. (2010). *Agile project management: Creating innovative products, Second edition.* Upper Saddle River, NJ: Addison-Wesley.

[2] Sliger, M., & Broderick, S. (2008). *The software project manager's bridge to agility.* Upper Saddle River, NJ: Addison-Wesley.

[3] Derby, E., & Larsen, D. (2006). *Agile retrospectives: Making good teams great.* Raleigh, NC: The Pragmatic Bookshelf.

[4] Kerth, N. L. (2001). *Project retrospectives: A handbook for team reviews.* New York: Dorset House Publishers.

[5] Cockburn, A. (2007). *Agile software development: The cooperative game, Second edition.* Upper Saddle River, NJ: Addison-Wesley.

[6] Highsmith, J. (2010). *Agile project management: Creating innovative products, Second edition.* Upper Saddle River, NJ: Addison-Wesley.

[7] Kerth, N. L. (2001). *Project retrospectives: A handbook for team reviews.* New York: Dorset House Publishers.

[8] Derby, E., & Larsen, D. (2006). *Agile retrospectives: Making good teams great.* Raleigh, NC: The Pragmatic Bookshelf.

[9] Ibid.

[10] Ibid.

[11] Ibid.

[12] Kerth, N. L. (2001). *Project retrospectives: A handbook for team reviews.* New York: Dorset House Publishers.

[13] Derby, E., & Larsen, D. (2006). *Agile retrospectives: Making good teams great.* Raleigh, NC: The Pragmatic Bookshelf.

[14] Kerth, N. L. (2001). *Project retrospectives: A handbook for team reviews.* New York: Dorset House Publishers.

[15] Cockburn, A. (2007). *Agile software development: The cooperative game, Second edition.* Upper Saddle River, NJ: Addison-Wesley.

[16] Ibid.

[17] Appleby, T., Stenbeck, J. G., & Berthot, B. (In press). *The agile maturity model* (AMM). La Mesa, CA: GR8PM.com.

[18] Ibid.

How to Pass the Exam... the First Time!

Chapter Highlights

This chapter covers the following topics:

- The PMI Code of Ethics and Professional Conduct
- What the ACP exam tests
- Getting to the test; filling out the application
- The testing environment

We begin our coverage of How to Pass the Exam with the ***PMI Code of Ethics and Professional Conduct*** because it is a guaranteed part of every PMI exam. Integrating professional and social responsibilities is an assumed part of every question that a student will face on the exam so being comfortable with the Code is important.

Integrate Professional and Social Responsibilities

Recognize Professional and Social Responsibilities

Whether a project manager is using traditional or agile approaches to accomplish the goals of the organization, it is important to be aware of, and to honor, the professional and social responsibilities that are the duty of those striving to achieve excellence. Project management, as a career field, enjoys the respect that is due to a profession that impacts so many lives in so many countries in so many ways. The respect that project management demands today, results from the hard work and dedication of countless individuals over the past five decades. The sacrifices of the past create a duty for project management practitioners to continue to serve their communities with the highest standards of ethical behavior.

Developing a solid understanding of the PMI Code of Ethics and Professional Conduct furnishes comprehensive guidelines for the behavioral norms that should be used as a basis for interactions with all stakeholders. It should also help project managers move forward with confidence that they are adhering to the highest standards of excellence. It aides Project Managers when making appropriate ethical decisions during interaction with the public, customers, and any other stakeholder of the organization that they represent.

The PMI Code of Ethics and Professional Conduct

The PMI Code of Ethics and Professional Conduct provides a framework for ethical practices beyond the project management profession by relating the most important values – responsibility, respect, fairness, and honesty – to the behavior that will help each individual practitioner become better recognized as a professional.

To view or obtain a copy of the code of ethics and professional conduct, visit the PMI global web site at **www.pmi.org**.

Based on experience with the PMP Exam, it is reasonable to expect between 9% and 12% of your final score on the ACP Exam will include questions from this content area. Thus, their importance for passing the exam is significant. While the difficulty of handling these questions is not high, it requires attention and proper preparation to master them.

PMI's philosophy regarding ethics and professional conduct is that the project manager should always act as a leader, deal directly with issues, act ethically and legally, and be open and up-front in communications. In order to do well on the exam, it is wise for students to recognize that PMI is not asking, "What *would* you do in your organization?" Rather, PMI is asking, "What *should* you do?"

Situational questions that present hard choices are a favorite tactic employed by PMI to test your understanding of ethical and professional conduct. For example, the situation described in the question may present a small violation that will be painful for the project manager to resolve. The answer that PMI expects you to choose will resolve the issue quickly, openly, and fairly. Alternately, PMI may present a situation or a problem which could be ignored instead of confronted. The answer that PMI expects to be chosen will deal with the problem directly. So when you are taking the ACP exam, remember that PMI expects you to be a leader who directly faces painful problems and solves them quickly, openly and fairly.

Since it is impossible for us to provide training that could cover every possible ethical scenario, below we provide high level instruction and guidelines focused on a general understanding of a project manager's professional responsibility.

One of the best things a student can do to prepare for this important section of the exam is visit the PMI website, download a copy of the code of conduct, and read through it multiple times.

 As you study the code, you will notice that there are **aspirational standards** and **mandatory standards,** which are not mutually exclusive. Therefore, a single violation may breach both. Take the time to acquire a clear understanding of the similarities and differences between the two levels of the standards.

 You may also notice that the code does not apply to everyone who calls themselves a PM - it only applies to project managers who choose to affiliate with PMI, whether they are certified or not! However, for the purposes of the exam, it is safest to assume that all persons identified or named in a question should choose to follow the code.

The Four Values – Responsibility, Respect, Fairness, and Honesty

 Responsibility focuses on laws, regulations, policies, and ethics as mandatory. It is safest to "take the high road" in questions where the scenario requires that doing the right thing will be very difficult for you professionally. Aspirational responsibility and the questions associated with it, generally require the project manager to take a significant step above the mandatory level. The questions will often require the project manager to do what they said they will do, including taking ownership of actions that caused mistakes.

 Respect focuses on the project manager showing esteem to others. While doing this in the workplace may be challenging, on the exam it should be a bit easier. PMI is strongly aligned to multiculturalism and so questions on the test tend to show this bias. Questions will often provide a situation where the project manager is expected not to impose his personal beliefs or culture on others. In fact, "politically correct" answers are usually correct on the exam.

Because of the PMI commitment to protecting confidentiality of client information, intellectual property, trade secrets, personal information, and project information, the mandatory standard for negotiating in good faith and not abusing others is tied into the value of respect. Aspirational respect and the questions associated with it, generally require the project manager to move beyond "not imposing" and into "embracing and valuing" other cultures and opinions.

 Fairness focuses on the project manager being careful to avoid conflicts of interest and discrimination. The questions on the exam may require a project manager to go out of his or her way to avoid even the *perception* of impropriety by taking actions that may seem unnecessary. Discrimination questions often concentrate on the project manager potentially passing over one candidate in favor of another due to age, gender, or some other illegal or unethical preference. Aspirational fairness questions will require the project manager to make decisions in a transparent and open way that treats everyone equally and examines the project manager's own impartiality.

 Honesty focuses on the mandatory standard of never deceiving others. For the exam, think of it as if you were in court and you took an oath to tell the truth, the whole truth, and nothing but the truth. Aspirational honesty takes the additional step of not only being truthful, but creating an environment where others are also encouraged and safe to be truthful.

For the purposes of the exam, and in real life, always do the right thing even if it is painful or tempting to avoid it. Be especially suspicious of answers to questions that offer you an easy way out or present a shortcut.

The only possible exception to this rule is questions dealing with work in another country where their customs, although not illegal or unethical in any way, are not the norm in the U.S. or Western Europe. Remember that if it is illegal or unethical in any way, it is wrong and you must deal with that correctly. Otherwise, the customs of the host nation where the work is being performed should be honored.

Endorsing Responsibilities to the Profession

Endorsing responsibilities to the profession begins with compliance with all applicable laws as well as organizational rules and policies. Embracing those responsibilities goes beyond simple compliance and involves a personal choice to uphold and honor the ideals described in the PMI Code of Ethics and Professional Conduct.

In real life, as well as to pass the ACP exam, it is useful to apply the following guidelines:

- When you make, or fail to make, a decision, take ownership of the consequences that result from your choice.
- When you act, or fail to act, take ownership of the consequences that result from your choice.
- Before accepting a project assignment, be sure your background, experience, skills, and qualifications are consistent with the requirements that will be needed to professionally complete the project.
- Once you have accepted a project assignment, be sure to fulfill the commitments you have undertaken and to do what you have said you will do.
- Always honor the duty to protect proprietary and confidential information that may be provided to you.
- Always disclose conditions or circumstances that could be perceived as a conflict of interest (or even just create the appearance of impropriety) to clients, customers and stakeholders.
- Always provide truthful, accurate information concerning your qualifications and services.
- Always respect intellectual property developed or owned by others, and abide by professional standards for the knowledge and work of others.
- Promptly report possible violations of the PMI Code of Ethics and Professional Conduct, and cooperate with PMI to collect and handle information related to a possible violation.

Safeguarding Responsibilities to Customers and the Public

Safeguarding responsibilities to customers and the public involves a personal choice to uphold the highest standards for confidentiality, conflicts of interest, and public representations in the media, advertising, and other forms of communication.

In real life, as well as to pass the ACP exam, it is useful to apply the following guidelines:

- Always provide truthful representations in advertising, public statements, estimates, and descriptions of services and their expected results.
- Abide by the laws, regulations, rules, and policies that apply to your work, in both professional and volunteer activities.
- Always negotiate in good faith and fulfill your commitments.
- Always respect the property and rights of others, including intellectual property rights such as copyrights, trademarks, and other confidential or sensitive information.

- Always protect the interests of clients, customers, and other stakeholders, so that any conflict of interest does not compromise their legitimate expectation of your professional judgment.
- Never offer or accept inappropriate payments, gifts, compensation, or other types of personal gain.

Observing Other Responsibilities

The PMI Code of Ethics and Professional Conduct is not the only source of responsibilities that project managers must observe. PMI has identified several additional sources of professional and social responsibility.

In real life, as well as to pass the ACP exam, it is useful to apply the following guidelines:

- Always adhere to the best appropriate ethical and legal standards in order to set a positive example for others to follow. Contribute to the high regard for integrity attributed to project management professionals.
- Whenever possible, share professional expertise and experience to help others increase their skills and competence to advance the shared body of knowledge in the field of project management.
- Whenever possible, contribute to a culture of understanding and respect by sharing information regarding successes, challenges, and obstacles overcome in order to help others improve their professional skills.
- Always strive to understand the truth, create an environment for others to safely disclose the truth, and demonstrate fairness and transparency in decision making.
- Never deceive others by making false or misleading statements, providing incomplete or inaccurate information, or withholding contextual information that would alter the understanding of the receiving party. Never support, condone, tolerate, or accept such behavior by other parties.

One final tip to remember is that PMI expects organizations to be accountable for impacts on the community, environment, economy and society when making decisions. So if you encounter a question where the scenario shows that the project would benefit, but society or the environment would suffer, the correct answer is to avoid all such situations. In the event that the situation in the question requires such a choice, the project manager should disclose the situation to the appropriate authorities and, if necessary, resign from the project.

This section of the exam will be difficult for students not properly prepared or who go into the exam with the wrong mindset about workplace ethics. For example, laziness or professional negligence should not be tolerated, but that does not mean that expectations won't vary between different cultures and from country to country. If a student is not careful, it is easy to approach questions with a sense of "fairness" about work standards that are inappropriate to the host location in the exam question.

How to Pass the Exam...the First Time!

Luckily, passing the ACP exam on the first try has nothing to do with luck and everything to do with preparation. It was our goal for this book, along with the exam simulator and flashcards, to contain everything needed to prepare at a level that exceeds the challenge of the ACP exam. Our expectation is that any student who uses these materials with a modicum of discipline will leave the exam saying, "That was too easy!" Really, that is what we expect, and we hope you'll let us know when that is your experience.

The Key is the 5 Ps

We have all heard the old adage about the 5 Ps – Proper Preparation Prevents Poor Performance – so realize you must have a study plan with defined expectations and schedule time to fulfill it like any other project. Figure 11.1 presents a sample study plan that maps both essential tasks and estimated time.

Task	Calculation	Time
Create a study notes document on your computer for recording new terms and concepts, especially the ones that were confusing		10min
Read each chapter and record Study Notes	10 x 2hr	20hr
Complete the chapter tests and exercises	10 x 1hr	10hr
Document misunderstandings in Study Notes	10 x 1hr	10hr
Take a 40 question online exam after chapters 1–4	4 x 1hr	4hr
Take an 80 question online exam after chapters 5–7	3 x 2hr	6hr
Take a 120 question online exam after chapters 8–10	3 x 3hr	9hr
Study incorrect answers and record lessons in Study Notes		5hr
Study the topics in your Study Notes and practice the process grid		10hr
Document your strategy for the real exam and run a simulation		3.5hr
Repeat study/test cycle until average score is 85% or greater		15hr
Total		**92.6hr**

Figure 11.1 Sample PMI-ACPSM exam study plan.

So proper preparation will likely take around 93 hours of self-study so a best practice is to have an accountability partner (aka a "study buddy") that commits to a mutual schedule for preparation and sets a test date at the same time you do!

A common short cut is to attend a formal preparation class, but you will need to decide which approach best suits your constraints. Regardless of which approach you choose, be sure to take one (but no more than one) day off before the real exam to let your mind rest. Then go forth and conquer! Afterwards, please email us at CustServ@gr8pm.com so we can help you celebrate passing!!

Proper preparation requires emulating the look, feel and experience of the actual test as closely as possible. The study plan outlined above assumes the use an online exam simulator because the real ACP exam is computer-based and the simulator creates an important experiential learning opportunity.

As we noted in Chapter 2, proper preparation also requires memorizing the Agile Project Management Processes Grid™. Reproducing the Agile PM Processes Grid™ from memory is one of the best test preparation exercises a student can practice. It is well suited to practicing over lunch, during breaks, and periodically throughout the day. Memorize a single, specific mnemonic and make it visually wild or, better yet, a crazy mental cartoon with motion and sound. Draw those 5 vertical and 7 horizontal lines, write the first letter in each column and row, and begin filling in everything you can remember. Doing so extends your study time and reinforces your learning.

What the Exam Tests

First of all, please be very clear about one thing: **exactly what the ACP exam will test is not disclosed by PMI** and will continue to be "under development" for the foreseeable future. PMI's initial pilot is over and the test is now administered and scored using industry-standard methods as with the PMP exam.

The ACP is different from PMI's other exams, like those for the PMP, CAPM, PgMP, and other certifications, because those can be traced back to *A Guide to the Project Management Body of Knowledge (PMBOK®) Fourth Edition.*[1] Unfortunately, there was no similar, authoritative guide for the Project Management *Agile* Body of Knowledge until this book was written.

Instead, PMI announced a list of 11 books, written by various luminaries from the agile sphere, as the basis for the ACP exam. That body of work covers 3,888 pages and has a total cost of $507.85, as shown in Figure 11.2. While mastering all that content is a daunting enough challenge, the fact that the authors have *differing* and sometimes opposing opinions about an agile standard or practice makes it immensely more challenging to prepare for the exam. The good news is that the three authors of this book, who together hold Project Management Professional (PMP) credentials, Agile Certified Practitioner (PMI-ACP) certifications, Certified Scrum Master (CSM) certifications, a Certified Scrum Product Owner (CSPO) certification, and a Certified Scrum Professional (CSP) certification, have read every one of those 3,888 pages. Approaching the content from different perspectives, together we have analyzed, integrated and aligned that content to create this comprehensive, usable, and accessible exam preparation book. We also identified where the authors of the eleven books on PMI's list had opposing, conflicting, or varying views and we highlighted them for you, the student.

The result is that this book provides a comprehensive explanation of everything that can reasonably be expected to appear on the exam.

Title:	Price	Pages
Agile Estimating and Planning	$54.99	368
Agile Retrospectives: Making Good Teams Great	$29.99	200
Agile Project Management: Creating Innovative Products	$49.99	432
Agile Project Management with Scrum	$39.99	192
Lean–Agile Software Development: Achieving Enterprise Agility	$39.99	304
The Software Project Manager's Bridge to Agility	$49.99	384
Agile Software Development: The Cooperative Game	$59.99	504
Coaching Agile Teams	$42.99	352
Becoming Agile: In an Imperfect World	$44.99	408
The Art of Agile Development	$39.99	440
User Stories Applied: For Agile Software Development	$54.99	304
	$507.85	3,888

Figure 11.2 PMI's recommended ACP book list.

A Passing Grade

You need to understand that *exactly* what is considered a ***passing grade*** has also not been announced. Based on the standard for the PMP credential exam, you can reasonably assume that a passing score will likely be 61 percent. And since PMI has announced that the exam will have 120 multiple-choice questions, a passing score will probably require 74 correct answers within the prescribed three hour time period.

Question Allocation on the ACP Exam

During the exam, you may anticipate that:2

- Knowledge and Skills will be covered in 50 percent of the questions and will be drawn from 43 identified Knowledge Areas.
- Tools and Techniques will account for the other 50 percent of the questions and will be drawn from 50 different components.

Use a Testing Strategy

Don't Get Stuck

The ACP is a timed exam. Therefore, it is important to not get stuck on any particular question. Keep focused on the fact that you do not need a 100% score to pass the exam. While PMI has not announced exactly what a passing score will be, it is reasonable to assume it will likely be 61 percent or 74 correct answers from the 120 multiple-choice questions within the prescribed three hour time period.

The simple, or easier, questions are designed to be answerable by most test takers and will make up about 30 percent of the exam (i.e., about 36 questions). With adequate preparation, you should expect to score nearly 95 percent on them.

The moderate questions are designed to begin separating proficient students from inadequately prepared students and will make up about 40 percent of the exam (i.e., about 48 questions). With this book and an adequate amount of preparation time, students should expect to get about 80 percent of these questions right.

The hard questions are designed to be challenging for most test takers and will make up about 30 percent of the exam (i.e., about 36 questions). With adequate preparation, you should expect to score at least 50 percent on them.

Using this book you have become a properly prepared student and should get at least 90 questions correct. Based on the standard from other PMP credential exams, it is reasonable to assume that a passing score will require 74 correct answers. Using the formulas just described [(36*95%) + (48*80%) + (36*50%)] a properly prepared student should get 90 questions correct. That leaves a margin of error of 16 questions, or almost 22 percent, above the minimum required.

You have about 1.5 minutes for each of the 120 questions and since most of them will take much you will have plenty of time - at the end - for the longer, harder, scenario type questions. But it does not mean you can be foolish with your time. Use your time wisely.

How to "Guess" Better

The testing software application allows you to mark questions for review for time efficiency. Here is a simple test taking strategy that you should begin practicing while you are taking your practice exams and using the online exam simulator:

- For a Simple question   =   Answer it; Do not mark it for review
- For a Moderate question =   Answer it; Consider marking it for review
- For a Hard question   =   Answer it; Mark it for review

Hard questions come in two types, **scenario-based questions** and those that ask for the **best answer among several correct answers.** For the first type, scenario-based questions, **skip to the end** of the paragraph and **read the question first.** Then, return to the beginning of the paragraph and read the scenario looking for the answer to the question. Review **all four** choices, eliminating obviously incorrect ones, and select from the remaining, possibly correct answers. Mark your choice, mark for review, and move on to the next question. As you continue through the test, you may find a statement in a subsequent question that helps you answer one you have marked for review. If so, note it on your scrap paper for use during your review.

For the second type of hard questions, ones that ask for the best answer among several correct answers, review **all four** choices, eliminate any obviously incorrect ones, and select from the remaining, possibly correct answers. Mark your choice, mark for review, and move on to the next question. Again, as you continue through the test, if you find a statement in a succeeding question that helps you answer a previous one, note it on your scrap paper for use during your review.

For **Moderate questions,** remember research has shown that the majority of prepared test takers' first reaction has the **highest probability** of being **correct.** Thus, use caution when considering changing your answers. If you have a note on your scrap paper from something you found after the question, use it to reanalyze the question. Otherwise, trust your first reaction and move on. (If you aren't sure how it affects you, track your changes on the practice exams and analyze your tendency.)

Every question is scored, so unanswered questions are *automatically* incorrect. Since there is no additional penalty for an incorrect answer, it is important to answer every question, even if you are guessing. A guess has a statistical chance of being correct at least 25% of the time. If you can eliminate incorrect choices, you improve the odds of your guess to 33% or even 50%. Leaving a question blank will always result in a 0% chance of being correct.

You should expect to encounter a few questions on the exam that you do not know how to answer. Do not agonize over them and let them waste your precious time! Even with proper preparation and a good test taking technique, there will be questions where you have to make an educated guess. Just do it! Don't get upset or let it undermine your confidence. Remember, each question is less than 1% of your score, so even if you hit a block of difficult questions, don't get alarmed or discouraged, just answer them, mark them for review, and keep moving. Time management is a very real part of passing the exam…so practice it as part of your preparation!

Manage the Exam

Every question is scored, so *unanswered* questions are automatically *incorrect.* Since there is no additional penalty for an incorrect answer, be sure to answer every question, even if you are guessing.

Expect to encounter a few questions on the exam that you do not know how to answer. Even with proper preparation and a good test taking technique, there will be questions where you have to make an educated guess. Just do it! Don't get upset or let it undermine your confidence. Remember, each question is less than 1% of your score, so even if you hit a block of difficult questions, don't get alarmed or discouraged, just answer them, mark them for review, and keep moving. Time management is a very real part of managing the exam…so practice it as part of your preparation!

Getting to the Test

Fill Out the Application!

Once you start filling out the application, you have 90 days to finish it on the PMI website. Once submitted, PMI has up to ten days to review the application for completeness and notify you of any deficiencies that need to be corrected or addressed. Once your application is approved as properly completed, you will be required to submit payment for your certification fees (see www.PMI.org for current amount). After you pay your certification fees, the system will notify you of your eligibility to sit for the exam, or inform you that you have been selected for audit. If your application is selected for audit, you have up to 90 days to provide the requested audit materials. PMI will process your audit materials within seven (7) days. In these situations, your eligibility to sit for the ACP Exam begins after successful completion of the audit.

From the date your application is approved, you have one (1) year of *eligibility*. You can take the multiple-choice exam up to three (3) times during that year.

Once you have passed the exam and been certified, your *certification cycle* begins. To maintain your certification, you must complete and report 30 professional development units (PDUs) within the 3-year certification cycle and pay the required renewal fees. (See www.PMI.org for specifics about the PDU requirements.)

Application Requirements

When you apply for the ACP Exam at PMI's website you will go through a multi-step application process:

PMI-ACP Application

- Provide a Contact Address
- Provide Contact Email and Phone
- Provide Your Name as it should appear on the Certificate (when you pass!)
- Provide Attained Education information (You must be at least a High School graduate.)

PMI-ACP Requirements Overview

- To be eligible, you are required to document work experience in both general and agile project environments as well as Agile Project Management education. If you are already a PMP, documenting the required 2,000 hours of general project management experience will be waived or pre-approved.

Agile Project Experience must:

- Be a minimum of 1,500 hours
- Be within 2 years of the application date
- Show a minimum of 8 months of experience, excluding gaps between projects and overlapping experiences like two projects during the same time period.

For recording experience, the application form on the website asks for the Project Title, Start Date, and End Date. Then, it provides drop down menus for you to select Project Role and Primary Industry. On the next four pages it asks the Organization Details for whom you managed the project.

- Page 1 – Job Title, Organization Name, Address, and Phone
- Page 2 – Contact Name, Contact Relationship (drop down menu), Email and Phone
- Page 3 – Fill in the number of Agile Experience Hours
- Page 4 – Name Your Role (Fill in the blank) and Summarize the Project in 300 to 1,100 characters.

Agile Project Management Education:

- Must be a minimum of 21 contact hours of formal training or instruction in Agile Project Management
- Must be completed at the time of the application
- Has no time limit on how long ago the instruction took place

For recording education, the application form asks for the Course Title, Institution Name, Start Date, End Date, and Qualifying Hours.

The Certification Application/Renewal Agreement is then displayed and you must check "I Agree" in order to proceed.

Finally, before you can "Submit" the application, you must check a box indicating, "All information that I have provided is accurate and complete."

Once PMI has approved your eligibility to sit for the exam you will receive an email letting you know and giving you instructions on how to contact the Prometric testing center and schedule your exam.

The Testing Environment

PMI uses the services of Prometric Inc., a testing services company, to administer the exam. These exams are considered proprietary and are taken very seriously, so it's important that you know and follow the rules.

When you arrive at the Prometric Testing Center, you must have two signature-bearing forms of identification to be admitted into the testing center. One form must be government-issued, with a photograph and signature.

The photograph with signature bearing identification may include:

- Valid driver's license
- Valid passport
- Valid military ID

The signature bearing identification may include:

- Credit card
- Bank (ATM) card

Examples of *unacceptable* identification are:

- Library card
- Social security card
- Driver's license stating *James* Ward with a credit card stating *Jim* Ward.

There is *no flexibility on the identification requirements*, so bring valid identification!

When you enter the testing area there is no talking during the exam and you are not allowed to bring anything in with you – nothing! No notes, books, papers, cell phones, PDAs, pagers, calculators – nothing! PMI considers their exams high-security and therefore Prometric considers it high-stakes. Don't bet on bending the rules, you will lose.

While you are taking the test, you will be monitored, observed, and audio and video taped to eliminate any sort of cheating. Don't let it distract or bother you.

The test itself will be delivered on a standard Windows PC running Prometric's proprietary testing application. If you specified special needs as part of your application, they will accommodate those needs. Otherwise, it is a pretty typical testing application. It begins with a tutorial on how to use it.

The Time Limit

The maximum time allowed for completing the exam is 3 hours.

The good news is that 3 hours is 180 minutes, which means you have about 1.5 minutes for each of the 120 questions. Since most of the questions will take much less than 1.5 minutes it means you will have plenty of time for the longer, harder, scenario type questions. But it does *not* mean you can be foolish with your time. Use a good test taking strategy to manage your time.

The bad news is that 3 hours is a long exam, so you must manage your physiology with planned breaks and nutrition. To keep your mind sharp you will need periodic stretch breaks and maybe a snack. Use your practice exams to work out the details of what is most helpful for you. Remember that taking a test while the clock is ticking induces stress and can inhibit your performance. Be sure to use a computer-based exam simulation as part of your preparation so you can get comfortable with pacing yourself and working against a timed deadline.

The exam ends automatically at 3 hours, but you may choose to finalize and submit it sooner if you have completed all the questions to your satisfaction.

When you pass, PMI will send a confirmation email as described in Chapter 11 and will mail you all the official information, including a certificate. If you do not pass, you may retake the exam up to two additional times during your year of eligibility. If you do not pass by the third attempt, you must wait one year to reapply.

After Taking the Exam

Now that the PMI-ACP exam pilot is over, test takers will learn their results immediately upon completion. In most situations, the testing site will provide you with a stamped copy of your results.

PLEASE, please, please send us a quick e-mail and let us know you passed! We take great joy from hearing about your success. Some students even send us a photo of them, their proof of passing from Prometric, and the nice bottle of red wine they are enjoying. We'd sure enjoy and welcome yours too! If you send it to CustServ@gr8pm.com it will be circulated for all of us to share…and you might even discover a small congratulatory gift arriving for you within a few days.

Email Confirmation of Passing

Once PMI has confirmed that you passed the PMI-ACP exam, you will receive an email.

Until you receive your certificate package, you may confirm that you hold the ACP certification by going to https://certification.pmi.org/ and logging into your PMI account.

Figure 11.3 approximates what you will see on the PMI web site.

PMI-ACP Certified
You are a PMI-ACP in good standing

PMI-ACP Number 1234567

PMI-ACP certification holder since 30 Jan 2012
PMI-ACP certification valid through 29 Jan 2015

Figure 11.3. Once You Pass the Exam, You Will See a Confirmation Similar to This.

Chapter Close-Out

Terminology Matching Exercise

In the blank column to the left of the Term, fill in the letter that identifies the correct Definition or Description.

	Term		Definition / Description
	1. Agile Ethos	A	One of the "four values" focusing on the project manager being careful to avoid conflicts of interest and discrimination.
	2. ACP®	B	Project Management Professional
	3. PMI's Code of Ethics	C	Project Management Body Of Knowledge
	4. PMP®	D	Agile Certified Practitioner
	5. PMBOK®	E	The outline for ethical practices within the project management profession.
	6. Fairness	F	Satisfy the customer through early and continuous delivery of valuable solutions.
	7. Highest priority	G	Empowering teams is central to realizing the goal of a successful project
	8. Responsibility	H	One of the "four values" focusing on the mandatory standard of never deceiving others
	9. Respect	I	Certified Scrum Master
	10. Honesty	J	One of the "four values" focusing on laws, regulations, policies, and ethics as mandatory
	11. CSM®	K	One of the "four values" focusing on the project manager showing esteem for others
	12. CAPM®	L	Program Management Professional
	13. PgMP®	M	Certified Scrum Professional
	14. CSPO®	N	Certified Associate in Project Management
	15. CSP®	O	Certified Scrum Product Owner

Crossword Puzzle

Hints:

ACROSS
- 4 Project Management Professional
- 8 Satisfy the customer through early and continuous delivery of valuable solutions.
- 10 Certified Scrum Product Owner
- 11 Certified Scrum Master
- 12 Project Management Body of Knowledge
- 13 Agile Certified Practitioner
- 15 The value focused on the project manager showing esteem for others.

DOWN
- 1 The value focused on the mandatory standard of never deceiving others.
- 2 Program Management Professional
- 3 The outline for ethical practices within the project management profession.
- 5 The value focused on being careful to avoid conflicts of interest and discrimination.
- 6 Certified Scrum Professional
- 7 Empowering teams is central to realizing the goal of a successful project.
- 9 The value focused on laws, regulations, policies, and ethics as mandatory.
- 14 Certified Associate in Project Management

Word Search

Word Search - 15 Words to find:

- ACP
- AGILEETHOS
- CAPM
- CODEOFETHICS
- CSM
- CSP
- CSPO
- FAIRNESS
- HIGHESTPRIORITY
- HONESTY
- PGMP
- PMBOK
- PMP
- RESPECT
- RESPONSIBILITY

S	C	E	T	A	H	E	R	O	P	E	C	B	C	L	P	P	_	Y	H
S	N	B	H	S	P	P	Y	E	P	O	S	P	M	P	H	M	N	E	H
K	S	F	C	A	A	E	P	M	S	M	P	F	A	I	R	N	E	S	S
T	E	H	O	A	N	I	I	M	M	P	O	O	O	S	P	S	R	E	I
R	L	I	D	G	O	C	S	M	B	P	P	T	K	C	C	N	C	P	C
E	H	G	E	I	S	E	T	S	F	P	I	C	E	I	I	S	C	H	I
S	H	H	_	L	C	O	R	A	S	T	M	M	H	P	Y	A	C	I	P
P	O	E	O	E	P	P	H	O	N	E	S	T	Y	T	S	E	P	G	S
O	T	S	F	_	Y	F	N	H	I	I	E	T	I	N	E	H	T	H	P
N	E	T	_	E	Y	Y	T	H	M	_	C	L	G	S	S	C	R	E	O
S	_	_	E	T	O	H	O	A	F	H	I	A	O	R	L	_	S	S	H
I	H	P	T	H	E	K	L	O	O	B	H	O	N	E	S	P	P	T	E
B	F	R	H	O	F	_	_	L	I	S	P	E	C	S	P	O	M	_	O
I	A	I	A	S	P	E	B	S	T	K	P	E	E	O	E	P	B	P	O
L	I	O	T	S	D	T	N	I	R	E	S	P	E	C	T	O	O	R	H
I	R	R	P	O	M	O	A	G	I	L	E	_	E	T	H	S	K	I	Y
C	N	I	C	O	P	L	P	N	P	E	E	M	E	O	S	T	P	O	C
P	R	T	T	S	E	I	E	C	R	G	P	M	P	O	N	P	C	R	P
E	S	Y	E	O	K	C	H	T	G	A	M	S	M	F	M	F	S	I	E
_	E	R	T	R	R	A	_	E	C	H	P	P	S	S	I	M	P	I	G

Chapter Practice Test

1. You are the project manager of the JKN Project. The project customer has requested that you inflate your cost estimates by 25 percent. He reports that his management always reduces the cost of the estimates so this is the only method to get the funding needed to complete the project. Which of the following is the best response to this situation?

    A. Do as the customer asks to ensure the project requirements can be met by adding the increase as a contingency reserve
    B. Do as the customer asks to ensure the project requirements can be met by adding the increase across each task
    C. Do as the customer asks by creating an estimate for the customer's management and another for the actual project implementation
    D. Complete an accurate estimate of the project. In addition, create a risk assessment on why the project budget would be inadequate

2. You are about to begin negotiations on a new project that is to take place in another country. Which of the following should be your guide on what business practices are allowed and discouraged?

    A. The project charter
    B. The project plan
    C. Company policies and procedures
    D. The PMP Code of Professional Conduct

3. One of your project team members reports that he has taken and sold copies of a commercial software application that your company produces because he needed to pay for his daughter's school tuition. He says he has paid back the money by working overtime without reporting the hours worked so that his theft remains private. What should you do?

    A. Fire the project team member
    B. Report the team member to his manager
    C. Suggest that the team member report his action to human resources
    D. Tell the team you're disappointed in what he did and advise him not to repeat that behavior in the future

4. You are the project manager for the Log Cabin Project. One of your vendors is completing a large portion of the project. You have heard a rumor that the vendor is losing many of its workers due to labor issues. In light of this information, what should you do?

    A. Stop work with the vendor until the labor issues are resolved
    B. Communicate with the vendor in regard to the rumor
    C. Look to secure another vendor to replace the current vendor
    D. Negotiate with the labor union to secure the workers on your project

5. You are completing a project for a customer in a foreign country. It is customary in this host country to honor the project manager of a successful project with a gift. Your company policy does not allow project managers to accept gifts having a value greater than $50 from any entity. At the completion of the project, the customer presents to you, in a public ceremony, a new car. Which of the following should you do?

   A. Accept the car since it is customary in the host country and to refuse it would be an insult to your hosts.
   B. Refuse to accept the car as it would violate your company's policies regarding how business is to be conducted
   C. Accept the car and then return it, in private, to the customer.
   D. Accept the car and then donate the car to a charity in the customer's name.

6. You have a project team member who is sabotaging your project because he does not agree with it. Which of the following should you do?

   A. Fire the project team member
   B. Present the problem to management
   C. Present the problem to management with a solution to remove the team member from the project
   D. Present the problem to management with a demand to fire the project team member

7. You are a project manager within an organization that completes software development projects for other entities. You have plans to leave your company within the next month to launch your own consulting business, which will compete with your current employer. Your company is currently working on a large proposal for a government contract that your new company could also benefit from. What should you do?

   A. Resign from your current job and bid against your employer to get the contract
   B. Decline to participate due to a conflict of interest
   C. Help your employer prepare the proposal
   D. Inform your employer that you will be leaving the company within a month and it would be inappropriate for you to work on the current proposal

8. You have just taken over a large software development project for your company. As you are reviewing material from the previous project manager you discover that he made a $200,000 payment to a consultant and that the payment was not approved in accordance with company policies. What should you do?

   A. Inform your manager of the situation
   B. Have the consultant return the payment
   C. Do nothing as the consultant did work that was acceptable
   D. Do nothing and continue the practice of the previous PM as the company policy regarding payment of consultants is not productive

9. You are assigned to lead a large software development project implementing an Extreme Programming (XP) approach. The work is to take place at one of your company's facilities located in a foreign country. You are informed that you will have to pay local police a fee before the construction workers are permitted to begin work on the team's colocated work areas. The police say that they will have to coordinate traffic on the narrow street in front of your building to accommodate the large trucks required by the construction company. What should you do?

    A. Do not pay the fee as it is a bribe
    B. Pay the fee
    C. Do not co-locate your teams and use the facility as is
    D. Do not pay the fee as it was not part of the original construction contract

10. You have just been assigned to take over an agile software development project that should be over halfway complete. After meeting with the team and seeing the completed code, you realize that the project is far behind where it should be. Customer participation in iteration and release demos has been minimal and sporadic and the team's velocity has been consistently lower than anticipated. It is obvious that the project will take at least twice as long to complete as originally believed yet the customer believes the project to be on schedule. What is your best course of action?

    A. Inform the customer of the situation and the likely timeline to complete the remaining work
    B. Make up the lost schedule without informing the customer. Since customer participation in demos is minimal, you can be caught up before anyone knows you were behind
    C. Add resources to your team to increase velocity
    D. Authorize overtime and add more stories to each iteration

11. You are leading one team in a large multi-team agile software development project and are attending a management project status meeting with other product owners representing the other agile development teams. One of the product owners is reporting that his team has been delivering code consistently and on time since the start of the project. You know this is not true as much of his code feeds your team and features have been frequently late and pushed to following iterations. What should you do?

    A. Meet with the project manager to inform him of the situation
    B. Discuss the situation with the human resources manager
    C. Report the situation to your boss
    D. Discuss the situation with the other product owner

12. The PMI Code of Ethics and Professional Conduct applies to all of the following except _____.

    A. Individuals who hold the title of project or program manager, but are not certified or affiliated with PMI
    B. Non-certified PMI members
    C. Certified PMPs
    D. People who have completed the application process, but have not yet taken a certification exam

13. The four values that PMI considers most important to the project management community and upon which the PMI Code of Ethics and Professional Conduct is based are _____.

    A. Responsibility, loyalty, fairness and respect
    B. Loyalty, profitability, fairness and honesty
    C. Responsibility, respect, fairness, and honesty
    D. Diversity, responsibility, fairness, and honesty

14. You are working on an agile software development project that required your customer to provide a large amount of confidential domain related data in order for your team to proceed with its work. You've been contacted by a local university doing research related to your customer's field and they've asked you for data to support their research. Some of the data requested is part of the confidential domain related data provided by your customer. What should you do?

    A. Contact your customer and request permission to disclose the data
    B. Disclose the data as it is always best to support academic research
    C. Provide a summary of the data
    D. Supply the data, but alter it such that its source cannot be determined

15. You are managing an agile project consisting of several teams of which one is located in a foreign country. The team located in the foreign country has a much more generous vacation and holiday schedule than the other teams on the project. What is your best course of action?

    A. Require the other teams to make up any time lost by the foreign team
    B. Require the foreign team to work at the same velocity as the other teams
    C. Match the foreign country team's vacation and holiday schedule so that all teams are equal
    D. Take the foreign country team's vacation and holiday schedule into account during iteration and release planning and schedule work accordingly

16. A colleague confides to you that he has been posing as an ACP. He tells you that he enjoys the recognition and has been offered many opportunities and sees no reason to go through the hassle of taking the exam and getting certified. What should you do?

    A. Report the situation to your colleague's management
    B. Report the situation to your colleague's HR director
    C. Report the situation to PMI
    D. Ignore the situation as your colleague told you in confidence and he's doing no harm

17. You are a member of an Extreme Programming (XP) team and you discover that one of the programmer pairs has been altering tests so that their code passes. They've done this because they were having trouble with their section of the code and they didn't want to negatively impact the team's velocity. What should you do?

    A. Bring the situation up at the next daily standup
    B. Discuss the problem with the offending programmer pair
    C. Bring the situation to the attention of the product owner
    D. Ignore the situation as your colleagues had the team's best interest in mind

18. You are on a team tasked with choosing a software vendor for a major government contract that your company has won. The choice has been narrowed down to three vendors with one seeming significantly better than the other two. The leading vendor happens to be owned by your brother-in-law and while you don't feel that this has impacted your ability to fairly evaluate the vendors, neither your management nor colleagues are aware of this relationship. What should you do?

    A. Disclose the relationship immediately and remove yourself from the evaluation team
    B. Say nothing as the appearance of a conflict of interest may negatively impact the contract
    C. Say nothing as you are a professional and are capable of making an unbiased decision
    D. Disclose the relationship after the selection as it did not affect your selection decision

19. The purpose of the PMI Code of Ethics and Professional Conduct is _____.

    A. To provide a framework for disciplinary action for PMI members as required
    B. To instill confidence in the project management profession and to help an individual become a better practitioner
    C. Provide an ethical model for other organizations to use
    D. To provide an ethical framework for certified PMPs to work within.

20. Taking ownership for the decisions we make or fail to make, the actions we take or fail to take, and the consequences that result is an example of which of the core values of the PMI Code of Ethics and Professional Conduct?

    A. Responsibility
    B. Diversity
    C. Loyalty
    D. Honesty

Answers – Terminology Matching

1:G, 2:D, 3:E, 4:B, 5:C, 6:A, 7:F, 8:J, 9:K, 10:H, 11:I, 12:N, 13:L, 14:O, 15:M

Answers – Crossword Puzzle

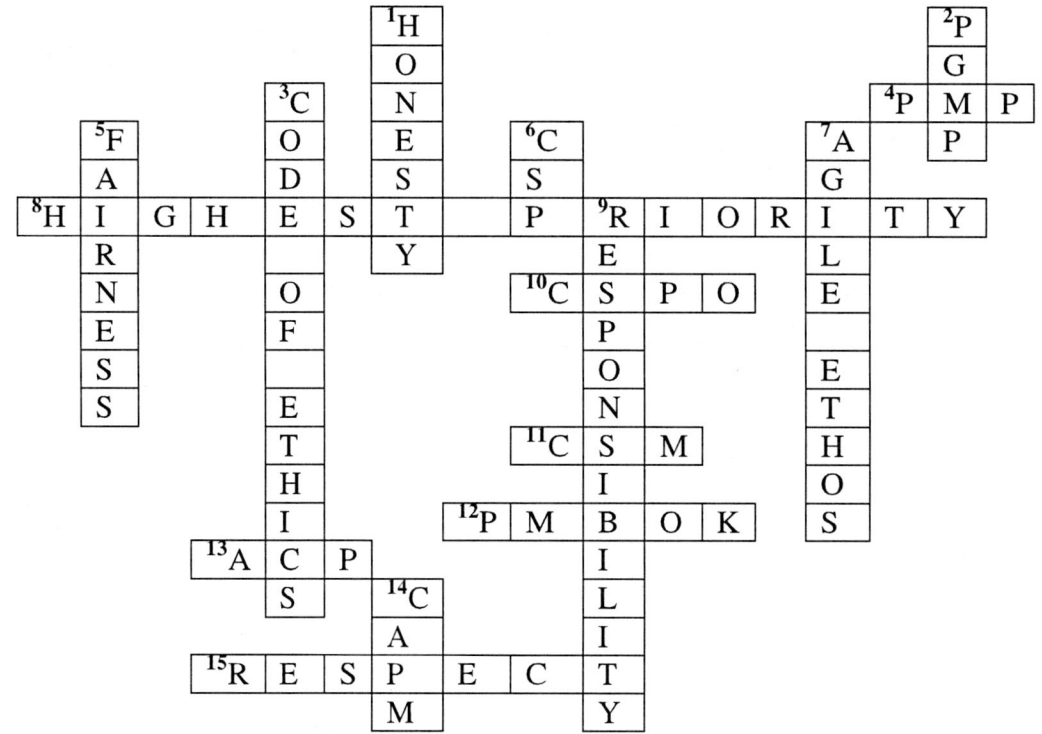

Answers – Word Search

Word Search - 15 Words to find:

ACP	AGILEETHOS	CAPM
CODEOFETHICS	CSM	CSP
CSPO	FAIRNESS	HIGHESTPRIORITY
HONESTY	PGMP	PMBOK
PMP	RESPECT	RESPONSIBILITY

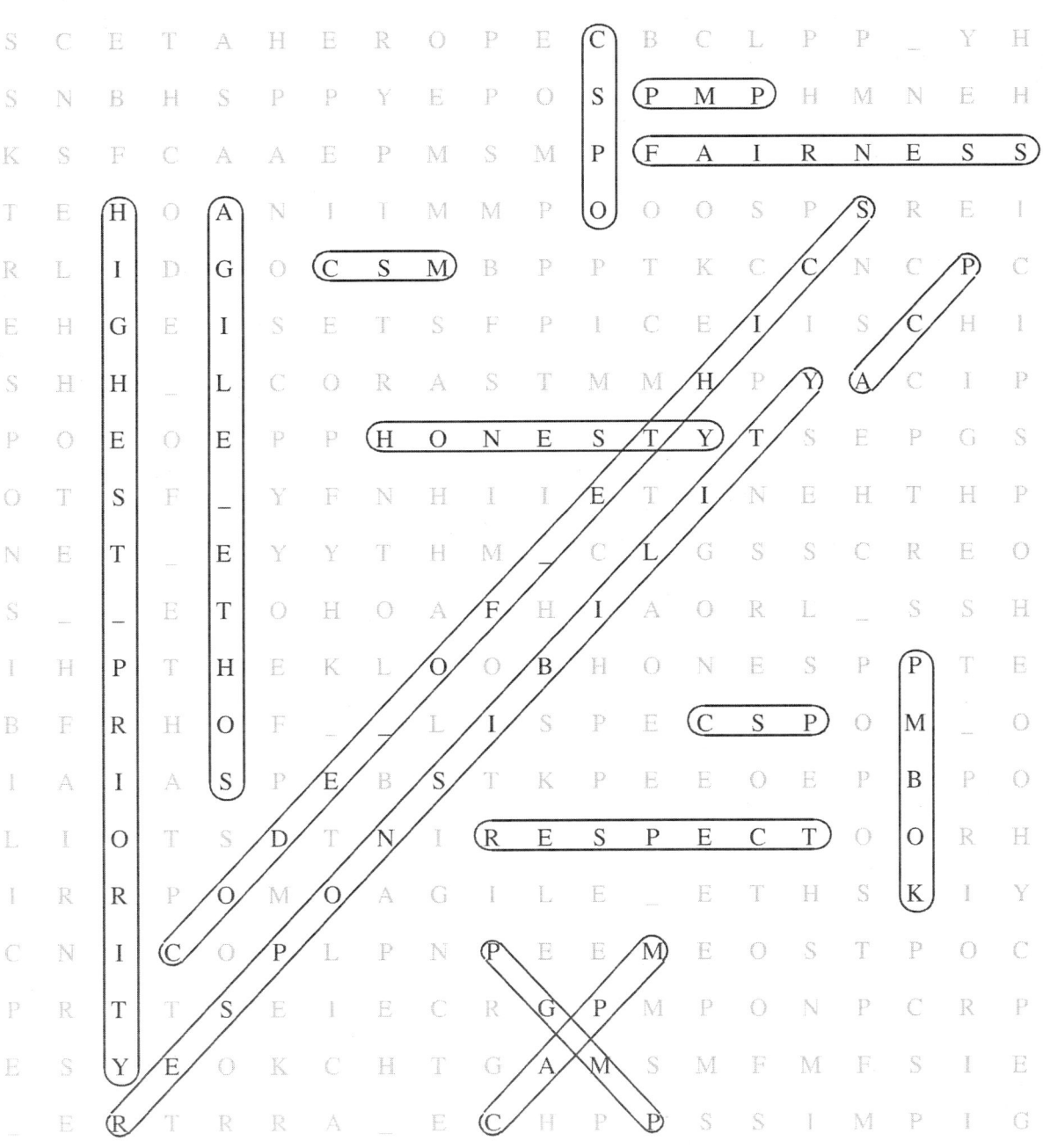

Answers – Practice Test

1. **D.** It would be inappropriate to bloat the project costs by 25 percent. A risk assessment describing how the project may fail if the budget is not accurate is most appropriate. A, B, and C are all incorrect because these choices are ethically wrong. Every ACP should always provide honest estimates of the project work.

2. **C.** The company policies and procedures should guide the project manager and the decision he makes in the foreign country. A and B are incorrect because these documents are essential, but usually do not reference allowed business practices. D is incorrect as the PMP Code of Professional Conduct provides general guidelines of professional behavior, but the company's policies and procedures contain specific rules defining how the organization will conduct business.

3. **B.** This situation calls for the project team member to be reported to his manager for disciplinary action. A is inappropriate because the project manager may not have the authority to fire the project team member. C is inappropriate because the project manager must take action to bring the situation to management's attention. D is also inappropriate because there are no formal disciplinary actions taken to address the problem.

4. **B.** The project manager should confront the problem by talking with the vendor about the rumor. A is incorrect because the action is based on an unconfirmed rumor and would delay the project and possibly cause future problems. C is incorrect and may violate the contract between the buyer and seller. D is also incorrect as the agreement is between the vendor and the performing organization, not the labor union.

5. **B** is the best answer. Although this solution may seem extreme, it is the best answer because to accept the car in public would give the impression that the project manager has violated company policy. In addition, accepting the car would appear to be a conflict of interest for the project manager. A, C, and D are all incorrect. Accepting the car, even with the intention of returning it or donating it to charity, would be in conflict with the company's policies regarding the acceptance of gifts.

6. **C.** The situation regarding the project team member that is causing the problems should be presented to management with a solution to remove that team member from the project. Remember, whenever the project manager must present a problem to management, he or she should also present a solution to the problem. A is incorrect because it likely is not the project manager's role to fire the project team member. B is incorrect because it does not present a solution for the problem. D is incorrect because the project manager's focus should be on the success of the project. By recommending that the project team member be removed from the project, the problem is solved from the project manager's point of view. Management, however, may come to the decision on their own accord to dismiss the individual from the company altogether. In addition, a recommendation from the project manager to fire someone may be outside the boundary of the human resource's procedure for employee termination.

7. **D.** Of the choices presented, this is the best answer. You should inform your employer of your intent to leave the organization and work on similar projects to avoid a conflict of interest. A is incorrect because you would have a conflict of interest. Information gained about your current employer's proposal (such as price and methods) would be ethically

wrong. B is incorrect because there is no rationale offered to explain what the conflict of interest may be. C is incorrect because a conflict of interest exists by preparing the proposal for your future competition.

8. **A.** The project manager is taking action on a potentially unethical situation and informing management of the potential issue. **B** does not address the problem and is unlikely to be successful and may needlessly damage your relationship with the consultant. **C** and **D** also are incorrect as no action is taken to address the problem.

9. **B.** This is a fee for service and paid to a local government agency and is therefore not a bribe. **A** is incorrect because the fee is not a bribe. **C** is incorrect as it would greatly impede the success of your project. **D** is incorrect because the fee is in fact legitimate and required.

10. **A.** You have a responsibility to maintain honest, fair, and open communications with the customer. **B** would be dishonest and would likely fail. **C** and **D** do not address the issue of honestly informing the customer of the current situation and would again, very likely fail.

11. **D.** Professional and social responsibility obligates you to confront the problem and attempt to resolve it with the other product owner and confirm whether or not your assessment of the situation is correct. **A** or **C** might be the *next* step depending on the outcome of your conversation with the other product owner. **B** would be inappropriate.

12. **A.** The PMI Code of Ethics and Professional Conduct applies to all PMI members as well as anyone who is certified by PMI, has applied to take a certification exam, or who serves or is affiliated with PMI in any official capacity. The code does not apply to individuals who are not certified by or are in no way affiliated with PMI.

13. **C.** The values that the global project management community defined as most important were: responsibility, respect, fairness, and honesty. The Code is based on these four values.

14. **A.** Your responsibility is to protect the data that was provided by your customer with the understanding of confidentiality and intended for a specific use. Providing the data to a third party should not be done without the specific permission of your customer. Choices **B**, **C**, and **D** might be next steps.

15. **D.** Respect for the culture and customs of the foreign team makes this the correct answer. Fairness would make **A** and **B** incorrect while responsibility to your company and customer would make **C** a less than optimal choice.

16. **C.** You have an obligation per the PMI Code to report the situation to PMI. **A** and **B** are incorrect as they do not meet your obligation to PMI. **D** is incorrect as it does nothing to address the situation.

17. **C.** Inform the Scrum Master of the situation and allow him or her to resolve the issue. **A**, **B**, and **D** involve ignoring the situation or bringing it up in public and possibly causing unnecessary damage to the team so they are incorrect.

18. **A.** Disclose the relationship immediately as even the appearance of a conflict of interest is potentially damaging. The PMI code also requires that you avoid conflicts of interest. **B** and **C** are incorrect as they don't address the appearance of a conflict of interest. **D** is incorrect because the action takes place "after the fact" and will likely be more damaging.

19. **B.** The purpose of this Code is to instill confidence in the project management profession and to help an individual become a better practitioner.

20. **A.** Of the four values that make up the foundation of the Code, responsibility, respect, fairness, and honesty, taking ownership of our actions and their results is an example of responsibility..

---

[1]Project Management Institute. (2008). *A guide to the project management body of knowledge (PMBOK® guide), Fourth edition.* Newtown Square, PA: Author.

[2]Project Management Institute. (2011). *PMI agile certification examination content outline.* Newtown Square, PA: Author.

CHAPTER 12

Comprehensive Exams

Exam #1

1. Initiating a project in an agile environment requires getting input from stakeholders and setting priorities according to their values. The output of collecting, refining, and prioritizing input from stakeholders, customers, end users, and the team produces a(n) _____.

   A. Product backlog
   B. Team velocity
   C. User story
   D. Iteration plan

2. Based on the concept of *sufficiency-to-purpose,* an intermediate work product needs:

   A. To be only good enough to help the team move forward
   B. To be complete as measured by a definable metric
   C. To be made better when resources allow it
   D. To be as realistic a model as possible to have intrinsic value

3. When should re-estimating take place?

   A. When progress is slower than expected
   B. When the customer/proxy is not happy with the estimated completion date
   C. When velocity is lower than expected for the most recently completed iteration
   D. When the relative size of one or more stories has changed

4. Agile teams typically perform planning at three levels - _____ planning, _____ planning, and _____ planning.

   A. Story, iteration, release
   B. Release, iteration, daily
   C. Cost, schedule, scope
   D. Iterative, estimated, progressive

5. In Scrum, the responsibility for prioritizing stories _____.

   A. Belongs completely to the customer/proxy
   B. Is exclusively that of the Product Owner
   C. Is shared among the whole team, but the effort is led by the Product Owner
   D. Is shared between the sponsor and end user

6. In agile planning, the use of iterations is intended to reduce the risk of _____.

   A. Exceeding the authorized budget
   B. Failing to meet customer requirements
   C. Developing the wrong product
   D. Delivering the product late

7. Prior to a retrospective, an agile team may wish to review its _____ and adjust them as needed to apply in the retrospective.

    A. "Caves and commons" layout
    B. Values and working agreements
    C. Pairings
    D. Organizational process assets

8. The staged contract allows for built-in checkpoints to provide the customer/proxy visibility and _____ decision points along the way.

    A. Go/no-go
    B. Scope control
    C. De facto
    D. Plan-driven

9. According to the Agile Manifesto, within a development team the most efficient and effective method of conveying information is _____.

    A. The daily stand-up meeting
    B. Information radiators
    C. Having colocated teams
    D. Face-to-face conversation

10. In Extreme Programming (XP), how is the quality of the team's programming evaluated?

    A. By examining the source code to ensure that all unit tests run at 100 % for checked-in code.
    B. By plotting the unit test percentages of checked-in code on a role-deliverable-milestone chart.
    C. By having the on-site customer/proxy sign off on the demonstrated, checked-in code.
    D. By peer review of the checked-in code.

11. In _____, the test or executable example is written before deciding how to design the code.

    A. Blitz planning
    B. Test-driven development
    C. Internal test collaboration
    D. External test collaboration

12. Each day, the team meets face-to-face for five to ten minutes to update each other on their status and any obstacles that are slowing them down. This is called the _____.

    A. Daily status report meeting
    B. Daily stand-up-meeting
    C. Daily retrospective meeting
    D. Daily planning meeting

13. It is the Scrum Master's responsibility to remove, or get someone to remove, whatever _____ the team mentions in the stand-up meeting.

    A. Chickens
    B. Noise
    C. Roadblocks
    D. Pigs

14. A period, usually two to four weeks, in which the project team codes and tests one or more small features resulting in potentially releasable software is referred to as _____.

    A. A timebox
    B. A story
    C. An iteration
    D. A theme

15. For an organization, being agile requires a balance between _____.

    A. Discipline and chaos
    B. Discipline and traditional project management
    C. Discipline and leadership
    D. Discipline and flexibility

16. A traditional project manager focuses on following the plan with minimal changes, whereas an Agile Project Manager _____.

    A. Focuses on processes
    B. Focuses on adapting successfully to inevitable changes
    C. Focuses on executing the plan
    D. Focuses on ways to change the plan

17. When project leaders focus on delivery, they add value to projects. When they focus on planning and control, they tend to add _____.

    A. Overhead
    B. Value
    C. Creativity
    D. Subject matter expertise

18. The agile iteration process can be best defined by four key terms:

    A. Iterative, feature-based, timeboxed, and incremental
    B. Initiate, produce, develop, and ship
    C. Enhance, design, produce, and ship
    D. Envision, feature-based, schedule, and iterative

19. Getting the right people,; articulating the product vision, boundaries, and team roles; collaborating; insisting on accountability; fostering self-discipline; and steering rather than controlling – are characteristic of what kind of teams?

    A. Well-organized teams
    B. Framing teams
    C. Self-directing teams
    D. Self-organizing teams

20. In agile projects, the correct scope is not a set of defined requirements, but the _____ for a releasable product.

    A. Tradeoff matrix
    B. Articulated product vision
    C. Preliminary scope statement
    D. Elevator statement

21. As a component of the agile framework layer, _____ management focuses on planning, execution, and team leadership during short individual timeboxes.

    A. Human resource (HR)
    B. Project
    C. Iteration
    D. Portfolio

22. During the Envision phase of the Agile Project Management Model (APM) delivery approach, an exploration factor acts as a barometer of the uncertainty and risk of a _____.

    A. Product
    B. Plan
    C. Project
    D. Possibility

23. A _____ or a story is defined as a piece of a product that delivers some useful and valuable functionality to a customer.

    A. Feature
    B. Pareto factor
    C. Sprint
    D. Release

24. A _____ is a list of capabilities, features, and stories that the product team has identified.

    A. Sprint
    B. Story
    C. Feature
    D. Backlog

25. In release planning, stories are assigned to iterations, based primarily on _____.

   A. Requirements and schedule
   B. Customer value and risk
   C. Time and schedule constraints
   D. Marketability and time constraints

26. Use of _____ iterations at the end of the agile project increases the reliability of the schedule, particularly with high exploration-factor projects.

   A. Buffer
   B. Risk transference
   C. Full
   D. Specialty

27. On agile projects, planning artifacts such as expenditure budgets may be finalized only after the _____ plan is complete.

   A. Backlog
   B. Iteration
   C. Release
   D. Retrospective

28. A sprint plan is a(n) _____ work plan for a Scrum team; it usually spans 1 to 4 weeks.

   A. Week-to-week
   B. Day-to-day
   C. Quarter-to-quarter
   D. Hour-to-hour

29. System change requests (SCRs) such as software defects and maintenance requests may be added as stories and included in the _____.

   A. Release plan
   B. Sprint plan
   C. Architecture
   D. Product backlog

30. The question, "Is it feasible for this project to deliver a quality releasable product within the identified constraints of scope, schedule, and cost?" can be answered by referring to the _____ plan.

   A. Iteration
   B. Backlog
   C. Feature
   D. Release

31. On your Extreme Programming (XP) team, an orderly process occurs in which pairs of programmers get the latest code from the server, do their work, run all the tests to confirm their code works, and then check in their changes. This process, called _____, occurs several times a day.

    A. Continuous integration
    B. Exploratory testing
    C. Root cause analysis
    D. Test driven development (TDD)

32. The practice of confirming that the build and tests succeed before moving on to your next task is referred to as _____.

    A. Asynchronous integration
    B. Continuous integration
    C. Synchronous integration
    D. Exploratory testing

33. The biggest problem with asynchronous integration is that _____.

    A. It inflates team velocity
    B. It tends to result in broken builds
    C. It is difficult for programmers to implement
    D. It makes the work of testers more difficult

34. On an Extreme Programming (XP) team, when a programmer updates her sandbox with files from the tip (or head) of the repository she is _____.

    A. Updating her sandbox with the highest priority files checked into the repository
    B. Updating her sandbox with files containing the latest changes checked into the repository
    C. Updating her sandbox with the largest files in the repository
    D. Updating her sandbox with files from another team

35. On an Extreme Programming (XP) team, sometimes a programmer will _____ his sandbox to throw away his changes and return to the point of his last update. This is handy when the programmer has broken his local build and can't figure out how to get it working again.

    A. Revert
    B. Delete
    C. Merge
    D. Branch

36. Sometimes the agile team is directed to generate specific documentation that has business value but isn't otherwise necessary for the team to do its work. In this case, the best approach would be to _____.

    A. Shield your team from this unproductive work by requesting that others outside the team do this work
    B. Create all required documentation at the end of the project
    C. Schedule the documentation as a story and create, estimate, and prioritize it just as you would any other story
    D. Have the project manager and Product Owner create all documentation that isn't required by the programmers to do their jobs

37. Weick's principle of _____ tells us that delivering running, tested, useful code at regular intervals is a motivating reward for the project team.

    A. Small wins
    B. Intrinsic motivation
    C. Extrinsic motivation
    D. Intermittent reinforcement

38. A(n) _____ displays project-related information in a place where passersby can see it.

    A. Dashboard report
    B. Information radiator
    C. Key performance indicator (KPI)
    D. Balanced scorecard (BSC)

39. All of the following are typical uses of an information radiator EXCEPT:

    A. To show vacancies when a project team member leaves
    B. To show the results of the project's periodic reflection workshop
    C. To show everyone the user stories delivered or in progress
    D. To show the work breakdown and assignments for the next iteration

40. Agile fixed-price contracts may base payments on which of the following unit of delivery?

    A. Function points
    B. Story points
    C. Incremental acceptances
    D. All of the above

41. Given the choices below, what is the main difference between the colors of Crystal (Crystal Clear, Crystal Yellow, and Crystal Orange)?

    A. Sustained velocity over time
    B. There is no significant difference, with the terms originating in different places
    C. Iteration length
    D. Team size

42. What two types of tests are considered part of fully automated regression testing?

    A. Unit tests and team tests
    B. Unit tests and functional tests
    C. Unit tests and user acceptance tests (UAT)
    D. User acceptance tests (UAT) and peer review tests

43. _____ is when designers in one location send specifications and tests to programmers in another location, usually another country.

    A. Offshore development
    B. Distributed development
    C. Open-source development
    D. Colocated development

44. _____ refers to a steering committee of evaluators who meet periodically to monitor a program of projects.

    A. Program modification
    B. Program governance
    C. Board of directors
    D. Project scope approval board

45. On your Extreme Programming (XP) team, the best approach to fixing bugs is to _____.

    A. Fix bugs on the last two days of the iteration
    B. Fix bugs whenever it is convenient, but before the end of the project
    C. Address and fix bugs as soon as they are discovered
    D. Go back and clean up the bugs after release so team velocity is not impacted

46. A _____ provides a central repository that helps coordinate changes to files and also provides a history of changes.

    A. Version control system
    B. Burn-up chart
    C. Coding standard
    D. Retrospective

47. You've just noticed a problem that threatens to impact the success of your Extreme Programming (XP) team's iteration. The best approach is to _____.

    A. Address the problem with the team at the end of the iteration
    B. Address the problem yourself so as not to impact team productivity
    C. Apprise the team as soon as possible so that the entire team has a chance to help solve the problem
    D. Ignore the problem until the iteration retrospective

48. _____ occurs when an organization asks a software development team to build something for the organization's own use.

    A. Vertical-market software
    B. Outsourced custom development
    C. Personal development
    D. In-house custom development

49. _____ is software that is intended to be used across a wide range of industries.

    A. Vertical-market software
    B. Horizontal-market software
    C. Outsourced custom development
    D. In-house custom development

50. A daily meeting where all participants specifically describe what they did yesterday, what they plan to do today, and what problems are preventing them from making progress can be described as a _____.

    A. Retrospective
    B. Daily Scrum
    C. Daily reflective workshop
    D. Project review

51. Typically generated by most agile teams when they update their release plan, a _____ is an excellent way to get a bird's-eye view of the project, as it shows progress and predicts a completion date.

    A. Burn-up chart
    B. Story board
    C. Coding standard
    D. Retrospective

52. Most software is built for a particular industry, such as healthcare, that has its own specialized rules for doing business. The software must implement such rules exactly per industry standards to be considered successful. These rules are _____ rules, and knowledge of these rules is _____ knowledge.

    A. Domain; Expert
    B. Intrinsic; Extrinsic
    C. Domain; Domain
    D. Focused; Focused

53. The bulk of the Extreme Programming (XP) team consists of software developers in a variety of specialties. Each of these developers contributes directly to creating working code. To emphasize this, XP typically refers to all developers as _____.

    A. Coders
    B. Subject matter experts (SME)
    C. Programmers
    D. Software specialists

54. Some organizations like to assign people to multiple projects simultaneously. This practice is referred to as _____ and is not recommended when using most agile methodologies.

    A. Fractional assignment
    B. Multiple tasking
    C. Extreme tasking
    D. Agile assignments

55. _____ is the total amount of imperfect design and implementation decisions in your project.

    A. Timeboxing
    B. Technical debt
    C. Subcode
    D. Code surplus

56. _____ is a simple way of mapping estimates to the calendar and is the total of the estimates for the stories completed in an iteration.

    A. Velocity
    B. Timeboxing
    C. Refactoring
    D. Progressive elaboration

57. Retrospectives can be conducted during crucial milestones throughout the project. However, the most common retrospective is the _____ retrospective.

    A. Project
    B. Iteration
    C. Release
    D. Surprise

58. You are new to agile and have been invited to watch an experienced Extreme Programming (XP) team conduct an iteration retrospective. You observe the team gathered at a whiteboard silently arranging and rearranging index cards that appear to have notes written on them. The activity you are observing is referred to as _____.

   A. Brainstorming
   B. Mind mapping
   C. Argumentation
   D. Mute mapping

59. During the agile retrospective, why is it important to debrief every activity?

   A. Debriefing gives the facilitator time to document the outcome of each activity
   B. Debriefing gives the customer/proxy an idea of how the team approached the work
   C. Debriefing helps the team form insights and decisions from the retrospective
   D. Debriefing gives the team data to put on the next information radiator

60. How can a project leader improve on facilitation skills needed for agile retrospectives?

   A. Observe others who excel at facilitating meetings
   B. Practice facilitating other types of meetings
   C. Facilitate a meeting and have an expert facilitator observe and give you feedback
   D. All of the above

61. The _____ activity, often used during retrospective closing, is intended to provide the retrospective facilitator with team feedback to improve skills and processes.

   A. Helped, Hindered, Hypothesis (HHH)
   B. Appreciations, Strengths, Weaknesses, and Deltas
   C. Appreciations, New Information, Legacy Data, and Hope and Wishes
   D. Appreciations, Legacy Data, Complaints with Recommendations, and Hopes and Wishes

62. In organizing a large release or project-level retrospective, the responsibilities of the retrospective facilitator include all of the following EXCEPT:

   A. Deciding who to invite
   B. Writing the post-retrospective report
   C. Extending the invitation
   D. Educating new participants

63. A user story must be valuable to whom?

   A. The user or customer
   B. The Scrum Master
   C. The project team
   D. The developer

64. Tools used by the Scrum team to establish a shared product vision include:

    A. Elevator Statement, Product Release Plan, and Press Release
    B. Product Data Sheet, Elevator Statement, and Product Release Plan
    C. Elevator Statement, Product Vision Box, and Press Release
    D. Press Release, Magazine Review, and Product Release Plan

65. In the middle of a four-week sprint, the Product Owner comes to the Scrum master and the team telling them he has become aware of a critical story that must be added to the sprint. If the proposed change cannot be kept out of the sprint:

    A. The additional story and the related story points should be added to the current sprint and burn-down chart.
    B. The current sprint should be abnormally terminated and restarted with the new story added.
    C. The additional story and the related story points should be added to the current sprint and burn-down chart only if the business makes additional resources available to the team.
    D. The situation described is a hybrid project and must be approved by the Product Owner, Scrum Master, and team before any changes can be made.

66. During retrospectives, a team may employ a _____ activity to help it look at factors affecting a proposed change. In conducting the activity, the team first defines a state they want to achieve and then breaks into groups to identify factors that may either restrain or drive the desired change.

    A. Detractor
    B. Tightrope Balancing
    C. Blitz Planning
    D. Force Field Analysis

67. A full cycle of design-code-verify-release practiced by Extreme Programming (XP) teams that is contained within a one to three week timebox is a(n) _____.

    A. Iteration
    B. Phase
    C. Story
    D. Theme

68. When applying Extreme Programming (XP) methods, the term "last possible moment" refers to _____.

    A. The moment at which time the project is officially late
    B. The end of an iteration
    C. The moment at which failing to make a decision eliminates an important alternative
    D. The latest possible release date

69. In a tradeoff matrix, agile project constraints are categorized as:

    A. Fixed, Functional, Flexible
    B. Factual, Functional, Flexible
    C. Fixed, Firm, Flexible
    D. Flexible, Functional, Financial

70. Which of the following statements is true about an abnormally terminated sprint?

    A. All work from the terminated sprint is undone
    B. Management may terminate the sprint if organizational priorities change
    C. The agile team may terminate the sprint if they feel they cannot meet the sprint goal
    D. All of the above

71. During an agile retrospective, one activity that might be helpful during the Generate Insights phase is that of constructing a fishbone diagram. The fishbone diagram facilitates the team's _____ analysis.

    A. Factor
    B. Root cause
    C. Spectral
    D. Multivariate

72. Extreme Programming (XP) is one method used by agile project teams. When using XP, analysis, design, coding, testing, and even deployment _____.

    A. Are done simultaneously and occur with rapid frequency
    B. Are planned and defined in detail at the start of every iteration
    C. Are not used as they are methods used in traditional software development
    D. Are less important due to the extreme speed of XP

73. Some stakeholders may want more detail than the vision statement provides, but not the extreme detail of the release and iteration plans. For these stakeholders, a _____ summarizes planned releases and the significant features in each one.

    A. Burn-up chart
    B. Roadmap
    C. Coding standard
    D. Retrospective

74. Extreme Programming (XP) teams will sometimes describe a story as being "done-done." This term means _____.

    A. The code is completed, but not tested
    B. The code is complete, but failed testing
    C. The code is complete and tested, but contains minor known bugs
    D. The code is complete, tested, bug free and can be released to the customer

75. An agile project's _____ comes from the release plan and is the aggregated total costs from its respective iterations.

    A. Internal rate of return (IRR)
    B. Budget
    C. Cost baseline
    D. Present value

76. A(n) _____ sprint in the last release of a project may be a way for the Scrum team to address some final finishing features.

    A. Optimizing
    B. Buffer
    C. Handoff
    D. Hardening

77. In an agile environment, _____ and facilitation replaces command-and-control project management to foster the development of the project team.

    A. Servant leadership
    B. Negotiation
    C. Laissez-faire leadership
    D. More democracy

78. A risk _____, which examines the effectiveness of risk responses, is conducted as part of the retrospective meeting.

    A. Review
    B. Debriefing
    C. Analysis
    D. Audit

79. _____ focuses on seven principles: eliminating waste, amplifying learning, deciding as late as possible, delivering as fast as possible, empowering the team, building integrity in, and seeing the whole.

    A. Agile Unified Development
    B. Feature-Driven Development
    C. Lean Software Development
    D. Complex Adaptive Systems Development

80. How does the agile team mitigate the threat of scope creep?

    A. By using iteration and release retrospectives to allow the customer/proxy to make changes to the backlog and to priorities.
    B. By identifying a single customer/proxy, or Product Owner, to make decisions
    C. By employing set-based design
    D. By implementing Open Space meetings

81. The _____ is the total number of story points planned for a release.

    A. Planned Percent Complete (PPC)
    B. Performance Measure Baseline (PMB)
    C. Actual Percent Complete (APC)
    D. Schedule Baseline

82. At the end of each iteration, a product _____ is provided to interested stakeholders, as well as a review and a retrospective on how the iteration went.

    A. Audit
    B. Display
    C. Walk through
    D. Demonstration

83. The agile approach to human resource planning is to establish _____ teams with mutual accountability, and allow them to _____ within a framework that requires regular team retrospection.

    A. Collaborative; Self-organize
    B. Cross-functional; Self-organize
    C. Globalist; Communicate
    D. Cross-functional; Self-flagellate

84. In an agile environment, having the project manager conduct individual performance reviews is considered a conflict of interest, as it violates the agile project manager's _____ role.

    A. Functional
    B. Subject-matter expert
    C. Servant leadership
    D. "Seagull"

85. The agile use of highly visible information radiators, stems from Lean Manufacturing's use of a signaling system called _____.

    A. Six Sigma
    B. Kanban
    C. Just-in-Time (JIT)
    D. Shu-Ha-Ri

86. One way to mitigate productivity variation for an agile team is to:

    A. Track team velocity
    B. Track financial burn rate
    C. Track the voluntary turnover rate of the project team
    D. Track team hours charged to specific project codes

87. The _____ is total number of sprint points completed (potentially shippable increments) divided by the total number of story points planned.

   A. Actual Percent Complete (APC)
   B. Planned Percent Complete (PPC)
   C. Performance Measurement Baseline (PMB)
   D. Schedule Baseline

88. When the team allocates an iteration to prepare the formal documentation and other deliverables that production requires, including attending final approval meetings, this is called a(n) _____ iteration.

   A. Hardening
   B. Hybrid
   C. Optimizing
   D. Handoff

89. How does the agile team mitigate against intrinsic schedule flaw?

   A. By identifying a single customer/proxy, or Product Owner, to make decisions
   B. By reevaluating the release plan at the end of each iteration, to see if the team is on target
   C. By employing set-based design
   D. By implementing Open Space meetings

90. The payback period is _____.

   A. The amount of time required to earn back the initial investment
   B. The period of time in which new business is won from a competitor
   C. The time in which a capital investment loan must be repaid
   D. The time it takes to complete an iteration

91. One method to reduce risk for both contracting parties is to include clauses that allow for _____ decisions at the end of each iteration. This protects the customer if the agile seller does not deliver as agreed and the agile seller if the customer does not provide needed input.

   A. Select-or-reject
   B. Reward-or-punishment
   C. Continue-or-cancel
   D. Make-or-buy

92. During the agile retrospective, it is the responsibility of the _____ to monitor their working agreements so that the retrospective leader may focus on facilitating.

   A. Customer/proxy
   B. Functional manager
   C. Tester
   D. Team

93. A(n) _____ is a single page summary of key project management information, product capabilities, and business and quality objectives.

    A. Project data sheet
    B. Flexibility matrix
    C. Team working agreement
    D. Information radiator

94. The core values and principles of Agile Project Management (APM) are applicable to project teams of what size?

    A. 5 to 9 members
    B. Any size
    C. Up to 50 members
    D. Up to 100 members

95. What factors drive release plans?

    A. Stories and iterations
    B. Backlogs and features
    C. Customer value and risk
    D. Products and risk

96. In an agile project, story cards are used to _____.

    A. Provide basic information about stories
    B. Provide test cases for stories
    C. Provide performance estimates for stories
    D. Provide baseline milestone dates for stories

97. A plan that defines the features the team will build in advance, but where the release date is uncertain is referred to as a _____ plan.

    A. Variable release date
    B. Feature-defined
    C. Timeboxed
    D. Scopeboxed

98. One effective way to improve team velocity is to _____.

    A. Reduce the duration of daily stand-up meetings
    B. Improve customer/proxy involvement
    C. Reduce the frequency of daily stand-up meetings
    D. Increase the number of stories planned per iteration

99. The amount of slack that you build into your iteration plan depends on the _____ of the problems that your project team experiences.

   A. Randomness
   B. Number
   C. Complexity
   D. Difficulty

100. Sometimes used synonymously with epic, a _____ describes a high-level business or product function that is complete and valuable.

   A. Feature
   B. Release
   C. Capability
   D. Theme

101. In Scrum, the _____ sequence is frequently used by teams when providing value point estimates for stories.

   A. Pareto
   B. Fibonacci
   C. Pearson product-moment
   D. Dover-Calais

102. _____ is an approach of continuous improvement, which has periodic releasable timeframes and does not require strict iteration lengths for all stories.

   A. Just-in-Time (JIT)
   B. Quality
   C. Kaisen
   D. Kanban

103. _____ is one of the best known of the Lean principles.

   A. Estimating work accurately
   B. Eliminating waste
   C. Delivering product on time
   D. Providing a guiding principle

104. _____ is the cause of most product failures.

   A. Market risk
   B. Lack of requirements
   C. Failure to adhere to the chosen development methodology
   D. Technical risk

105. Which system strives to minimize work-in-process and maximize business value creation?

    A. Lean
    B. Test-Driven Development
    C. Waterfall
    D. Six Sigma

106. A project manager is drawing process-flow diagrams to try to add value for a customer. What tool is the project manager trying to use?

    A. Waterfall map
    B. Agile map
    C. Value stream map
    D. Lean principles map

107. The idea behind applying Lean principles in software development is to have _____ agility.

    A. Product
    B. Enterprise
    C. Feature
    D. Team

108. A variation of Scrum is _____, which is an enhancement that results from embedding Scrum with Lean thinking.

    A. Scrum++
    B. Waterfall
    C. Scrum#
    D. Agile

109. A Scrum team is typically guided by a _____ who can be guiding the team as an agile coach.

    A. Product Owner
    B. Project Champion
    C. Customer/proxy
    D. Scrum Master

110. When preparing for Scrum sprint planning, the agile coach's two essential jobs are:

    A. Facilitating a structured meeting agenda and ensuring Product Owner engagement
    B. Creating the meeting checklist and ensuring attendance of subject-matter experts
    C. Preparing the burn-down chart and ensuring Product Owner engagement
    D. Prioritizing the user stories and ensuring Product Owner engagement

111. In a Scrum environment, the Product Owner can impact agile team efficiency by _____.

    A. Not speaking during the daily stand-up meetings
    B. Establishing priorities and value on behalf of the customer
    C. Providing story estimates during planning poker sessions
    D. Reading all posted information radiators prior to sprint retrospectives

112. In Scrum, forecasting the financial value of a theme is the responsibility of _____.

    A. The Product Owner
    B. The Product Owner, but it is a responsibility shared with all other team members
    C. Senior management
    D. Senior management and the customer/proxy

113. In Scrum, the notion of a reciprocal commitment refers to:

    A. The business committing to deliver some specified amount of functionality and the team committing to not change priorities during the sprint.
    B. The Scrum Master committing to deliver some specified amount of functionality and the customer/proxy committing to not change priorities during the sprint.
    C. The Scrum Master committing to deliver some specified amount of functionality and the Product Owner committing to not change priorities during the sprint.
    D. The team committing to deliver some specified amount of functionality and the business committing to not change priorities during the sprint

114. In a Scrum environment, John is writing a project data sheet. What sections should be included in the project data sheet?

    A. Elevator Statement, Risk Register, Performance Attributes, Tradeoff Matrix
    B. Elevator Statement, Stakeholder Analysis, Performance Attributes, Tradeoff Matrix
    C. Elevator Statement, Customer Attributes, Performance Attributes, Tradeoff Matrix
    D. Elevator Statement, Scope Statement, Customer Attributes, Tradeoff Matrix

115. For the agile project team, when obstacles are addressed as part of the daily stand-up meeting, this is considered _____ risk management. When risks are charted on a white board or flip chart, this is exemplary of _____ risk management.

    A. Organic, Overt
    B. Overt, Organic
    C. Original, Overt
    D. Obvious, Overt

116. Scrum is a specific framework for creating an effective _____ development process

    A. Lean
    B. Waterfall
    C. Agile
    D. Kanban

117. During the "Gather Data" phase of the agile retrospective, the data should include both hard facts and the _____ of team members.

   A. Feelings
   B. Myers-Briggs Type Indicator (MBTI) profiles
   C. Attitudes
   D. Opinions

118. A(n) _____ shows the relative importance of project constraints, where only one of these constraints may be "fixed."

   A. Project data sheet
   B. Trade-off matrix
   C. Team working agreement
   D. Information radiator

119. Senior management has two projects they want your Extreme Programming (XP) team to complete in the next six months. The priorities of the two projects are roughly the same and it is up to you to determine how to schedule the work. Your best approach would be to _____.

   A. Use either the serial or parallel approach, as it has no impact on the teams productivity
   B. Work on both projects simultaneously, completing stories from both projects during each iteration
   C. Work on both projects simultaneously, switching from one project to the other each month until both are complete
   D. Work on one project at a time, releasing the first project and then the second one in sequence

120. The smallest set of functionality that provides value to your market, whether that market is internal users or external customers is referred to as a _____.

   A. Basic feature set (BFS)
   B. Minimal set of functionality (MSF)
   C. Minimally marketable feature (MMF)
   D. Basic market value (BMV)

Exam #2

1. What characterizes a method such as Adaptive Software Development or Crystal as being high-tolerance?

    A. High-tolerance methods suggest the use of standards but call for team members to form consensus on the minimal compliance needed
    B. High-tolerance methods require project leaders to enforce strict adherence to practices they consider effective
    C. High-tolerance methods require project leaders to ignore to practices they consider ineffective
    D. High-tolerance methods require project leaders to abandon the method when they discover false adherence to discipline

2. For product development in an agile environment, what is the purpose of planning?

    A. To produce a schedule that is acceptable to the customer/proxy
    B. To reduce overall project risk
    C. To find the best answer to the question of what to build
    D. To ensure that all project requirements are validated

3. The use of story points _____.

    A. Is easier than ideal planning
    B. Promotes cross-functional behavior
    C. Requires the use of subject matter experts
    D. Is not a preferred agile planning method

4. Which of the following statements about Extreme Programming (XP) is correct?

    A. The programmer owns the story's priority and the design estimate
    B. The programmer owns the story's priority; the customer/proxy owns the design estimate
    C. The customer/proxy owns the story's priority; the programmer owns the design estimate
    D. The story's priority and the design estimate are the shared responsibility of customer/proxy and programmer

5. When following the appropriate sequence for feature development, the _____, _____ features should be developed first.

    A. High-value, low-risk
    B. Low-value, high-risk
    C. Low-value, low-risk
    D. High-value, high-risk

6. A(n) _____ is a meeting where the team gathers after completing an increment of work to inspect and adapt their methods and teamwork.

   A. Iteration
   B. Release planning session
   C. Retrospective
   D. Wireframe

7. According to the Agile Manifesto, the highest priority that drives agile teams is based on the philosophy of _____.

   A. Satisfying the customer
   B. Delivering in iterations
   C. Maximizing the customer's competitive advantage through process improvement
   D. Maintaining an ethical and transparent demeanor

8. _____ is considered a critical element of Crystal Clear.

   A. Colocation
   B. A static team size of nine (9) members
   C. Having twice-a-day stand-up meetings
   D. Adherence to the "caves and common" room layout

9. An agile approach to planning _____.

   A. Fully defines product features early in the project
   B. Results in plans that encourage change and that are easily changed
   C. Focuses on the plan documents rather than the planning process
   D. Results in a fully defined schedule and budget

10. The authors of the Agile Manifesto wrote, among other things, that they value _____.

    A. Working software that is extensively documented
    B. Comprehensive contract negotiations to reduce uncertainty
    C. Strictly following a detailed project plan
    D. Individuals and interactions over processes and tools

11. Retained revenue is revenue that _____.

    A. Is generated from new product development
    B. Is retained from increased operational efficiencies
    C. An organization will lose if the project or theme is not developed
    D. Is retained from the business of a new customer

12. The amount an investor has today to generate a known amount in the future is called the _____.

    A. Present value
    B. Future value
    C. Investment value
    D. Prior funding

13. Whereas waterfall methods deliver _____ at the end of the project, agile projects deliver it quickly and incrementally throughout the project.

    A. Solutions
    B. Value
    C. Output
    D. Communications

14. Agile values tell us that responding to change is more important than following a _____.

    A. Plan
    B. Guide
    C. Manual
    D. Requirement

15. The "Agile Triangle" constraints pertain to _____ goals.

    A. Value, Quality, and Risk
    B. Schedule, Cost, and Quality
    C. Time, Cost, and Scope
    D. Value, Quality, and Constraint

16. Effective teams cover four key subject areas in their retrospectives:

    A. Project, plan, requirement, and test
    B. Meeting, collaborate, report, and close
    C. Product, process, team, and project
    D. Product, plan, people, and execute

17. When using the Agile Project Management Model (APM) delivery approach, the Explore phase delivers _____.

    A. Story estimates
    B. Product stories
    C. Sprints
    D. Backlog features

18. When using the Agile Project Management Model (APM) delivery approach, the product of the Speculate phase is a _____ based on capabilities or stories to be delivered.

    A. Release plan
    B. Release product
    C. Release phase
    D. Release feature

19. The purpose of the product backlog is to expand the product _____.

    A. Features
    B. Vision
    C. Release
    D. Elevator statement

20. The purpose of _____ is to provide a simple medium for gathering basic information about stories, recording high-level requirements, developing work estimates, and defining acceptance tests.

    A. Feature cards
    B. Sprint cards
    C. Story cards
    D. Release cards

21. A _____ presents a roadmap of how the team intends to achieve the product vision within the project objectives and constraints identified in the project data sheet.

    A. Release plan
    B. Feature plan
    C. Story plan
    D. Sprint plan

22. On an agile project, when schedule problems occur, cutting _____ reduces scope. On waterfall projects, when schedule problems occur, _____ are cut, affecting quality.

    A. Value; Staff
    B. Testing; Tasks
    C. Iterations; Requirements
    D. Stories; Tasks

23. When going from traditional to agile project management, the project plan is replaced by the _____ plan, which addresses management concerns about project constraints such as schedule, value, and cost.

    A. Sprint
    B. Release
    C. Backlog
    D. Risk mitigation

24. A sprint plan is a(n) _____ work plan for a Scrumteam; it usually spans 1 to 4 weeks.

    A. Day-to-day
    B. Week-to-week
    C. Quarter-to-quarter
    D. Hour-to-hour

25. Agile stories may be estimated either in _____ terms (i.e., story points) or _____ terms (i.e., hours).

    A. Relative; Absolute
    B. Feature; Calendar
    C. Weighted; Calendar
    D. Feature; Absolute

26. During retrospectives, the purpose of having the team generate insights is to:

    A. Eliminate any variance from proscribed agile methods
    B. Groom the product backlog for the next iteration
    C. Make improvements for the next iteration
    D. Ascribe blame to those not on the agile team

27. Agile development methodologies focus on creating success in which three of the following areas?

    A. Technical, organizational, and business
    B. Personal, technical, and organizational
    C. Personal, organizational, and marketing
    D. Marketing, business, and software

28. _____ is an agile activity that brings together testing, coding, design, and architecture.

    A. Task oriented development (TOD)
    B. Feature driven planning
    C. Test-driven development (TDD)
    D. None of the above

29. You have just been assigned two testers to support your Extreme Programming (XP) agile project team. You should assign the testers to _____.

    A. Develop detailed tests to be used by the team at the end of each iteration
    B. Test each feature prior to release at the end of each iteration
    C. Develop detailed tests to be used by the team at the end of each iteration
    D. Work as integral members of the project team to help the team maintain high quality code, avoid or detect and correct bugs, avoid gaps in the software and improve the overall software development process

30. When does the agile project team update the release plan cost baseline?

    A. During the release retrospective
    B. After each iteration
    C. During the last daily stand-up meeting of the release
    D. Only upon customer/proxy request

31. Each of the following is a useful goal for an agile retrospective EXCEPT:

    A. Determine how to persuade HR to eliminate performance appraisals
    B. Understand reasons behind missed targets
    C. Find ways to improve our responsiveness to customers
    D. Discover what we were doing well

32. A _____ is a list of capabilities, features, and stories that the product team has identified.

    A. Test case
    B. Deliverable
    C. Backlog
    D. Use case

33. A(n) _____, or story, is a product component that provides some valuable functionality for the customer.

    A. Task
    B. Test case
    C. Iteration
    D. Feature

34. Your Extreme Programming (XP) team is planning its project and you have the option of doing two large releases or a number of smaller more frequent releases. Your best approach would be to _____.

    A. Do infrequent large releases as this tends to add value and reduce risk
    B. Do frequent smaller releases as it tends to add value and reduce risk
    C. Do one or two large releases as this is the preference of most customers
    D. Do either, as release size and frequency are unrelated to project success

35. A plan that defines the release date in advance, but where the features to be included in the release remain uncertain is referred to as a _____ plan.

    A. Timeboxed
    B. Scopeboxed
    C. Variable release date
    D. Feature-defined

36. When applying the concept of last responsible moment to the Extreme Programming (XP) planning process, the best approach is to _____.

    A. Use the longest planning horizon possible
    B. Use a tiered set of planning horizons having long planning horizons for general plans and short planning horizons for specific, detailed plans
    C. Use the shortest planning horizon possible
    D. Not consider planning horizon length, as it is not applicable when applying the concept of last responsible moment to planning

37. A release planning method that tends to work best in stable environments and in which the entire plan is created in advance is referred to as _____ planning.

    A. Predictive release
    B. Timeboxed
    C. Scopeboxed
    D. Variable feature

38. On an Extreme Programming (XP) team, the _____ deals with organizational emergencies and support requests so the other programmers can focus on programming. He has no other duties and does not work on stories or the iteration plan.

    A. Product manager
    B. Product owner
    C. Batman
    D. Lead programmer

39. You are conducting a planning meeting with your new Extreme Programming (XP) team when one of your programmers asks how the team should schedule time to fix bugs. Your best response would be to tell her _____.

    A. To ignore the bugs, as the testers will fix them prior to release
    B. Not to worry because XP methodology eliminates bugs so there are none to fix
    C. To batch the bugs up for fixing in a later iteration
    D. To fix bugs as soon as you find them, preferably as you work on each task, as this time is part of the overhead of your iteration

40. Stories that are written from the on-site customer/proxy's point of view, and provide something that the customer cares about are said to be _____.

    A. Customer-focused
    B. Customer-centric
    C. Detailed and complete
    D. Accurate

41. Sometimes programmers will not be able to estimate a story because they do not know enough about the technology required to implement the story. In this case, a story to research that technology must be created. This type of story is typically referred to as a _____ story.

    A. Non-functional
    B. Documentation
    C. Spike
    D. Bug

42. The number of story points a team can complete in an iteration can best be described as the team's _____.

    A. Velocity
    B. Minimally marketable feature (MMF)
    C. Timeboxed plan
    D. Scopeboxed plan

43. One very effective way to improve team velocity is to _____.

    A. Reduce the duration of daily stand up meetings
    B. Reduce the frequency of daily stand up meetings
    C. Pay down technical debt.
    D. Increase the number of stories planned per iteration

44. Extreme Programming (XP) assumes that customers have the most information about _____, what best serves their organization, while programmers have the most information about _____, what it takes to implement and maintain features.

    A. Planning; Costs
    B. Value; Costs
    C. Costs; Requirements
    D. Planning; Requirements

45. The primary disadvantage to payback period is that _____.

    A. It complicates the development of themes
    B. It can be easily determined by competitors
    C. It is difficult to calculate
    D. It fails to take into account the time value of money

46. Threshold (or must-have) features are defined as _____.

    A. Features that must be present in the product for it to be successful
    B. Features that meet the minimum requirements
    C. Features that senior management have directed to be included in the product
    D. Features that will save the developers the greatest amount of development time

47. When using Extreme Programming (XP) practices, a list of your project's unique risks is referred to as a _____.

    A. Risk strategy
    B. Risk census
    C. Risk plan
    D. Risk mitigation

48. Improving the performance or amount of a threshold (or must-have) feature will _____.

   A. Produce a significant savings in developer time
   B. Produce a large increase in customer satisfaction
   C. Have little impact on customer satisfaction
   D. Increase team velocity

49. In the context of Extreme Programming (XP) risk management, _____ tell you when the risk will come true.

   A. Risk census
   B. Risk plan
   C. Transition indicators
   D. Risk mitigation

50. "Exciters and delighters" are those features that provide great satisfaction, often adding a price premium to a product. The lack of an exciter or delighter in a product will have what impact on customer satisfaction?

   A. Will likely result in complaints to senior management
   B. Will increase customer satisfaction
   C. Will cause a significant and very negative change in customer satisfaction
   D. Will not decrease customer satisfaction below neutral

51. It may be necessary to split a user story into multiple, smaller parts when _____.

   A. The user story is too large to fit within a single theme
   B. The user story is too large to fit within a single iteration
   C. Senior management thinks the user story is too large
   D. The project plan calls for multiple smaller user stories

52. Release planning is _____.

   A. The process of creating a very high-level plan that covers a period longer than an iteration
   B. The process of creating a very focused and detailed plan that covers several iterations
   C. The process of planning each iteration
   D. Done at the end of a project prior to final release of the product

53. During release planning, _____.

   A. The process in which software is released to the customer is defined
   B. Individual task assignments are defined
   C. User stories are clearly understood and the process of disaggregating into engineering tasks should begin
   D. It is too early, and some user stories may be insufficiently understood to be disaggregated into engineering tasks.

54. Your Extreme Programming (XP) team is nearing the end of an iteration and it is now obvious that one of the stories will not be complete as the iteration ends. You should _____.

    A. Include the partially completed code as part of the iteration deliverables and explain to the customer that the code will be completed when time permits
    B. Discard the partially completed code and start the story from scratch in a future iteration if the story is still wanted
    C. Extend the iteration finish date to allow the code to be completed
    D. Define the code as complete at the iteration finish as the iteration end date defines completeness rather than the state of the code

55. An iteration plan is created in an iteration planning meeting. This meeting should be attended by _____.

    A. The customer/proxy and the technical team leads
    B. The product owner, customer/proxy, and senior management
    C. The product owner, analysts, programmers, testers, database engineers, user interaction designers, and so on
    D. Only the most senior members of the project team

56. New functionality and capabilities that were added during the iteration are demonstrated to stakeholders during _____.

    A. The iteration review meeting
    B. The team reflective workshop
    C. The stakeholder meeting
    D. Customer buy-off

57. In velocity-driven iteration planning, the team estimates its velocity based on its performance during recent iterations and to determine how many story points should be planned into the current iteration. In commitment-driven iteration planning, _____.

    A. The team commits to completing the number of stories determined by the product owner during the current iteration
    B. The team is asked to add stories to the iteration one by one until they can commit to completing no more
    C. The team commits to completing all story points in the current iteration
    D. The team commits to always completing all story points in each iteration

58. The _____ is the total number of planned iterations multiplied by iteration length.

    A. Actual Percent Complete (APC)
    B. Planned Percent Complete (PPC)
    C. Performance Measure Baseline (PMB)
    D. Schedule Baseline

59. How does the agile team mitigate the threat of scope creep?

    A. By using iteration and release retrospectives to allow the customer/proxy to make changes to the backlog and to priorities.
    B. By identifying a single customer/proxy, or product owner, to make decisions
    C. By employing set-based design
    D. By implementing open space meetings

60. _____ focuses on seven principles: eliminating waste, amplifying learning, deciding as late as possible, delivering as fast as possible, empowering the team, building integrity in, and seeing the whole

    A. Complex Adaptive Systems Development
    B. Agile Unified Development
    C. Lean Software Development
    D. Feature-Driven Development

61. One method to reduce risk for both contracting parties is to include clauses that allow for _____ decisions at the end of each iteration. This protects the customer if the agile seller does not deliver as agreed and the agile seller if the customer does not provide needed input.

    A. Select-or-reject
    B. Reward-or-punishment
    C. Make-or-buy
    D. Continue-or-cancel

62. The length of a project's iterations determines _____.

    A. The complexity of the feature to be designed
    B. How often the software can be shown (in potentially shippable form) to users and customers
    C. The length of the longest individual story
    D. The total number of features that can be completed for a given project

63. Iteration length should be chosen _____.

    A. To maximize the amount, frequency, and timeliness of feedback to the whole team
    B. To accommodate the schedule of the customer/proxy
    C. Randomly as it has no impact on overall project execution
    D. To minimize the complexity of the completed features

64. One of the main goals in selecting an iteration length is _____.

    A. Finding one that accomplishes the work as quickly as possible
    B. Finding one that encourages everyone to work at a consistent pace throughout the iteration
    C. Finding one that is acceptable to the customer
    D. Finding one that puts an optimal amount of stress on the team so that they are motivated to do their best work

65. One of the challenges of planning a release is estimating the velocity of the team. An ideal way to forecast velocity is to _____.

   A. Use subject-matter experts from outside the team to estimate velocity
   B. Run several iterations and then estimate velocity from the observed velocity during the iterations run
   C. Utilize the experience of senior management to estimate velocity
   D. There is no way to accurately estimate velocity and attempting to do so is not a productive use of resources

66. In an agile project, the two types of buffers are _____.

   A. Feature buffers and iteration buffers
   B. Iteration buffers and release buffers
   C. Feature buffers and schedule buffers
   D. Schedule buffers and iteration buffers

67. A risk _____, which examines the effectiveness of risk responses, is conducted as part of the retrospective meeting.

   A. Audit
   B. Review
   C. Debriefing
   D. Analysis

68. Which of the following are valid ways for the agile project manager to ensure that project status is reported to the customer in accordance with the contract?

   A. An open-door invitation to observe the daily stand-up meetings
   B. Informal documentation (e.g., burndown charts, iteration summaries, task board webcam)
   C. Formal documentation (e.g., reports)
   D. All of the above

69. In agile projects, since the customer/proxy drives the priority of the requirements, such priorities may change at any time EXCEPT:

   A. During release planning
   B. During a release retrospective
   C. During the ongoing iteration
   D. During an iteration retrospective

70. On an Extreme Programming (XP) team using a version control system, there is typically a master storage area for all the team's files and their history. This _____ is stored on the version control server and each stand-alone project should have its own.

   A. Coding standard
   B. Repository
   C. Retrospective
   D. Roadmap

71. On an Extreme Programming (XP) team using a version control system, a _____ is what team members work out of on their local development machines; it contains a copy of all the files in the repository from a particular point in time

    A. Retrospective
    B. Coding standard
    C. Sandbox
    D. Branch

72. Traditional (i.e., waterfall) development is considered a(n) _____ approach whereas agile is often referred to as a(n) _____ approach.

    A. Plan-Driven, Value-Driven
    B. Disciplined, Undisciplined
    C. Planned, Reactive
    D. Plan-Driven, Customer-Driven

73. Whereas a release plan is a high-level _____ for a collection of iterations, an iteration plan is more of a _____ to help the agile team accomplish the specific iteration goals.

    A. Tactical plan, Strategic plan
    B. Strategic plan, Tactical plan
    C. Work breakdown structure (WBS), project schedule
    D. Architecture, Walking skeleton

74. A(n) _____ iteration is one where the agile team prepares for the final rollout of a project.

    A. Buffer
    B. Handoff
    C. Optimizing
    D. Hardening

75. On an Extreme Programming (XP) team, who is responsible for maintaining the build script?

    A. All the programmers are responsible for maintaining the script
    B. The on-site customers are responsible for maintaining the build script.
    C. The product owner is responsible for maintaining the build script
    D. The build script is automated and updated automatically by software

76. The _____ is total number of sprint points completed (potentially shippable increments) divided by the total number of story points planned.

    A. Performance Measurement Baseline (PMB)
    B. Planned Percent Complete (PPC)
    C. Actual Percent Complete (APC)
    D. Schedule Baseline

77. Developing in increments, integrating with other people's code, and refactoring code are made easier by having _____.

    A. Unit tests
    B. Automated test suites
    C. Functional tests
    D. User acceptance testing (UAT)

78. A daily meeting where all participants specifically describes what they did yesterday, what they plan to do today, and what problems are preventing them from making progress can be described as a _____.

    A. Retrospective
    B. Daily Scrum
    C. Daily reflective workshop
    D. Project review

79. In Scrum, the responsibility for prioritizing stories _____.

    A. Belongs completely to the customer/proxy
    B. Is exclusively that of the product owner
    C. Is shared among the whole team but the effort is led by the product owner
    D. Is shared between the sponsor and end user

80. It is the Scrum Master's responsibility to remove, or get someone to remove, whatever _____ the team mentions in the stand-up meeting.

    A. Chickens
    B. Noise
    C. Roadblocks
    D. Pigs

81. In Scrum, forecasting the financial value of a theme is the responsibility of _____.

    A. The product owner
    B. The product owner, but it is a responsibility shared with all other team members
    C. Senior management
    D. Senior management and the customer/proxy

82. How does the agile team mitigate against intrinsic schedule flaws?

    A. By identifying a single customer/proxy, or product owner, to make decisions
    B. By reevaluating the release plan at the end of each iteration, to see if the team is on target
    C. By employing set-based design
    D. By implementing Open Space meetings

83. For the agile project team, when obstacles are addressed as part of the daily stand-up meeting, this is considered _____ risk management; when risks are charted on a white board or flip chart, this is exemplary of _____ risk management.

    A. Organic, Overt
    B. Overt, Organic
    C. Original, Overt
    D. Obvious, Overt

84. The practice of starting your next task immediately after starting the build, without waiting for the build and tests to succeed is referred to as _____.

    A. Exploratory testing
    B. Continuous integration
    C. Synchronous integration
    D. Asynchronous integration

85. According to osmotic communication strategy:

    A. Team members should be sequestered from everyone else to avoid unnecessary communication
    B. Communication between people decreases radically when their walking distance exceeds the length of a school bus
    C. Team members who need to communicate should sit near each other so that they overhear each other in their background hearing and can respond quickly to the information flow around them
    D. It may be appropriate to balance multiple communication strategies to foster success of the agile team

86. Tools used by the Scrum team to establish a shared product vision include:

    A. Elevator Statement, Product Release Plan, and Press Release
    B. Product Data Sheet, Elevator Statement, and Product Release Plan
    C. Elevator Statement, Product Vision Box, and Press Release
    D. Press Release, Magazine Review, and Product Release Plan

87. In Scrum, the notion of a reciprocal commitment refers to:

    A. The business commits to delivering some specified amount of functionality and the team commits to not changing priorities during the sprint.
    B. The Scrum Master commits to delivering some specified amount of functionality and the customer/proxy commits to not changing priorities during the sprint.
    C. The Scrum Master commits to delivering some specified amount of functionality and the product owner commits to not changing priorities during the sprint.
    D. The team commits to delivering some specified amount of functionality and the business commits to not changing priorities during the sprint.

88. In the middle of a four-week sprint, the Product Owner comes to the Scrum Master and the team and tells them that he has become aware of a critical story that must be added to the sprint. If the proposed change cannot be kept out of the sprint:

   A. The additional story and the related story points should be added to the current sprint and burndown chart.
   B. The current sprint should be abnormally terminated and restarted with the new story added.
   C. The additional story and the related story points should be added to the current sprint and burndown chart only if the business makes additional resources available to the team.
   D. The situation described is a hybrid project and must be approved by the Product Owner, Scrum Master, and team before any changes can be made.

89. In a Scrum environment, John is writing a project data sheet. What sections should be included in the project data sheet?

   A. Elevator Statement, Risk Register, Performance Attributes, Tradeoff Matrix
   B. Elevator Statement, Stakeholder Analysis, Performance Attributes, Tradeoff Matrix
   C. Elevator Statement, Customer Attributes, Performance Attributes, Tradeoff Matrix
   D. Elevator Statement, Scope Statement, Customer Attributes, Tradeoff Matrix

90. Which of the following statements is true about an abnormally terminated sprint?

   A. All work from the terminated sprint is undone.
   B. Management may terminate the sprint if organizational priorities change
   C. The agile team may terminate the sprint if they feel they cannot meet the sprint goal.
   D. All of the above

91. The number sequence 1, 2, 3, 5, 8, 13, etc. is called what?

   A. Fibonacci
   B. Pearson product-moment
   C. Pareto
   D. Dover-Calais

92. The agile way of dealing with uncertainty is frequent _____ based on progress to date and new information gathered during development iterations.

   A. Re-planning
   B. Reiteration
   C. Reworking
   D. Refactoring

93. _____ is an approach of continuous improvement which has periodic releasable timeframes and which does not require strict iteration lengths for all stories.

   A. Just-in-Time (JIT)
   B. Quality
   C. Kaisen
   D. Kanban

94. Sometimes used synonymously with epic, a _____ describes a high-level business or product function that is complete and valuable.

    A. Feature
    B. Release
    C. Capability
    D. Theme

95. In Scrum, the _____ sequence is frequently used by teams when providing value point estimates for stories.

    A. Pareto
    B. Fibonacci
    C. Pearson product-moment
    D. Dover-Calais

96. The Fibonacci sequence is a series of numbers that is used in what Scrum activity?

    A. Planning poker
    B. Walking skeleton
    C. Release planning
    D. Team reflection workshop

97. In agile, the notion of looking ahead to learn the unknown and to reduce uncertainty is called _____.

    A. Specifying
    B. Sprinting
    C. Spreading
    D. Scanning

98. In agile, setting a fixed time limit to overall development efforts is referred to _____.

    A. Scheduling
    B. Timeboxing
    C. Specifying
    D. Timekeeping

99. _____ is one of the best known of the Lean principles.

    A. Estimating work accurately
    B. Eliminating waste
    C. Delivering product on time
    D. Providing a guiding principle

100. Which framework subscribes to the following belief: "Most errors are due to the system within which people work rather than to the individuals themselves?"

   A. Agile
   B. Crystal
   C. Lean
   D. Waterfall

101. _____ is the cause of most product failures.

   A. Market risk
   B. Lack of requirements
   C. Failure to adhere to the chosen development methodology
   D. Technical risk

102. Which system strives to minimize work-in-process and maximize business value creation?

   A. Lean
   B. Test-Driven Development
   C. Waterfall
   D. Six Sigma

103. A project manager is drawing process-flow diagrams to try to add value for a customer. What tool is the project manager trying to use?

   A. Waterfall map
   B. Agile map
   C. Value stream map
   D. Lean principles map

104. One way of determining which aspects of a product can be delivered quickly is by identifying the _____, that is the smallest amount of functionality that makes sense to deliver to market

   A. Minimum demand features
   B. Maximum customer demands
   C. Maximum marketable features
   D. Minimum marketable features

105. A variation of Scrum is _____ which is an enhancement that results from embedding Scrum with Lean thinking.

   A. Scrum++
   B. Waterfall
   C. Scrum#
   D. Agile

106. Scrum is a specific framework for creating an effective _____ development process

    A. Lean
    B. Waterfall
    C. Agile
    D. Kanban

107. What kind of organizations adhere to the philosophy that doing things just before they need to be done eliminates waste?

    A. Sales and marketing organizations
    B. Lean organizations
    C. Agile organizations
    D. Software development organizations

108. When preparing for Scrum sprint planning, the agile coach's two essential jobs are:

    A. Facilitating a structured meeting agenda and ensuring product owner engagement
    B. Creating the meeting checklist and ensuring attendance of subject-matter experts
    C. Preparing the burn down chart and ensuring product owner engagement
    D. Prioritizing the user stories and ensuring product owner engagement

109. A Scrum team is typically guided by a _____ who can be guiding the team as an agile coach.

    A. Product Owner
    B. Project Champion
    C. Customer
    D. Scrum Master

110. For an organization, being agile requires a balance between _____.

    A. Discipline and chaos
    B. Discipline and traditional project management
    C. Discipline and leadership
    D. Discipline and flexibility

111. When project leaders focus on delivery, they add value to projects. When they focus on planning and control, they tend to add _____.

    A. Overhead
    B. Value
    C. Creativity
    D. Subject matter expertise

112. In agile projects, the correct scope is not a set of defined requirements, but the _____ for a releasable product.

    A. Tradeoff matrix
    B. Articulated product vision
    C. Preliminary scope statement
    D. Elevator statement

113. In release planning, stories are assigned to iterations, based primarily on _____.

    A. Requirements and schedule
    B. Customer value and risk
    C. Time and schedule constraints
    D. Marketability and time constraints

114. On agile projects, planning artifacts such as expenditure budgets may be finalized only after the _____ plan is complete.

    A. Backlog
    B. Iteration
    C. Release
    D. Sprint

115. During the agile retrospective it is the responsibility of the _____ to monitor their working agreements so that the retrospective leader may focus on facilitating.

    A. Customer/proxy
    B. Functional manager
    C. Tester
    D. Team

116. A(n) _____ is a single page summary of key project management information, product capabilities, and business and quality objectives.

    A. Project data sheet
    B. Flexibility matrix
    C. Team working agreement
    D. Information radiator

117. A(n) _____ shows the relative importance of project constraints, where only one of these constraints may be "fixed."

    A. Project data sheet
    B. Trade-off matrix
    C. Team working agreement
    D. Information radiator

118. On your Extreme Programming (XP) team, an orderly process occurs in which pairs of programmers get the latest code from the server, do their work, run all the tests to confirm their code works, and then check in their changes. This process, called _____, occurs several times a day.

    A. Continuous integration
    B. Exploratory testing
    C. Root cause analysis
    D. Test driven development (TDD)

119. Typically generated by most agile teams when they update their release plan, a _____ is an excellent way to get a bird's-eye view of the project, as it shows progress and predicts a completion date.

    A. Burn-up chart
    B. Story board
    C. Coding standard
    D. Retrospective

120. Most software is built for a particular industry, such as healthcare, that has its own specialized rules for doing business. The software must implement such rules exactly per industry standards to be considered successful. These rules are _____ rules, and knowledge of these rules is _____ knowledge.

    A. Domain; Expert
    B. Intrinsic; Extrinsic
    C. Domain; Domain
    D. Focused; Focused

Answers– Exam #1

1. **A.** The process requires taking input from stakeholders and setting priorities according to their values. In order to do that successfully the agile framework recognizes and responds to the demand to engage stakeholders in structured, meaningful discussions that help them clarify and articulate their values and priorities. The output of collecting, refining, and prioritizing input from stakeholders, customers, end users, and the team produces a product backlog.

2. **A.** Each activity should reach a level of being sufficient-to-purpose. Intermediate work provides no direct value to the customer but should be evaluated in terms of its sufficiency i.e. does it inspire the team.

3. **D.** Re-estimating should occur only when the relative size or significant information regarding one or more of the stories has changed.

4. **B.** Agile teams use three levels of planning: release planning, iteration planning, and daily planning. The release plan accounts for the schedule of the release, typically a three to six month window. An iteration plan lays out the plan for a single iteration, typically two to four weeks. A daily plan is defines work the team is committed to accomplish in a single day and is typically confirmed at the daily stand up meeting.

5. **C.** The Product Owner leads the effort of prioritizing the stories however this is done with the input of the entire team all of whom share responsibility for the priority of the stories.

6. **C.** The iterative approach is intended to significantly reduce or eliminate the risk of developing the wrong product. Short iterations provide the opportunity for frequent customer/proxy review and input thus reducing the risk of developing a product or features that are not of optimal value to the customer.

7. **B.** A team's values and agreements should apply to the retrospective as well as to the team's work. As with the work process, values may need to be reiterated and agreements reviewed or adjusted to improve the effectiveness of the retrospective.

8. **A.** Staged contracts allow for better customer visibility and provide go/no-go decision points that can be used to adjust the contract to preserve optimal value for both the customer and the contractor.

9. **D.** Face to face communication is the most reliable and effective method of conveying information to and within a team.

10. **A.** In XP, code is written and tested simultaneously and thus code that works 100% is an indication of the quality of the team's work.

11. **B.** In test driven development, the test, or executable example, is written before deciding how to design the code.

12. **B.** The daily stand up meeting is conducted each day and is intended to provide an opportunity for each team member to state what he will work on today, what he has completed since the last stand up meeting, and what impediments to progress he has before him.

13. **C.** It is the responsibility of the Scrum Master to remove any roadblocks impeding progress that the team has identified. Roadblocks are typically identified and discussed at the daily stand up meeting.

14. **C.** Agile teams work in iterations, which are short (usually two to four week) timeboxed periods in which they produce working code that is demonstrated at the end of each iteration.

15. **D.** Agile project management requires a balance between discipline and flexibility in order to be successful. Discipline in order to produce high quality work quickly and efficiently and flexibility in order to accommodate the inevitable changes that will occur.

16. **B.** Agile project managers focus on effectively adapting to inevitable changes that will occur during a project. Effectively adapting to change helps to provide a high value product to the customer.

17. **A.** Project leaders who focus on project deliverables tend to add value while an excessive focus on plans and control tends to increase overhead.

18. **A.** The four key terms describing an iteration are iterative, feature-based, timeboxed, and incremental. Iterative implies that a partial version of a product is created and expanded upon in successive periods. The iteration focuses on developing the required features progressing incrementally and completing the work in a specific well defined time period.

19. **D.** A self-organizing team generally exhibits all the traits mentioned in the question. A self directing team implies the team is self-led which involves a different set of characteristics.

20. **B.** It is generally very difficult to precisely define the project scope at the beginning of a project. Agile projects therefore focus on developing and working to an articulated product vision i.e a releasable product.

21. **C.** Iteration Management focuses on the day-to-day management of a short iteration rather than the overall management of the project.

22. **C.** An exploration factor is used to help understand the uncertainty and risk of a project.

23. **A.** A feature or story is typically defined as a segment or part of a product that provides some useful and valuable functionality to a customer.

24. **D.** A backlog is a list of capabilities, features, and stories that the product team has identified that will be developed and will provide value to the customer.

25. **B.** Release planning attempts to schedule stories in the order of the value created for the customer/proxy and the risk involved in development. High value, high risk stories are typically planned first.

26. **A.** Planning in one or more buffer iterations towards the end of a project or release provides a way of accommodating changes or dealing with risk events without jeopardizing the project end date. In addition, as stories are assigned based on value and risk, stories assigned to the end of the iteration may be dropped if necessary with minimal impact to customer value.

27. **C.** Common project management planning artifacts such as expenditure budgets are typically finalized after the release plan is complete.

28. **B.** A sprint plan is a day-to-day work plan for a development team. Iteration lengths vary from 1 to 4 weeks, with a two week iteration being typical.

29. **D.** SCRs and other new tasks are added to the product backlog in order to preserve the integrity of the current sprint and to be in agreement with the commitments of the team and the organization.

30. **D.** A release plan is developed by the product teams, typically with input from managers and sponsors. Bringing a management perspective to release planning can also help the team to appreciate issues and the key release criteria that are important to management.

31. **A.** A version control system allows an orderly process called continuous integration in which developers get the latest code from the server, do their work, test their code, and check in their changes. This process is typically repeated several times per day by each programmer pair.

32. **C.** Synchronous integration confirms that the build and tests succeed before moving on to the next task. The build should be relatively fast (no more than 10 minutes) for synchronous integration to work optimally.

33. **B.** The biggest problem with asynchronous integration is that it tends to result in broken builds. If the build breaks it tends to be disruptive to the progress of the rest of the team particularly if other team members have checked out code that later turns out to be broken.

34. **B.** Files from the tip or head of the repository contain the latest changes that have been checked in.

35. **A.** A programmer will revert his or her sandbox to throw away changes and return to the point of the last update. This is helpful when the local build fails and the cause cannot be determined and can sometimes be more productive than trying to debug the code.

36. **C.** When specific documentation is required for a project, the work of creating that documentation should be treated as any other story and estimated and prioritized accordingly.

37. **A.** The principle of "small wins" is a powerful motivator and describes the practice of completing small tasks frequently thus inspiring and motivating the team.

38. **B.** An information radiator is a display of information conspicuously posted in an area where it can be easily viewed by many people.

39. **A.** Typical information radiator information includes the work breakdown and assignments for the upcoming increment, the results of the project's periodic reflection workshop, and the user stories delivered or in progress.

40. **D.** Fixed price contracts can have many and various units of delivery as long as there is agreement between thecustomer and contracted company as to the definition, schedule, and payments related to the units of delivery.

41. **D.** The difference is in team size with: Crystal Clear (3-8 people), Crystal Orange (30-50 people) and Crystal Yellow (15 – 30 people)

42. **B.** Fully automated regression tests include either unit or functional tests and sometimes both.

43. **A.** The practice of designers in one location sending specifications and tests to programmers in another location, often in another country, is referred to as offshore development.

44. **B.** The practice of having a steering group of evaluators meet periodically to watch over a set of projects is referred to as program governance.

45. **C.** Bugs should be fixed as soon as they are discovered which will improve both quality and productivity.

46. **A.** When working as a team it becomes necessary to coordinate source code, tests, and other important project artifacts. A version control system provides a vehicle to coordinate changes to files and document a development history.

47. **C.** The entire team should be informed when a significant problem is encountered to allow the whole team to participate in finding a solution.

48. **D.** In-house custom development occurs when management directs the team to develop something for the organization's own use and is common in IT development.

49. **B.** Software that is developed for use across a wide range of industries is referred to as horizontal-market software.

50. **B.** The daily Scrum is a short (15 minutes or less) meeting where each team member describes what they accomplished since the last Scrum, what they plan to do today, and what impediments are preventing progress.

51. **A.** A burn-up chart, typically created during update of the release plan and including work completed and work remaining, is an excellent way to get a big picture overview of project status.

52. **C.** Software that operates in a particular industry, such as accounting, will have its own specialized rules of operation and must implement those rules faithfully and exactly in order to be successful. These rules are domain rules, and knowledge of these rules is domain knowledge.

53. **C.** On XP teams, all software developers are called programmers to emphasize the variety of specialties required by the team and the fact that all team members contribute directly to creating working code.

54. **A.** Fractional assignment refers to the practice of assigning people to multiple projects simultaneously and is considered a less productive approach to project work.

55. **B.** The amount of less than optimal design and implementation decisions in your project is referred to as technical debt and includes band aids, quick fixes, and code that is no longer necessary for the software to function.

56. **A.** Velocity represents the amount of work or story points completed in an iteration and provides a simple way of correlating story estimates to the calendar.

57. **B.** The most common retrospective is the iteration retrospective. This retrospective is conducted at the end of every iteration and is intended to help the team develop changes to their process that will make future iterations more successful.

58. **D.** Mute mapping is a great way to categorize many ideas quickly. The exercise should take about ten minutes and is intended to help the team develop ideas that will make future iterations more successful.

59. **C.** Debriefing helps the team develop ideas and insights that are intended to help the team make changes to their process that will make future iterations more successful.

60. **D.** Facilitating other kinds of meetings, observing other people who are effective at leading meetings and working with groups, and soliciting feedback are good ways to improve facilitation skills.

61. **A. Helped, Hindered, Hypothesis** helps the retrospective leader get feedback to improve the team's processes. This approach helps identify items that either helped or hindered the project work and, in addition, helps the team to develop ideas for how things might be done differently to improve the next iteration.

62. **B.** The retrospective facilitator has three primary tasks consisting of deciding who to invite, extending the invitation, and educating new participants.

63. **A.** User stories must be valuable to users or customers - not developers. Developer stories should be rewritten to reflect value to users or customers.

64. **C.** Tools used by the Scrum team for establishing a shared product vision include the product positioning map, the product vision box, the elevator statement, the press release, the product data sheet, and the magazine review.

65. **B.** In Scrum, if a change proposed during an ongoing sprint cannot be kept out, the sprint should be terminated abnormally and restarted. This is an extreme circumstance and should not be done very often.

66. **D.** During a force field analysis the team defines a desired state they want to achieve and breaks into small groups to work to identify the factors that could either hinder or promote the change they desire. A list of factors is created and the group assesses the relative strength of each supporting and inhibiting factor.

67. **A.** An iteration for an XP team consists of the full cycle of design-code-verify-release.

68. **C.** An XP team delays commitment until the last responsible moment which is defined as the moment at which failing to make a decision eliminates an important alternative.

69. **C.** In a tradeoff matrix, agile project constraints are categorized as fixed, firm, or flexible. Only one constraint (i.e., time, scope, or cost) may be fixed.

70. **D.** Teams can abnormally terminate a sprint if they feel they cannot meet the sprint goal. Management can abnormally terminate a sprint if organizational priorities change. When abnormally terminating a sprint, all work from the current sprint is undone and the code base reverts to what it was prior to the sprint termination. Then the team must begin the work of planning the next sprint.

71. **B.** A fishbone diagram is a tool that is useful to a team in helping to determine the root cause of a problem.

72. **A.** On an XP team, analysis, design, coding, testing, and deployment occur with rapid frequency and are performed simultaneously. This approach helps the XP team to more consistently and predictably deliver high quality code.

73. **B.** A roadmap provides a high level or summary view of releases and the significant features planned for each release.

74. **D.** The term "done done" refers to code that is completely written, tested and bug free and that can be released to the customer.

75. **C.** The cost baseline is created by aggregating the total costs for all items in each iteration.

76. **B.** The last iteration prior to a release is typically the buffer iteration and provides a practical way for new teams to create a space in which to address some final finishing features.

77. **A.** A servant leadership approach rather than one of command and control is preferred in an agile environment to facilitate optimal team performance.

78. **D.** A risk audit is conducted as part of the retrospective meeting in order to evaluate the effectiveness of risk responses with the goal of improving risk management in future iterations.

79. **C.** Lean Software Development focuses on the following seven principles: eliminating waste, amplifying learning, deciding as late as possible, delivering as fast as possible, empowering the team, building integrity in, and seeing the whole.

80. **A.** An agile approach attempts to minimize scope creep by involving the customer/proxy and allowing the code to be evaluated frequently (at the end of each iteration) and providing an opportunity for customer/proxy input allowing the backlog to be adjusted based on priority reflecting customer value.

81. **B.** Performance Measurement Baseline (PMB) is defined as the total number of story points planned for a release. Performance will be measured, in part, by a team's ability to complete the number of story points that were planned to be completed in an iteration.

82. **D.** Working code is demonstrated to interested stakeholders at the end of each iteration to confirm progress and value and to allow for adjustments to the backlog to ensure that the team continues to deliver optimal customer value.

83. **B.** The agile approach emphasizes the use of cross-functional teams allowing them to self-organize within a framework in order to facilitate optimal performance. The use of regular retrospectives is also encouraged in order to continuously improve performance.

84. **C.** Because the agile methodology encourages the servant leadership approach in order to optimize team performance, having the agile project manager conduct individual performance appraisals is considered an unhealthy conflict of interest.

85. **B.** Highly visible information radiators are used to create real time communication throughout the project. This concept is was derived from Lean Manufacturing's use of a signaling system called Kanban. These information radiators are typically seen in the form of graphs, tables, burn-down charts, task boards, or other displays that show the current status of the project.

86. **A.** Tracking velocity is one way to help mitigate productivity variation in an agile team. After several iterations an accurate team velocity should be determined and used to accurately plan future iterations.

87. **A.** Actual Percent Complete (APC) is defined as the total number of sprint points completed divided by the total number of story points planned.

88. **D.** A hand off iteration is often used to prepare the formal documentation and other deliverables that production requires. New features are typically not implemented during this iteration instead, hand-off and final approval meetings are attended, documentation prepared, and other support tasks accomplished.

89. **B.** Intrinsic schedule flaw generally refers to the common tendency to underestimate the size of the product being built. The agile approach mitigates this by reevaluation of the release plan at the end of each iteration to confirm that the team is still on target.

90. **A.** The payback period is defined as the amount of time required to earn back the initial investment.

91. **C.** Under a contract containing continue or cancel language based on successful completion of each iteration, the customer may cancel if the seller is failing to make deliveries as agreed, and the seller may cancel if the customer is not providing input to the team at the agreed upon frequency and level of detail.

92. **D.** The team should be responsible for monitoring their working agreements during the retrospective which will allow the leader to focus on facilitating.

93. **A.** A Product Data Sheet (PDS) is typically a single-page summary of key business and quality objectives, product capabilities, and project management information related to the project.

94. **B.** The core values and principles of Agile Project Management (APM) are applicable to projects of any size and while adjustments and special techniques may be required to manage large teams the agile core values and principles will still apply.

95. **C.** Good release planning should always be driven by customer value and risk.

96. **A.** Story cards is to provide an easy way to document basic information about stories including high level requirements, work estimates, and acceptance test definition.

97. **D.** Two basic planning approaches are defined by scope boxed plans and timeboxed plans. A scope boxed plan defines required features but leaves the release date undefined while a timeboxed plan sets a release date but leaves the specific features undefined.

98. **B.** Increasing customer/proxy involvement and communication with the development team will almost always improve velocity.

99. **A.** The amount of slack required is driven by the complexity of the work as complexity generally implies an increased or varying number of unknowns thus increasing randomness and variation in velocity. An adequate amount of slack should be built in to account for the complexity and reduce variations in team velocity.

100. **C.** A capability is defined as a high-level business or product function that is complete and valuable. The term capability is sometimes used synonymously with the term epic.

101. **B.** A Fibonacci series is defined as a sequence of numbers where the sum of the preceding two numbers equal the third number as in 1, 2, 3, 5, 8, 13. A Fibonacci series is sometimes used as a range of points from which to choose relative estimates for story effort during agile planning.

102. **D.** The term Kanban came from the Japanese process for continuous improvement and the name has been applied to an approach to software development which combines ideas from lean development and from Goldratt's theory of constraints.

103. **B.** One of the best known Lean principles is "eliminate waste." That's not a law as much as it is something you should do, as a rule.

104. **A.** Most product failures are caused by market risk. This is not because marketing people are less competent than designers, but rather because market risk is a much tougher problem than technical risk.

105. **A.** Lean extends Agile to create a system that helps minimize work-in-process and maximize the speed at which business value is created.

106. **C.** The value stream map is a Lean tool that practitioners use to analyze the value stream. Value stream mapping involves drawing pictures of the process streams and then using them to look for waste

107. **B.** Team agility is necessary but not sufficient. Enterprise Agility requires team Agility; but team Agility is only a means to an end – Enterprise Agility. Enterprise Agility enables a company to deliver higher quality products and services to their customers at a faster rate than their competition. This is a strong competitive advantage in any industry.

108. **C.** Scrum# is an enhancement of Scrum that results from embedding Scrum with Lean thinking.

109. **D.** A Scrum Master can also act as an agile coach when he or she goes beyond getting agile practices up and running and moves into actively facilitating and helping the team to pursue continuously improving performance.

110. **A.** The two primary jobs of a coach when preparing for sprint planning are to ensure product owner participation and to facilitate a structured meeting agenda.

111. **B.** A good product owner can positively impact agile team efficiency by establishing priorities and value on behalf of the customer.

112. **B.** Forecasting the financial value of a theme is primarily the responsibility of the product owner however the entire team should participate in the process and share in the responsibility.

113. **D.** In Scrum, the notion of a reciprocal commitment refers to the team's commitment to delivering some specified amount of functionality and the business's commitment to not changing priorities during the sprint.

114. **C.** Typical sections of the project data sheet include: Identification (of the Scrum Master and Product Owner), Elevator Statement, Customer Attributes, Customer Benefits, Feature/Ability to, Performance Attributes, Major Milestones, and Tradeoff Matrix

115. **A.** Organic risk management refers to the process of risk being developed by the team as part of the project life cycle such as during the daily standup. Displaying risk status on a chart is an example of overt risk management.

116. **C.** Scrum is a framework for creating an effective Agile development process. It is based on the belief that software development must be controlled by responding to feedback received during the course of development.

117. **A.** Feelings should always be included in the data gathering process as feelings tell what's important to people about the facts and about the team. Thorough data gathering, including both facts and feelings, will improve results of the retrospective and lead to improved performance in future iterations.

118. **B.** The trade-off matrix shows the relative importance of the three constraint areas of scope, schedule, and cost and is used both in agile and traditional project management.

119. **D.** Work on only one project at a time as switching tasks has a substantial cost and is likely to greatly reduce team productivity.

120. **C.** A minimum marketable feature, or MMF, is the smallest set of functionality that provides value to your market applying to both internal and external customers.

Answers–Exam #2

1. **A.** High tolerance methods suggest the use of standards but allow the team to reach consensus on their processes and procedures and make adjustments based on what they learn in their retrospectives.

2. **C.** The purpose of planning in an agile product development environment is to answer the question of what to build. The planning process considers features, resources, cost, and schedule as well as accounting for risk and complexity.

3. **B.** Estimating in story points can help teams learn to work cross-functionally. A story-point estimate needs to be a single number that represents work from all required team members and thus requires high-level discussions about all the work involved which in turn promotes cross-functionality.

4. **C.** In the XP environment decisions about a story's priority belong to the customer/proxy and decisions regarding design estimates are made by the programmer to create the most efficient development process possible while maximizing customer value.

5. **D.** The high-value, high-risk features should be developed first as this delivers the most value to the customer and by addressing the high risk features early overall project risk is significantly reduced.

6. **C.** A *retrospective* in the agile community is described as a meeting in which the team reviews its methods and results (typically at the end of an iteration) and generates ideas that will improve their performance on future work.

7. **A.** The Agile Manifesto was written along with a set of 12 principles one of which specifically states that: *Our highest priority is to satisfy the customer through early and continuous delivery of valuable software.*

8. **A.** Co-location is required in Crystal Clear such that the entire team must sit in the same room or adjacent rooms to optimize the exchange of information and to take advantage of osmotic communication.

9. **B.** The agile approach focuses on the planning process rather than the plan documents and embraces the idea that change is to be expected, designing plans such that the plans can be easily changed and adjusted as new knowledge is developed.

10. **D.** Agile teams value individuals and interactions over processes and tools. The philosophy of the individuals who wrote the agile manifesto is such that it puts a very high value on the capability of individuals and believes that talented individuals will always overcome mediocre processes and tools to produce great software.

11. **C.** Retained revenue refers to the revenue an organization will lose if the project is not developed and is separate from both new and incremental revenue.

12. **A.** The amount of money needed to invest today to produce a specific amount of money in the future is called the present value.

13. **B.** Traditional waterfall methods deliver value at the end of the project where agile methodology attempts to deliver value incrementally throughout the project.

14. **A.** Agile values state that responding to change is more important than following a plan as change is to be expected as a normal part of project work.

15. **D.** The agile triangle constraints are goals defined as value, quality, and constraints. The goals are that the team builds a releasable produce (value), builds a reliable, adaptable product (quality), and achieves value and quality goals within acceptable time and cost constraints.

16. **C.** The four key subject areas that should be covered in a retrospective are product, process, team, and project. The idea of the retrospective is to uncover opportunities for improvement in those areas with the goal being to improve performance of future iterations.

17. **B.** The Explore phase delivers product stories.

18. **A.** The Speculate phase produces a release plan based on capabilities or stories to be delivered.

19. **B.** The purpose of creating a product backlog is to provide a means to expand the product vision, through an iterative process of defining and evolving requirements resulting in a product feature list or backlog.

20. **C.** Story cards are a tool used by agile teams to provide an easy way to gather basic information about stories or product features. The cards typically contain high-level requirements, work estimates, and acceptance test definitions.

21. **A.** A release plan creates a high level view or roadmap describing how the team will accomplish the product vision based on the project objectives and constraints defined in the project data sheet.

22. **D.** In traditional project management, when schedule problems occur, the tendency is to cut tasks to relieve schedule pressure with the risk of negatively impacting quality. On agile projects, schedule pressure is reduced by cutting stories which reduces scope and is much less likely to impact quality.

23. **B.** Agile project managers do not create a project management plan but instead develop a release plan. The release plan accounts for value, schedule, cost, and risk but does so with a process and format that differs from that of the traditional project management plan.

24. **A.** A sprint plan is a day-to-day work plan for a development team. Iteration lengths vary from 1–4 weeks, with a two week iteration being typical.

25. **A.** Stories represent features that are desirable and valuable to the customer. These features or stories can be estimated either in relative terms using story points or in absolute terms using hours.

26. **C.** The purpose of generating insights during the retrospective is to make improvements in the way the team executes future work.

27. **B.** Agile development focuses on achieving personal, technical, and organizational successes. This philosophy is based in part on the belief in the value of individuals and that by creating an environment where individuals can grow personally and technically the organization will benefit significantly.

28. **C.** Test-driven development (TDD) is an activity that simultaneously combines testing, coding, design, and architecture to more effectively develop product and is frequently supported by paired programming.

29. **D.** Testers contribute to helping the team produce high quality code by using exploratory testing and performing root-cause analysis to help improve the process to prevent similar bugs from occurring in the future. Testers should be an integral part of the development team.

30. **B.** The release plan cost baseline is updated after each iteration to make use of information from the retrospective and to account for customer/proxy input on feature value and priority.

31. **A.** The purpose of the agile retrospective is to evaluate the team's processes with the goal of making changes that will improve the success of future iterations. Looking at the processes of the HR department is well beyond the scope of the team's retrospective.

32. **C.** The product team identifies a list of capabilities, features, and stories that are to be developed. This list is referred to as the backlog and a backlog is typically maintained for both the current iteration and the product.

33. **D.** In the agile environment, a feature or story is defined as a piece of a product that delivers some functionality of value to a customer.

34. **B.** Agile philosophy in general and Extreme Programming (XP) in particular always favors shorter duration projects with frequent releases as a means of delivering customer value sooner and of reducing risk.

35. **A.** Two basic approaches to planning are to develop scopeboxed plans or timeboxed plans. A scopeboxed plan defines the features the team will build but the exact release date is undefined. A timeboxed plan defines the release date but the specific features contained in that release will be undefined.

36. **B.** The planning horizon determines how far a team looks into the future. Many project managers try to plan every requirement for the entire project at the beginning of the project, thus using a very long planning horizon. To plan at the last responsible moment, use a tiered set of planning horizons. Use long planning horizons for general plans and short planning horizons for specific, detailed plans.

37. **A.** Predictive release planning is the classic alternative to adaptive release planning. In predictive release planning, the entire plan is created in advance. This can work in stable environments, but tends to be problematic in dynamic environments where frequent changes occur.

38. **C.** In most organizations the team has a legitimate need to provide ongoing support for ad hoc requests. In order for the team to proceed with the work of the iteration uninterrupted, one programmer can be assigned to be the batman. "Batman" is a military term and refers to a soldier assigned to deal with chores so that other soldiers can focus on their duties. On an

XP team, the batman deals with organizational emergencies and support requests so the other programmers can focus on programming. This programmer has no other duties and does no project work while assigned as the batman.

39. **D.** Bugs should be fixed as soon as they are discovered. The time required to fix the bugs is considered part of the overhead of the iteration. For bugs that are too big to fix during the iteration, create story cards and schedule them for the next iteration.

40. **B.** Stories should be customer-centric and written from the on-site customer's point of view to ensure the team is creating a product that optimizes value to the customer.

41. **C.** Sometimes programmers won't be able to estimate a story because they don't have enough information regarding the technology to be used to implement the story. When this situation occurs, programmers are required to research the technology in order to learn enough to implement the story. The work required for this research is defined and scheduled as a story and is referred to as a spike story.

42. **A.** A team's velocity is defined as the number of story points the team can complete in an iteration.

43. **C.** Technical debt is the most common problem encountered by agile teams and has a greater impact on team productivity than any other factor. Creating high quality code (low technical debt) will improve velocity dramatically.

44. **B.** Extreme Programming (XP) teams assume that customers have the most information about value while the programmers have the most information about costs. A successful plan needs to take into account information from both groups.

45. **D.** The main disadvantage to payback period is that it fails to take into account the time value of money which can be a concern as money received in the future is not valued as highly as money paid out today. In addition payback period does not measure the profitability of a project but only when the money invested will be recovered.

46. **A.** Threshold or must have features are those that must be present in the product for it to be successful.

47. **B.** The risk census is a list of risks that are specific or unique to the project and is focused on these rather than on more generic risks such as a flawed release plan, technical problems, ordinary requirements growth, and employee turnover.

48. **C.** Threshold features are defined as those that must be present for the product to be successful. Customer satisfaction will not be significantly impacted by improving the performance or amount of threshold features.

49. **C.** Transition indicators tell the team when a risk event is about to occur similar to a risk trigger in traditional project management.

50. **D.** Exciters and delighters are those features that are often used to add a price premium to a product but whose absence will not decrease customer satisfaction below neutral.

51. **B.** A user story should be split when it is too large to fit within a single iteration.

52. **A.** Release planning is the process of creating a very high-level plan that covers a period longer than an iteration and will typically include a large number of iterations depending on the length of the iterations and size of the project.

53. **D.** Release planning is a high level planning effort typically done at a time when some user stories may be insufficiently understood to be disaggregated into engineering tasks. Stories are broken down into engineering tasks at the start of the iteration in which they are to be implemented.

54. **B.** With a true timeboxing approach, the software is either accepted or thrown away at the timebox deadline. This practice makes it clear that the code must be acceptable at all times and helps to minimize the accumulation of technical debt.

55. **C.** An iteration plan is created in an iteration planning meeting which should be attended by the entire team as everyone has responsibility for completion of the work in the iteration and all should participate in the planning process.

56. **A.** New functionality andcapabilities that were added during the iteration are demonstrated to stakeholders at the iteration review meeting. All stakeholders and any other interested parties are welcome to attend as valuable feedback is often gathered here.

57. **B.** In commitment driven iteration planning the team is asked to add stories to the iteration one by one until they can commit to completing no more. Selecting stories one by one allows the team to split each story into tasks and with the tasks estimated, the team determines whether or not to commit to delivering that story during the iteration.

58. **D.** The Schedule Baseline is determined by the total number of planned iterations multiplied by iteration length.

59. **A.** An agile approach attempts to minimize scope creep by involving the customer/proxy and allowing the code to be evaluated frequently (at the end of each iteration) and providing an opportunity for customer/proxy input allowing the backlog to be adjusted based on priority reflecting customer value.

60. **C.** Lean Software Development focuses on the following seven principles: eliminating waste, amplifying learning, deciding as late as possible, delivering as fast as possible, empowering the team, building integrity in, and seeing the whole.

61. **D.** Under a contract containing continue or cancel language based on successful completion of each iteration, the customer may cancel if the seller is failing to make deliveries as agreed, and the seller may cancel if the customer is not providing input to the team at the agreed upon frequency and level of detail.

62. **B.** The length of the iteration determines how often the software can be shown (in potentially shippable form) to users and customers. In addition, iteration length determines how often progress can be measured as well as how often revisions to the plan can be made.

63. **A.** Iteration length should be chosen to maximize the amount, frequency, and timeliness of feedback to the whole team. The length chosen may vary depending on the work, organization, resources, etc. However, two weeks is typical.

64. **B.** An optimum iteration length is one that encourages the team to work at a consistent pace throughout the iteration. Sometimes when an iteration is too long there is a tendency to go slowly in the beginning leading to a crisis environment near the end of the iteration which is less productive.

65. **B.** One of the best ways to forecast velocity is to run several iterations and then estimate velocity based on the observed velocity. Provided nothing changes with the team, this method should provide an accurate estimate of velocity for future iterations.

66. **C.** Including buffers is a form of risk mitigation that helps protect the project from the impact of the uncertainty. Feature buffers provide some flexibility on the features that need to be completed in a release while a schedule buffer provides time to resolve risk events.

67. **A.** A risk audit is conducted as part of the retrospective meeting in order to evaluate the effectiveness of risk responses with the goal of improving risk management in future iterations.

68. **D.** Agile principles require close coordination with the customer/proxy and a high degree of transparency supported by the use of information radiators. This philosophy makes use of both formal and informal documentation as well as encouraging frequent customer/proxy visits and participation in the development process.

69. **C.** In agile projects, the customer/proxy works closely with the team and drives the priority of the requirements however, the team commits to deliver the agreed upon features at the end of the iteration and the customer/proxy and management agree to not direct changes to the ongoing iteration.

70. **B.** The master storage for all the team's files and file history is referred to as the repository. The repository typically resides on the version control server and is unique to each individual project.

71. **C.** Team members work out of a sandbox which is located on their local development machines (and never on a shared drive). Programmers will typically download files from the repository to the sandbox for use in developing new code.

72. **A.** Traditional project management sometimes tends to focus more on the project plan than on the value delivered to the customer. On an agile project, the priority of the development is based in part on the value the customer/proxy puts on the features to be developed and thus tends to be more value driven than the traditional project management approach.

73. **B.** The release plan is a high-level strategic plan and covers a number of iterations. An iteration plan is a detailed plan specifically describing the work to be done by the team during the iteration making the iteration plan more tactical in nature.

74. **D.** Agile teams will commonly set aside an iteration to use for preparation of the product for final release. This iteration is referred to as a hardening iteration.

75. **A.** As the code evolves the build script should evolve with it making all the programmers responsible for maintaining the build script.

76. **C.** Actual Percent Complete (APC) is defined as the total number of sprint points completed divided by the total number of story points planned.

77. **B.** Automated test suites reduce problems encountered by programmers integrating other people's code when developing in increments and thus significantly reduce refactoring issues.

78. **B.** The daily Scrum is a short (15 minutes or less) meeting where each team member describes what they accomplished since the last Scrum, what they plan to do today, and what impediments are preventing progress.

79. **C.** The Product Owner leads the effort of prioritizing the stories however this is done with the input of the entire team all of whom share responsibility for the priority of the stories.

80. **C.** It is the responsibility of the Scrum Master to remove any roadblocks impeding progress that the team has identified. Roadblocks are typically identified and discussed at the daily stand up meeting.

81. **B.** Forecasting the financial value of a theme is primarily the responsibility of the product owner however the entire team should participate in the process and share in the responsibility.

82. **B.** Intrinsic schedule flaw generally refers to the common tendency to underestimate the size of the product being built. The agile approach mitigates this by reevaluation of the release plan at the end of each iteration to confirm that the team is still on target.

83. **A.** Organic risk management refers to the process of risk being developed by the team as part of the project life cycle such as during the daily standup. Displaying risk status on a chart is an example of overt risk management.

84. **D.** Synchronous integration confirms that the build and tests succeed before moving on to the next task. A synchronous integration consists of starting the next task immediately after starting the build, without waiting for the build and tests to succeed.

85. **C.** When utilizing osmotic communication, people who need to communicate frequently should be located such that they overhear each other's background conversations. This allows everyone to contribute and respond quickly to the information flow around them.

86. **C.** Tools used by the Scrum team for establishing a shared product vision include the product positioning map, the product vision box, the elevator statement, the press release, the product data sheet, and the magazine review.

87. **D.** In Scrum, the notion of a reciprocal commitment refers to the team's commitment to delivering some specified amount of functionality and the business's commitment to not changing priorities during the sprint.

88. **B.** In Scrum, if a change proposed during an ongoing sprint cannot be kept out, the sprint should be terminated abnormally and restarted. This is an extreme circumstance and should not be done very often.

89. **C.** Typical sections of the project data sheet include: Identification (of the Scrum Master and Product Owner), Elevator Statement, Customer Attributes, Customer Benefits, Feature/Ability to, Performance Attributes, Major Milestones, and Tradeoff Matrix.

90. **D.** Teams can abnormally terminate a sprint if they feel they cannot meet the sprint goal. Management can abnormally terminate a sprint if organizational priorities change. When abnormally terminating a sprint, all work from the current sprint is undone and the code base reverts to what it was prior to the sprint termination. Then the team must begin the work of planning the next sprint.

91. **A.** Estimating points for individual stories are often limited to a short series of possible numbers (e.g., 1, 2, 3, 5, 8, 13). A common sequence used is the Fibonacci sequence where each numbers is equal to the sum of the two preceding numbers.

92. **A.** Frequent re-planning based on progress to date and new information is one way in which agile methods deal with uncertainty.

93. **D.** The Kanban came from the Japanese process for continuous improvement and the name has been applied to an approach to software development which combines ideas from lean development and from Goldratt's theory of constraints.

94. **C.** A capability is defined as a high-level business or product function that is complete and valuable. The term capability is sometimes used synonymously with the term epic.

95. **B.** A Fibonacci series is defined as a sequence of numbers where the sum of the preceding two numbers equal the third number as in 1, 2, 3, 5, 8, 13. A Fibonacci series is sometimes used as a range of points from which to choose relative estimates for story effort during agile planning.

96. **A.** Planning poker is an estimating technique used by agile teams to estimate relative story size. A Fibonacci sequence is commonly use to establish the range of numbers from which to choose story points.

97. **D.** Scanning is basically the proactive, and early gathering of information and looking ahead with the goal of reducing uncertainty and risk.

98. **B.** The practice of setting a fixed time limit to overall development efforts and allowing specific features to remain undefined for the time being is sometimes referred to as timeboxing.

99. **B.** One of the best known Lean principles is "eliminate waste." That's not a law as much as it is something you should do, as a rule.

100. **C.** According to Lean principles, errors are due to the system within which people work rather than to the individuals themselves.

101. **A.** Most product failures are caused by market risk. This is not because marketing people are less competent than designers, but rather because market risk is a much tougher problem than technical risk.

102. **A.** Lean extends Agile to create a system that helps minimize work-in-process and maximize the speed at which business value is created.

103. **C.** The value stream map is a Lean tool that practitioners use to analyze the value stream. Value stream mapping involves drawing pictures of the process streams and then using them to look for waste.

104. **D.** By identifying minimum marketable features (MMFs), the smallest amount of functionality that makes sense to market, allows us to determine which aspects of a product can be delivered quickly.

105. **C.** Scrum# is an enhancement of Scrum that results from embedding Scrum with Lean thinking.

106. **C.** Scrum is a framework for creating an effective Agile development process. It is based on the belief that software development must be controlled by responding to feedback received during the course of development.

107. **B.** Just-in-Time (JIT) is a principle governing Lean organizations.

108. **A.** The two primary jobs of a coach when preparing for sprint planning are to ensure product owner participation and to facilitate a structured meeting agenda.

109. **D.** A Scrum Master can also act as an agile coach when he or she goes beyond getting agile practices up and running and moves into actively facilitating and helping the team to pursue continuously improving performance.

110. **D.** Agile project management requires a balance between discipline and flexibility in order to be successful. Discipline in order to produce high quality work quickly and efficiently and flexibility in order to accommodate the inevitable changes that will occur.

111. **A.** Project leaders who focus on project deliverables tend to add value while an excessive focus on plans and control tends to increase overhead.

112. **B.** It is generally very difficult to precisely define the project scope at the beginning of a project. Agile projects therefore focus on developing and working to an articulated product vision i.e a releasable product.

113. **B.** Release planning attempts to schedule stories in the order of the value created for the customer and the risk involved in development. High value, high risk stories are typically planned first.

114. **C.** Common project management planning artifacts such as expenditure budgets are typically finalized after the release plan is complete.

115. **D.** The team should be responsible for monitoring their working agreements during the retrospective which will allow the leader to focus on facilitating.

116. **A.** A Product Data Sheet (PDS) is typically a single-page summary of key business and quality objectives, product capabilities, and project management information related to the project.

117. **B.** The tradeoff matrix shows the relative importance of the three constraint areas of scope, schedule, and cost and is used both in agile and traditional project management.

118. **A.** A version control system allows an orderly process called continuous integration in which developers get the latest code from the server, do their work, test their code, and check in their changes. This process is typically repeated several times per day by each programmer pair.

119. **A.** A burn-up chart, typically created during update of the release plan and including work completed and work remaining, is an excellent way to get a big picture overview of project status.

120. **C.** Software that operates in a particular industry, such as accounting, will have its own specialized rules of operation and must implement those rules faithfully and exactly in order to be successful. These rules are domain rules, and knowledge of these rules is domain knowledge

GLOSSARY

A-EVM: *See Agile earned value management.*

Abnormally terminated sprint: A scrum iteration that is discontinued, either because the team cannot meet the sprint goal or because organizational priorities change.

Acceptance criteria: Measurable terms defining how a user story can satisfy customer expectations.

ACP: Agile Certified Practitioner, a certification offered by the Project Management Institute.

Active listening: Intentionally focusing on who is speaking in order to understand what is said and what is meant.

Actual Cost (AC): An agile earned value management (A-EVM) measure, AC is the actual cost of work completed during an iteration.

Actual day: A standard working day in a specific work environment.

Actual Percent Complete (APC): An agile earned value management (A-EVM) measure, APC is the number of story points completed (s) divided by the total number of story points planned (Sp). In terms of a formula, APC = s/Sp

Adaptation: Allowing requirement or design issues to arise and then building them into the product.

Adaptive planning: As commonly practiced, entails incremental delivery cycles or iterations.

Affinity estimating: A technique employed to quickly and easily estimate a large number of user stories.

Agile coaching levels: Agile coaching occurs on two levels, individual and team.

Agile cycle time: The start-to-finish time required to complete a potentially shippable increment of the solution.

Agile Earned Value Management (A-EVM): An adaptation of the widely recognized and used EVM toolset.

Agile Ethos: The notion that empowering teams is central to realizing the goal of a successful project.

Agile Manifesto values:

Individuals and Interactions	over	Processes and Tools
Working Software	over	Comprehensive Documentation
Customer Collaboration	over	Contract Negotiation
Responding to Change	over	Following a Plan

Agile Modeling (AM): A practice-based methodology for effective modeling of software-based systems.

Agile planning levels: Release planning, iteration planning, and daily planning.

Analysis paralysis: The fear of moving forward until the project's agile models are perfect.

Anchoring: The undue influence exerted on a team by a single strong-willed member whose opinion is an outlier, often because of an undisclosed agenda.

Applied simplicity: Principle used in Agile Modeling (AM) to focus on only creating models that address the current facet of the problem, thus avoiding large, unwieldy models.

Artifacts: Deliverables or work products resulting from the agile process. Examples include: Vision statement, flexibility matrix, product backlog, user stories, and team agreements.

Backlog: A list of capabilities, features, and stories that the product team has identified for use in both release and iteration planning.

Barely sufficient: The philosophy that advocates doing only what is necessary to achieve success.

BART analysis: When performing a BART analysis, agile coaches focus on the impact of four dimensions on team dynamics: **B**oundary, **A**uthority, **R**ole, and **T**ask.

Batman: On an Extreme Programming (XP) team, the "Batman" deals with organizational emergencies and support requests so that the other developers can focus on programming work.

Blitz planning: An index card-based planning session in which the sponsor, business expert, expert user, and developers together build the project map and timeline, including tasks and dependencies.

Bottleneck: A term adapted from the Theory of Constraints, a bottleneck is a finite resource that when over allocated, impedes progress on the project.

Buffer: A margin for error around an estimate, used where there is significant uncertainty.

Buffer iteration: An iteration in the last release of a project that allows the agile team to address some final finishing features.

Buffer types: There are two types of buffers, feature buffers and schedule buffers.

Burn chart: A time-based graph of features to be completed over time and features completed so far.

Burn-down chart: Shows the work remaining, like number of story points or ideal days, in the project or release. Burn-down charts are used most often for iterations and typically reflect the results of the team's daily meeting.

Burn-up chart: Shows the work completed, again in story points or ideal days for the project or release. Burn-up charts are used most often for releases and typically reflect features or deliverables completed.

Business case: A written document that explains how the use of resources is aligned with the accomplishment of a goal or the implementation of a needed change.

CAPM: Certified Associate in Project Management, a certification offered by the Project Management Institute.

Caves and commons area: The team is located in a "commons" area to foster osmotic communication but members may retreat to a private "caves" area when they need quiet or personal space.

Central feature list: A rough sketch or a superset used for planning the first iteration and release.

Certified Scrum Master (CSM): One of the most widely recognized agile certifications, the CSM is issued by the Scrum Alliance.

Coach: An Extreme Programming (XP) team leader who helps the team reach its potential and encourages discipline in XP practices.

Code freeze: An agile team may initiate a code freeze only during an ongoing iteration, to prevent unapproved scope changes.

Code of Ethics: The outline for ethical practices within the project management profession.

Coding standards: Everyone on the agile team codes to the same standards and conventions. Considered a core XP practice.

Colocation: Placing the project team in close proximity (i.e., in the same room or in adjacent rooms) to facilitate communication.

Collective code ownership: A practice where everyone shares responsibility for the quality of the code, allowing anyone to make necessary changes anywhere. Considered a core XP practice.

Compliance documentation: Documentation necessary to appease external bodies such as regulatory agencies but which has little value in communicating customer value to the agile development team.

Cone of uncertainty: Term used to describe how customers must traverse through an ambiguous process where they move between experiences that sub-optimally solve their problem in order to find the experiences that optimally solve it.

Continue-or-cancel clauses: Contract stipulations where the customer may cancel if the agile seller fails to deliver and the agile seller may cancel if the customer does not provide input and priorities.

Continuous integration: All product changes (i.e.. to the code base) are integrated at least daily. Unit tests have to run at 100% both pre and post-integration. Considered a core XP practice.

Cooperative Game goals: Delivering the software and creating an advantageous position for the next game

Cowboy coding: Considered the least disciplined of agile methodologies.

CRACK: The acronym "CRACK" describes an effective agile product owner: **C**ommitted, **R**esponsible, **A**uthorized, **C**ollaborative, and **K**nowledgeable.

Cross-functional team: A team composed of members who have all the functional skills and specialties needed to complete a project.

Crystal: A family of agile frameworks that vary based on project size and criticality.

Crystal color schemes: Going from lighter (Clear) to darker (Maroon) indicates increased "heaviness" in terms of the number of people involved, criticality, and project-level priorities.

Crystal named color schemes: Clear, Yellow, Orange, Red, Maroon

CSD: Certified Scrum Developer, a certification offered by the Scrum Alliance.

CSM: Certified Scrum Master, a certification offered by the Scrum Alliance.

CSP: Certified Scrum Professional, a certification offered by the Scrum Alliance.

CSPO: Certified Scrum Product Owner, a certification offered by the Scrum Alliance.

Cumulative flow diagram (CFD): A tool for understanding project execution and using that insight to improve performance. It reduces risk due to workload imbalance by spreading it more evenly, creating a more effective and sustainable pace.

Customer-centric stories: Stories that are written from the on-site customer's point of view, and provide something that the customer cares about.

Customer satisfaction: The result of delivering a product, service, or information that meets customer requirements.

Cycle time: The time (weeks, months, or years) required to deliver capabilities. A properly implemented agile framework should minimize cycle time.

Daily scrum: A 15 minute daily meeting where all participants specifically describe what they did yesterday, what they plan to do today, and what problems are preventing them from making progress. A scrum-specific type of daily stand-up meeting. Also called *morning scrum*.

Daily stand-up meeting: Each day, the team meets face-to-face for a maximum of fifteen minutes to update each other on their status and on any obstacles that are slowing them down. Also called *daily scrum* and *morning scrum*.

Dashboard: An integrated assemblage of metrics that have meaning to the team, to the customer/proxy, and to key stakeholders. Often displayed as a visual control for the team.

Date-driven project: One that must be released by a certain date but for which the feature set is negotiable. See *Timeboxed plan*.

Decomposition: Involves breaking large features into smaller stories and tasks.

Defect repair iteration: An iteration devoted exclusively to fixing product defects (e.g., software bugs).

Deferring commitment: Decisions are made at the right time; synonymous with "last responsible moment."

Definition of done: Defines specific metrics or acceptance criteria for each user story.

Demonstration (Demo): See *Product demonstration*.

Discipline: The level of adherence (on a high/low continuum) to the agile methodology's prescribed structure and processes.

Discounting: The process of moving future amounts back into their present value.

Done-done: An agile state of being when the code is complete, tested, and bug free and can be released to the customer.

DSDM: Dynamic Systems Development Method

Dynamic Systems Development Method (DSDM) phases: Pre-project, Project Lifecycle, and Post-Project

Earned Value (EV): An agile earned value management (A-EVM) measure, EV is the budgeted cost of work completed during an iteration.

Earned Value Management (EVM): A program management technique that integrates scope, schedule, and resource consumption information in order to measure project performance against planned cost metrics.

Elevator statement: A brief, structured product vision statement that gives the team the ability to explain the project concisely to someone "in an elevator."

Emotional intelligence: Popularized by Daniel Goleman, emotional intelligence distinguishes an effective leader from a merely competent one and is characterized by the presence of its components – self-awareness, self-regulation, motivation, empathy, and social skills.

Epic: A high-level, valuable business or product function that typically is broken down into smaller user stories for inclusion in an iteration.

Erg-second: A "unit" of agile measure that captures the cost in both labor and time to get a project-related question answered.

Escaped defects: Product defects that go undiscovered by (or "escaped from") the agile project team during the development and quality assurance (QA)/testing process.

ESVP: Retrospective check-in activity where participants identify attitudes toward the retrospective as one of an Explorer, Shopper, Vacationer, or Prisoner.

Exciters and delighters: Features that provide great customer satisfaction, often adding a price premium to a product.

Exploratory 360°: A Crystal methodology technique where a pre-project safety check is performed.

Exploratory spike: A story used to overcome complexity challenges by creating speculative possible solutions to test. The goal of a spike is to solve a difficult technical problem or to learn enough to posit another solution that will solve it. Also called *spike*.

Extreme Programming (XP): A programmer-centric framework focused on technical practices that promote skillful software development. XP is considered a high-discipline agile method that applies techniques and practices with extreme rigor as long as doing so improves results.

Extreme Programming (XP) quality: All checked-in code must pass unit tests at 100% at all times.

Face-to-face (F2F) conversation: The most efficient and effective method of communication for agile teams.

Facilitating: Supporting the agile team's self-organization and enhancing its ability to deliver real business value to the customer.

Fairness: The value focused on being careful to avoid conflicts of interest and discrimination; one of the four hallmarks of the PMP® Code of Ethics and Professional Responsibility.

FDD: Considered the most "tightly wrapped" Agile framework.

Feature: A product component that provides some valuable functionality for the customer, typically accomplished in one or more agile stories.

Feature breakdown structure (FBS): Depicts the backlog of features for release and iteration planning in a way that enhances communication with the customer by avoiding techno-jargon.

Feature development priorities: High-value, high-risk features deliver the most value and eliminate risks.

Fibonacci sequence: A non-linear number series (1, 2, 3, 5, 8, 13, 21, 34, 55, etc.) where the next number is derived by adding the previous two, defined by the equation $Fn = Fn\text{-}1 + Fn\text{-}2$. Used by scrum teams during "planning poker" when providing value point estimates for user stories.

Fist of five: An agile consensus-building activity. During team votes, showing more fingers (1 to 5) demonstrates increased agreement with the question posed, with five fingers meaning, "Strongly agree."

Fixed, firm, orflexible: In a flexibility matrix, agile project constraints are categorized as fixed, firm, or flexible. Only one constraint (i.e., time, scope, or cost) may be fixed.

Flexibility matrix: A grid which shows the relative importance of project constraints (i.e., scope, schedule, cost, quality) in terms of fixed, firm, or flexible; only one constraint may be fixed. Also called trade-off matrix.

Flow: The continuous delivery of value to customers. Similar in concept to throughput from the Theory of Constraints.

Flux: The level of change (on a high/low continuum) that is occurring with the project requirements or code.

Force Field Analysis: A retrospective activity where the team first defines a state they want to achieve and then breaks into groups to identify factors that may either restrain or drive the desired change.

Forecasted velocity: An estimate (or forecast) of team velocity when it is either impossible or impractical for the team to run an iteration, and they do not yet have any historical observations.

Forty (40) hour work week: Considered a core XP practice, the development team works a standard 40 hour week. A maximum of one week of overtime is allowed. If additional overtime is needed, this is considered a serious failure of the agile process and must be evaluated.

Fractional assignment: Assignment of people to multiple projects simultaneously, a practice not recommend when using most agile methodologies.

Free-for-all: Along with round-robin and silent individual generation of ideas, the three brainstorming activities that may be performed during agile retrospectives.

Gemba: A Japanese term for the place where value-added work is being done. Examples include the developer team room and the customer's office.

Greenfield project: A project where the team is creating a new codebase from scratch. Also the preferred method of implementing Extreme Programming (XP) for the first time in an organization.

Handoff iteration: An iteration used to prepare the formal documentation and other deliverables that production requires, including attending final approval meetings.

Hard commitment: In Scrum, describes when the team has finalized their analysis, agreed they can succeed, and commits to the specific set of features that will be delivered to the Product Owner at the end of the iteration.

Hardening iteration: An iteration where the agile team prepares for the final rollout of a project. Also called *Iteration H*.

Heavyweight team: An agile team focused solely on new development and not supporting existing operations; often used on pilot projects or when onboarding agile methods.

Highest priority: The highest priority of the agile team is to satisfy the customer through early and continuous delivery of valuable solutions.

Honesty: The value focused on the mandatory standard of never deceiving others; one of the four hallmarks of the PMP® Code of Ethics and Professional Responsibility.

Hybrid iteration: An iteration where a significant part is reserved for non-development work (e.g., defect repair, unplanned items, etc.).

Hybrid project: Project in which agile and traditional development methodologies are combined, or one in which multiple agile methods are combined.

Ideal day: The amount of time per day that a team member would spend on a project if working full speed without any interruptions, vacations, or other competition for her time.

Ideal scrum team size: 5 to 9 members (i.e., 7 + 2)

Identifying stakeholders: Identifying all stakeholders is important because they hold the power to provide or deny access to the resources needed by the agile team to fulfill the vision of the project.

Impediment backlog: A visible list of obstacles prioritized according to the severity with which they are blocking the team. Also called risk backlog.

Incremental revenue: Additional revenue that may be obtained from existing customers.

Information radiator: Any visual display in the project workspace that concentrates important project information where anyone can see and evaluate it.

INVEST: The acronym "INVEST" represents the qualities of a good user story: Independent, Negotiable, Valuable, Estimatable, Sized Appropriately, and Testable.

Invitation opening: A non-leading, open-ended question ("What did you notice during the stand-up meeting this morning?") that gives team members the opportunity to provide a thoughtful response.

Iteration: A period, usually one to four weeks, in which the agile team codes and tests one or more small features resulting in potentially releasable software. Also called sprint by scrum practitioners.

Iteration 0: A planning iteration used for accomplishing technical setup, establishing agile methods and roles, and creating a product vision.

Iteration backlog: The prioritized, detailed task list for the current iteration that the team promises to deliver to the sponsors at the end of the iteration. Also called sprint backlog.

Iteration H: *See Hardening iteration.*

Iterative development: The agile practice of delivering increments of the solution early and often.

Iteration plan: Combines a timebox with detailed work effort descriptions.

Ivory tower architecture: An architecture or design developed in isolation from the agile team responsible for following it.

Kanban: A continuous improvement approach which has periodic releasable timeframes and which does not require strict iteration lengths for all stories.

Kanban board: A visual display of the scheduling process and the limits set on work-in-process (WIP) and new work that is being "pulled" through the development system.

Knowledge worker: Term coined by management guru Peter Drucker to describe employees who have, distribute, and control knowledge in an organization. Management theory asserts that challenge and not financial compensation is the main motivator for knowledge workers. Most agile team members are considered knowledge workers.

Law of large numbers (LLN): The statistical concept that the larger the sample of observations used to predict the behavior of a variable, the smaller the expected deviation in outcomes. Thus, a large series of observations is the best method to transform unpredictable and chancy individual outcomes into stable, predictable cases for a large group. Also called Bernoulli's law.

Linear feature: Linear features are so named because customer satisfaction is correlated linearly with the quantity of the feature.

Listing stakeholders: Listing stakeholders and their interests in a project is the "most obvious secret" to success that is commonly overlooked.

Microtouch intervention: A practice whereby the project leader gets team members to make acceptably small changes that they do not mind and which causes the team to become more aligned in the same direction.

Minimum marketable feature (MMF): The smallest amount of functionality that makes sense to deliver to market.

MoSCoW analysis: A feature prioritization technique which represents:
    M: Must have
    S: Should have
    C: Could have
    W: Won't have

Morning scrum: See Daily scrum.

Must-have features: See Threshold features.

Mute mapping: A practice where an Extreme Programming (XP) team gathers at a whiteboard to silently arrange annotated index cards; often performed at iteration retrospectives. A type of Silent generation of ideas.

Obstacle: Any roadblock or impediment that slows down team members during an iteration.

On site customer: Considered a core XP practice, the development team has continuous access to an on site customer. For commercial software with many external stakeholders, an internal proxy may be used.

Open space meeting: A self-organized meeting where the participants set the topic and agenda, typically to solve a problem.

Optimizing the whole: A Lean principle that emphasizes continuous improvement by addressing whole entities or processes rather than individual problems or symptoms.

Organic risk management: Risk management resulting inherently from using agile practices such as release planning, short iterations, and the daily stand-up meeting, where obstacles are addressed daily.

Overt risk management: Specific risk management strategies employed to identify, track, and mitigate project risk, such as constructing and maintaining a risk board.

Pair programming: An Extreme Programming (XP) practice where two programmers are paired at a keyboard, with one person (the driver) coding and the other person (the navigator) thinking. Considered a core XP practice.

Participatory decision making: A creative process where ownership of decisions belongs to the team, and where finding effective options that everyone can support is the focus.

Payback period: The amount of time required to earn back an initial investment of cash.

PDCA: Plan-Do-Check-Act cycle.

Performance Measure Baseline (PMB): An agile earned value management (EVM) measure, Performance Measure Baseline (PMB) is the total number of story points planned for a release.

Personal safety: Describes an environment where team members may both innovate and come to friendly disagreements without fear of repercussions or personal attacks.

PgMP: Program Management Professional, a certification offered by the Project Management Institute.

Pigs and Chickens: In scrum, "pigs" are the people on the scrum team. All others with a vested interest but who do not participate are "chickens."

Planned Percent Complete (PPC): An agile earned value management (A-EVM) measure, Planned Percent Complete (PPC) is the number of the current sprint (n) divided by the total number of planned sprints (T), or n/T.

Planned Value (PV): An agile earned value management (A-EVM) measure, PV is the budgeted cost of work planned for an iteration.

Planning Game: A technique whereby the sponsors write story cards that call for creating new program features, the developers estimate the time it will take, and the customers prioritize the stories. Considered a core XP practice.

Planning poker: A consensus-based game that employs the Delphi method; team members individually estimate user stories through use of numbered cards, followed by discussion, until consensus is achieved.

PMBOK: The Project Management Institute's Project Management Body Of Knowledge

PMI: The Project Management Institute, the largest professional association of project managers.

PMP: Project Management Professional, a certification offered by the Project Management Institute.

Portfolio management: An organizational approach of selecting the most important products to create and enhance.

Predictive release planning: A release planning method in which the entire plan is created in advance and which tends to work best in environments that are low in flux.

Present value: The amount an investor has today to generate a known amount in the future.

Pre-assignment: Pre-assignment of team members is necessary when the project is dependent on specific expertise and that expertise is in short supply.

Process-centric: Pertaining primarily to the agile process.

Product backlog: A prioritized list (of features or tasks) of all the things the agile team needs to do. It is an artifact similar to the product specification or requirements list in traditional project management and it represents the customer's vision of the product.

Product backlog grooming: The practice of preparing the backlog for the next iteration planning meeting by adding stories, refining existing stories, and estimating stories as needed.

Product demonstration: The meeting where the agile team demonstrates working features to the customer/proxy, key stakeholders, and selected end users.

Product Owner: In scrum, the "voice of the customer" or customer proxy representing stakeholders and the business, who sets the priorities of the deliverables.

Product roadmap: An artifact which shows how the product is intended to evolve over time.

Product theme: Each project has an underlying theme or metaphor, which provides an easily remembered naming convention. Considered a core XP practice.

Product vision box: May be thought of as a product box on a store shelf with whatever graphic images and narrative content is necessary to convey its purpose.

Product vision exercises: Two exercises for refining the product vision are designing a product box and writing an elevator statement.

Product-centric: Pertaining primarily to product development.

Project chunking: The agile practice of taking large projects and breaking them down into smaller pieces that reduce risk and add customer value sooner. Also called chunking.

Project constraint: A restriction on the degree of freedom in providing a solution. Examples include cost and time constraints.

Project data sheet (PDS): A single page summary of key project management information, product capabilities, and business and quality objectives, the project data sheet is the minimum documentation for an agile project's objectives.

Pulling: A concept from Lean manufacturing, pulling refers to a "make to order" (MTO) supply chain philosophy where production is based on actual demand.

Pushing: A concept from Lean manufacturing, pushing refers to a "make to stock" (MTS) supply chain philosophy where production is not based on actual demand.

Reciprocal commitment: The team commits to delivering specified functionality and the business commits to not changing priorities during the iteration.

Refactoring: Constantly improving a product's internal design (e.g., rewriting code) without changing its behavior to make the product more reliable and adaptable. Considered a core XP practice.

Reflective workshop: See Team reflective workshop.

Release: A release occurs when a product is ready to use. An agile release is similar to a traditional project milestone, with the deliverable being a specified set of working features. The release may be internal to the organization or there may be formal deployment to customers and end users.

Release plan: A timebox equivalent to a traditional project schedule.

Release planning: The process of creating a very high-level plan that covers a period longer than an iteration.

Release planning inputs: The three inputs to agile release planning are:
1. Prioritized, estimated product backlog
2. Velocity measurement (or estimate)
3. Product vision

Release planning output: The release plan is the main output of release planning.

Repository: A master storage area for all the team's files and their history; typical of Extreme Programming (XP) projects.

Respect: The value focused on the project manager showing esteem for others; one of the four hallmarks of the PMP® Code of Ethics and Professional Responsibility.

Responsibility: Taking ownership of one's decisions, actions, and related outcomes; one of the four hallmarks of the PMP® Code of Ethics and Professional Responsibility.

Responsibility, Respect, Fairness, and Honesty: The four hallmarks of the PMP® Code of Ethics and Professional Responsibility; adhering to them builds trust.

Retained revenue: Revenue an organization will lose if the project or theme is not developed.

Retrospective: A process-centric meeting where the team gathers after completing an increment of work to inspect and adapt their methods and teamwork.

Retrospective structure: The structure of an agile retrospective is:
1. Establish retrospective parameters
2. Assemble data
3. Develop insights
4. Make decisions
5. End retrospective

Risk audit: Examines the effectiveness of risk responses and is conducted as part of the retrospective meeting.

Risk board: An overt risk management visual control where the status and severity of risks are documented and maintained by the agile team. As with story boards, risk boards may be physical or virtual.

Risk census: A list of the project's unique risks, particularly when using Extreme Programming (XP) practices.

Risk-adjusted backlog: Occurs when the customer/proxy and key stakeholders provide the agile team with feature priorities that take legal or regulatory requirements into consideration.

Risk-based spike: An experiment specifically designed to assess the probability of an event occurring.

Round-robin: Along with free-for-all and silent individual generation of ideas, the three brainstorming activities that may be performed during agile retrospectives.

Rules of engagement: Establish norms and expectation for team member's treatment of one another.

Sandbox: The local development area for each team member, it contains a copy of all the files in the team repository from a recent snapshot in time.

Satisfy the customer: According to the Agile Manifesto, the highest priority that drives agile teams.

Scanning: The agile practice of looking ahead to learn the unknown and to reduce uncertainty.

Schedule Baseline (SB): An agile earned value management (A-EVM) measure, SB is the total number of story points planned for a release.

Science of simplicity: Maximizing the amount of work *not* done, by eliminating what is unnecessary and focusing on only what is essential.

Scopeboxed plan: A plan that defines the features the team will build in advance, but where the release date is uncertain.

Scrum: A project management framework (often used to develop software) that uses iterative cycles and incremental deliverables to develop solutions.

Scrum Alliance: A professional organization of scrum professionals and practitioners.

Scrum Master: A scrum team member who ensures the process is understood and followed, shields the team from outside interference, and removes impediments for the team.

Scrum project roles: The three essential roles for a scrum project are: 1) Product Owner; 2) Scrum Master; and 3) Team.

Scrum#: A variation of scrum, which is an enhancement that results from embedding scrum with Lean thinking.

Self-organized team: The agile team makes all tactical and implementation decisions, operating under the principle that those closest to the work know best how to organize it.

Self-regulating questions: Internal questions posed by the agile project manager to ease the transition from a traditional environment to an agile one, or from a technical role to a facilitator role. Examples of such questions include "What am I feeling?" and "Are my biases interfering with the team's goals or the agile process?"

Self-transcendent: A term used to describe the agile team's empowerment to make decisions to get the work done and to strive continuously to "find the limit."

Servant leader: An agile project leader or facilitator who makes his highest priority that of serving the needs of the team.

Seven Principles of Lean:
1. Eliminating waste
2. Amplifying learning
3. Deciding as late as possible
4. Delivering as fast as possible
5. Empowering the team
6. Building integrity in
7. Seeing the whole

Showing empathy: A part of active listening, acknowledging that people's feelings of loss or frustration are valid.

Shu Ha Ri: Japanese concept, which is used as a model for mastering agile, means "Follow the rule, break the rule, and be the rule."

Shuffle time: The time is takes to move from one activity to another during agile retrospectives.

Silent generation of ideas: Along with free-for-all and round robin, the three brainstorming activities that may be performed during agile retrospectives.

Simple design: Employ the simplest possible design to get the job done. Considered a core XP practice. See also *Barely sufficient*.

Sizing: An estimating technique that definesthe relative measure of the effort involved with delivering a particular user story.

Small releases: Begin with the smallest useful feature set. Release early and often, adding a few features with each iteration. Considered a core XP practice.

Splitting user stories: A user story should be split when it is too big to fit within a single iteration.

Sprint: *See Iteration.*

Sprint Backlog: *See Iteration backlog.*

Story: A self-contained element that typically corresponds to an individual product feature and represents one to two days of work. Also called *user story*.

Story board: Visual control that shows the status of user stories, often with index cards. The story board may be a physical board on a wall or white board or it may be a virtual table in one of many available commercial software applications. The stories are typically aligned in status columns such as Not Started, In Progress, In Testing, and Done and are moved on the board as their statuses change. Also called *story map* or *task board*.

Story points: Quantify work effort and complexity relative to other stories to provide a high-level indicator of how difficult development will be.

Sufficient-to-purpose: An intermediate work product that needs to be only good enough to help the agile project team move forward.

Sustainable pace: Allowing agile teams to work at a pace that can be sustained for the long term; this practices avoids team burnout and improves quality and team morale.

Swarming: The practice of bringing together all of the people (and their insights) needed to define a roadmap, thus decreasing the overall time required to complete the product.

Synchronous integration: The practice of confirming that the build and tests succeed before moving on to the next task.

Tacit knowledge: Undocumented knowledge that people retain in their heads about the project and the organization; such knowledge may be technical, historical, or procedural.

Task board: *See Story board.*

TDD: A software development process that is an agile project management tool, not a framework.

Team reflective workshop: A process-oriented forum during an iteration to correct flawed agile processes, to introduce new ones, or to augment working agreements.

Team working agreements: Standards that the agile team defines for how it will work, which are often displayed on information radiators. Examples include:
"If the build is broken then the entire team stops to fix it."
"We resolve to be on time for team meetings!"
"Always remember that the customer is part of the working team."
"We are not *done* until the use cases are written and tested."

Technical debt: The total amount of imperfect design and implementation decisions in the project.

Test-driven development (TDD): The test, or executable example, is written before deciding how to design the code. Considered a core XP practice.

Theory of Constraints: A management approach (popularized by Eli Goldratt) used to improve the output of a system by identifying, resolving, and managing a system's constraints.

Threshold features: Features that must be present in the product for it to be successful. Also called *must-have features*.

Timebox: There are several types used in agile project management; the highest level one is a roadmap.

Timeboxed plan: A plan that defines the release date in advance, but where the specific features that the release will include are negotiable.

Timeboxing: Setting a fixed time limit to overall development efforts while letting other elements (e.g., scope) vary.

Trade-off matrix: *See Flexibility matrix.*

Transition indicators: In Extreme Programming (XP) risk management, triggers that tell you when the risk has materialized.

Trend analysis: Utilizes historical data to evaluate patterns or trends in the data over time.

User Story: *See Story.*

Value stream: A set of activities required to analyze, design, and build a product from concept to launch.

Value stream mapping: A technique developed in the Lean manufacturing field to analyze (and potentially redesign) the flow of materials and information required to deliver a product or service to the customer.

Variance analysis: Involves comparing actual data versus estimated or planned expenditures of a specified measure. Time, cost, and resource constraints are the focus of traditional variance analyses. The goal of a variance analysis is to ascertain the causes of the observed variances and their impact on the project.

Velocity: The number of story points an agile team can complete in an iteration.

Velocity estimate methods: 1) Use historical values; 2) Run an iteration; and 3) Forecast velocity.

Velocity-driven iteration planning: The team estimates how many story points should be planned into the current iteration based on its actual velocity during recent iterations.

Venture-capital financing model: The sponsor provides a round of financing for a certain amount of work, and the contracted company must produce results in order to get more funding.

Visual control: In Lean, a visual tool (e.g., Kanban signal card) for controlling an activity or process. When adopted by agile teams, similar to an information radiator.

Walking Skeleton: A Crystal methodology technique in which there is a tiny implementation of the system that performs a small end-to-end function, linking the main architectural components.

Wastes in software development: Per Lean principles, the two biggest wastes in software development are: 1) Delays; and 2) Building what is not needed.

Weick's Principle of Small Wins: Delivering running, tested, useful code at regular intervals is a motivating reward for the project team.

Wideband Delphi: A consensus-based technique for estimating work effort, derived from the Delphi method originated by the Rand Corporation in the 1940s as a forecasting tool.

Wireframes: Stemming from the website development world where fast, emergent designs are a mandatory part of succeeding, wireframes are visual guides starting with a skeletal structure or framework, layering on additional facets of the desired solution.

Work-in-process (WIP): A concept borrowed from Lean, refers to the set of unfinished items being developed or waiting in the backlog which, by definition, produce no business value until they are finished.

Working agreements: *See Team working agreements.*

Working software: In Lean thinking, working software is the most valuable indicator of project status.

XP: *See Extreme Programming.*

INDEX

— A —

abnormally terminated sprint 318, 342, 365
acceptance criteria 63, 68, 81, 83, 84, 101, 102, 109, 110, 111, 126, 142, 157, 191, 200, 236, 258, 267, 268, 269, 271, 276, 365, 368
active listening 67, 68, 83, 85, 93, 365, 377
activities 10, 22, 29, 34, 38, 39, 40, 42, 45, 73, 78, 81, 96, 99, 102, 104, 108, 110, 121, 122, 128, 129, 132, 146, 152, 157, 177, 190, 191, 194, 198, 199, 219, 221, 234, 258, 260, 261, 262, 267, 282, 370, 376, 377, 378
    Brainstorming 104, 152, 370, 376, 377
        Check-In 369
        Circle of Questions 262
        Color Code Dots 106
        ESVP 262, 369
        Fishbone Diagram 104
        Force Field Analysis 105, 152, 370
        Helped, Hindered, Hypothesis 264
        Learning Matrix 106, 152, 216
        Mad Sad Glad 262
        Planning Game 35, 50, 373
        Prioritize with Dots 105
        Satisfaction Histogram 263
        SMART Goals 262
        SWOT Analysis 262
        Timeline 297, 366
        Working Agreements 99, 108, 110, 149, 150, 151, 222, 260, 263, 378, 379
actual day 128, 129, 133, 135, 137, 141, 143, 365
adaptation 23, 33, 127, 137, 142, 191, 238, 365
adaptive planning 71, 73, 101, 108, 111, 185, 189, 193, 217, 365
affinity estimating 131, 133, 135, 138, 139, 141, 143, 144, 365
agile coaching 365
    individual 10, 24, 25, 69, 75, 127, 129, 130, 133, 138, 143, 148, 157, 158, 161, 193, 194, 222, 258, 263, 265, 267, 280, 370, 372, 373, 376, 377
    team 4, 5, 7, 8, 16, 17, 18, 21, 22, 23, 25, 26, 29, 30, 32, 33, 34, 35, 36, 37, 38, 39, 40, 41, 42, 43, 44, 45, 46, 62, 63, 64, 65, 67, 70, 71, 72, 73, 74, 75, 76, 77, 78
agile earned value management (A-EVM) 238, 239, 365, 369, 373, 376
agile ethos 4, 5, 6, 7, 71, 80, 81, 189, 201, 365
Agile Manifesto 6, 69, 71, 99, 108, 365, 376
agile modeling (AM) 15, 32, 44, 59, 192, 366
agile planning and estimating 15, 20
agile planning levels 366
Agile Unified Process (AUP) 40
    disciplines 41, 189
    phases 32, 40, 60, 191, 369
    philosophies 40

— B —

backlog 34, 39, 45, 46, 62, 63, 70, 81, 82, 96, 97, 98, 99, 102, 103, 105, 107, 108, 110, 111, 127, 128, 130, 131, 132, 133, 134, 135, 138, 141, 142, 143, 147, 148, 150, 157, 159, 161, 176, 177, 178, 182, 187, 188, 189, 198, 200, 216, 218, 223, 236, 237, 241, 244, 258, 366, 370, 371, 374, 375, 376, 377, 379
barely sufficient 66, 67, 83, 110, 265, 366, 377
BART analysis 366
Batman 333, 358, 359, 366
Barton, Brent 244
Beck, Kent 33
Benefield, Gabrielle 74
Berthot, Bryan 158, 265
Blackburn, Thomas 244
Boehm, B. 144
bottleneck 131, 132, 181, 368
brainstorming
    free-for-all 104, 370, 376, 377
    round robin 199, 377
    silent generation of ideas 104, 372, 377
Broderick, Stacia 244
buffer iteration 353, 366
burn chart 187, 188, 206, 207, 366
    burn-down chart 150, 158, 185, 186, 187, 198, 217, 220, 223, 266, 317, 324, 366
    burn-up chart, 351, 364
business case 68, 71, 72, 83, 85, 178, 179, 366

— C —

caves and commons area 367
central feature list 100, 112, 367
Certified Associate in Project Management 292, 293, 366
Certified Scrum Developer 368
Certified Scrum Master (CSM), 12
Certified Scrum Product Owner (CSPO) 285
Certified Scrum Professional (CSP) 285
Christensen, Clayton 104
    heavyweight teams 104
coach 35, 74, 75, 81, 146, 147, 149, 166, 172, 194, 259, 263, 276, 324, 345, 355, 363, 364, 367
Cockburn, Alistair 41, 66, 92, 110, 148, 265
code freeze 367
Code of Ethics, PMI 279, 280, 282, 283
Cohn, Mike 78
Collins, Jim 80
collective 35, 39, 44, 192, 200, 213, 367
compliance documentation 367
cone of uncertainty 33, 65, 66, 80, 83, 85, 127, 142, 191, 195, 367
Constantine, Larry 40, 60
continue-or-cancel clauses 367
contracts 69, 70, 157, 158, 235, 236, 246, 254, 312, 348, 350
cooperative game goals 367
Covey, Stephen 175
cowboy coding 367
CRACK 367
critical chain 18, 60
cross-functional teams 4, 5, 37, 71, 155, 158, 162, 353
Crystal, i 20, 31, 41, 42, 265
    Crystal color schemes 367

cumulative flow diagram (CFD) 183
customer 6, 16, 17, 18, 20, 21, 23, 24, 25, 26, 27, 29, 30, 33, 34, 35, 36, 37, 45, 63, 64, 66, 69, 70, 71, 72, 73, 74, 75, 76, 77, 78, 80, 81, 82, 96, 98, 99, 100, 101, 102, 103, 105, 107, 108, 109, 110, 111, 127, 128, 130, 131, 136, 139, 142, 143, 144, 146, 147, 148, 152, 153
customer collaboration 6, 69, 71, 177, 235, 365
customer satisfaction 18, 95, 157, 335, 359, 368, 369, 372
customer-centric stories 368

— D —

daily scrum 86, 314, 340, 351, 361, 368, 372
    See daily stand-up meeting
daily stand-up meeting 99, 149, 185, 219, 373
dashboards 173, 174
date-driven project 368
    See timeboxed plan
decomposition 99, 102, 107, 108, 112, 114, 368
deferring commitment 26, 27, 54, 55, 59, 368
definition of done 46, 63, 83, 85, 108, 110, 111, 125, 258, 267, 268, 269, 271, 276, 368
    done-done 110, 112, 114, 116, 122, 318, 368
DeGrace, Peter 32
Deming, W. Edwards 23, 24, 36
demonstration (demo)
    See product demonstration
Derby, Esther 146, 260, 261
discipline 19, 29, 33, 44, 76, 108, 110, 111, 146, 152, 195, 237, 263, 265, 283, 308, 309, 327, 345, 349, 364, 367, 368, 369
discounting 368
Drammissi, Joseph 10
Drucker, Peter 80, 372
Dynamic Systems Development Method (DSDM) 369

— E —

earned value (EV) 239, 250, 251, 254
earned value management (EVM) 11, 215, 235, 238, 239, 249, 250, 254, 373
elevator statement 69, 72, 93, 152, 153, 154, 309, 317, 325, 330, 341, 342, 346, 352, 355, 362, 369, 374
emotional intelligence (EI) 76
epic 323, 343, 354, 363, 369
erg-second 369
Erlang, Agner Krarup 214
escaped defects 220, 224, 225, 229, 233, 369
exploratory 360
exploratory spike 222, 229, 234, 369
Extreme Programming (XP) 8, 15, 33, 130, 143, 146, 297, 366, 367, 369, 370, 372, 373, 375, 378
    continuous integration 35, 191, 194, 195, 196
    estimation 126, 129, 130, 142, 155, 194
    quality 17, 18, 22, 24, 25, 26, 28, 35, 36, 37, 40, 41, 60, 67, 69, 70, 71, 74, 76, 78, 79, 81, 87, 93, 101, 110, 148, 153, 155, 157, 177, 191, 193, 216, 220, 223, 236, 265, 307, 310, 322, 323, 329, 330, 331, 342, 346, 348, 349, 351, 352, 354, 355, 357, 358, 359, 364, 367, 369, 370, 374, 377
    roles 32, 33, 34, 35, 39, 43, 59, 68, 69, 70, 72, 75, 147, 158, 221, 222, 223, 224, 236, 258, 266, 276, 309, 371, 376

— F —

face-to-face (F2F) communication 66, 92, 149, 151, 161, 201, 213
facilitating 75, 84, 89, 94, 146, 193, 222, 263, 316, 321, 324, 345, 346, 352, 354, 355, 364, 369
    facilitator role 146, 147, 149, 161, 166, 172, 173, 193, 259, 376

retrospectives 75, 94, 99, 104, 106, 108, 117, 122, 123, 137, 146, 147, 149, 155, 161, 168, 173, 174, 200, 201, 208, 216, 219, 221, 222, 234, 259, 261, 263, 264, 267, 272, 276, 277, 278, 315, 316, 317, 319, 325, 329, 331, 337, 353, 356, 370, 372, 376, 377
fairness 280, 281, 283, 292, 294, 298, 301, 303, 304, 369, 375
Feature Driven Development (FDD) 37, 54
    Feature sets 22, 38, 54, 58, 101
    Feature Set Progress Report iv, 39, 40
features 19, 22, 26, 28, 35, 37, 38, 39, 40, 45, 46, 53, 62, 63, 70, 72, 76, 79, 96, 97, 98, 99, 100, 101, 102, 107, 108, 128, 147, 148, 154, 155, 157, 158, 176, 178, 185, 187, 190, 200, 216, 217, 222, 223, 236, 237, 238, 240, 241, 244, 258, 267, 366, 368, 369, 370, 371, 372, 373, 374, 375, 376, 377, 378
    development priorities 34, 370
    exciters and delighters 335, 359, 369
    linear 80, 94, 129, 133, 134, 143, 183, 195, 370, 372
    minimum marketable feature (MMF), 18, 101, 102, 372
    must-have 334, 335, 372, 378
    threshold 34, 67, 334, 335, 359, 372, 378
Fibonacci sequence 76, 94, 128, 129, 130, 133, 138, 143, 343, 362, 363, 370
Fist of five 370
flexibility matrix 64, 71, 152, 153, 154, 366, 370, 378
    fixed, firm, and flexible constraints iv
flow 23, 24, 25, 36, 62, 81, 87, 93, 131, 139, 144, 155, 156, 157, 176, 179, 181, 182, 183, 185, 189, 201, 368, 370, 378
flux 45, 107, 108, 111, 132, 189, 370, 374
Ford, Henry 23, 25, 80, 81
fractional assignment 315, 351, 370

— G —

Gantt, Henry 23
gemba 370
Goldratt, Eliyahu
    Theory of Constraints iv, 36, 60, 354, 363, 366, 370, 378
Greenfield project 370
ground rules. *See rules of engagement*

— H —

hard commitment 5, 63, 371
Highsmith, Jim 76, 258, 259
honesty 280, 281, 371, 375
hybrid projects 4, 19, 265, 266, 371

— I —

ideal day 128, 129, 133, 135, 137, 141, 143, 371
ideal scrum team size 371
INVEST 79, 82, 136, 178, 212, 357, 371
incremental revenue 357, 371
information radiators 149, 150, 151, 161, 217, 219, 221, 222, 260, 261, 264, 361, 378
    monitoring 217, 264, 277, 354, 364
    invitation opening 371
Ishikawa diagram. *See Activities, Fishbone Diagram*
iteration backlog 39, 45, 63, 70, 81, 92, 102, 105, 108, 110, 111, 127, 128, 130, 142, 147, 150, 182, 187, 216, 218, 223, 236, 371, 377
Iteration H 103, 371
iteration plan 22, 74, 101, 112, 136, 196, 199, 237, 372
iteration review 22, 78, 99, 199, 200, 216, 223, 336, 360
iteration 5, 16, 17, 22, 23, 30, 39, 40, 50, 51, 52, 53, 54, 55, 57, 58, 63, 70, 71, 72, 73, 74, 75, 76, 78, 81, 96, 97, 99, 100, 101, 102, 103, 104, 105, 106, 107, 108, 110, 111, 127

    defect repair 103, 108, 368, 371
    goals 29, 68, 75, 79, 101, 146, 148, 151, 158, 161, 176, 177, 180, 185, 193, 194, 260, 263, 367, 376
    handoff 108
    hardening 103, 108, 258, 371
    hybrid 4, 8, 9, 103, 108, 116, 117, 132, 265, 266, 268, 270, 272, 275, 277, 317, 321, 342, 371
    planning 10, 15, 16, 17, 18, 20, 21, 23, 28, 35, 38, 62, 63, 71, 72, 73, 74, 75, 77, 81, 82, 96, 97, 98, 99, 100, 101, 102, 103, 104, 106, 107, 108, 109, 110, 111, 126, 127, 128, 129, 130, 132, 133, 134, 135, 137, 138, 141, 142, 143, 144, 145, 146, 147, 149, 152, 154, 155, 161, 176, 177, 178, 180, 185, 188, 189, 190, 191, 193, 197, 204, 217, 218, 219, 237, 238, 239
    traditional (standard)
    QA/testing 103, 108, 220, 224
iterative development 29, 30, 62, 73, 157, 372
ivory tower architecture iv, 372

— J —

Jobs, Steven 18
Jones, Daniel 24

— K —

Kanban 132, 133, 135, 141, 185, 189, 190, 372, 379
Kanban board 132, 133, 135, 141, 189, 372
knowledge worker 80, 372

— L —

Law of large numbers (LLN) 126, 372
Lean software development (LSD) 15, 36, 54
    Optimize the whole 25, 37, 71
    Seven Principles of Lean 377
    & Theory Constraints
linear features 372
Little, John 182, 183

— M —

Martin, Roger 80
McKenna, Jeff 32
microtouch intervention 372
minimum marketable feature (MMF) 18, 101, 102, 372
Moore, Geoffrey 152
MoSCoW analysis 372
morning scrum. *See Daily Scrum*
must-have features 372, 378
mute mapping 316, 351, 372

— N —

Nonaka, Ikujiro 32

— O —

obstacle 217, 218, 219, 223, 372
    See impediment backlog
    removal and risk management
O'Callaghan, Mike. *See impediment backlog*
Ohno, Taiichi 24
open space meeting 149, 222, 373
Optimize the whole 25, 37, 71
organic risk management 149, 195, 355, 362, 373

overt interventions 96
overt risk management 150, 160, 219, 220, 223, 373, 375

— P —

pair programming 34, 35, 39, 55, 56, 59, 373
participatory decision making 66, 80, 81, 82, 109, 110, 127, 194, 373
payback period 321, 334, 354, 359, 373
Performance Measure Baseline (PMB) 320, 336, 373
personal safety 75, 83, 85, 373
pigs and chickens 373
Plan-Do-Check-Act (PDCA) cycle
Planned Percent Complete (PPC) 373
Planned Value (PV) 239
Planning game 35, 262, 373
Planning poker 129, 130, 132, 133, 135, 138, 141, 143, 144, 176, 370, 373
point-based engineering 66
portfolio management 26, 374
pre-assignment 72, 83, 374
predictive release planning 374
present value 368, 374
process-centric 46, 64, 95, 155, 200, 221, 222, 223, 259, 265, 374, 375
product backlog 39, 45, 46, 62, 63, 70, 81, 82, 96, 97, 98, 99, 103, 105, 107, 108, 110, 127, 128, 142, 147, 148, 150,
    159, 176, 177, 178, 189, 200, 237, 258, 306, 366, 374, 375
    grooming of
    risk-adjusted
product demonstration 216, 223, 368, 374
Product Owner 12, 23, 29, 33, 45, 62, 63, 69, 70, 71, 81, 96, 115, 123, 130, 136, 139, 149, 153, 154, 201, 249, 285,
    367, 368, 371, 374, 376
product roadmap 96, 97, 100, 374
product vision box 64, 72, 152, 153, 374
product vision exercises 374
product-centric 46, 216, 223, 374
Project Management Professional (PgMP) 11, 12, 47, 283, 285, 373
progressive elaboration 54, 55, 86, 99, 107, 108, 117, 118, 122, 167, 208, 315
project chunking 374
project constraints   153, 158, 172, 318, 326, 330, 346, 352, 370
    & flexibility matrix
project data sheet (PDS) 88, 93
Project Management Body of Knowledge (PMBOK) 10, 15, 18, 19, 20, 31, 47, 266, 285, 373
Project Management Institute (PMI) 11, 53
Project Management Professional (PMP) 11, 12, 47, 283, 285, 373

— R —

Rational Unified Process (RUP) 40
reciprocal commitment 110, 127, 136, 142, 374
refactoring 34, 35, 40, 138, 191, 195, 375
Reinertsen, Don 183
release 16, 17, 18, 21, 22, 34, 35, 39, 40, 43, 70, 71, 72, 73, 74, 75, 96, 97, 98, 99, 100, 101, 102, 103, 107, 108, 127,
    136, 142, 147, 149, 150, 154, 155, 158, 159, 161, 176, 178, 180, 181, 185, 187, 190, 197, 200, 217, 219, 220,
    236, 237, 238, 240, 241, 244, 246, 258, 259, 260, 263, 264, 267
    release plan iv, 22, 100, 101, 102, 127, 136, 142, 150, 176, 180, 197, 200, 217, 237, 238, 241, 375
release planning 17, 75, 96, 98, 100, 101, 102, 107, 108, 149, 154, 155, 178, 180, 298, 366, 373, 374, 375
    inputs 39, 96, 98, 102, 110, 155, 157, 375
    output 16, 17, 62, 82, 176, 375, 378
    & agile planning levels 376

        & JIT progressive elaboration 107, 108
repository 109, 375, 376
respect 37, 76, 280, 281, 282, 283, 375
responsibility 3, 35, 63, 70, 81, 157, 177, 237, 258, 271, 276, 280, 281, 283, 367, 369, 371, 375
retained revenue 375
retrospectives
        activities 104
        release and project level 264, 267
        schedule 22, 35, 39, 40, 43, 67, 77, 81, 100, 101, 112, 139, 153, 197, 216, 223, 238, 239, 240, 242, 243, 260, 261, 266, 267, 284, 289, 366, 369, 370, 375, 376
        structure   41, 128, 133, 137, 139, 142, 158, 178, 192, 201, 238, 260, 261, 266, 267, 368, 370, 375, 379
risk audit 375
risk board 149, 150, 219, 373, 375
risk census 375
risk management 4, 145, 160, 175, 219, 223, 266, 335, 378
        organic 30, 96, 99, 149, 161, 194, 195, 198, 219, 223, 228, 229, 325, 341, 355, 362, 373
        overt 96, 149, 150, 160, 197, 198, 219, 220, 223, 228, 233, 325, 341, 355, 362, 373, 375
risk-adjusted backlog   148, 161, 163, 165, 171, 198, 376
risk-based spike 196, 197, 203, 205, 214, 376
round-robin 104, 370, 376
rules of engagement 76, 83, 166, 376

— S —

sandbox 196, 311, 339, 350, 361, 376
satisfaction histogram 263
satisfy the customer 6, 356, 371, 376
scanning 11, 83, 87, 93, 196, 376
Schedule Baseline (SB)
scopeboxed plan 98, 112, 115, 121, 334, 358, 376
Scrum 8, 9, 11, 12, 15, 19, 20, 22, 23, 29, 31, 32, 33, 36, 39, 44, 45, 63, 74, 82, 96, 102, 110, 127, 128, 129, 130, 136, 142, 143, 146, 149, 150, 153, 154, 178, 192, 199, 201, 216, 222, 265, 266, 285, 364, 365, 367, 368
        artifacts 39, 40, 41, 43, 44, 78, 152, 155, 178, 191, 192, 200, 260, 364, 366
        ceremonies 6, 82, 191, 204
Scrum Alliance (SA) 19, 58
Scrum Guide 178, 206, 212, 214
Scrum Master 8, 11, 12, 19, 23, 33, 130, 146, 149, 154, 199, 201, 216, 266, 285, 367, 368, 376
Scrum of Scrums 222
Scumniotales, John 32
self-organized team 376
self-regulating questions 146, 376
self-transcendent 376
servant leader 259, 376
set-based concurrent engineering (SBCE) 66
Seven Principles of Lean 377
showing empathy 377
Shu Ha Ri 8, 377
shuffle time 261, 377
silent generation of ideas 104, 372, 377
sizing 81, 82, 110, 126, 127, 128, 129, 130, 131, 132, 133, 135, 139, 141, 142, 143, 188, 194, 241, 377
        activities
Simini, Leonardo 158
Sliger, Michelle 244
spike, 2
sprint. *See iteration*
sprint backlog. *See iteration backlog*

Stahl, Leslie 32
stakeholders 17, 22, 23, 33, 35, 40, 41, 42, 44, 46, 62, 63, 64, 65, 66, 67, 69, 73, 78, 79, 82, 96, 98, 100, 103, 111, 129, 143, 148, 149, 153, 155, 156, 158, 161, 185, 192, 193, 198, 199, 200, 207, 213, 216, 223, 225, 226, 228, 230, 233, 234, 258, 264, 277, 280, 282, 283, 306, 318, 320, 336, 348, 353, 360, 368, 371, 372, 374, 376
    engagement 61, 62, 63, 64, 65, 66, 67, 74, 76, 80, 82, 83, 95, 96, 99, 121, 155, 166, 216, 222, 223, 230, 234, 258, 324, 345, 376
    identifying 19, 72, 73, 76, 77, 78, 96, 98, 99, 127, 155, 157, 167, 173, 178, 191, 202, 222, 223, 224, 319, 321, 337, 340, 344, 363, 371, 378
    listing 64, 83, 85, 372
Stenbeck, John 10, 265
story 63, 67, 68, 76, 81, 82, 98, 99, 100, 103, 105, 107, 108, 109, 110, 111, 127, 128, 129, 130, 131, 132, 133, 134, 135, 137, 138, 139, 141, 142, 143, 144, 147, 148, 159, 178, 180, 181, 185, 187, 188, 190, 196, 197, 217, 218, 219, 221, 223, 236, 238, 239, 240, 241, 258, 259, 267
    estimates. *See sizing*
    format 10, 69, 109, 152, 185, 200, 357
    prioritization 98, 99, 100, 105, 121, 157, 163, 164, 188, 192, 372
    splitting 104, 189, 377
story board 107, 108, 110, 122, 181, 258, 314, 347, 377, 378
use for estimating WIP
story map. *See story board*
story points 76, 82, 98, 103, 110, 128, 129, 130, 132, 133, 135, 137, 138, 141, 142, 143, 147, 148, 159, 185, 217, 218, 219, 223, 241, 258, 259, 365, 366, 373, 376, 377, 379
sufficient-to-purpose 348, 377
Sulaiman, Tamara 244
sustainable pace 181, 183, 203, 204, 368, 377
Sutherland, Jeff 32
swarming 180, 203, 205, 377
synchronous integration 311, 341, 350, 362, 378

— T —

tacit knowledge 221, 224, 225, 227, 229, 232, 234, 378
Takeuchi, Hirotaka 32
task board. *See story board*
team reflective workshop 99, 118, 123, 147, 149, 172, 222, 234, 336, 375, 378
team working agreements 149, 150, 151, 222, 263, 378, 379
technical debt 157, 378
test-driven development (TDD) 43, 358
Theory of Constraints 36, 60, 366, 370
timebox 16, 21, 22, 32, 71, 73, 74, 100, 101, 102, 127, 136, 142, 236, 259, 260, 265, 267, 372, 375, 378
timeboxed plan 97, 368, 378
timeboxing 378
Tillman, Pat iii
Toyoda, Kiichiro 23, 24
Toyoda, Sakichi 23, 24
trade-off matrix. *See flexibility*
    matrix 30, 64, 71, 77, 106, 152, 153, 154, 216, 266, 366, 370, 378
transition indicators 378
trend analysis 219, 220, 223, 378

— U —

User story. *See story*

— V —

value stream 24, 25, 26, 131, 155, 156, 157, 181, 189, 190, 193, 378
value stream mapping 155, 156, 157, 378

variance analysis 128, 158, 219, 223, 379
velocity 97, 98, 102, 128, 129, 159, 194, 200, 216, 217, 218, 219, 220, 223, 237, 238, 241, 244, 260, 297, 298, 370, 375, 379
    forecasted 218, 230, 234, 370
    velocity-driven iteration planning 218, 336, 379
venture-capital financing model 379
visual controls 151, 155, 158, 185, 194, 217

— W —

WAG. *See wild ass guess (WAG)*
Walking Skeleton 379
wastes in software development 379
Weick, Karl
    Principle of small wins 67, 148, 379
Wideband Delphi 129, 130, 132, 133, 135, 138, 141, 143, 379
Wild ass guess (WAG) 196, 197
wireframes 192, 193, 379
Womack, James 24
work-in-process (WIP) 131, 132, 181, 182, 372
working agreements, *See team working agreements*
working software, 43

— X —

XP. *See Extreme Programming*